MANAGING HUMAN RESOURCES IN RECREATION, PARKS, AND LEISURE SERVICES

MANAGING HUMAN RESOURCES
IN RECREATION, PARKS,
AND LEISURE SERVICES

David F. Culkin
Sondra L. Kirsch
North Carolina State University

Macmillan Publishing Company
NEW YORK

Collier Macmillan Publishers
LONDON

Macmillan Publishing Company
866 Third Avenue, New York, New York 10022

Collier Macmillan Canada, Inc.

Library of Congress Cataloging in Publication Data
Culkin, David F.
  Managing human resources in recreation, parks, and leisure services.

  Includes bibliographies and index.
  1. Recreation—United States—Personnel management.
2. Parks—United States—Personnel management.
I. Kirsch, Sondra L.   II. Title.
GV181.5.C84   1986   790'.0973   85-25452

Printing: 3 4 5 6 7 8   Year: 6 7 8   1 2 3 4 5

ISBN 0-02-326320-2

Acknowledgments: p. xvii, figure I.1, from Wendell L. French: *The Personnel Manage-
ment Process*, Fifth Edition, copyright © 1982 Houghton Mifflin Company. Used with
permission; p. 53, figure 3.4, from *National Personnel Guidelines*, National Recreation and
Park Association, copyright © 1978. Reprinted by permission; p. 59, figure 3.6, from
Principles of Management, Henry L. Sisk, copyright © 1969 by South-Western Publishing
Co., Cincinnati, p. 377. Reprinted with modifications by permission of South-Western
Publishing Co.; p. 92, figure 4.6, reprinted by permission of the National Recreation
and Park Association and the California Park and Recreation Society, Inc.; p. 133, figure
6.1, reprinted by permission of the *Harvard Business Review*. Exhibit from "How to
Choose a Leadership Pattern" by Robert Tannenbaum and Warren H. Schmidt (May/
June 1973). Copyright © 1973 by the President and Fellows of Harvard College; all
rights reserved; p. 160, figure 7.1, from *Managerial Attitudes and Performance*, Lyman W.
Porter and Edward E. Lawler, copyright © 1968 by Richard D. Irwin, Inc., Homewood,
IL, p. 17. Adapted by permission; p. 175, figure 8.6, from Dale Yoder, *Personnel Man-
agement and Industrial Relations*, Sixth Edition, © 1970, p. 237. Reprinted by permission

To Our Students

Preface

The problem is simple. Most park, recreation, and leisure service professionals require a considerable understanding of the principles and practices needed to manage full-time, part-time, and seasonal personnel and volunteers. Unfortunately, most professionals have not had sufficient training and development in this area. (We know what it is like; we both have been in management positions and faced personnel problems. This textbook would have helped us. We hope it will help current and future recreation professionals to solve their personnel problems.)

We teach a course at North Carolina State University that covers essentially all the material found in this book. The students are receptive, and it is one of the most popular courses in our curriculum. We feel confident that they will be much better managers someday because of this exposure to the fundamentals of managing personnel.

We have never been happy with the textbooks available for this course. The business administration texts on personnel are manufacturing- and sales-oriented. Personnel management texts are designed for students and professionals in the personnel management field. The public administration texts on personnel tend to emphasize large municipal government operating procedures.

While writing this book, we constantly asked the question, "What do recreation managers need to know in order to manage their personnel effectively?" Hopefully, the result is a book that is substantive and practical but easy to digest. Obviously, we could not cover everything, but the reader should certainly get a solid foundation on which to build.

We are grateful to our colleague and friend, Dr. Richard Gitelson, who contributed a chapter on motivation. A number of people in park and recreation agencies provided us with forms, manuals, examples, and ideas. It would be impossible to acknowledge them all, but we owe a special thanks to Roger Brown, Greensboro, North Carolina; Ronald Chase, Cincinnati, Ohio; Eric Reickel, Oakland County, Michigan; Karen Boriss, Metropolitan Dade County, Florida; and Ron Ferris, North Lauderdale, Florida. We would also like to thank Betty West, Sarah Jones, and Kimberly Golombisky for critiquing sections of the manuscript. A final "thank you" goes to our typists, Christian Kirsch, Reggi Powell, and Ann Rouse.

David F. Culkin
Sondra L. Kirsch

Contents

Appendixes

Introduction

Every park and recreation manager performs a variety of activities. Perhaps the most essential of these activities is the management of human resources. Every person associated with an organization, directly or indirectly, is a resource. These people might be program instructors, park managers, attendents, or office personnel. They might have full-time, part-time, seasonal, or volunteer status. It is a mistake to assume that these people will automatically fit together into a cohesive, coordinated team. Furthermore, it is an error to assume that people will automatically perform the *appropriate tasks* and perform those tasks in the most *desirable manner*. An effective team effort is essential to the operation of any organization, and it is the responsibility of the manager to make this happen.

Process Management

Henri Fayol, a Frenchman, was one of the earliest authors in the field of managerial theory. Fayol saw management as the process by which an organization channels its resources toward the accomplishment of predetermined goals. Managers performed those *functions* that were necessary to keep this process going. Today, most disciples of the Process School of Management have agreed that the primary functions of a manager are:

1. *Planning:* establishing goals and determining how the goals of the organization are to be achieved.

2. *Organizing:* arranging and allocating the resources needed to accomplish organizational goals.
3. *Staffing:* obtaining the type of people needed to accomplish the established goals.
4. *Directing:* leading, guiding, and assisting people as they carry out the activities of the organization.
5. *Controlling:* monitoring and evaluating activities and taking corrective action as needed.

Virtually every activity performed by a manager falls within one of these five functions. They are not unique to any one field or any particular type of manager; they are performed by all managers in all organizations. By performing these five functions, park and recreation managers are able to convert organizational resources into programs, services, facilities, and parks. The resources might consist of land, equipment, buildings, or people. *In this book we focus on the planning, organizing, staffing, directing, and controlling of people in order to achieve organizational goals* (see Figure I.1).

As shown in Figure I.2, these five functions follow a logical pattern and this book reflects that pattern. After the first two chapters present an introduction to the legal aspects of managing personnel, Chapter 3 focuses on planning and organizing for personnel. Chapters 4 and 5 collectively cover the many aspects of staffing an organization. Chapters 6 and 7 focus on directing personnel. The controlling function is a complex area that is dealt with in Chapter 8, "Performance Appraisal," Chapter 9, "Compensation," Chapter 10, "Training and Development," Chapter 11, "Discipline and Grievances," and Chapter 12; "Employee Separations." The last two chapters, "Collective Bargaining" and "Employee Well-Being," cover two areas that directly affect *how* managers function when dealing with personnel.

Use of Terms

In this book the terms *managing human resources* and *managing personnel* are used interchangeably. These terms, however, are not synonymous with the term *personnel management,* which is a professional occupation. Many of the organizations that provide recreation services, with the exception of some of the smaller ones, have personnel departments. The purpose of a personnel department is to provide support services for all other units in the organization in matters related to personnel.

A typical personnel department provides technical advice to managers, assists in the development of personnel policies, processes and maintains records, and performs research needed to solve problems and to for-

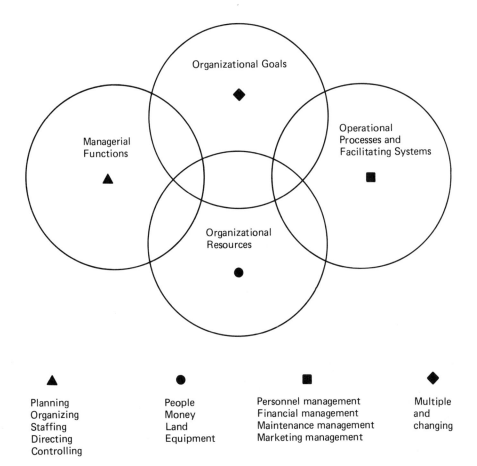

Planning
Organizing
Staffing
Directing
Controlling

People
Money
Land
Equipment

Personnel management
Financial management
Maintenance management
Marketing management

Multiple
and
changing

Figure I.1   Major aspects of organization.

mulate personnel-related plans. In some organizations, personnel management functions are the part-time responsibility of one person. In other organizations, especially larger ones, the personnel unit consists of a number of well-trained specialists.

The relationship between the recreation manager and the people in the personnel unit is often a complex matter. Recreation professionals must keep in mind that the personnel unit is only a support service; it is always the responsibility of the recreation manager to oversee the day-to-day operation of his or her staff. We frequently discuss specific aspects of this important relationship between the recreation manager and the personnel department. If an organization has no personnel unit, managers will be forced to carry out *all* personnel-related functions. To keep our discussions concise and manageable, in this book we assume that the recreation manager does have access to a personnel department.

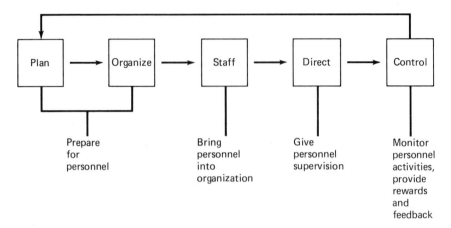

Figure I.2   The five functions of managing.

The term *supervisor* is usually associated with the lowest level of management. In the early days of the Industrial Revolution, the supervisor's primary responsibility was to watch the workers carefully and make sure that they did their jobs. Today, most people working at the lowest level of management do not have their jobs defined so narrowly. For example, they may also be asked to make decisions in the areas of finance, resource allocation, policy development, and public relations. Also, the need for understanding the management of human resources is not confined to the lowest level of management. Every manager, including the top manager, is responsible for the supervision of people lower in the organization. Every manager, from top manager to supervisor, needs to have a basic understanding of the principles of managing personnel. In this book, we use the terms *manager* and *supervisor* interchangeably—with one exception: If the area of discussion pertains primarily to the first-line manager only, we emphasize the use of the term *supervisor*.

Throughout this book we attempt to provide basic information, principles, and methods that have application to a wide variety of recreation operation. Professionals in private for-profit, private nonprofit, and public recreation should be able to relate to most of the material presented. The terms *recreation, recreation and parks,* and *leisure services* are used interchangeably to refer to the entire field of recreation, parks, and leisure services. Also, keep in mind that even though most of our discussion and examples focus on full-time personnel, the material generally pertains also to part-time and seasonal personnel as well as volunteers.

MANAGING HUMAN RESOURCES IN RECREATION, PARKS, AND LEISURE SERVICES

1

Legal Environment: Equal Employment Opportunity

What do laws, regulations, and court decisions have to do with supervising personnel? The answer to this question, clearly revealed in this chapter and Chapter 2, is "a great deal." In a spirited effort to correct some of the serious social problems in American society, a significant amount of our nation's legal activity over the past half century has focused on employment practices. Although the laws that attempt to correct unfair employment practices have not always achieved their objectives, they are reflected in a significant part of each park, recreation, and leisure organization's policies and procedures.

All of us, concerned about the people we work with as well as the people we serve, have both a moral and a legal obligation to carry out fair employment practices. To function otherwise places ourselves and our organizations outside the law and enhances the risk of facing investigation or litigation by some federal or state regulatory agency. In addition, unfair employment practices frequently foster resentment, anger, and frustration in our work force and do nothing to promote the worth and dignity of each individual human being.

Unfortunately, it is very difficult to keep track of our legal obligations. Even the well-intended person may violate the law because he or she is unaware of exactly what the law requires. But, as we all know, ignorance of the law is no excuse. Hence the purpose of this chapter is to provide the park and recreation professional with a broad overview of the most important legal aspects of managing leisure service personnel.

If legal problems arise, most park and recreation managers will have access to the expertise of lawyers and personnel specialists. It is to our advantage, however, to prevent legal problems from arising in the first place, and we cannot expect lawyers and personnel specialists to constantly monitor our day-to-day activities. We need at least a basic knowledge of the legal aspects of managing personnel. An understanding of this chapter is a good starting point, but ultimately, managers should (1) continue to read and keep current with changing laws, and (2) develop a good working relationship with their lawyers and personnel specialists in order to anticipate and eliminate potential problems.

We opened this chapter by referring to laws, regulations, and court decisions. All three taken together make up the legal environment. Laws are usually written in broad terms, and an agency under the executive branch of government is assigned the task of writing the specific regulations that put the new law into action. The agency assigned to this task is either a new agency created by the law or an already existing agency. Court decisions also come into play in that they assess the constitutionality of laws and interpret their meaning.

Considerable attention is devoted in this book to equal employment opportunity because many of the laws in this area have only recently been enacted and because the principles behind equal employment opportunity are fundamental and influence all aspects of personnel planning, management, and supervision.

The reader will soon understand why this chapter is presented in the beginning of this book. On numerous occasions, throughout the book, we will refer back to this chapter. Compliance with the law will frequently dictate what we do and how we do it in the area of human resource management.

Equal employment opportunity (EEO) refers to the responsibility of organizations and managers to keep the work environment free from discrimination. Everyone has the right to obtain work, earn fair wages, and receive fair treatment in all areas on the basis of ability, work performance, and potential to learn on the job. One persistent stumbling block in accomplishing the objectives of EEO is the existence of prejudices. In order that the reader may better understand how prejudices can lead to employment discrimination and why the United States has experienced so much legislation pertaining to discrimination in the past twenty years, a brief discussion of the history of employment discrimination in the United States is presented.

U.S. History of Employment Discrimination

Following the Civil War, the Fourteenth Amendment to the Constitution was passed to guarantee everyone the right to equal protection of the law. Initially, however, this amendment was neither obeyed nor enforced. During the middle decades of the twentieth century, antidiscrimination orders were issued by Presidents Roosevelt, Truman, and Eisenhower, and thirty-one northern states passed antidiscrimination laws. On occasion, even the judicial branch of government addressed discrimination. In the 1940s the Supreme Court banned several state laws that discriminated against minorities. Nevertheless, these legal actions did not stem the flow of pervasive discrimination in housing, education, recreation, and employment because government did not seek to enforce the laws.

Frequently, employment practices were discriminatory. Too often, recruitment for new employees was conducted primarily by word of mouth, or it was aimed at specific schools or newspapers that did not represent minorities. Although discrimination was not always the intent of these practices, the recruitment results eliminated most minorities from knowing about position openings.

If prospective minority applicants did learn about job vacancies, they were confronted with complicated application blanks which too often asked unfair questions, making the applicant appear inferior. For example, some application blanks inquired about the heritage and education achievements of the parents. A question about the length of time at present residence inferred that something might be wrong with a person who had moved frequently. Those questions referring to home ownership focused on the poor economic status of many minority members. Similarly, questions concerning years of education and degrees earned were often intimidating to those having little education. Columns of questions concerning political memberships and drinking habits required the applicant to acknowledge personal life-styles.

The criteria used to screen applicants were equally discriminatory. Unskilled jobs often required high school degrees, thus eliminating culturally and economically disadvantaged candidates. Tests were frequently used which might ask applicants to solve algebraic problems when only simple math would be required on the job. An applicant who could verbalize in English and follow spoken instructions might not be able to read or write English well enough to pass the test.

Traditionally, therefore, only the backbreaking, dirty jobs were available and sought by blacks and immigrants: jobs such as collecting trash, cleaning streets, working in blast furnaces, or cleaning homes. Educated blacks took jobs for which they were over qualified. Learning that certain organizations and certain jobs were closed to them, minorities confined job hunting to low-status occupations and today still tend to be apprehensive about applying for jobs that claim "Equal Opportunity Employer."[1]

Similar standards existed for training and promotion practices. Many blacks and immigrants were excluded from apprenticeships in the building trades because those trades required a high school degree and the passing of examinations.[2] In the south, two seniority rosters were frequently kept: one for white employees and one for black employees. Blacks could not seek white positions and whites could not seek black positions. White jobs were better paid, however, and offered better working conditions.[3]

Many blacks and women, once they were hired, often faced dead-end jobs. Agencies and companies could show compliance to equal employment opportunity legislation by calling attention to their minority representatives in personnel departments or public relation offices. If women or blacks were promoted to supervisory or management positions, complaints from subordinates, requests for transfers, or resignations frequently resulted. As late as 1983, in one southern community where the elected officials announced the appointment of a female parks and recreation director, the park maintenance men threatened to resign rather than work for a woman. Such working environments tend to discourage women and minorities from seeking better-paying positions.

It took the courageous actions of individual black leaders and the civil rights movement to draw serious attention to the problems of discrimination in this country. As early as 1945, one young black Air Force officer challenged segregation regulations at Duke Field, Kentucky. Later he faced charges of mutiny when he and a fellow black officer tried to integrate the officer's club. The charges were eventually dropped, and Daniel (Chappie) James, Jr. went on to become the first black four-star general in the history of this country. Thurgood Marshall, the attorney for young "Chappie," became the first black Supreme Court justice, and William Coleman, the law student who assisted Marshall, became U.S. Secretary of Transportation in the 1970s.[4] It was not until 1963 when hundreds of thousands of civil rights' supporters demonstrated in Washington, D.C., before a television audience of millions, that the federal government sought to right past wrongs. That was the turning point, particularly for blacks. President Kennedy and then President Johnson pushed for civil rights legislation, and the Civil Rights Act was passed in July 1964.

Today, the legal spotlight continues to focus on blacks, ethnic minorities, and women in its search for discrimination. But other minority groups are also demanding attention and an end to bias in hiring and personnel practices. Persons with handicaps frequently face discrimination. Although social attitudes are changing, persons suspected or known to be homosexuals are shunned because of possible embarrassment to the agency. The culturally disadvantaged, the hard-core unemployed, and older workers of all races and ethnic heritage also continue to feel the sting of prejudice and discrimination.

Prejudice and Discrimination Defined

Prejudice

An attitude of hostility directed against an individual, a group, or race, because of their supposed characteristics.[5]

Webster's definition for the word *prejudice* offers a meaning most closely associated with the past history of discrimination in the United States. For the purpose of discussion in this book, the word *prejudice* means those emotional beliefs, usually unfavorable, from which a person literally prejudges all members of a particular minority group.

Prejudices do not necessarily lead to acts of discrimination. A person who prejudges another person, but allows that other person to move about and live as he or she wishes, is not discriminating. In our society, personal beliefs are highly valued, as long as those beliefs do not infringe on the rights of others. Consequently, *laws to change the acts of discrimination should not begin by trying to change personal beliefs.* It was evident from the discussion on past employment practices that prejudices were not legislated away because of constitutional amendments, presidential orders, or state legislation. Only the acts of discrimination can be made illegal; specific acts toward specific minority groups.

An awareness of one's prejudices sometimes prevents acts of discrimination. Putting oneself into the shoes of a minority person, even for a short while, can lead to better understanding of the frustrations and problems of minority-group members. The classic example is the role-shift study conducted by sociologist John Howard Griffin. Griffin darkened his skin in order to pass himself off as a southern black man. He learned that constant rejection eventually leads to self-image and behavioral changes, and he eventually became fearful, clumsy, and self-rejecting in his role as a black man. In his book, *Black Like Me,* Griffin concluded that those characteristics which whites assign to blacks are not the result of differences in races, but rather the result of differences in environmental factors.[6]

In 1973, leaders of the National Recreation and Park Association sat, traveled, and functioned in wheelchairs for one day at the national congress. They experienced the humiliation of entering fancy hotels through back street service entrances. Once inside the buildings they traveled down halls lined with smelly containers of garbage, and moved across kitchens full of busy personnel not inclined to make intruders in wheelchairs feel welcome. Why the charade? To sensitize park and recreation leaders to both the physical and attitudinal barriers facing those confined to wheelchairs. The "back-door" route was the only access to the main meeting rooms for those in wheelchairs attending the congress. Today, because of legislation, many of the physical barriers have been removed for those with handicapping conditions. The attitudinal barriers remain, however.

Discrimination

The definition of discrimination has undergone three distinct changes in recent decades.

1. The courts initially defined the word as "committing harmful acts against a person because he belongs to a group that is disliked."[7] The emphasis was on the word "because," which implied that the intent was to treat someone differently based on his or her group membership.
2. When it became difficult to prove that someone intended to harm another person, the courts defined discrimination as "unusual treatment" or treating persons differently because of their race, color, gender, religion, or national origin.[8] The emphasis shifted from the "prejudicial intent to harm" to the actual treatment of employees. Different treatment was the commonly accepted definition, referred to as "disparate treatment." It was assumed that inequalities would be eliminated by removing different treatment based on race, color, and sexual awareness of employers and supervisors. Thus the same standard of employment was applied to all applicants and all employees. But this definition led to unequal results. When equal standards, such as requiring a high school diploma, were applied to everyone, it resulted in unequal effects on certain minority groups.
3. The term *disparate effect* emerged as the third, more realistic definition of discrimination. This definition emerged from the famous Supreme Court case, *Griggs* v. *Duke Power Co.* (1971). Duke Power used what was believed to be a neutral, color-blind technique in determining promotions. Every applicant was treated the same, blacks and whites. Everyone had to pass two nationally recognized tests. A passing score was considered the national median score for high school graduates. This equal treatment, however, resulted in unequal impact on blacks, who were less likely to have a high school education and consequently, less likely to pass the tests.[9] The Duke Power Company had evidently interpreted the Civil Rights Act to mean that the use of any test from a reputable publisher of psychological tests was permitted by law. For a description of the key excerpts from Title VII of the Civil Rights Act, see Appendix C.

Disparate Effect. The Supreme Court addressed the definition of disparate effect when it interpreted Congress's intent to eliminate not only disparate treatment over discrimination, but also those practices that, while appearing to be equal, lead to unequal consequences for different groups. "Under the Act [Civil Rights Act], practices, procedures, or tests neutral on their face and even neutral in terms of intent cannot be maintained if they operate to 'freeze' the status quo of prior discriminatory employment practices."[10] Although Duke's tests were not intended to discriminate, the Court ruled that the tests operated to exclude blacks. Good intentions, therefore, are not sufficient reasons to excuse employers from violating the law. Congress was directing the law to the *consequences* of employment practices, as well as intent. Thus disparate treatment and disparate impact are both illegal discriminatory practices (see Figure 1.1).

It is useful to review those EEO laws, regulatory directives, and court decisions which attempted to rectify past employment injustices. The legal implications of EEO have changed the role of everyone who supervises anyone in park and recreation organizations. A supervisor no longer may make decisions based exclusively on personal feelings or prejudices.

WHAT IS DISCRIMINATION?

Disparate treatment: members of one group overtly and intentionally treated differently than members of another group. If a Hispanic employee leaves the center early without permission four times and is discharged, but an Anglo co-worker leaves work the same number of times and is not fired, the result is disparate treatment for the Hispanic.

Disparate effects: indirect or unintentional adverse impact on members of one group who are deprived employment opportunities because of a particular rule or practice. Requiring a high school degree in order to work as a park laborer would rule out a disproportionate number of blacks and naturalized citizens because a greater proportion of these groups never obtain high school diplomas.[11] This requirement results in disparate effects for affected minorities.

WHAT IS PREJUDICE?

An emotional belief whereby an individual literally prejudges all members of a particular minority group. If a man works with an illogical, overly emotional female, he may prejudge all women, believing that they all think illogically and emotionally. These personal beliefs may lead to actions which infringe upon the rights of others.

Figure 1.1 Definitions of the terms *discrimination* and *prejudice*.

Civil Rights Act of 1964, Title VII, as Amended by the Equal Employment Opportunity Act of 1972

A black maintenance laborer with a high school diploma worked for a park district six years, receiving good performance evaluations. He was never offered an opportunity to attend training programs, nor was he ever notified about vacancies in better-paying positions. After witnessing the third promotion of white employees with less seniority, and noting that their expenses had been paid to attend a maintenance workshop prior to each of their promotions, the black complained to his supervisor. The response was, "Aren't you happy in your present job? I didn't think you wanted extra training or a promotion."

Was the supervisor guilty of unfair equal employment opportunity practices under the law?

The Civil Rights Act of 1964, especially Title VII, Sec. 703, provides the cornerstone for EEO employment. This law makes it unlawful for employers to hire, refuse to hire, discharge, or discriminate in employment practices against anyone because of race, color, religion, sex, or national origin. In other words, acts of discrimination, whether deliberately planned or accidentally executed, are illegal.

The supervisor of the black laborer, previously cited, was guilty of unintentional discrimination. He was unaware that the aim of equal opportunity legislation extends beyond the mere hiring of blacks. The law also attempts to remove discrimination in staffing procedures which have adverse effects on minorities or women. It never occurred to this supervisor to promote the black laborer or train him for another job.

Title VII offers three exceptions in which preferential hiring is permitted. Recent court decisions have interpreted these exceptions very narrowly. If an employer can demonstrate that religion, sex, or national origin are *bona fide occupational qualifications* (BFOQs), necessary to perform the job and necessary to maintain the normal operation of that particular business, the employer may hire according to one of these three conditions. Thus recruitment for a female wet nurse, male sperm donor, or female shower–sauna room attendant would be permitted. Race and color are not permissible exceptions in the law.

Initially, the category of sex was not included in the bill, but in an attempt to prevent passage, southern congressmen tacked on the word "sex," thinking that the bill wouldn't pass if "sex" were included as one of the protected groups.[12] They might have been more successful in stopping the Civil Rights Act if they had inserted the word "baldness" instead of "sex." But elected officials from those states that had already passed antidiscrimination laws did not consider the issue of sex discrimination a joke, and they voted to pass the bill into law. Older persons and those with handicapping conditions were not included in the act.

> The purpose of Title VII was expressed very well by the Supreme Court in its decision in the *Griggs* v. *Duke Power Company,* 1971.
>
> The objective of congress in the enactment of Title VII is plain from the language of the statute. It is to achieve equality of employment opportunity and remove barriers that have operated in the past to favor an identifiable group of white employees over other employees. Congress did not intend by Title VII, however, to guarantee to every person a job regardless of qualifications. In short, the Act did not command that every person be hired simply because he was formerly the subject of discrimination or because he is a member of a minority group. What is required by Congress is the removal of artificial, arbitrary and unnecessary barriers to employment when the barriers operate invidiously to discriminate on the basis of racial or other impermissible classification.[14]

Consideration for these minority groups was addressed in later legislation.

As amended by the Equal Employment Opportunity Act of 1972, Title VII of the Civil Rights Act applies to all educational institutions, state and local governments, employment agencies, all private employers, unions with fifteen or more employees or members, and to joint labor–management apprenticeship and training programs. Exemptions from the law included businesses that for most of the year hire fewer than fifteen employees and certain tax-exempt private clubs. The act also forbids discrimination in the federal executive branch, along with those competitive civil service positions in the judicial and legislative branches.[13]

Equal Employment Opportunity Commission

To administer and enforce the Civil Rights Act, a new independent federal organization was created, the Equal Employment Opportunity Commission (EEOC). The five members on the commission are appointed for five years by the president with the consent of Congress. Originally, EEOC only investigated complaints of alleged discrimination and, through conciliation, persuasion, and negotiation, tried to resolve charges. When these methods failed, EEOC lacked authority to take cases to court. This lack of authority was the major weakness of the 1964 Civil Rights Act. Employers often ignored the Civil Rights Act and EEOC, hoping that wronged individuals would not have the knowledge or financial resources to pursue their complaints through litigation.[15] The Equal Employment Opportunity Act of 1972 addressed these weaknesses and extended the authority of the EEOC, enabling it to take organizations directly to federal district courts.

EEOC has two primary functions: (1) processing complaints of discrimination, and (2) issuing written guidelines that govern employment practices. The function of processing complaints includes three steps.

1. *Investigation.* If a person believes that he or she has been the victim of discrimination, the person has 180 days from the date the alleged discriminatory act took place to file a complaint with EEOC. In some states, the person must first file a charge with the appropriate state agency, waiting sixty days before filing with EEOC. In addition, interested organizations may file class action suits on behalf of individuals who they believe have been victims of discrimination. The number of cases filed each year has grown from 8,000 in 1973 to 58,754 new discrimination complaints in 1981.[16] The backlog of cases numbers in the tens of thousands each year.

   After a person files a complaint, EEOC examines the documentation, looking for evidence of disparate treatment or disparate impact. The agency may refer the case to appropriate state or local deferral agencies for investigation. The commission must give notice of a complaint to the employer within ten days after it is filed. Usually, a visit to the employer's organization is made, people are interviewed, and records are examined. After all the evidence is collected, EEOC decides whether or not there is "probable cause" that Title VII was violated.

2. *Conciliation.* If EEOC finds no probable cause, the complainant is notified and he or she may file a lawsuit against the employer in a federal district court. If probable cause is found, EEOC will try to settle the problem through conciliation with all parties involved. During 1981, more than 38,000 persons received benefits under the enforcement of Title VII, the Equal Pay Act, and the Age Discrimination Act.[17] More than $91 million was claimed for the victims of employment discrimination. EEOC has been able to obtain pretrial reconciliation in almost forty-nine out of fifty cases.[18]

3. *Litigation.* When conciliation fails, EEOC may file suit in a federal district court against the employer. Usually, however, EEOC drops the matter because litigation is costly and time consuming.[19] This last step is usually reserved for cases where there is a good chance that large cash awards for the complainant will be awarded, or where the court might provide new interpretation on the law. EEOC filed 452 litigation cases in U.S. federal courts in 1981, an increase of 24 percent over previous years. Monetary benefits from court cases amounted to more than $70 million.[20]

The second function of EEOC is to issue procedural regulations or provide technical assistance, interpreting Title VII to employers. Technical assistance may be sought by employers to help them identify discriminatory features in their employment system.

The most significant regulations have been the 1978 *Uniform Guidelines on Employee Selection Procedures,* procedures that govern all employment decisions.[21] Because pencil-and-paper testing was the screening and selection technique that traditionally barred minority applicants from jobs, so-called "tests" were carefully reviewed by federal agencies. The Uniform Guidelines state (1) that any test which is used to screen or select applicants or to promote continuing employees must be reasonably related to successful job performance of the position for which the applicant is applying, and (2) there should be empirical evidence which demonstrates that the test actually predicts important job behavior necessary in accomplishing tasks. The guidelines do not focus only on paper-and-pencil tests. They include screening techniques used to qualify applicants, such as personal and work history, education, scored interviews, scored application blanks, and interviewer's rating scales.

Equal Pay Act of 1963, as Amended by the Equal Opportunity Act of 1972 and 1977

In 1973, a female recreation superintendent was promoted to county park and recreation director after the male director resigned. The three-step increase in salary was not made at the time of her promotion, although the duties and responsibilities remained the same for the director's position. When she sought to correct this oversight, she was told, "We have decided to reclassify the director's position down *three steps from what it had been previously. Consequently, you are not entitled to any salary increase."*
Did this action violate EEO laws?

The county that acted to pay the female director three steps less in salary than the former male director was in conflict with the Equal Pay Act. The female director held the same position and performed the same responsibilities as her predecessor; therefore, she was entitled to the same salary.

The Equal Pay Act of 1963 and the Equal Opportunity Acts of 1972 and 1977 were all amendments to the Fair Labor Standards Act of 1938 (see Appendix A). To avoid confusion over the different titles of the same law, we will refer to the law as the Equal Pay Act.

This act provides even broader coverage than the Civil Rights Act of 1964. It covers all state and local governments and public agencies, schools, hospitals, and businesses with sales in excess of $362,500. Under the Equal Pay Act, all employers are required to pay equal wages to men and women performing similar work. The law defines similar work as:

> Equal work on jobs, the performance of which requires equal skill, effort, and responsibility, and which are performed under similar working conditions, except where such payment is made pursuant to (i) a seniority system; (ii) a merit system; (iii) a system which measures earnings by quantity or quality of production. [sec. 6, Fair Labor Standards Act].

Equal work does not necessarily mean identical working conditions, that is, skill, effort, and responsibility. The issue is not always one of exact duties in exactly the same environment, but whether or not any differences in duties are significant enough to warrant different wages. Should a male community center director be paid more than a female community center director because his center has 5,000 more square feet, offers different facilities, and requires an extra person to assist in operating the center? Probably not, because all major job functions, levels of responsibility, and required education and experience remain the same for both centers.

The Equal Pay Act does permit employers to pay differential wages when wages are based on established seniority or merit systems. If the male center director had been a center director several years longer than the female center director, the agency can pay him a higher salary, as a result of legitimate longevity pay increases. Similarly, if two center directors were hired at the same time, but the male employee performed in an outstanding manner the first year while the female employee only performed her duties satisfactorily, the agency with an established merit system could reward the male employee with a greater salary increase.

Another important aspect of the Equal Pay Act relates to differential pay according to the risk of bodily harm on the job. Some organizations provide greater renumeration to the employee facing possible danger. This may not be considered legal. For example, one agency requires rangers to assign camp sites, collect fees, patrol park areas, present interpretive programs, and perform related duties. Male rangers in that agency are more frequently scheduled to patrol isolated park sites late at night, and occasionally encounter disorderly park patrons breaking park regulations. Although both male and female rangers are charged to patrol park areas, the likelihood of the male ranger finding himself in a potentially confrontive situation late at night is greater. The courts generally have been unsympathetic to situations such as the one just cited, where male employees have been paid higher wages than females based on the possibility that the males are exposing themselves to greater danger.[22] A number of court cases have resulted in back-pay awards to women who were targets of unequal pay discrimination.

Initially, the enforcement of the Equal Pay Act was the responsibility of the Wage and Hour Division of the U.S. Department of Labor, but that authority was transferred to the Equal Employment Opportunity Commission in July 1979.

Age Discrimination in Employment Act of 1967, as Amended in 1978

> "Tom, don't be angry about not being considered for the golf superintendent's job. Carl is fifteen years younger than you and has more energy. Besides, a guy at age 52 doesn't need all that added stress and responsibility."
> How does this statement violate the law?

The Age Discrimination in Employment Act of 1967 (ADEA), as amended in 1978, prohibits job discrimination against workers between 40 and 70 years of age. This act covers private employers with twenty or more employees and state, federal, and local governmental units. Since 1979, the EEOC has been the investigating and enforcement agency for this act.

The main purposes of the 1978 Amendments were to raise the forced retirement age from 65 to 70 and to eliminate mandatory retirement for federal employees. Congressional proponents of the act argued that depriving healthy older workers of the right to work amounted to "ageism," no different than racism or sexism, especially since the life expectancy for Americans has risen more than ten years in the past twenty-five years. The age of 65 was initially chosen arbitarily by Chancellor Bismark in 1889 when he had to define old age for the first national pension program. A few years later, Great Britain adopted that same age for their program and then the United States followed in 1935 with the Social Security Act. There has never been a medical reason for choosing the age of 65. In 1900, only one out of every twenty-five Americans was 65 or older. In 1975 that figure was one out of ten, and within the next five decades, it will be one out of every six persons. There are more than 23 million Americans over age 65 today.[23]

One of the similarities between Title VII of the Civil Rights Act and ADEA is the exemption from the law for bona fide occupational qualification (BFOQ). Employers may engage in disparate treatment because of age, and the courts have been more permissive in considering age as a BFOQ than they have for race or sex, particularly when safety is a consideration. The Supreme Court in both *Usery* v. *Tamiami Trail Tours, Inc.* (1976) and *Hodgson* v. *Greyhound Lines, Inc.* (1974) has ruled that age can be a BFOQ in hiring bus drivers if the employer can provide some evidence that older persons are less safe drivers. The evidence does *not* have to be statistically documented. One bus company claimed that for most people, physical changes begin around age 40 and these changes have adverse effects on driving skills and thus increase the risk of accidents. The Court agreed with the bus company and a maximum 40-year age limit was imposed on new hires for drivers.

However, scientific evidence in recent years has proven many generalizations based on age to be false. There is evidence that contradicts the view that all older employees lose their faculties with aging, are resistant to change, are unable to handle stress, and experience more safety and absenteeism problems.[24] Some studies show that older workers are less prone to accidents than younger employees, have a better attitude toward their supervisor, offer the employer additional maturity and experience, and are equal to young employees in the quality and quantity of their work.[25]

In most situations, age discrimination has been unsupported and blatant, and the courts have acted on complaints in increasing numbers since the passage of the act. A supervisor cannot expect the courts to defend his preference for younger workers based on his belief that younger workers have more drive and energy. Therefore, the reason given Tom in the introductory statement violates Section 4(a)(1) (see Appendix D). The supervisor was depriving Tom of a promotion opportunity based on his age, and Section 4 states that this is unlawful. Tom has every right to apply for a better position and be evaluated on credentials other than age.

Presidential Executive Orders 11246 and 11375

A construction company contracted with Central City Parks and Recreation to develop a new community park. Half the monies for the $350,000 contract came from a federal grant. It was noted by black leaders who represented Central City's 31 percent black population, that only one black was employed by the construction company. This was particularly distressing to them because the city's unemployment rate was 11.7 percent. When the leaders complained to the director of parks and recreation, she responded, "I sympathize with your position, but there's nothing I can do since I don't hire the men that work for the contractor."

Was she correct?

Presidential executive orders are directives issued by U.S. presidents which have the force of law, even though Congress did not enact them. Some of these orders pertain to EEO and federal contracts with private organizations. Local and state governments who receive federal monies are also covered.

In 1941, President Franklin D. Roosevelt was the first president to try to prohibit employment discrimination nationally. Through executive order, he created a Fair Employment Practices Committee which investigated complaints of discrimination in defense industries that held federal contracts. The committee settled thousands of cases by conciliation, but it lacked the authority to enforce the executive order. Those presidents who followed Roosevelt established similar committees, but it was not until President Kennedy took office that an investigating committee was given the authority to cancel government contracts or to penalize contractors who chose to continue to discriminate in employment practices.[26]

In 1965, President Johnson issued Executive Order 11246 (amended two years later by Executive Order 11375), which required that government contractors and subcontractors who supply a service to a governmental agency and receive a payment in excess of $10,000 per year must ban all discriminatory actions against protected groups identified in Title VII of the Civil Rights Act. The order now covers handicapped workers as well. To ensure compliance with the order, these contractors are regularly audited by the Office of Federal Contract Compliance Programs (OFCCP), through regional offices of the Department of Labor. Reports of violations or complaints are also made to OFCCP.

It is important to note here that Executive Orders 11246 and 11375 also apply to all state and local governments with fifteen or more full-time employees. Why? Because these units of government receive federal payments from programs such as federal revenue sharing. Thus park and recreation departments receiving federal monies from any federal agency are responsible for those private contractors who contract for facility development, operations, maintenance, or programming. If a private contractor discriminates in any employment practice and a violation is reported (or a complaint made, as in the previously cited Central City scenario), the park and recreation agency could be investigated by OFCCP, become involved in a formal hearing or lawsuit, and possibly lose federal financial support.

Those contracts over $50,000 and those contractors who hire fifty or more employees are specifically addressed in the orders. Not only are these contractors prohibited from discriminatory actions, but they are also required to develop and implement an affirmative action program. The mandated affirmative action programs require contractors and subcontractors to take three distinct actions designed to increase employment opportunities for minorities and women. These three actions are to:

1. Compare minority employment within the contractor's organization with availability of qualified minorities in the local labor market, and determine if there is fair representation of minorities in each job category within the organization.

2. Develop numerical goals and timetables to correct any underutilization of minorities found to exist.
3. Establish action plans to implement the goals and timetables.[27]

In the first action, each contractor must conduct an analysis to determine the number and percentage of minorities and women in each affected job category. These figures must then be compared to the availability of qualified minorities and women in the labor market in which the contractor works. If the job category figures do not match the labor market availability figures, the contractor must take corrective measure to hire more women and/or minorities.

In the second distinct action, the contractor must develop numerical hiring goals and establish timetables in which to meet those goals. These goals and timetables then become operating targets for recruiting, hiring, promoting, and training women and minorities.

Next, a contractor must demonstrate that every effort has been made to recruit employees in minority communities, searching for minority candidates who meet minimum job qualifications. The regulations do not mandate that every contractor be successful in implementing the goals and timetables, only that they make an effort, in good faith, to obey the executive order.

It is clear that Executive Orders 11246 and 11375 require the employer to conduct more analysis, reporting, record maintenance, and compliance than Title VII, particularly in regard to affirmative action. Park and recreation departments participating in federal funding programs are not exempt from these directives.[28] Agencies should not award contracts to contractors who do not provide evidence of earnestly implementing established affirmative action programs. To do otherwise jeopardizes the legal and financial position of the park and recreation agency.

Vocational Rehabilitation Act of 1973, as Amended in 1974

A young college graduate with a dual degree in natural resource management and recreation and certification in wilderness survival skills applied for a seasonal position as a back-country ranger. The response to his inquiry about why he was not considered for the position was, "You are a diabetic and we can't take a chance that you might endanger yourself or others out in the 'brush' if you should require medical care."

Was the agency justified, legally, in offering this reason for not hiring the applicant?

The minority group to most recently claim discrimination and seek protection under the law is that group of persons known as "handicapped individuals." For them, the Vocational Rehabilitation Act of 1973 (as amended in 1974) is their counterpart of Title VII in prohibiting employment discrimination. The Vocational Rehabilitation Act (VRA) covers federal agencies and government contractors.

- Section 503, as amended in 1974, requires employers with contracts or subcontracts over $2,500 to include affirmative action clauses in the contracts. If the contract is $50,000 or more and the employer has at least fifty people on the payroll, the employer must also submit affirmative action plans for hiring the handicapped.
- Section 504 covers any program that receives federal financial aid and prohibits organizations that receive funds from discriminating against the handicapped in employment. This section of the law does not require an affirmative action plan.[29]

It is difficult to identify the exact number of handicapped persons in the United States. Some figures include partial disabilities such as hypertension, diabetes, and heart disease, bringing the figure up to as high as 36 million. Other figures are as low as 20 million. As the social stigma is reduced for persons with disabilities, the disabled are publicly acknowledging their conditions and adding their numbers to the records. Vietnam veterans with disabilities have also been added to recent figures concerning persons who are handicapped, and improved medical care has increased the average life span and thus the potential for developing disabling conditions that once killed individuals.[30] Consequently, the labor force now includes a growing number of disabled workers, a figure as high as 7 million.[31] One estimate of the total loss of earnings because of discrimination against disabled white males is $4.5 billion.[32]

Section 503 of the VRA is enforced by the Department of Labor's Office of Federal Contract Compliance Programs (OFCCP). In 1980, 91 percent of 300 companies surveyed by the Department of Labor were not in compliance with Section 503.[33] Enforcement has been slow because many questions remained, and still remain, unanswered. For example, what exactly is a handicapped person? What kinds of jobs can persons with different impairments safely perform, even with reasonable accommodation on the part of the employer? What about alcoholics and drug dependents?

The definition of a handicapped individual is quite broad and confusing. The handicapping condition can be physical, mental, or emotional. It does not have to be visible and can include certain illnesses, such as diabetes, heart disease, epilepsy, and cancer.[34] Alcoholism and drug dependency are also covered, together with 600 other conditions.[35]

If a person currently has a handicap which substantially limits one of life's major activities, such as self-care, ambulation, communication, or employment, that person is protected under VRA. Furthermore, if someone has a past record of a handicap (or considers himself or herself handicapped), that person is also protected under this law. These broad definitions have elicited comments such as, "Who is not handicapped?"

The interpretation of "reasonable accommodation" in the law is another area that is not self-explantory, nor easily adapted to a standard regulation. Department of Labor guidelines expect the contractor to make reasonable accommodations to the physical and mental limitations of an applicant or employee, unless an undue hardship would be imposed on the business. "Business necessity" and "financial expense" are two factors that can be considered in not being able to accommodate the handicapped person. If the organization cannot afford any changes to accommodate an applicant, the law does not mandate it to do so. Each individual employer's circumstances are different. Nor does reasonable accommodation mean that the contractor must tolerate lower job performance from the handicapped person, accept lower productivity, or endanger others by placing a handicapped worker in the work environment. It does mean that inexpensive assistance devices could be purchased or alterations to the work site provided to accommodate an employee in a wheelchair.

In the case of the diabetic applicant who was not considered for the position of back-country ranger, the agency could be courting a lawsuit for discrimination. Diabetes is one of the handicaps for which OFCCP has settled out of court in cases of employment discrimination.[36] The agency had the right to ask the applicant if he had any physical handicap that might impair his ability to perform his duties, but not until after the agency had decided that the applicant did or did not meet all the necessary requirements for the position. If the applicant was not considered for the position solely because of his diabetic condition, he could claim discrimination because his nonhandicapping qualifications were never considered, nor was he able to demonstrate that a diabetic in the "brush" is not a medical risk, nor that it requires reasonable accommodation on the part of the agency.

Vietnam Assistance Act and Veterans' Preference Laws

A female applied for a position at a coastal state park and was told she was one of five top candidates and would be called soon for an interview. When she was never notified, she contacted the park superintendent and learned that two veterans had "bumped" her from the interview list.

Did the state park system violate federal law?

There are over 30 million living veterans in this country from World Wars I and II, Korea, Vietnam, and peacetime. It has been of particular concern to the federal government that the Vietnam-era veterans have experienced the greatest discrimination in the labor market. Their number exceeds 9.7 million service personnel, a figure much higher than that of many individual ethnic minority groups.[37] The reasons for discrimination toward this group will not be addressed in this chapter, but it is interesting to note that only 32.3 percent of the Vietnam-era veterans actually experienced service in Vietnam.[38]

The Vietnam-era Veterans Readjustment Assistance Act of 1974 parallels the Vocational Rehabilitation Act. It requires federal contractors to take affirmative action to hire and promote Vietnam veterans, it prohibits employment discrimination, and it is enforced by the Department of Labor. The legislation mandates that employers who hold federal contracts of at least $10,000 must employ qualified disabled veterans and those nondisabled veterans who were on active duty for more than 180 days between August 1967 and May 1975.

All veterans (except those entering military service after October 1976) continue to receive five points of credit on competitive examinations and placement for federal civil service jobs, and ten points if they are disabled veterans. According to a number of women's groups, this practice of veterans' preference has resulted in half the federal civilian jobs being held by veterans. These womens' groups claim that veterans preference is a form of discrimination against women because the military draft and combat duty regulations exclude women, and social mores inhibit women from entering the armed forces.[39]

Title VII of the Civil Rights Act specifically exempts veterans' perference laws now found in all states, as well as the federal government. In other words, such preferential laws are recognized by Title VII as appropriate because they provide compensation to those who spent time in active military service. Because these laws are neutral on the matter of gender, the Supreme Court has also upheld preferential laws for veterans, ruling that such laws are constitutional even when they provide an "overwhelming" advantage to males.[40]

The state park system, therefore, did not violate federal legislation when it followed its state veterans' preference law and placed two qualified veterans on the list ahead of the female. Whenever veteran applicants meet minimum job qualifications, they may be given a point advantage, even if such practice appears to discriminate against women and those male nonveterans who may have been disqualified from military service because of some disability. The example given did violate good recruiting and selection personnel practices. An applicant should not be kept anticipating a promised call for a job interview. She should have been notified when her position changed on the list of applicants.

Pregnancy Discrimination Act of 1978

A female recreation director for a private industrial corporation took all her vacation and sick leave to have her second child. Because the company's insurance policy did not include pregnancy disability benefits, which would have paid her a percentage of her salary while she was out having the child, she planned to return to work immediately after childbirth. However, medical complications ensued, and when she finally returned to work two months later, she learned the company had hired someone else in her position.

Was this action fair? Was it legal?

Legislation passed in 1978 amends Title VII of the Civil Rights Act of 1964 and attempts to eliminate employment discrimination against pregnant employees. The Pregnancy Discrimination Act (PDA) relates primarily to employee benefit plans, and requires that women who are affected by pregnancy, childbirth, or any subsequently related medical conditions will receive the same benefits as any other disability in the fringe benefit program of the employer. Although pregnant women are not disabled because they are pregnant, there is a period of disability associated with every childbirth. Medical insurance must now cover pregnancy as fully as it covers other medical disability conditions.[41]

PDA has caused much discussion and controversy. It will certainly increase the cost of employee benefit plans and may also discourage employers from pursuing a vigorous affirmative action plan for women. This 1978 Amendment to Title VII of the Civil Rights Act represents the conclusion of a long emotional battle on the issue of pregnancy. Earlier regulations gave pregnant women the right to continue to work while pregnant, and the right to take a leave of absence for childbirth so that they could return to their jobs. The law says that employers may not discriminate against pregnant women or women who may become pregnant.

The adversaries of such regulations say that pregnancy is a voluntary condition and can be planned, and many women (50 percent) do not return to work. Thus disability benefits result in severence pay for those women who do not return to work. Furthermore, when a woman is disabled due to pregnancy or childbirth, someone must be assigned to assume her duties. Temporary replacement costs are an additional expense for the employer. Adversaries claim that businesses may have to reduce medical and disability benefits for both men and women, or if the employer does not have any such plan, he may choose not to establish one because of PDA. Thus PDA could result in a setback for all employee benefits progress.[42] Proponents of the law claim that it was discriminating not to pay benefits for a disability that affects only women, and that disability benefits are paid for other voluntary conditions, such as alcholism and drug addiction. These arguments raise the question: How equal do different classes of people have to be treated under the law in order not to discriminate?

In the case of the female recreation director, the company prior to PDA would have been within their legal rights not to provide pregnancy disability benefits in their insurance coverage. The Supreme Court in *General Electric* v. *Gilbert* (1976) struck down an EEOC guideline, Sex Discrimination—Part 1604. This guideline stated that pregnancies were temporary disabilities and should be covered under any health plan. The Court ruled that such guidelines were in conflict with interpretations of the Equal Pay Act, and that difference in benefit plans between men and women were legal. However, with the passage of PDA two years later, Congress mandated that pregnancy be treated like any other disability in health insurance plans.

Thus, if the industrial corporation provided 60 percent salary benefits for sixty days for any disability, the female recreation director would be entitled to those same benefits the two months she experienced medical complications following childbirth. Furthermore, the corporation could not discharge her from her position during that time period, even if she had used all sick and vacation leave. Explanations of the guidelines can become complex and will not be explained in detail here. Each case should be considered independently with EEOC prior to any discharge decision, to avoid a future complaint or lawsuit.

Sexual Harassment Guidelines, Title VII

"Sarah, I'll be happy to pay for your N.R.P.A. Congress registration fee and give you administrative leave to go, if you want to share my room for five days while we are in Kansas City." Sarah filed a complaint against her boss.
Will anyone take her complaint seriously?

This supervisor is demonstrating an overt act of sexual harassment. He is requesting implied sexual favors as a prerequisite condition to granting approval and financial support for professional development opportunities. Sexual harassment is a form of discrimination in violation of Title VII of the Civil Rights Act of 1964. Recent guidelines issued in 1980 by EEOC place the responsibility on the employing agency, as well as the supervisor, to provide a work environment free from unwelcome sexual advances. Sarah has a valid complaint against both her boss and the organization for whom they work.

Like Title VII, the guidelines cover all employers who hire fifteen or more employees, all public agencies, and educational institutions and hospitals. EEOC enforces these guidelines and will notify the employer when a complaint is filed. Although charges are not made public, neither the employer not the complainant is bound to confidentiality. These guidelines do not have the force of law, but they closely parallel already existing court decisions which state that employers are responsible for the actions of their employees.

What is sexual harassment? Personal relationships between employees do not necessarily constitute sexual harassment. It is only when the relationships include unwelcome sexual advances, requests for sexual favors, and other verbal or physical conduct that occurs when:

1. Submission to such conduct is explicitly or implicitly implied as a prerequisite to employment.
2. Submission to or rejection of such conduct is used as a basis for employment decisions, such as assignments, training, pay, and so on.
3. Such conduct creates an atmosphere where the employee's work performance is disturbed, or where the employee feels intimidated, or where she or he finds the behavior hostile or offensive.

The following examples *might* constitute sexual harassment:

• Unnecessary patting or pinching.
• Constant brushing against another's body.
• "Friendly" arms around the shoulder.
• Remarks about clothing, body, or sexual activities.

A number of court cases have ruled that sexual harassment is in violation of Title VII, and several courts have awarded back pay to the plaintiff. The courts have also stated that an employee does not have to demonstrate that tangible job benefits such as pay, promotion, or discharge were at stake in not submitting to sexual harassment. The employee only has to demonstrate that the unwanted conduct affected his or her work or created an offensive work environment. This principle was the deciding factor in the case of *Hensen* v. *City of Dundee* (1982). The court ruled that when an employee's psychological well-being is affected because the work environment becomes offensive due to sexual harassment, the employee does not have to demonstrate the loss of tangible job benefits. The employer is guilty of violating Title VII.[43]

To comply with the guidelines and avoid embarrassing lawsuits, employers should develop a clearly written policy prohibiting sexual harassment. First, this policy should include a grievance procedure which initially guarantees confidentiality. Employees do not want to fear retribution for filing complaints. The next step is to communicate both the policy and the grievance procedures to all employees through pamphlets, hearings, staff meetings, and memorandum. Both males and females need to know they do not have to tolerate sexual harassment on the job, and that the employer's position is one where guilty persons will be disciplined. The last step is more difficult and requires that employees, especially men, become more sensitive to behavior that might be construed as sexually harassing. Liability can be reduced if the employer has a history of discouraging sexual harassment in the work environment. This means investigating complaints and dealing appropriately with guilty employees. Knowledge of sexual harassment without taking action to correct it places the employer in violation of the law.

How widespread is sexual harassment? General studies have documented that more than 70 percent of all respondents to surveys have experienced overt physical harassment and sexual remarks.[44] The majority of these respondents regarded this behavior as a serious employment problem but felt that if they complained to their supervisor, nothing would be done.

The problem of sexual harassment in the work environment will persist as long as some males and females see other people as sex objects instead of as people needing and deserving respect. It is up to the employer and each supervisor to eliminate conscious and overt behavior which is unwanted by an employee and which fits the definition of sexual harassment.

Summary and Recommendations

1. The primary purpose of EEO legislation is to ensure that every person has the right to fair treatment as a job seeker and as an employee.
2. Employment practices shall be based on a person's ability, work performance, and potential to learn the job rather than on his or her age, sex, race, religion, color, national origin, or handicapping condition.
3. An employment practice is discriminatory if it (a) treats people differently, or (b) leads to unequal consequences for different groups.
4. The Civil Rights Act of 1964 outlawed discriminatory acts regardless of whether they are deliberately planned or accidentally executed.
5. The EEOC, established by the 1964 Civil Rights Act, has responsibility for (a) issuing the regulations that ensure compliance with the Act, and (b) processing complaints of discrimination.
6. Under the Equal Pay Act, employers are required to pay equal wages to men and women performing similar work requiring similar skill, effort, and responsibility.

7. Employers may pay differential wages when those wages are based on an established seniority or merit system.
8. Whereas both the Civil Rights Act and the Age Discrimination Act provide for exemptions from the law for "bona fide occupational qualifications" (BFOQs), employers and supervisors should exercise caution in taking advantage of these permissible exceptions. Remember, race and color are not permissible BFOQs.
9. Park and recreation agencies should not award contracts to contractors who cannot provide evidence of obeying presidential executive orders which serve to eliminate employment discrimination. Ignorance of discriminatory practices is not excusable under the law.
10. Employers are expected to make reasonable accommodations for the physical and mental limitations of job applicants or employees, unless an undue financial hardship would be imposed on the hiring organization. The laws do not expect the employers to jeopardize the safety or health of employees and the public in order to hire a person with a disabling condition.
11. State and federal veterans' preference laws were passed to compensate those who spent time in active military service. These laws have been upheld as legal by the Supreme Court and the Civil Rights Act.
12. Organizations that provide employee disability health insurance benefits must provide the same benefits for pregnant employees who may be absent from work due to pregnancy- or childbirth-related medical problems.
13. Employers should develop written policies and grievances and disciplinary procedures concerning sexual harassment. These must be communicated to all employees. Knowledge of sexual harassment without taking measures to eradicate it places the employer in violation of the law.

Discussion Topics

1. Why should park and recreation organizations want to comply with EEO?
2. What is adverse impact? What are ways that organizations can avoid adverse impact charges? Why is *Griggs* v. *Duke Power* recognized as an important case in the area of adverse impact discrimination?
3. What is meant by "job relatedness" and "business necessity"? How might these concepts apply to organizations providing leisure services?
4. Under what conditions would "good-natured fun" constitute sexual harassment?

5. Under what conditions can an employer be held responsible for sexual harassment of its employees?
6. Do you agree or disagree with the following statements? Explain your rationale.
   (a) "Brotherhood cannot be legislated."
   (b) "The courts have no right to impose AAP quotas to remedy past wrongs."
   (c) "The discrimination in employment problem has been rapidly reduced in recent years."
7. When could employees make a case for reverse discrimination?
8. Should government impose a mandatory retirement age? Provide an argument against such an act. What rationale exists for government intervention?
9. What is the difference between prejudice and discrimination?
10. Assume that you are the manager of a county athletic program. You are responsible for hiring, training, supervising, and evaluating a staff of full-time and part-time personnel. List a number of discriminatory practices that you should avoid.

Notes

1. Jack Halloran, *Supervision: The Act of Management* (Englewood Cliffs, N.J.: Prentice-Hall, Inc., 1981), p. 307.
2. George Strauss and Leonard R. Sayles, *Personnel: The Human Problems of Management*, 4th ed. (Englewood Cliffs, N.J.: Prentice-Hall, Inc., 1980), p. 439.
3. Ibid.
4. Robert Calvert, *Affirmative Action: A Comprehensive Recruitment Manual* (Garrett Park, Md: Garrett Park Press, 1979), p. 281.
5. *Webster's New Collegiate Dictionary* (Springfield, Mass.: G. & C. Merriam Co., 1975), p. 987.
6. Jack Halloran, *Applied Human Relations: An Organizational Approach* (Englewood Cliffs, N.J.: Prentice-Hall, Inc., 1978), p. 438.
7. H. C. Jain and P. J. Sloane, "The Structure of Labor Markets, Minority Workers and E.E.O. Legislation," *International Journal of Social Economics* 3 (1981): 109.
8. Ibid.
9. Richard D. Arvey, *Fairness in Selecting Employees* (Reading, Mass.: Addison-Wesley Publishing Co., Inc., 1979), p. 67.
10. *Griggs* v. *Duke Power Co.*, United States Supreme Court Decision (401 U.S. 424), 1971.
11. Margaret Butteriss, revised by Karl Albrecht, *New Management Tools* (Englewood Cliffs, N.J.: Prentice-Hall, Inc., 1979), p. 143.
12. Arvey, *Fairness in Selecting Employees*, p. 42.

13. Arthur N. Frakt and Janna S. Rankin, *The Law of Parks, Recreation Resources, and Leisure Services* (Salt Lake City, Utah: Brighton Publishing Co., 1982), p. 220.
14. *Griggs* v. *Duke Power Co.*
15. Arthur A. Sloane, *Personnel: Managing Human Resources* (Englewood Cliffs, N.J.: Prentice-Hall, Inc., 1983), p. 77.
16. Armando M. Rodriguez, "A Look at EEO," *Labor Law Journal* 33 (May 1982): 262.
17. Ibid., p. 263.
18. Calvert, *Affirmative Action*, p. 298.
19. James Ledvinka, *Federal Regulation of Personnel and Human Resource Management*, Kent Human Resource Management Series, Richard W. Beatty, University of Colorado at Boulder, Series Consulting Editor (New York: Van Nostrand Reinhold Company, Inc., 1982), p. 30.
20. Ibid.
21. These 1978 guidelines were adopted by the EEOC, Civil Service Commission, Department of Labor, and Department of Justice, and can be read in the *Federal Register*, August 25, 1978.
22. Frakt and Rankin, *The Law of Parks, Recreation Resources, and Leisure Services*, p. 224.
23. Halloran, *Supervision*, p. 314.
24. Ledvinka, *Federal Regulation of Personnel and Human Resource Management*, p. 73.
25. Edwin B. Flippo, *Personnel Management*, 5th ed. (New York: McGraw-Hill Book Company, 1980), p. 45.
26. Dale S. Beach, *Personnel: The Management of People at Work*, 4th ed. (New York: Macmillan Publishing Company, 1980), p. 266.
27. Sloane, *Personnel*, 86.
28. Frakt and Rankin, *The Law of Parks, Recreation Resources, and Leisure Services*, p. 225.
29. Ibid., p. 222.
30. Gopal C. Pati and Glenn Morrison, "Enabling the Disabled," *Harvard Business Review* (July–August 1982): 82.
31. Flippo, *Personnel Management*, p. 47.
32. Richard I. Lehr, "Employer Duties to Accommodate Handicapped Employees," *Labor Law Journal* 31 (March 1980): 175.
33. Gopal C. Pati and John I. Adkins, "Hire the Handicapped—Compliance Is Good Business," *Harvard Business Review* (January–February 1980): 180.
34. Ledvinka, *Federal Regulation of Personnel and Human Resource Management*, p. 79.
35. Pati and Adkins, "Hire the Handicapped," p. 180.
36. Flippo, *Personnel Management*, p. 48.
37. *Statistical Abstracts of the United States: National Data Book and Guide to Source* (103rd Edition), U.S. Department of Commerce, Bureau of the Census (Washington, D.C.: U.S. Government Printing Office, 1982–1983), p. 366.
38. Ibid.
39. Strauss and Sayles, *Personnel*, p. 446.

40. Frakt and Rankin, *The Law of Parks, Recreation Resources, and Leisure Services,* p. 227.

41. Ledvinka, *Federal Regulation of Personnel and Human Resource Management,* p. 62.

42. Paul S. Greenlaw and Diana L. Foderaro, "Some Further Implications of the Pregnancy Discrimination Act," *Personnel Journal* (January 1980): 43.

43. James Koslowski, "Employer Liability for Sexual Harassment in the Workplace," in *Parks and Recreation* (Alexandria, Va.: National Recreation and Park Association, April 1983), p. 24.

44. Bernice R. Sandler and Associates, "Sexual Harassment: A Hidden Problem," *Educational Record* (Winter 1981): 52–53.

2

Legal Environment: Employee Concerns

While EEO legislation has received the most attention in recent decades, federal laws and regulations have influenced human resource management since the 1920s, when the federal government and court actions attempted to intervene in the disputes between organized labor and employees (see Figure 2.1). Just as Chapter 1 focused on EEO legislation, this chapter attempts to give the reader an overview of the magnitude of governmental legislation in labor relations, health and safety benefits, and compensation and civil liberties: legislation that also influences the supervision and management of park, recreation, and leisure service employees. An awareness of these laws may be all that is required of first-line supervisors. But as the professional accepts greater responsibility within the organization, moving up into middle and top management, the need to interact with attorneys, personnel, and labor relations specialists is magnified and additional information and training should be sought. At all levels, supervisors should understand the significance that these laws play in maintaining a work environment which will maximize employee motivation and which will respond to employee concerns for safety, benefits, and personal rights.

Labor Relations

In Chapter 13 we delve into labor issues in more detail, discussing the relationship between each law and personnel practices. The following

EMPLOYMENT LEGISLATION

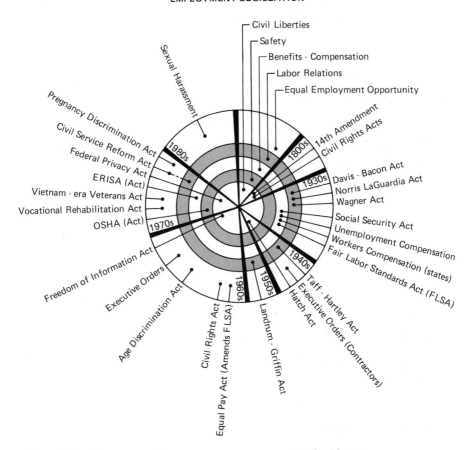

Figure 2.1   Summary of human resource management legislation.

discussion provides only a brief description of the most important labor laws.

National Labor Relations Act of 1935 (Wagner Act)

The primary purpose of this law was to give employees more bargaining power. Known as the Wagner Act, it has served as the basic federal statement of policy toward labor–management relations. Chapter 13 provides the reader with additional details on this law. To administer the Wagner Act, the National Labor Relations Board (NLRB) was established. The NLRB investigates and decides on employers' unfair labor practices and is responsible for conducting union representation elections.

Labor–Management Relations Act of 1947 and 1974 (Taft–Hartley Act)

Congress passed this law after employers complained that the Wagner Act not only favored unions too much, but failed to address unfair union practices. Thus the Taft–Hartley Act, as it is frequently called, attempted to establish a balance of power between the labor union and the employer. One of its most notable provisions recognized the right of employees not to join unions. It also prohibits strikes during national emergencies.

Labor–Management Reporting and Disclosure Act of 1959 (Landrum–Griffin Act)

In an effort to prevent improper union practices and the abuse of power by some union officials, the Landrum–Griffin Act was passed to protect employees and regulate the internal affairs of unions. It included provisions that controlled union elections, membership dues, and member conduct.

Federal Employees and Labor Relations

Although employees in the private sector have been governed by federal legislation for fifty years, federal government employees were excluded from those labor relations laws discussed previously in this section. Only in the past twenty years were federal employees protected under executive orders, and only in the past few years were they covered by congressional law.

President Kennedy in 1962 established the first labor relations regulations for federal employees. Executive Order (EO) 10988 recognized employees' right to organize and collectively bargain, although employees were forbidden to strike. Agency heads had the final authority over all grievances. Orders 11491, 11616, and 11838 amended EO 10988, clarified collective bargaining regulations, and created a Labor Relations Council to hear appeals and discuss personnel practices and working conditions. Federal employees still did not have the same rights as those of workers in the private sector, however, because they could not bargain for salaries or benefits, and their respective agency heads still made the final decisions on all matters.

The Civil Service Reform Act, passed by Congress in 1978, superseded previous executive orders and became the basic law governing labor relations for federal employees. Presidents cannot refine, change, or interpret it. This is a major change from previous practices. One member of the Federal Labor Relations Authority (FLRA) has referred to the act as "the most significant development in federal personnel administration since the passage of the Civil Service Act in 1883."[1] The act created the FLRA, modeled after the NLRB. This new, independent, bipartisan authority is not directed by any other federal agency. Rather, it has the final say in resolving labor disputes and interpreting the Civil Service Reform Act. Agency heads no longer have this authority. Only the courts offer a higher authority on any FLRA decision. Still excluded from arbitration are matters pertaining to salary, benefits, examination, and appointments.

State and Local Government Employees

Most states have passed laws pertaining to the collective bargaining rights of state and local public employees, although the coverage and permissiveness varies from state to state. While some state laws protect all public employees, others only specify and cover certain groups, while exempting other groups.[2] Many states forbid employees to strike and will fine or jail strike leaders. The rights of public-sector employees, as those rights relate to collective bargaining, have not been as extensive as those in the private sector, but the greatest growth in unionization in recent years has been public-sector labor organizations.[3]

Health and Safety

It is important for the reader to understand that each supervisor must accept responsibility for maintaining a healthy and safe work environment. In Chapter 14 we discuss the principles of health legislation and provide a framework to help the supervisor better understand how to assume and affirmatively pursue that responsibility. Workers' compensation and the Occupational Safety and Health Act represent the major health-related legislation. They are included here only to identify for the reader all pertinent employment legislation in this chapter.

Workers' Compensation Laws

Until 1970 and the passage of the Occupational Safety and Health Act, health and safety on the job had been governed exclusively by individual state laws, although some effort had been made by the federal government to control safety conditions in certain industries. Workers' compensation laws vary considerably from state to state, but certain provisions are similar in all states. These laws are designed to compensate employees for job related illnesses or injuries, whether temporary or permanent; to provide rehabilitation services to reclaim the injured worker's capabilities; and to award death benefits to survivors.

Not all states make employer participation compulsory. In some cases, employers are self-insured. Where the employer does provide coverage for employees, the employer pays all the costs through insurance premiums based in part on a rate set according to the organization's past safety and health record. The employer, through each supervisor, must maintain a safe work site in order to reduce accidents and thereby reduce workers' compensation costs, a figure that exceeds $16 billion per year.[4]

In most states, there is a workers' compensation board which decides disputed claims, generally as to what is a compensable injury. Since some of these injuries can be avoided or their numbers reduced through employer cooperation and supervisory vigilance, a full discussion is provided in Chapter 14.

Generally, part-time recreation and park employees, however short their period of work, are covered by workers' compensation if the employer is contributing financially to a program. Volunteers would not usually be covered unless (1) the insurance company agrees and/or extra premiums were paid, or (2) the volunteer receives some form of recompense, such as a free lunch, free use of facilities, or a stipend. Court cases have supported the contention that when the work is performed within the course of business hours and represents an integral part of the recreation operation, the person should be covered, like any other wage-earning employee.[5]

The issues are not as clear on whether an independent contractor performing an integral service for the recreation organization and, working under the supervision of the employer, should receive compensation for injuries.[6]

Although state workers' compensation laws have not always been adequate, there has been a trend in recent years to revise state laws and resolve existing problems. For this reason, there is strong opposition to any move by the federal government to intervene and govern such systems[7] (see Figure 2.2).

WHIRLPOOL CORPORATION v. MARSHALL (1980)

Following an on-the-job death of an employee, a foreman ordered two workers to perform the same hazardous duties. The workers refused, claiming that the conditions surrounding the assignment were unsafe. When they were formally reprimanded and sent home without pay, they challenged this action in court. The Supreme Court decided that the employees were justified in refusing to work under those conditions, which posed risk of injury or death, and under circumstances where there was not time for the workers to appeal to the employer or to the Occupational Safety and Health Administration.

Figure 2.2   Insubordination is justified when a work environment fails to meet OSHA standards.

Occupational Safety and Health Act of 1970

It was not until the 1960s that the federal government seriously concerned itself with safety in the private sector. Prior to the passage of the Occupational Safety and Health Act of 1970 (OSHA), employee safety was regulated by state workers' compensation laws; laws often obsolete and lacking in enforcement. As a result of a coal mine explosion in 1968 and a significant increase in injuries on the job during the previous decade, unions became active in lobbying for job-safety legislation. Congressional lawmakers were convinced that work environments were unsafe after hearing considerable evidence on black lung disease, work accidents, and job-related mortality rates.

The purpose of OSHA is to preserve human resources by ensuring, as far as possible, safe and healthy working conditions for all workers. State workers' compensation laws are designed to assist the worker after an accident, but OSHA regulations are designed to reduce the risk of accidents in the first place. This means that each nongovernment recreation employer must furnish his or her employees with a place of employment free from recognized hazards that are likely to cause physical harm or death. Each employee must abide by the prescribed standards or face prescribed disciplinary action specifically permitted in OSHA regulations. The federal government regulates the employer, but the employer, through supervision, must ensure that employees are in compliance with the OSHA standards. Employees of federal, state, and local government are excluded in this law.

The administration and enforcement of this act is vested in the Occupational Safety and Health Administration within the Department of Labor. This agency establishes the standards, conducts on-site inspections, and issues citations for OSHA violations. An independent review commission functions like a court to hear appeals, and a national institute conducts safety standards research and trains inspectors.

The act itself is very brief, but the technical and complex regulations and standards number in the thousands and fill volumes. It would be impossible to provide the reader with all the basic provisions in the regulations and standards as they pertain to parks and recreation.

Benefits and Compensation

Benefits other than wages did not exist at the turn of the century. Now they can consume as much as 30 to 35 percent of the employer's payroll. Because they are so widely accepted as part of the cost of hiring labor, the term "fringe benefits" is no longer appropriate. No one would argue that benefits vary from employer to employer, some being more generous than others. The discussion on how those benefits can vary is provided in Chapter 9. This section merely identifies federal legislation and regulations that govern basic benefits and unemployment compensation.

Social Security Act of 1935

The Social Security Act of 1935 was passed near the end of the Great Depression, following public concern over economic security. It now covers approximately 90 percent of all wage earners in this country.[8] Only the military, federal employees, railroad workers, and some state and local public employees do not participate in the program. Initially, the plan was designed to force workers, through payroll deductions matched by the employer, to save for old age. At age 65 the worker could retire and receive a modest pension to supplement his or her own savings. Today, the plan not only covers retired workers, but provides benefits to survivors of deceased workers, pays disability benefits, and covers payments for medical and hospital care for those 65 years of age or older. The employers' contribution to the pension is the part that is considered a benefit.

It is no secret that this federal program is financially overextended and has become the focus of much adverse attention. There are several reasons for this criticism. To keep up with the increased number of retired persons and the expanded programs, payroll deduction taxes for both the employee and the employer have risen sharply, and are expected to reach 7.15 percent. There are currently seven people employed for every Social Security recipient, and the projected ratio of three to one is predicted in the next decade by some authorities.[9] No one is happy to pay more taxes and take home less money.

The average monthly pension is the same for everyone, reflecting periodic adjustments based on the Consumer Price Index. Payments are not in proportion to what was paid into the system. In order to maintain a retirement life-style that is similar to preretirement life-style, many workers have had to invest in other pension plans as well. These workers recognize that retirees have had difficulty living exclusively from Social Security income. With increased payroll deduction taxes and fear of not being able to support oneself on a Social Security pension, Americans are criticizing the management of the Social Security trust fund, which now experiences greater expenditures than revenues, a situation that could eventually deplete the fund.

Employee Retirement Income Security Act of 1974

The Employment Retirement Income Security Act (ERISA) attempts to regulate the internal management of the 300,000 private pension plans now in existence in order to protect the employees who have contributed to the plans.[10] Not every employer is required to have a plan, but those who offer their employees this benefit are regulated by the federal government under this law. The financial solvency of every retirement pension plan approved by ERISA is now guaranteed by the Pension Benefit Guarantee Corporation, an entity created by ERISA. This corporation will continue to make payments on each retired member of a pension plan should their plan be terminated or should their former employer go bankrupt. Congress appropriates money to the corporation and income is also generated from insurance fees paid by all employers. Employers must pay an annual fee for each of their participating employees and must file an annual report with the Secretary of Labor.

Like OSHA, this law is very lengthy, complex, and highly technical. Some employers claim that pension plans are more expensive now because the law demands so much. This may be true, but workers can now retire without fear that their pension program will not be able to pay out benefits when they most need the money.

Unemployment Compensation

The seasonal nature of recreation in both the private and public sectors places an economic strain on the underemployed park or recreation worker who can find work only during specific months of the year. It can also place a burden on the employer, who must pay higher unemployment taxes. For these reasons, the reader should know how some management decisions make an impact on unemployment compensation rates: decisions such as whether to hire seasonal employees rather than full-time workers, and whether to fire or retain an employee.

Title IV of the Social Security Act of 1935 actually forced the states into enacting unemployment compensation laws. The federal government imposed a federal payroll tax on every employer, but permitted the employer to pay the tax into a state plan instead of paying the tax to the federal government. To keep the tax money in the state, each state established its own unemployment compensation plan by 1937.

Not only do the tax rates differ from state to state, but the tax rate for each employer also varies, based on the employer's own record of unemployment payments to discharged employees. This is referred to as an *experiencing rating system*. By terminating fewer employees, the employer pays taxes based on a lower rate. Rates might be as low as 1 percent or as high as 6 percent paid on a portion of the total payroll.[11] Some states, such as Michigan, treat public employers as reimbursing employers and unemployment payments are paid to the state equal only to those unemployment payments made to discharged employees the preceding year by that particular employer.

The federal government sets minimum standards for both the dollar amount of weekly payments and for the length of time that payments should be made to each unemployed person. The government also requires states to establish a state employment service and to develop a plan to train and find jobs for handicapped workers.

To receive payments, a worker must:

1. Have worked a specified period of time for the employer.
2. Have been terminated through no fault of his or her own and not for on-the-job misconduct, or because the worker chose to leave without a good reason.
3. Have filed for benefits.
4. Be available and able to work should the state employment service locate another job.
5. Be making reasonable effort to find employment in the same or similar line of work.

Thus, if an athletic specialist, terminated from a local recreation agency, met all these conditions, the employment service would expect him to be seeking work at hospitals, prisons, private clubs, or industries. But if a seasonal interpreter for the National Park Service met all the first four conditions, she would probably find it difficult to find similar work in an isolated area near the National Park that had formerly hired her.

Civil Liberties

A number of state and federal laws protect individual privacy, including the First, Fifth, and Fourteenth Amendments to the U.S. Constitution. The issues of personal privacy have been very controversial in the work environment. These issues include freedom of expression, loyalty oaths, private life and morals, political activities, the use of the lie detector, and access to employee records.

Freedom of Speech

The First Amendment guarantees freedom of speech for every citizen. A number of conflicting court decisions have clouded this issue, however, as it relates to government employees, such as recreation workers, who may choose to publicly criticize their supervisors or elected officials. A so-called *balancing test* is usually applied in court cases on this issue. The balancing test examines the rights of employees as citizens to comment on public matters against any evidence that a public official is unable to continue to provide services to the public. If a public official is unable to serve the public satisfactorily as a result of an employee's unfavorable remarks, the courts are not sympathetic to the employee's claim that "freedom of speech" was violated.[12] Where employee statements do not affect their own performance, disrupt the harmony of the workplace, violate employer confidentiality, or damage the reputation of the agency, the courts have generally supported the employee's right to make public statements about the activities of the employer.

Loyalty Oaths

Prior to the 1960s the swearing of loyalty oaths was upheld by the U.S. Supreme Court as a reasonable requirement for governments to impose on employees.[13] But a number of court decisions in the 1960s struck down the constitutionality of loyalty oaths, as well as affidavits, as a prerequisite for employment. It is no longer advisable to ask employees to take oaths of allegiance or to sign affidavits which state that they have never been a member of an anti-American organization.

Morals and Private Life

Not too many years ago, social attitudes, laws, and even court sanctions endorsed the discharge of employees for immoral conduct: behavior such as extramarital relations, openly living together without a marriage contract, and homosexuality. As the courts shifted their position and demanded that immoral conduct be related to job performance, public attitudes also changed.[14] Today, laws against homosexuality are being repealed or ignored, and some cities are enacting EEO ordinances protecting homosexuals.[15] Federal courts have ruled that homosexuals cannot be discharged just because they are homosexuals. But if they broadcast their preferential activities to the degree that the work environment is disrupted or the agency loses the public's confidence, the homosexual employees may be fired.[16] The precedent case of *Norton* v. *Macy* (1969) is the one still cited. The National Aeronautics and Space Administration (NASA) fired an employee for admitting to homosexual tendencies. The court ruled that NASA should reinstate the employee because he was a good worker, did not work in an area where security risks are involved, and did not publicly flaunt his behavior to attract public scandal for NASA.

Lie Detectors

The use of the polygraph, better known as the lie detector, has been banned in many states to protect job applicants and employees from giving information which they do not wish to give. It is also recognized that the instrument is only 75 percent accurate.[17] But while more and more states move to prohibit the use of lie detectors, many businesses are turning to this instrument in an effort to stem the rising costs of theft, computer tampering, and embezzlement, a figure estimated to be $40 billion in 1982.[18]

From a civil liberties perspective, the use of the lie detector on an unwilling employee or prospective employee is an invasion of privacy and violates the Fifth Amendment (privilege against self-incrimination) and the Fourth Amendment protection against unreasonable search. Labor arbitrators have upheld employees' refusal to take lie detector tests as insufficient grounds for discharge. The National Labor Relations Board and Unemployment Compensation Boards of Review have also rejected the results of such tests from evidence.[19]

It has been recommended that Congress legislate against the use of the lie detector, but this probably will not happen since so many business firms regard the machine as a partial solution to security problems.[20] Employers should note that the EEOC has ruled the use of lie-detector tests to be in violation of civil rights laws because they discriminate against nonwhite job applicants.

Employee Records

With the accumulation of so much information about employees in order to document and satisfy recent federal legislation and regulations, and with the increased use of credit cards and computers, the public has begun to express concern over uncontrolled access to personal records. The regulation of private employers on matters of this nature has been the legal province of each individual state. The Privacy Act of 1974 and the Freedom of Information Act of 1966 does attempt to govern public agencies and protect federal employees and private citizens.

The Privacy Act states that the dissemination of federal employee records is an invasion of privacy when the information is provided without the consent of the federal employee. The act limits disclosure of a person's records. Federal employees also have the right to determine what information is on file by reviewing their records, and to correct any misinformation or refute derogatory remarks. They may prevent the use of those records for any purpose other than that purpose for which the information was obtained.[21] The Freedom of Information Act mandates that federal agencies must respond within ten days to a request by a person for his or her personal records.

Since privacy has always been valued by Americans, it is reasonable to assume that additional privacy legislation will be enacted in the future. The private sector has been voluntarily changing their personnel practices to protect employees' records. An effort has been made to guarantee the employee the right to see his or her records, make appropriate adjustments, and know how the information will be used. Attention to the employee's rights of privacy has an effect on the day-to-day functioning of a supervisor. As a provider of information, the supervisor should never give information about an employee over the telephone. The supervisor should document all information that is released, and release objective facts only after obtaining written consent from the employee. Employees, on the other hand, should have access to their records and be able to challenge any false information.

Summary and Recommendations

1. Employees have the legal right to organize for their mutual benefit, but they may not be forced to join unions.
2. The Civil Service Reform Act of 1978 governs labor relations for federal employees. These employees are not permitted to arbitrate for salary, benefits, examinations, or appointments.

3. State laws covering public employees vary considerably in their permissiveness to bargain and strike.
4. Employees' health and safety are protected by state workers' compensation laws and the Occupational Safety and Health Act (OSHA) of 1970. OSHA serves to prevent accidents and state laws provide compensation after an accident.
5. The purpose of the Social Security Act is to provide income for retired workers and their survivors, to pay disability benefits, and to cover medical expenses for those age 65 or older. Most workers in the United States contribute to this program through mandatory payroll deductions.
6. The Social Security Act also forces every state to establish a statewide unemployment compensation program whereby unemployed workers receive a minimum stipend for a certain period of time. The employer pays a payroll tax into the state fund based on his record of unemployment payments to discharged employees.
7. The Employee Retirement Income Security Act of 1974 (ERISA) attempts to regulate the management of thousands of private pension plans so that workers can retire and be guaranteed the benefits they invested in pension plans during their working years.
8. Park and recreation employers should become familiar with state laws pertaining to workers compensation, unemployment compensation, and employee civil liberties. Personnel departments and legal advisors are in the best position to provide employers with this information as well as relevant interpretation of these laws.

Discussion Topics

1. Should federal employees have the right to bargain for salaries and benefits?
2. What is occupational health and safety? Provide several examples. Who is covered under OSHA?
3. How might an agency's unemployment compensation program be effected if it chooses to reduce its number of full-time employees and hire more seasonals?
4. Who should be responsible for the cost of employee benefits: employees, employers, state government, or the federal government?
5. Is the Social Security system meeting its original intent? Explain.
6. Why was the Employee Retirement Income Security Act of 1974 (ERISA) a significant piece of legislation?
7. List some important contemporary issues in the area of employee rights which have some relationship to leisure service organizations.

Notes

1. Henry B. Frazier III, "Labor–Management Relations in the Federal Government," *Labor Law Journal* 30 (March 1979): 131.
2. Arthur N. Frakt and Janna S. Rankin, *The Law of Parks, Recreation Resources, and Leisure Services* (Salt Lake City, Utah: Brighton Publishing Co., 1982), p. 212.
3. Randall S. Schuler, *Personnel and Human Resource Management* (St. Paul, Minn.: West Publishing Co., 1981), p. 397.
4. Arthur A. Sloane, *Personnel: Managing Human Resources* (Englewood Cliffs, N.J.: Prentice-Hall, Inc., 1983), p. 324.
5. Frakt and Rankin, *The Law of Parks, Recreation Resources, and Leisure Services*, p. 212.
6. Ibid., p. 246.
7. James Ledvinka, *Federal Regulation of Personnel and Human Resource Management*, Kent Human Resource Management Series, Richard W. Beatty, University of Colorado at Boulder, Series Consulting Editor (New York: Van Nostrand Reinhold Company, Inc., 1982), p. 153.
8. Sloane, *Personnel*, p. 342.
9. Schuler, *Personnel and Human Resource Management*, p. 312.
10. Sloane, *Personnel*, p. 352.
11. Ledvinko, *Federal Regulation of Personnel and Human Resource Management*, p. 245.
12. Felix A. Nigro and Lloyd G. Nigro, *The New Public Personnel Administration* (Itasca, Ill.: F. E. Peacock Publishers, Inc., 1976), p. 284.
13. Ibid., p. 288.
14. Ibid., p. 291.
15. George Strauss and Leonard R. Sayles, *Personnel: The Human Problems of Management*, 4th ed. (Englewood Cliffs, N.J.: Prentice-Hall, Inc., 1980), p. 446.
16. Ibid.
17. Dale S. Beach, *Personnel: The Management of People at Work*, 5th ed. (New York: McGraw-Hill Book Company, 1980), p. 209.
18. John A. Belt, "The Polygraph: A Questionable Personnel Tool," *Personnel Administrator* (August 1983): 65.
19. Ibid., p. 69.
20. Ledvinka, *Federal Regulation of Personnel and Human Resource Management*, p. 255.
21. Ibid., p. 12.

3
Planning and Organizing for Personnel

With this chapter we begin our discussion of the five human resource management functions first presented in the Introduction: planning, organizing, staffing, directing, and controlling. In this chapter we focus on *planning and organizing*.

As we pointed out in the Introduction, the five human resource management functions do follow a logical sequence, and for the sake of learning, they will be discussed in the order in which we named them. Keep in mind, however, that in the real world, these functions are highly interrelated and usually occur simultaneously. Consider the two functions discussed in this chapter: planning and organizing. As plans change, the organizational structure will need to be changed, and vice versa.

We start this chapter with a case study that sets up a scenario that will be used throughout the chapter. After the steps involved in planning for personnel are covered, we discuss how the organization's overall work load is first broken down into specific activities and then reassembled into a functional organizational structure.

Start with Goals

Human resource planning and organizing must be directed toward some purpose. That purpose, the starting point for our discussion and the guiding force that gives human resource planning and organizing its

Case Study

STATE PARKS NEED A PLAN

The division of state parks in a western mountain state operates 27 different parks, historic sites, reserves, and wildlife areas. The division was created in 1928 with six sites but remained small until just after World War II. The governor at that time, Tom McCloud, was a strong conservationist and pushed hard for expansion. As a result, twenty new sites were added, and within four years the operating budget quadrupled. A large group of professionals, mostly young men in their 20s, were hired to manage these new areas.

An informal arrangement within state government allowed the division to function independent of the state's personnel department. For many years the division's chief took care of the little personnel work that was necessary. If site managers had a personnel problem, it was usually resolved with one telephone conversation with the chief.

A year ago the governor appointed a special citizen task force to review the operation and management of its natural resource areas. The task force's report recommended that the state should take steps to attract more out-of-state tourists.

Stacy Valez, the division's chief for the last six years, quickly realized that the current personnel would be unable to meet these new challenges without considerable adjustment. After a great deal of soul searching, he identified some of the problem areas as follows:

- We are shorthanded in a number of staff positions, especially in the planning and programming sections.
- We lack expertise in certain critical areas. No one, for example, has a background or experience in marketing or research.
- The average age of our professional staff is 56. We need more young college graduates and a management training program.
- Our affirmative action record has been terrible: only one minority and no women professionals.

Valez said to himself, "What I need is a plan for putting together a work group that will enable us to meet these new challenges."

Question: What steps would you suggest that the chief take?

---

direction, is *the achievement of goals.* Goals are broad guidelines that provide overall direction.[1]

Having clearly defined goals is absolutely essential, not only for leisure service management, but for almost anything we do in life. In any given work situation we might have organizational goals, departmental goals, project goals, individual work goals, and individual career goals. In our case study, Chief Valez has been presented with a new organizational goal: attract more out-of-state tourists. This goal provides Valez with a certain amount of direction, but he is still a long way from having sufficient information to be able to plan and organize his personnel. The next step is to establish *objectives* for each goal. Objectives are specific targets that focus on the achievement of goals. For example, Chief Valez might work with his staff to establish a set of objectives for his new goal. Those objectives might include the following:

- To provide sixty lodge units in Alpha Park by January 1, 1990.
- To increase camp sites in Beta Park by 50 percent by August 1, next year.
- To provide a ski slope and support services at Gamma Park within two years.

A more specific discussion of how to write objectives is presented in Chapter 8.

Although more definitive than goals, objectives still do not tell us exactly what employees will do. Therefore, each objective needs to be broken down into a number of activities. For the objective "to provide sixty lodge units in Alpha Park by January 1, 1990," Valez might delineate the following activities to be done:

- Perform market analysis.
- Prepare master site plan.
- Develop construction specifications.
- Develop publicity material.
- Provide food service operation.
- Provide housecleaning service.

Activities are the units of work that must be accomplished in order to achieve an objective.

Human Resource Planning

Once Valez and his staff have clearly stated their objectives and compiled a complete list of all the activities to be accomplished, they are in a position to begin planning and organizing for personnel. This arrangement is depicted in Figure 3.1. As stated earlier, planning and organizing for personnel are two closely related procedures that usually happen simultaneously, but we will discuss planning first.

Human resource planning is the process of anticipating human resource needs and establishing a sound procedure for filling those needs. Four steps are involved in this process, and line managers have responsibility for three of them.

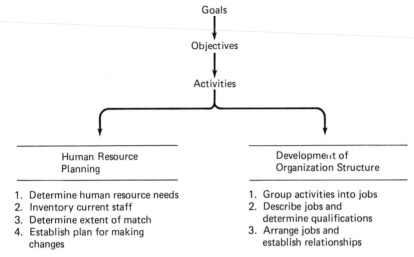

Figure 3.1 Human resource planning and organizing reflect organizational goals.

Determining Human Resource Needs

The first step is to forecast the number and type of employees needed by the organization. Several factors might influence the *number* of employees that will be needed. For example, if new facilities are acquired or constructed, programs are expanded, or the level of service is increased, it is very possible that more employees will be needed. As Chief Valez and his staff look over the long list of activities that will need to be accomplished to attract more out-of-state tourists, they may decide to request funding for one or more new positions. Some agencies, unlike the state parks unit in our case study, are forced to cut back on the size of their operations and find it necessary to transfer, retrain, temporarily lay off, or permanently lay off certain personnel.

Determining the *type* of staff that is needed can be an even more complicated task than determining the number that is needed. The term "type of staff" refers to the knowledge, skills, and abilities of the work group. Some public park and recreation organizations have switched from a direct provision approach to service delivery to a facilitator approach. This switch has allowed them to reduce the size of their full-time work force, but it has also forced them to change the *type* of employees that they hire. Employees that carry out a facilitator approach to service delivery need a different set of skills and abilities than do the employees that utilize the traditional direct provision approach.

In other cases, it might be that some important tasks are not now being performed because the agency's work group lacks the necessary knowledge. For example, an agency may not be administering construction contracts effectively because no one is knowledgeable about contract administration. Perhaps some changes in technology have occurred, but the organization is unable to utilize the new machinery because employees are unskilled in its use. A good example would be failure to use computers for such tasks as data-based management, mapping, financial analyses, networking, league scheduling, and facility use scheduling.

Inventorying Current Staff

The second step in the human resource planning process is to inventory and evaluate the current work force. The first step determined what was needed; the second step tells us what human resources are currently available to us. Up-to-date and complete information on each employee needs to be maintained in a usable form.[2] The information on employees should include:

- Individual demographics.
- Career progression.
- Knowledge, skills, and abilities.
- Training and education.
- Career goals.
- Trainability.
- Promotability.

Most of this information can be gathered through the annual or semi-annual performance appraisals and through periodic career counseling interviews. A chart such as the one shown in Figure 3.2 can be plotted to show the employee situation in an entire department.

Matching Needs with Inventory

The third step is to determine the extent to which the existing staff can fulfill the organization's needs. In other words, how well does the current work group match with current and future organizational needs? One park district in the midwest found that its maintenance personnel had slowly shifted from multipurpose generalists to highly focused specialists. Because these specialists were only able to perform a narrow scope of work activities such as carpentry, plant care, and painting, it greatly restricted management's capacity to obtain from its full-time employees a full day of work throughout most of the year. In this case, the work group's

Figure 3.2 Assessing promotion potential for management personnel.

Position	Current Occupant	Age	Promotability[a]	Current Personnel Capable of Filling Position
Level One				
Executive Director	D. Hooper	60	—	C. Korte, J. Riddle
Level Two				
Superintendent of Parks	C. Korte	57	A	
Superintendent of Recreation	J. Bonham	27	B	M. Patroni
Superintendent of Special Facilities	S. Stalnaker	61	C	L. Watts, M. Patroni
Support Services Manager	J. Riddle	51	A	L. Shenk, L. Watts, M. Patroni
Level Three				
Supervisor—North	N. Faessler	60	C	
Supervisor—South	C. Carlos	46	B	
Supervisor—Centers	D. Huisingh	30	C	
Supervisor—Programs	A. Barefoot	31	B	
Supervisor—Sports	L. Watts	47	A	
Supervisor—Culture	M. Patroni	29	A	
Business Manager	M. Johnson	50	C	
Planning Director	L. Shenk	45	A	

[a] A—Ready for promotion; B—currently lacks training and experience for promotion; C—questionable promotability.

47

knowledge, skills, and abilities did not match well with organizational needs.

Planning for Changes

It is invitable that an existing staff will never match perfectly with the human resource needs of the organization. *Thus the fourth step is to develop a plan to make changes in the work force.* Usually, the plan will involve *expanding, retraining,* or *reducing* the work group. Each of these areas is covered later in the book. The process of hiring new personnel is discussed in Chapters 4 and 5. Training and retraining employees is an often neglected but important area which we discuss in Chapter 10. Reducing a work force is a complicated and disconcerting task which is covered in Chapter 12.

Once Chief Valez and his staff have gone through the first three steps in the process, they are in a position to develop a plan for human resources. This might include:

- Expand the position of Park Superintendent to include responsibility for publicity.
- Establish a training program for Park Superintendents on publicity and advertising methods.
- Establish a new position: Market Analyst.
- Retrain L. Tuttle, a current member of the office staff, to perform database management with microcomputers.

Depending on the size of the operation and its level of management sophistication, various leisure service organizations handle human resource planning in different ways. In larger operations especially, the maintenance of data on individual employees and the overall work group (step 2) is done by the personnel unit. Primary responsibility for the other three steps usually rests with line managers, although the personnel unit may provide managers with assistance as needed. In small leisure service operations or units within large operations, all the human resource planning steps may be the responsibility of the unit manager or owner. Regardless of the particular situation, any manager with supervisory responsibilities should be familiar with the four steps: determine human resource needs, inventory current staff, match needs with inventory, and plan for changes.

Organizing

In addition to planning for personnel, managers need to develop the type of structure that will keep employees working together as a coordinated team, directed toward the achievement of organizational goals. This is organizing: the establishment of an organization structure among employees to promote a coordinated effort toward the achievement of organizational goals.[3] An organization structure is the result of organizing. It is the final product we hope to achieve. To develop organization structure, we first break down goals into objectives and objectives into activities, and then follow these steps:

1. Group activities into jobs.
2. Describe the jobs and the qualifications needed by the people who are to perform them.
3. Assign jobs to organizational units and establish the necessary relationships among jobs and units.

Figure 3.1 gives an overview of the organizing process.

Grouping Activities into Jobs

Recall that Chief Valez developed a list of activities for the objective "to provide sixty lodge units in Alpha Park by January 1, 1990." Some of these were:

- Perform market analysis.
- Prepare master site plan.
- Develop construction specifications.
- Develop publicity material.
- Provide food service operation.
- Provide housecleaning service.

In reality, this list would be much longer. If you were in Mr. Valez's position, how would you go about grouping the activities into specific jobs that can be assigned to employees? Your job would be much easier if you addressed the following:

- Which activities go together?
- Which ones use the same resources or space?
- Which ones closely depend on others?
- At what level in the organization should the activity be placed?
- What activities need supervision, and who should provide it?
- Who most needs to talk to and work with whom?
- What knowledge, skills, and abilities are needed to accomplish each activity?

Valez will probably give considerable time and thought to this matter, but eventually it will be possible to convert all of this information into real jobs. Thank goodness, Valez will probably not have to work at this task alone. The state's personnel unit probably has specialists who are experts at developing and defining jobs. But since most of these jobs will be either managerial or professional, the final decision about them will still have to be made by Valez and his people in the division. We cannot and should not expect specialists in the personnel unit to know a great deal about activities involved in the provision of lodging services in a state park. If the situation we had chosen to illustrate had involved lower-level personnel such as equipment operators, clerk-typists, lifeguards, or custodians, Valez could have expected the personnel unit to develop and define the jobs with minimal input from himself or his staff.

Job Descriptions

Once the activities have been grouped into jobs, it is common practice to prepare a job description, a written statement of each job. Typically, job descriptions are in two parts: job specifications and job qualifications.

Job Specifications

Job specifications are written summaries of what employees are expected to do and how they are to do it. Among the items often included as job specifications are:

- *Overall responsibilities:* a brief general statement of the major responsibilities of the position.
- *Duties:* the specific tasks to be performed.
- *Supervision:* a statement of what positions the employee supervises and by whom the employee is supervised.
- *Relationships and key contacts:* a description of the people with whom the person filling the position will work in performing assigned duties.
- *Working conditions and possible hazards:* a statement about any unusual working conditions or hazards.

Figure 3.3 presents the job description for a Recreation Supervisor.

Not all items have relevance to all positions. For example, "working conditions and possible hazards" may not be relevant to people working in a normal office situation. However, this item is very relevant to people who have to use power boats, operate park construction equipment, use horticultural and swimming pool chemicals, officiate contact sports, serve as lifeguards, work with those with mental and physical handicapping conditions, and deal with violators of the law.

Figure 3.3 Job description for a recreation supervisor.

FUN CITY PARK DISTRICT

Job Description

Position Title: Recreation Supervisor

Organizational Unit: Recreation Division

Overall Responsibilities:
   Responsible for the planning, organizing, and supervising the following
      program units:

Playgrounds   Show wagon
Mobile recreation   Special trips
Teens   Adult leisure education
Special events

Duties:
   Directs a wide variety of activities for his or her assigned units of
      responsibility
   Recruits, selects, directs, and evaluates recreation leaders and volunteers as
      needed.
   Conducts programs within adopted budget guidelines.
   Makes recommendations regarding the total Fun City recreation program
      and assists in the study of community wants and interests.
   Submits program reports, evaluations, inventories, and proposals to the
      superintendent of recreation.
   Establishes and maintains cooperative planning and work relationships with
      public and private nonprofit agencies serving Fun City, such as the
      YWCA, the school district, and the Chamber of Commerce.
   Provides all appropriate program publicity.
   Assists in the preparation of the budget and supporting material.
   Conducts workshops and in-service training programs as needed.
   Evaluates program areas using appropriate procedures.
   Reviews performance of leaders and volunteers and provides feedback as
      needed.
   Maintains current and acccurate records of assigned program units.
   Performs other duties assigned by the superintendent of recreation.

Supervision:
   Reports to the superintendent of recreation.
   Directly supervises part-time and seasonal leaders and volunteers.

Relationships and Key Contacts:
   Has frequent contact with the superintendent of recreation regarding goals
      and objectives, policy questions, and the coordination of program
      activities.
   Has frequent to moderate contact with the general public regarding
      program offerings.
   Has frequent contact with the other recreation supervisors regarding the
      coordination of program planning, scheduling, implementation, and
      evaluation.

(continued)

Figure 3.3 (*continued*)

> Has moderate contact with the news media and the general public
>   regarding publicity and public relations.
> Has occasional to moderate contact with other groups serving the public
>   regarding the provision of services.
>
> *Knowledge, Skills, and Abilities*
>   Ability to be flexible in all aspects of job responsibility.
>   Ability to communicate effectively.
>   Skill in the operation of audio-visual equipment.
>   Knowledge of basic management functions.
>   Ability to set goals and objectives.
>   Knowledge of the community's socioeconomic structure.
>
> *Education and Experience:*
>   Bachelor's degree in parks and recreation.
>
> *Special Requirement:*
>   Registered by a state professional park and recreation association.
>
> *Review and Approval:*
>   *Approved by* _____ *Date* _____
>   *Approved by* _____ *Date* _____

Job Qualifications

The second part of a job description consists of the *job qualifications:* the qualities and capabilities a person needs in order to perform the job. The job description in Figure 3.3 includes three categories of qualifications: knowledge, skills, and abilities (KSAs); education and experience; and special requirements. *Knowledge* is the acquired information background that a person must have to perform the job's duties and responsibilities. *Skills* refer to the capacity to use devices, machines, equipment, and work aids, such as a pool filter system, chemical sprayer, an Apple microcomputer, a kiln, topographic maps, and a radar gun. *Abilities* are the capacity to perform based on natural talent or acquired proficiencies. The ability to react quickly and calmly under emergency conditions is an example of an ability that is typically required of a park ranger.

Anyone who has ever applied for a job knows that *education and experience* are important job qualifications. Figure 3.4 lists several leisure service jobs and the education and experience typically listed as minimum qualifications. The last category of job qualifications, *special requirements,* refers to such items as a valid state motor vehicle operator's license, good physical condition and health, professional registration or certification, water safety instruction certification, and cardiopulmonary resuscitation certification.

Position	Education and Experience
Camp counselor	Successful completion of two years of study in a college or university of recognized standing; or graduation from high school and two seasons of not less than twelve weeks of experience in the required specialty; or any equivalent combination of education and experience.
Roving leader	An associate degree from an accredited college with major course work in recreation leadership or a closely related field; and two years of successful leadership experience or an equivalent combination of the above. Bachelor's degree preferred.
Golf course superintendent	Graduation from a college or university with specialization in agronomy preferred, and not less than two years of experience in the care of golf greens, fairways, and trees.
Naturalist	Graduation from an accredited four-year college or university with major course work in nature, botany, horticulture, floriculture, zoology, or a related field. Experience in nature work desirable.
Park planner	Graduation from an accredited college or university with a bachelor's degree in planning, civil engineering, landscape architecture, or a closely related field, and two years of professional planning experience. Graduate study in planning may be substituted for the two years' experience.

Figure 3.4 Education and experience requirements typically specified for certain recreation positions.

As pointed out in the discussion of equal employment legislation in Chapter 1, all job qualifications must be job related. For example, it would be appropriate to require a golf starter to have "a general knowledge of golf." It would be very inappropriate to require the golf starter to have "a college degree in parks and recreation" because it would be extremely difficult to demonstrate that a person with less education could not perform the job as well.[4] In other words, job qualifications must be based on the job specifications; doing otherwise would probably be construed as discriminatory.

Importance of Job Descriptions

In 1978, the local public park and recreation agencies in Illinois were surveyed regarding their job descriptions. Twenty-five percent indicated that their job descriptions did not present an adequate description of their jobs, over 22 percent communicated job descriptions verbally, and almost 50 percent failed to provide employees with accurate and complete job descriptions.[5] "Agencies have developed job descriptions with a minimum of input from employees, have borrowed job descriptions from other jurisdictions and have not utilized a systematic approach in the documentation of task statements or knowledge, skills and abilities."[6]

It is likely that these results would be similar if all leisure service agencies in the United States were surveyed. Apparently, many leisure service managers are unaware of the importance of complete and accurate job descriptions. In spite of the fact that they are difficult and time consuming to prepare, job descriptions are "necessary for effective organizational staffing and operation."[7]

First, clear and accurate job descriptions are vital because they serve as a concise delineation of each position in the organization. In addition, job descriptions are essential for the following:

- Position classification and compensation.
- Recruiting, testing, screening, and selecting employees.
- Orientation.
- Training and development.
- Performance appraisal.

All these areas are discussed later in the book, and we will frequently need to refer to clear and accurate job descriptions as our important starting point.

Preparing Job Descriptions

When writing the duties and responsibilities, it is important to use "precise action verbs."[8] Words such as "initiates," "submits," "assists," and "attends" give a clear picture of what is expected. Words such as "does" and "handles" do not.

The degree of detail that should be included in a job description is a matter for constant debate. If it is very specific, a job description is helpful for certain things, such as orienting a new employee. The new person will be able to understand exactly what is expected of him or her. This is especially valuable for a young or inexperienced employee, who might need considerable direction. But if the job description is very specific, it leaves very little room for flexibility or creativity. Also, as an organization's goals and plans change, a very specific job description will quickly become out of date. Most leisure service organizations have chosen to develop job descriptions that are only moderately specific. On those occasions when more specificity is needed, detailed information can either be incorporated into a supplemental job description or included in the unit's operating manual—the document that explains day-to-day operating procedures.

Job Analysis

Before we go further, an important matter needs to be clarified. Previously, we stated that job descriptions are prepared after the activities to be accomplished have been arranged into jobs. This is true. But after jobs exist for a time, it is imperative that they be analyzed periodically to determine their accuracy and relevance. This is called a job analysis— a systematic investigation of all aspects of a job to determine (1) its current effectiveness at meeting organizational goals, (2) the job specifications as they should exist, and (3) the job qualifications that accurately describe the qualities and capabilities needed to perform the job. The outcome of a job analysis usually entails a certain amount of adjustment in what a jobholder is to do and the description of that job. To summarize, new job descriptions are the product of jobs being formed, while revised job descriptions are the result of job analyses. The relationship among job formulation, job analysis, job descriptions, and other management activities is depicted in Figure 3.5.

Purpose of Job Analysis

The purpose of job analysis is to address three very important questions:

- What is the current content of this job; that is, what work is done and how is it being done?
- Is the content of this job what it should be to achieve organizational goals effectively?
- If current content is inappropriate, how should this job be designed?

To illustrate how these questions might be addressed, recall the case study on state parks. Chief Valez has been doing some serious thinking about his organization's new mandate. It would be nice to use the state

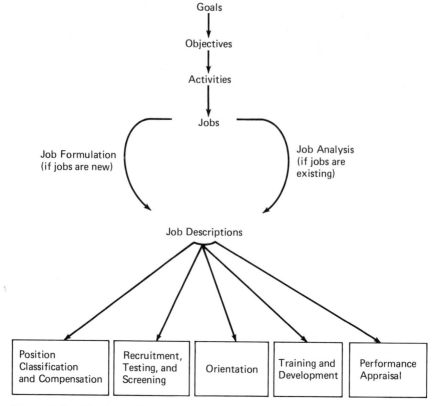

Figure 3.5   Job descriptions as a basis for other human resource management functions.

parks as a vehicle to attract more out-of-state tourists, but on the other hand, increased use of the parks might have a negative impact in a number of ways. For one thing, the increased number of park users might destroy certain fragile areas and disrupt plant and animal life.

Although the division does have an environmental assessment analyst, that person has been spending most of her time working on projects dealing with the acquisition of land for preservation purposes. Valez thought to himself, "It's been a long time since we did a job analysis of the environmental assessment analyst position. I think we need to do one." When doing this job analysis, each of the three questions we listed previously will need to be addressed. Perhaps this analysis will result in a change in the job and job description of the environmental assessment analyst to include certain new duties related to assessing the potential impact of increased park usage.

Responsibility for Job Analysis

Some park and recreation managers, because they have access to a personnel unit, allow job analysis to be performed by the personnel specialist. Other park and recreation managers do not have access to personnel units, but fail to perform job analyses either because they lack the ability or fail to understand its importance.

Managers should be involved in job analysis whether they oversee the entire process themselves or assist and advise the personnel unit.[9] In fact, one of the most significant benefits of job analysis is that it serves as an opportunity for managers and subordinates to discuss and debate the three questions mentioned previously. Areas of confusion, overlapping areas, and voids can be minimized or eliminated.[10] Leisure service managers should at least have a fundamental knowledge of how to perform a job analysis.

Performing Job Analysis

Brademas and Lowrey have developed a model job analysis procedure that appears to have great potential.[11] The employees whose jobs are to be analyzed and their immediate supervisors work together as a group to develop a preliminary statement for each of the key elements of a job. For example, in the state park system, Mr. Valez might ask his head of environmental interpretation and all the current environmental interpretors to work together. The key elements of a job analysis and an example of what the interpreters might generate for each of these elements is presented:

1. Overall responsibility.
   Example: Organizes, guides, and instructs groups in nature study and wildlife education.
2. Domain (a major area of job duties).
   Examples:
   Program planning.
   Scheduling.
   Evaluation.
3. Duties.
   Note: Each duty should begin with an action verb (prepare, consult, collect). Duties should reflect what needs to be done to best meet organizational goals.
   Examples:
   Domain: program planning.
   Duty: assesses the environmental features of the area.

Domain: scheduling.

Duty: conducts tours at those times that best explain the phenomena of nature.

Domain: evaluation.

Duty: maintains attendance records.

4. Supervision.

Examples:

Reports to the head of environmental interpretation.

Responsible for volunteer leaders.

5. Relationships and key contacts.

Example: Has occasional to moderate contact with park personnel to advise on matters of plant and animal life conservation.

6. Knowledge, skills, and abilities.

Example: Knowledge of botany and zoology.

7. Desired education and experience.

Example: Graduation from a four-year university with a major in recreation (interpretation concentration), botany, or zoology.

8. Special requirement.

Example: Cardiopulmonary resuscitation certification.

Hopefully, the reader has noticed that the key elements of a job analysis are also the main section headings for job descriptions. (Domains may or may not be included in job descriptions.) This further illustrates the close relationship between job analyses and job descriptions.

Once the job elements are developed, a preliminary job description can be prepared by the personnel unit or a small group of managers. This preliminary description should reflect the standardized language used in all the agency's job descriptions. Other review steps can be added to the Brademas–Lowrey model, depending on the agency size, policies, and the particular positions involved. The final version of a job description is usually subject to approval by upper-level management or policymakers.

Organizing Jobs

Now that we have assembled the jobs (step 1) and accurately described them (step 2), our third task is *to assign jobs to organizational units and establish the necessary relationships among jobs and units.* To do this we need to understand five key elements of organization structure: span of control, unity of command, chain of command, departmentation, and line and staff functions. In addition, organization charts can be an effective tool for understanding organization structure. We will present a discussion of organization charts first because this tool will also be used to help explain the five elements.

Organization Charts

An organization chart is a graphic illustration of an organization's formal structure.[12] Charts serve as a tool to indicate department names, identify the position that heads each department, and clarify how positions and departments are linked together.[13]

No one correct or best way to draw an organization chart exists. Since the purpose of a chart is to depict an organization's formal structure accurately, it should be drawn in whatever form or style best achieves that purpose. Some charts are circular, some horizontal (from left to right), and some are pyramidal. The most common arrangement among park and recreation organizations is vertical (from top to bottom). Positions and departments are indicated by rectangles. Lines, indicating the formal flow of decision making authority, connect these rectangles into a network. Generally, vertical charts are drawn so that positions with greatest authority are shown at the top and less important positions are shown at the bottom. Suggestions for the preparation of the traditional vertical organization chart are presented in Figure 3.6.

SUGGESTIONS FOR PREPARING AN ORGANIZATION CHART

1. Identify the chart fully showing the name of the organization, name of person responsible for preparation, name of person or group that granted authorization, and date of authorization.
2. Use rectangular boxes to show either an organizational unit or position.
3. For line units, vertical placement of rectangles show relative position in the organization hierarchy. No such pattern exists for staff personnel or units that may be incorporated into the organization in various locations.
4. Any given horizontal row of boxes should be of the same size and should include only those positions having the same organizational rank. This rule is frequently violated due to space limitations.
5. Vertical and horizontal solid lines are used to show the flow of line authority.
6. Use dashed or broken lines to show technical relationships or critical advisory channels (see Figure 3.7).
7. Lines of authority enter at the top center of a box and leave at the bottom center; they do not run through the box. Exception: The line of authority to a staff position may enter the side of the box (see Figure 3.7).
8. The title of each position should be placed in the box. The title should be descriptive and show function. For example, "supervisor" is not sufficient as it does not show function. The functional area (e.g., aquatics) should be included even though it is not a part of the official title. Titles should be consistent; if necessary, revise titles so that they are both consistent and descriptive.
9. Include the name of the person currently holding the position (optional).
10. Keep the chart as simple as possible; include a legend if necessary to explain any special notations. When preparing a separate chart for an organizational unit, include the superior to whom the unit reports.

Figure 3.6

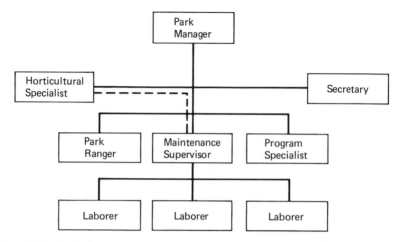

Figure 3.7   Vertical organization chart representing a small agency.

The need for an organization chart varies considerably according to the size of the organization. The small park operation depicted in Figure 3.7 has little need for a chart. A middle-sized organization such as the one shown in Figure 3.8 has a greater need for a chart. Figure 3.9 indicates a horizontally drawn chart for a resort operation. The need for this chart is obvious.

Benefits of Organization Charts.   The primary benefit of organization charts is that they inform people of the network of relationships that exist throughout the organization. Each person can see how his or her position fits into the entire structure. Recall that job descriptions specify key relationships for each position. But as each person studies his or her own job description, only a small part of the picture can be seen. Organization charts provide a summarized overview of the entire picture.

Another benefit is that it forces people preparing the charts to think about how the organization can be most effectively structured. In fact, the analysis and discussion that goes into the preparation of the chart may be more valuable than the chart itself. Finally, charts seem to be most beneficial for people in the middle of the organization because relationships at this level seem to be the most complex. "Without charts you are almost sure to have some overlapping of authority and responsibility among middle managers."[14]

Problems with Charts.   It should be kept in mind that the organization chart represents only the officially sanctioned organization structure. Communications and even decision making sometimes take place outside

Figure 3.8 Vertical organization chart depicting a medium size agency.

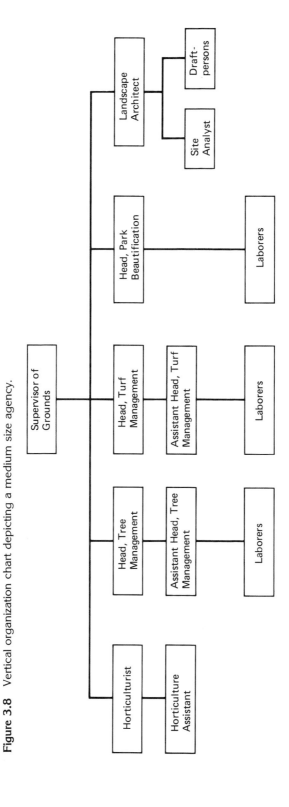

Figure 3.9 Horizontal organization chart depicting a large agency.

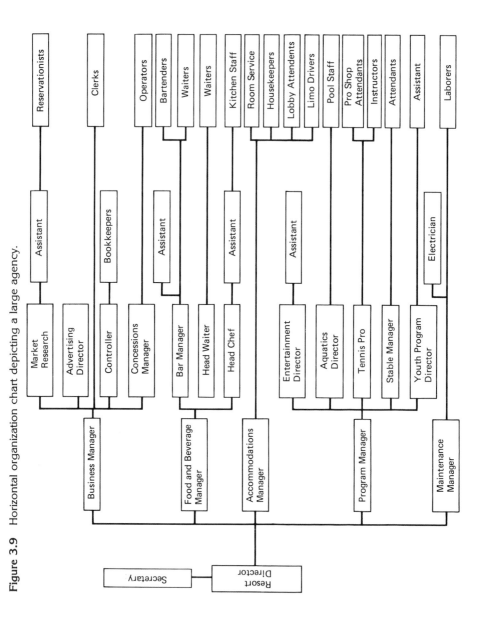

normal channels. When this occurs, the principle of *chain of command* is violated. This principle will be defined and discussed in a later section.

Because some problems exist with charts, some managers are reluctant to use them. For one thing, if charts are simple, they are easy to use but provide little information. If they provide a lot of information, they are more informative but more difficult to use. Also, charts are difficult to keep up to date, and an out-of-date chart only explains "what was." Another criticism is that it makes some people feel superior and others inferior. This is one of the points that Townsend makes:

> A chart demoralizes people. Nobody thinks of himself as *below* other people. And in a good company he isn't. Yet on paper there it is. If you have to circulate something, use a loose-leaf table of organization (like a magazine masthead) instead of a diagram with the people in little boxes. Use alphabetical order by name and by function wherever possible.[15]

We are not so sure of Townsend's criticism. If your immediate supervisor has considerably more authority and responsibility than you, would it not be normal to consider him or her your superior as an employee? Everyone is not equal in an organization and surely most people are mature enough to understand and accept this.

Circle Charts.   Townsend goes on to make a good point:

> In the best organizations people see themselves working in a circle as if around one table. One of the positions is designated chief executive officer, because somebody has to make all those tactical decisions that enable an organization to keep working. In this circular organization, leadership passes from one to another depending on the particular task being attacked—without any hang-ups.[16]

This circle approach can be extremely effective in many types of small leisure service operations. Picture a small local public park and recreation operation such as the one in Figure 3.10. The recreation supervisor is in charge of a major special event: an ice cream social for the whole community. Usually, this means that most of the planning, organizing, and implementing is the responsibility of the recreation supervisor and all work is carried out at a lower level in the organization with part-time people and volunteers.

If Townsend's circle approach were used, the entire staff, including the director, would participate and assume a share of the work. Decision-making authority for that particular event would rest with the recreation supervisor. Individuals would be "assigned" to tasks based on their capabilities and expertise. For example, the museum director, who has many contacts in the business community, might be in charge of finding a place to store a large amount of ice, and the director, who can be very

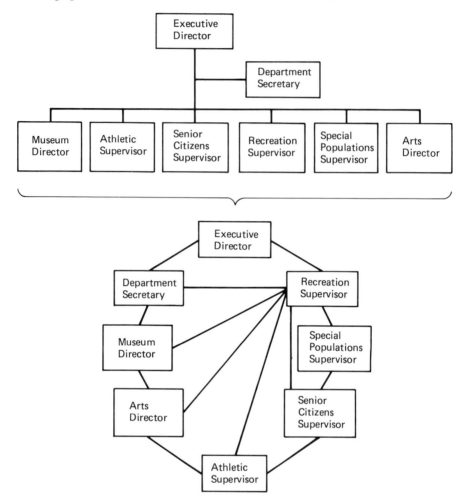

Figure 3.10   A vertical organization structure can be converted to a circular structure for projects and special circumstances.

persuasive, is in charge of getting volunteers. Although the director always retains ultimate decision-making authority, he or she does not exercise that authority unless necessary or appropriate.

This type of organization structure (1) makes everyone on the staff feel he or she has an important role to play in the organization, (2) allows maximum utilization of individual capabilities and expertise, and (3) keeps jobs dynamic and challenging. The major prerequisite to a successful circle structure is that "upper-level" personnel must be willing to allow "lower-level" staff to share power, albeit for short periods of time. Also, lower-level staff must be mature and capable of handling this type of arrangement.

Span of Control

How many subordinates should report directly to each manager? In the organization chart presented at the top of Figure 3.11, eleven people report to the director of intramurals. Is this too many, too few, or just the right number? The number of employees that a manager can supervise effectively is called span of control. The twelve positions in the top portion of Figure 3.11 are all arranged on two levels and because of the way it looks, it is referred to as a "flat" structure. The same twelve positions could be arranged into a "tall" organization (as depicted in the bottom of Figure 3.11) by narrowing the span of control and adding middle management personnel.

For decades, management theorists tried to determine the optimal span of control.

> Many writers on organization believe that the maximum number of subordinates a chief executive can normally supervise effectively is six to eight. For first-line supervisors of routine operations, the same writers would put the maximum limit at fifteen to twenty subordinates.[17]

These general rules have little relevance, however, unless certain factors are taken into consideration for each situation. These factors are:

- Amount of time that a manager must spend on activities other than supervision.
- Training and experience of the supervisor as well as the people being supervised.
- Extent to which clear policies and plans exist to guide the people being supervised.[18]
- Complexity and importance of the activities being performed.
- Extent to which activities are repetitive and routine.
- Amount of support staff assistance provided to both the supervisor and the subordinates.
- Geographic distance between the manager and his or her staff.

Advantages and Disadvantages.   Another way to look at span of control is to consider the effects created by tall and flat organization structures. Flat organizations, caused by wide spans of control, have the advantage of rapid information flow. Since only a few people are involved, messages can move quickly up and down through the network.

Figure 3.11 Comparison of "flat" and "tall" organization structures.

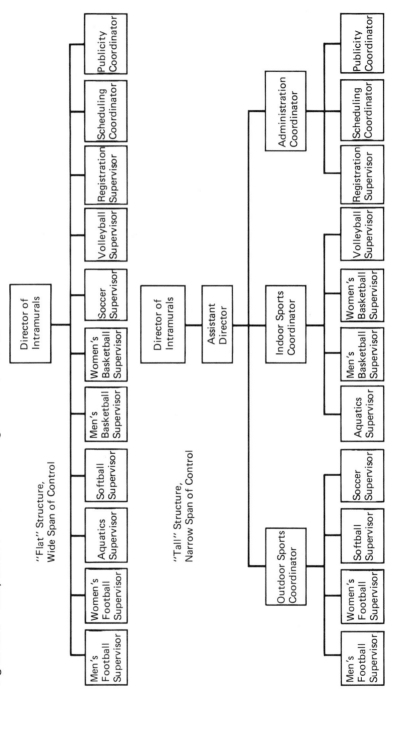

"Flat" Structure,
Wide Span of Control

"Tall" Structure,
Narrow Span of Control

In addition, decision making tends to be closer to the clientele—the people being served. Flat organizations also have fewer managers, which means less office space, fewer support staff, fewer salaries, and greater savings to the agency.

Flat organizations also have some disadvantages. Because a large number of subordinates report to one person, subordinates may have difficulty gaining access to their supervisor. Also, during a busy season or in a crisis situation, a considerable strain may be put on the normal decision-making process. In some cases, decisions may get delayed, and in other cases, weak decisions might be made because of inadequate time for analysis and discussion.

Tall organization structures, caused by narrow spans of control, usually result in faster, more efficient problem resolution.[19] Also, decisions are made at higher levels by generally more experienced managers. Since they have fewer people to supervise, managers have the time to become closely involved in their areas of responsibility and give very close supervision. But this can also be a serious disadvantage. In fact, this situation, usually referred to as *overmanagement*, is a serious problem in some leisure service agencies. When supervisors become too involved in specific day-to-day operations, it can stifle those subordinates who desire a more challenging and flexible role. In addition, when managers spend too much time on lower-level matters, upper-level matters such as policy development, goal setting, and organization planning can be badly neglected.[20]

In summary, no easy answer exists for the question of how many subordinates should report to one manager. The span of control needs to be tailored for each supervisory position, taking into consideration the seven factors we discussed previously. Koontz, O'Donnell, and Weihrich sum up the current thinking on the subject.

> The correct principle of span of management [span of control] is that there is a limit in each managerial position to the number of persons an individual can effectively manage, but the exact number in each case will vary in accordance with the effect of underlying variables and their impact on the time requirements of effective managing.[21]

Unity of Command

Luther Gulick, a name that every student of the history of recreation should immediately recognize, was a pioneer in management theory. In 1937, he wrote: "From the earliest times it has been recognized that nothing but confusion arises under multiple command."[22] By this he meant that each employee should have only one boss. Whenever an employee is required to take orders from more than one person, a real possibility exists that the orders will occasionally conflict.

Consider the following illustration that actually occurred in a local public park and recreation agency. A parks division employee was assigned to perform the interior maintenance work in a recreation center. The maintenance foreman instructed the employee to wax the ballet room floor on Tuesday afternoon when no one was scheduled to be using the room. On the same morning, the center director, a member of the recreation division, instructed the employee to spend Tuesday afternoon cleaning and preparing the arts and crafts room for a Wednesday morning special event. Early Wednesday morning, another member of the maintenance crew, who was following the instructions given to her, picked up the waxing equipment from the center and took it to a new location. On Wednesday afternoon, the foreman was angry when he inspected the center and found that the floor had not been waxed and the waxing equipment was gone.

If the principle of unity of command had been observed, the maintenance worker would report to either the center director or the foreman, but not to both. It would be up to these two people to communicate effectively and coordinate the work assignments of the maintenance employee.

Chain of Command

In an earlier section we pointed out that the lines of an organization chart indicate the formal flow of decision-making authority from the top to the bottom of an organization. One of these lines, going from the chief executive to the lowest level of personnel, is commonly referred to as a chain of command. We also stated that although organization charts represent the officially sanctioned arrangement, decision making sometimes takes place outside the chain of command.

We have used Figure 3.8 to illustrate. The *Landscape Architect* frequently has lunch with the *Horticulture Assistant*. Often they discuss current projects and exchange ideas. The *Head of Park Beautification* and the *Site Analyst* occasionally get together and decide which proposed beautification projects should be recommended for funding. These activities violate the principle of chain of command, which says communications and decision making should follow the lines of authority specified by the organization chart. In other words, supervisors have the right to direct the activities of the employees immediately below them in their chain of command.[23] In addition, subordinates do not have the right to deal directly with personnel outside their chain of command or jump over their supervisor and deal with their supervisor's superior.

Depending on the desires of top management, the principle of chain of command is rigidly followed in some organizations while in others it is almost completely ignored. Persons new to an organization would be wise to find out early how closely the principle of chain of command is followed.

In the typical leisure service operation, people are usually allowed to communicate outside the chain of command when the need exists. Actual decision making is usually viewed as more critical, however, and most managers will indicate to subordinates the types of decisions and kinds of circumstances that may warrant going outside the chain of command.

It is our opinion that this principle generally makes good sense and should not be needlessly violated. Sometimes employees attempt to jump over their immediate supervisor because they disagree with the directives they have been given by that person. This can be very risky. The supervisor may have very good reasons for his or her decisions and is not always in a position to explain those reasons fully to a subordinate. Impertinent subordinates may find themselves in serious trouble if they circumvent their superior without just cause.

Departmentation

When developing organization structure, consideration should be given to how similar jobs are arranged into work units. This process is referred to as departmentation. The work units might be called "divisions," "bureaus," "departments," "branches," or "units." For example, in a large leisure service operation, the largest work units might be referred to as "divisions," the subunits within divisions might be called "departments," and the sub-subunits might be called "units."

Different patterns can be used for grouping jobs. Four are most relevant to parks and recreation.

1. *Organizing by primary purpose.* Units are built around the major components of an agency's mission, such as parks, conservation, recreation, or fitness. Each unit would contain all the necessary elements to achieve that particular portion of the mission.[24]
2. *Organizing by process.* Units are arranged according to specialized skills, such as programming, purchasing, security, counseling, or public relations.
3. *Organizing according to territory.* Units are organized by geographic location, such as the sections of a linear parkway, the quadrants of a city, or the branch locations of a hospital.
4. *Organizing by clientele to be served.* Units reflect groups of people, such as teens, tots, seniors, young adults, or males and females.

Different patterns can be used at different levels of an organization. Figure 3.12 shows an organization arranged using all four patterns.

As you read through the description of the four patterns you may have perceived a certain amount of ambiguity. This is the major criticism of using these patterns to form departments. Is maintenance a primary purpose or a process? Is a program for the blind a clientele group or a primary purpose? Sometimes activities are hard to fit into neat categories; nevertheless, these four patterns do provide a basis for arranging activities into units for more effective handling.

Line and Staff

Another type of organization pattern deals with the concept of line and staff. Line personnel are all the people from the top to the bottom of the organization who are directly responsible for accomplishing the organization's mission. Their focus is outside the organization toward the clientele being served. Support staff are those persons who help the line staff work more effectively. Their services are rendered within the organization, not outside it. For example, the line personnel at a YWCA would be the director and all persons involved in programming for the membership. The support staff personnel would be the receptionist, secretary, bookkeeper, accountant, and maintenance personnel.

Most modern administrators feel no need to make a big distinction between line and staff. It would be easy to argue that all personnel are important for the achievement of an agency's mission regardless of whether they run a program directly or assist indirectly by signing up participants, mopping the floor, or sending out publicity. The important thing is not whether they fall into neat categories labeled "line" and "staff," but whether they fully understand their role in the organization and their work relationship with other people. Specifically, the work relationship should be clear concerning:

- Who is consulted.
- Who decides.
- Who acts.
- Who is informed of the results.
- Who reports.

Looking at Figure 3.9, the organization chart of a resort, it would be difficult to distinguish line and staff. But this distinction may not even be relevant if each person knows who is responsible for what and the degree of this responsibility. Organizations that emphasize effective communications, clearly defined objectives, cooperation, and mutual support will seldom have to debate questions of who is line and who is staff.

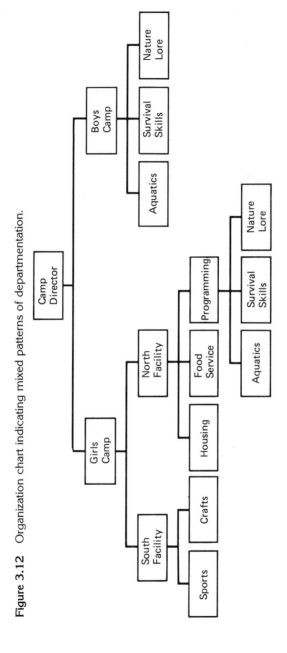

Figure 3.12 Organization chart indicating mixed patterns of departmentation.

Organizational Structure

Organizational structure can be thought of as the fabric that keeps an organization coordinated and directed toward the achievement of organizational goals. In this chapter we have described the three steps needed to design a structure and some key elements of organizing that must be considered. But no magic formula exists for designing an organization and no one best structure exists. Each operation must be shaped to fit its unique circumstances.

In some cases, organizations are highly structured and people within that organization are not allowed to shape the organization but asked only to "fit in" to what exists. In other cases, leisure service professionals will be required to play a key role in organizing whether it is an entire organization or only a small unit within an organization. In any case, a basic knowledge of organizing is quite important.

Summary and Recommendations

1. Human resource plans and organization structure are based on and shaped by organizational goals and objectives.
2. The purpose of human resource planning is to anticipate personnel needs and develop a plan for meeting those needs.
3. It is usually the responsibility of line managers to (a) forecast personnel needs, (b) determine if current personnel match those needs, and (c) make plans to correct problem areas.
4. Organizational structure is the fabric that keeps an organization coordinated and directed toward the achievement of organizational goals.
5. The basic procedures and concepts of organizing can be applied to small organizations and units within organizations as well as large operations.
6. Organizing is the process of breaking down broad goals into specific activities, arranging those activities into jobs, and then assembling those jobs into an organizational structure.
7. Job specifications are written summaries of what employees are expected to do and how they are to do it.
8. Job qualifications are the qualities and capabilities a person needs in order to perform a job.
9. Job specifications and qualifications are the two parts of a written job description.
10. Job analyses are done periodically to ascertain if jobs, as they are currently being done, are consistent with the goals of the organization.

11. Tall organizational structures can result in overmanagement, a serious problem in some leisure service agencies.
12. Each employee should usually have only one supervisor.
13. The principle of chain of command should not be violated in matters of decision making without very good reason.
14. It is not important that each job be labeled "line" or "staff," but it is important that employees understand their role in the organization and their work relationship with other people.

Discussion Topics

1. To assess whether you understand goals, objectives, and activities, develop one goal, two objectives, and four activities for a group to which you belong.
2. What role should a line manager play in the assembling and maintenance of complete information on each employee?
3. What is the purpose of organizational structure?
4. Which of the following activities are most closely linked together and could conceivably be assigned to specific jobs? Explain your rationale for the linkages.
   (a) Prepare master site plan.
   (b) Develop construction specifications.
   (c) Develop publicity material.
   (d) Provide food service operation.
   (e) Provide housecleaning services.
5. What are the usual sections of a job description? What is the difference between job specifications and job qualifications?
6. Describe the overall responsibilities and list five duties of a college student as they would be presented in a job description.
7. Describe the relationships and key contacts of a college student.
8. If you were director of intramurals, which of the two organizational structures presented in Figure 3.11 would you wish to have? Which structure do you feel would make the most efficient use of limited financial resources?
9. Review the list of seven factors that can influence the span of control that a manager can effectively handle. Develop a leisure service–related example that will explain each factor.
10. Give several examples of the types of decisions and kinds of circumstances that may warrant (a) going outside the chain of command or (b) jumping over an immediate supervisor.
11. Identify in Figure 3.12 the four patterns most frequently used in leisure services for grouping jobs in work units.
12. Does the park and recreation manager who is responsible for a small

operation and a small staff (five to seven people) have to be as concerned about organization structure as does the chief executive of large operation?

Notes

1. Monica Nolan, *Program Evaluation Procedure for Leisure Service Agencies* (Urbana-Champaign, Ill.: University of Illinois, 1981), pp. 8–9.
2. Robert L. Mathis and John H. Jackson, *Personnel: Contemporary Perspectives and Applications*, 3rd ed. (St. Paul, Minn.: West Publishing Co., 1982), p. 171.
3. Hyler Bracey, Aubrey Sanford, and James C. Quick, *Basic Management* (Plano, Tex.: Business Publications, Inc., 1981), p. 125.
4. Mathis and Jackson, *Personnel*, p. 159.
5. D. James Brademas and George Lowrey, Jr., *Manual for Systematically Developing Job Descriptions* (Urbana-Champaign, Ill.: University of Illinois, 1982), p. 2.
6. Ibid.
7. Mathis and Jackson, *Personnel*, p. 161.
8. Ibid., p. 157.
9. Ibid., p. 135.
10. Wendell L. French, *The Personnel Management Process*, 4th ed. (Boston: Houghton Mifflin Company, 1978), p. 176.
11. Brademas and Lowrey, *Job Descriptions*, pp. 6–9.
12. Ronald S. Burke and Lester R. Bittel, *Introduction to Management Practice* (New York: McGraw-Hill Book Company, 1981), p. 159.
13. Franklin G. Moore, *Management: Organization and Practice* (New York: Harper & Row, Publishers, Inc., 1964), p. 516.
14. Ibid., p. 517.
15. Robert Townsend, *Up the Organization* (New York: Alfred A. Knopf, Inc., 1970), p. 134.
16. Ibid.
17. William H. Newman, Charles E. Sumner, and E. Kirby Warren, *The Process of Management*, 2nd ed. (Englewood Cliffs, N.J.: Prentice-Hall, Inc., 1967), p. 133.
18. Harold Koontz, Cyril O'Donnell, and Heinz Weihrich, *Management*, 7th ed. (New York: McGraw-Hill Book Company, 1980), p. 344.
19. Ibid., p. 348.
20. Robert T. Golembiewski, *Behavior and Organization: O & M and the Small Group* (Chicago: Rand McNally & Company, 1962), p. 202.
21. Koontz, O'Donnell, and Weihrich, *Management*, p. 354.
22. Luther Gulick, "Notes on the Theory of Organization," in *Classics of Organization Theory*, ed. Jay M. Shafritz and Philip H. Whitbeck (Oak Park, Ill.: Moore Publishing Co., 1978), p. 57.
23. Robert W. Eckles, Ronald L. Carmichael, and Bernard R. Sarchet, *Supervisory Management*, 2nd ed. (New York: John Wiley & Sons, Inc., 1981), p. 55.
24. J. D. Williams, *Public Administration: The People Business* (Boston: Little, Brown and Company, 1980), p. 47.

4

Recruitment

The recruitment and selection of competent, productive personnel can pay a very high rate of return. A good staff is perhaps the most important single asset any organization can have. History has shown repeatedly that organizations rich in fiscal resources will fail miserably if they are staffed by incompetent personnel. Because employee recruitment and selection are so important, organizations ought to make careful, well-informed decisions in these areas. The purpose of this chapter and the next is to help leisure service managers (1) make better recruitment and selection decisions, (2) avoid costly mistakes, (3) comply with legal mandates, and (4) work effectively with the personnel specialists in a personnel unit.

What Is Recruitment?

The purpose of recruitment is to attract and interest a sufficient number of qualified people to apply for available positions with a particular park, recreation, or leisure organization.[1] This sounds easy but it is not. Recruitment involves much more than just finding at least one well-qualified person for each available position.

Recruitment involves developing contacts and maintaining ongoing communications networks to ensure adequate supplies of appropriately qualified people. Decisions must be made on which people sources produce the most qualified candidates, including minorities and women. Lists of schools, organizations, employment agencies, and other contacts must be regularly updated. Job announcements, ads, brochures, and bulletins must be designed for each position to attract specific segments of the labor market. Finally, personnel sources must be evaluated to determine whether or not they were successful sources for qualified candidates and productive employees.

When lower-level positions in a leisure service organization become available, the immediate supervisor usually does not have the authority to start recruiting automatically. The policymakers and upper-level management may want to consider alternatives to filling the position immediately. The supervisor's first responsibility usually is to submit to his or her supervisor a personnel requisition form such as the one presented in Figure 4.1. This procedure is a systematic way of asking higher authority to act on the question of how the work load will be accomplished. Notice how the form in Figure 4.1 addresses such matters as whether money is budgeted for the position, if the position constitutes an increase in staff, and how the position will be recruited.

Alternatives to Recruitment

Although the purpose of this chapter is to discuss recruitment, it should be kept in mind that not all employment needs have to be met by promoting current employees or hiring new ones. Recruitment and selection costs are high. One study estimated that an organization spends over $9,000 to fill each professional position. This expenditure includes travel expenses for interviews, an employment agency fee, relocation expenses, and the time and dollars lost orienting the new employee.[2]

To avoid these expenses, park and recreation organizations have sought alternatives to the traditional pattern of full-time, permanent personnel. Some organizations have chosen to pay their existing employees overtime to meet peak seasonal work requirements. The danger in prolonged use of overtime is that employees will become fatigued and experience less energy and enthusiasm. These behaviors have resulted in an adverse impact on the quality of work performance and on the relationships with fellow workers and the public. The employee working overtime for a long period of time is often the last person to recognize the signs of fatigue, personality change, and decline in work effort.

Contracting out entire services or particular job functions is another alternative that is used in the park and recreation field. It is cost-effective because recruitment and selection expenses are eliminated and because the agency does not have to pay for full-time employee fringe benefits, which represents an additional expense. This practice does have some pitfalls. The leisure service organization loses direct control over the employees hired by the contracting firm. Complaints from the public about contracted personnel cannot be processed and resolved; except through

Figure 4.1 Example of a personnel requisition form.

Personnel Requisition

Please print or type | Date

1 | Submitting supervisor | Authorizing manager | Date position desired | Requisition number
| | | Year Month Date |

2 | Job to be filled (title) | Department | Location

3 | Job code | P = Permanent
T = Temporary
S = Seasonal | if T or S: Job ends
Year Month Day | FT = Full time
PT = Part time | Grade | Rate or range | PO = To be posted
NP = No posting | RO = Recruit in organization
RL = Recruit locally
RN = Recruit nationally

4 | List 4 or 5 major tasks required to be accomplished in this position (Attach Job Description) | Minimum education level | Education major

Experience desired (in order of importance) | Years | | Years | | Years
1. | | 2. | | 3. | |

Special KSAs | 1. | | 2. | | 3. | | 4.

Special requirements (Weekend work, extensive travel, etc.)

5 | Approved | Date | Approved | Date | Comments

A personnel requisition must be submitted for every opening to be filled. It must be signed by the initiating supervisor and at least one higher-level authorizing manager.
Original pink, canary, and blue copies must be sent to the personnel office that serves the requesting unit. The green copy is for the authorizing manager.

6 | Position filled by | Social Security No. | Starting date
Year Mo Day | Starting rate or salary | Referral source

77

a third party, the contracting group. Even more critical is the possibility of gradual erosion of agency image and effectiveness if the contractor is not effective.

A third staffing alternative is the use of temporary employees who are on the payroll of temporary help agencies. These employees may not feel the same loyalty to the park and recreation organization as do full-time employees, and they may not understand the goals of a park, recreation, or leisure organization. In spite of these minor disadvantages, temporary help is sometimes a good alternative to full-time employment, especially in the area of clerical work. As work loads fluctuate, or as full-time employees take maternity, jury-duty, or vacation leave, temporary typists and other office specialists keep the operation going until business returns to normal. It has been estimated that 2.5 million workers have been placed in temporary positions each year by temporary help agencies.[3]

Commitment to Affirmative Action

Chapter 1 gave the reader some background and understanding of the mandates which have regulated and directed employers to demonstrate that their personnel practices are based only on the merit and qualifications of the individuals involved. Protected groups are to be hired proportionate to their representation, qualifications, and availability in the market area.[4]

To comply with equal employment opportunity (EEO) laws and to ensure proportional representation in their work groups, many leisure service agencies have committed themselves to programs of affirmative action. *Affirmative action means that the employer will make additional efforts to recruit, hire, and promote minorities, women, and those in legally protected groups.* Affirmative action greatly affects recruitment policies and procedures. Before continuing the discussion of recruitment, it is important to review the background material on affirmative action planning and programs. Important terms that should be reviewed are found in Figure 4.2.

- Are affirmative action programs really necessary? The answer is "yes."
- Does the law require every employer to develop one? The answer to this question is "no."

Affirmative action programs are necessary in three different employment situations, but they are mandated by law or court order in only the first two of these situations.

COMMONLY USED AFFIRMATIVE ACTION TERMS

Underutilization: minority-group members employed in significantly lower numbers than would be reasonably expected, based on their qualifications and availability for employment.

Goals: a numerical objective that the employer hopes to attain by identifying the number and types of anticipated job vacancies and the number of qualified minority applicants available in the recruiting area.

Quotas: required numbers of persons from minority groups that must be hired by a certain time.

Timetables: estimates of the time required to meet specific goals or quotas in relationship to anticipated job openings.

Parity: achievement of the same ratio between minority and nonminority employees as exists in the population.

Figure 4.2

1. Organizations found to have a history of employment discrimination by a federal or state court must take specific actions to eliminate discriminatory practices and correct underutilization of protected groups. The court normally requires the organization to develop an affirmative action plan (AAP) which identifies those specific actions that will be taken to correct the situation. Such plans may include establishing minority hiring goals, quotas, and timetables.

   Quotas have generated a flood of controversy in this country, but they are permissible under Title VII of the Civil Rights Act of 1964. Several prerequisites must exist before the courts will establish hiring quotas. (a) The employer must have a clear history of racial discrimination. (b) Quotas would be the only known remedy for the problem of discrimination. (c) The effects of meeting quotas will not result in reverse discrimination for a small identifiable group of nonminority persons, such as white males.

2. Companies with a federal contract greater than $50,000 must file an affirmative action plan with the Office of Federal Contract Compliance (OFCC). This is mandated under Executive Orders 11246 and 11375.[5] The AAP's are enforced by the OFCC and the Equal Employment Opportunity Commission (EEOC).[6] As we discussed in Chapter 1, any park and recreation agency using federal funds to pay contractors must make sure those contractors have affirmative action plans.

3. Organizations, both public and private, may voluntarily establish and adopt their own affirmative action program. In fact, most public agencies and governmental units have been implementing their re-

spective programs for over a decade. These organizations have taken this voluntary measure to ensure that they are complying to EEO laws, and to document that they have become equal opportunity–affirmative action employers.

Employers wanting to adopt their own affirmative action programs voluntarily should obtain the EEOC *Guidelines for Affirmative Action* to avoid possible future complaints of reverse discrimination.

Affirmative Action Plans

The affirmative action program that an organization undertakes is spelled out in an affirmative action plan (AAP). Each plan is tailored to the individual employer's work situation. A Veteran's Administration hospital in Newark, New Jersey; a YWCA in Miami, Florida; the Texas state park system; and the park and recreation department in Seattle, Washington, all require distinctively different plans and recruitment strategies.

The plans are result oriented, designed to achieve equal employment opportunity through specific actions taken by the employer (see Figure 4.3). The plans are not just token policies that exist only on paper. Furthermore, the plans include steps which the employer must take in order to ensure that the AAP is implemented.

ELEMENTS OF A SUCCESSFUL AFFIRMATIVE ACTION PLAN

- Adopt a strong affirmative action commitment through an officially adopted policy statement.
- Provide financial resources to implement the plan.
- Assign AAP responsibility to a top official, an affirmative action officer.
- Publicize the policy inside and outside the organization
- Analyze existing workforce for underutilization of minorities and women and discriminatory employment practices.
- Develop specific realistic objectives and timetables for hiring, promoting, and training.
- Develop actions to attain the objectives.
- Review and revise all employment practices to eliminate discrimination.
- Sensitize all supervisors and make them accountable for meeting the goals and eliminating discrimination.
- Establish internal reporting systems to monitor progress.
- Establish an internal grievance procedure.
- Actively recruit, train, and promote minorities and women.
- Periodically evaluate the effectiveness of the AAP and make appropriate adjustments.

Figure 4.3

Developing a Plan

The affirmative action plan should begin with an equal employment opportunity commitment on the part of the policy making board and top management. This commitment should take the form of a written policy statement that is officially adopted and publicized throughout the organization and to the recruitment market of potential employees. The commitment must include adequate staffing and financial support to develop, implement, and promulgate the plan. An affirmative action officer should be appointed to assist the organization in its preparation of an overall affirmative action program and in the specific development of a plan of action—the AAP.

A difficult step in preparing the AAP is to develop a profile of personnel both within the work group and in the overall work force in the area. A profile of current employees in the work groups should include the numbers of women, racial and ethnic minorities, handicapped veterans, and older workers in every job classification. This inventory of statistics will be analyzed to determine underutilization of target groups in all grades and in all positions in the organization.

Developing a profile of the work force in the area is a difficult task because the numbers of qualified and available workers in the market area are hard to obtain. The first hurdle to overcome is to define the market area. Would the market area for a suburban park district be the political boundaries of the suburban area or a much larger urban area known as a Standard Metropolitan Statistical Area (SMSA)? SMSAs have a higher percentage of minorities. The answer to this and related questions becomes complex and requires the assistance of personnel specialists. The autonomous public recreation agencies or private leisure agencies which have no personnel specialists should contact their local or state Equal Employment Opportunity Commission office. This agency will suggest where to find appropriate resources and census data. Many data are available on minorities and women in the population and in the work force of relevant labor market areas. But it may be more difficult to obtain statistics on specific skills available in a particular area.

Figure 4.4 represents a typical example of a park and recreation agency's personnel profile. Note the overutilization of women in secretarial-clerical positions. Also, note the consistent underutilization of blacks in all positions except the unskilled categories.

The next step in developing the AAP is to establish realistic timetables in which to recruit, train, and promote women and minorities so that they are no longer underutilized. A realistic goal for recruiting, training, and promoting black semiskilled and skilled workers in Figure 4.4 might be two years if there is a high turnover rate in those positions. It might take longer to meet parity for black supervisors and managers, however.

	Blacks		Women	
Job Category	Percent Utilized	Percent in Market	Percent Utilized	Percent in Market
Managers	0	8	1	20
Supervisors	1	10	2	35
Security-rangers	1	7	2	25
Secretary-clerical	4	20	100	95
Professional specialist	4	12	63	65
Skilled	7	15	0	12
Semiskilled	10	18	2	18
Unskilled	20	20	1	40

Figure 4.4 Profile of a hypothetical recreation group.

In middle-management positions, resignations and retirements probably would be slower; and there is not a pool of available blacks in the professional-specialists category from which promotions could quickly occur. The reverse situation exists for women where there is a readily available labor pool from which to promote women into supervisory and managerial positions.

Implementation

When the employer embarks on implementing an AAP, care should be taken not to be overzealous in righting past wrongs. Recruitment materials should not request "minority applicants only." Training and job promotion goals should not exclude opportunities for nonminority employees to advance in the organization.

The Affirmative Action Officer

The role of the affirmative action officer is very important in keeping the AAP alive and in meeting its objectives. This person promotes better understanding of minority cultures, conducts training sessions for managers and supervisors, and promotes the plan and its goals in the community. He or she assists in preparing job ads and recruitment materials so that language or pictures do not imply preferences for nonminority groups. A picture of a black officer on a highway billboard produced more black applicants for the Maryland State Police Department than from all other recruitment sources during the previous two years.[7] The affirmative action officer also prepares the necessary statistical reports for policymakers, the EEOC, OFCC, and other inquiring agencies.

Hiring from Within

Organizations usually have a choice concerning their hiring policy to fill new or vacant positions. In come cases, organizations will attempt to fill positions by recruiting from outside the existing work group. In other cases, organizations will always attempt to recruit from within their current pool of full-time, part-time, and seasonal employees. Each approach has certain advantages and limitations.

Advantages

Three major reasons exist for a policy of hiring from within the organization.

1. It fosters good employee morale by providing career ladders for advancement and more pay within the agency. When an employee fills an opening within the organization, it opens his or her former position for someone else to fill. This practice ensures a succession of advancement opportunities as people move up in the agency. Employees know that when someone retires or leaves the agency, there will be an opportunity for a higher-level position. Similarly, if a new position is created in upper management, several employees have the opportunity to benefit and advance.
2. An organization knows the strengths and weaknesses of its own employees. It is easier to evaluate knowledge, skills, abilities, and work behavior of current employees from personal records supervisors than those candidates interviewing from outside the organization. Working with known information reduces the risk of making a poor selection decision.
3. The period of time for employee orientation is reduced when persons from inside the organization are advanced to fill vacant positions. Current employees are already familiar with the goals, policies, procedures, and expectations of their employers. They can give their full attention to learning the new job, and they do not have to concentrate as much on environmental characteristics, lines of communication, and origins of resources. Since their adjustment time is shorter, they become more productive sooner.

Limitations

There are three inherent problems or limitations in *always* following a policy of filling vacancies from within the organization.

1. To ensure that the labor pool includes qualified individuals capable of moving up in the organization, there has to be an ongoing employee development program. Such a program teaches new skills and provides new information for the right employees at the right time in their careers. These comprehensive programs are not inexpensive. In the leisure services field, they generally mean overnight attendance at some workshop, conference, or school outside the agency' service area and, frequently, outside the state. Often, smaller agencies feel that they cannot afford to provide such training.
2. When the agency can afford training and development programs, it may not have enough employees with the potential ability to be trained and promoted into top management or specialized positions.
3. The third problem with *always* promoting from within is that all employees at all levels may tend to think and react alike. There is little opportunity to bring in fresh new ideas, except perhaps at entry-level positions. As subordinates move up in the organization, they bring to the new job the same thinking and practices under which they previously worked. This inbreeding situation over a long period of time will cause a leisure services agency to stagnate. An agency that never changes cannot possibly keep pace with the rapid socioeconomic changes of the twentieth century and will therefore provide less effective and beneficial leisure services to the public.

In light of the previous discussion, it would appear that the best policy for most agencies would be a flexible one in which the organization fills most positions from within, when qualified employees are available, but goes outside when appropriate talent is not available inside the organization. When filling upper-level positions, many agencies prefer to go outside to tap new ideas and bring fresh perspectives to the organization.

Internal Recruitment Procedures

Seeking qualified employees within the organization is usually the first step in the recruitment process. One of two methods is used. One involves posting or circulating job announcements throughout the agency several weeks before the agency recruits outside the agency. This is known as "job posting."[8] The vacancy is placed on bulletin boards and publicized in newsletters or special announcements. Employees are invited to apply. If current employees are interested in a particular opening, they may inform the immediate supervisor of the vacant position or the personnel unit. This may lead to sensitivities within an organization between supervisors and their respective subordinates. If the employee interested in changing jobs does not inform his immediate supervisor for fear of harassment or because he forgot, but does contact the supervisor of the vacant position, his immediate supervisor may feel piqued at both the subordinate and the supervisor of the vacant position.

To avoid those potential clashes, the personnel unit generally will serve as a clearinghouse to screen all applicants. The personnel unit can protect the confidentiality of applicants until it can be decided whether they are qualified enough to be actual candidates for the job. This unit also screens out those who are not qualified, to prevent an excessive number of applicants from taking the time of the supervisor of the position opening.[9] The principal value of this method of posting and circulating job announcements throughout the agency is that it gives every employee a fair chance to obtain a better job. It also helps reduce employee selection based on special deals or favoritism. Sometimes it may be difficult to decide between two or three equally qualified employees. When this occurs, those who are not chosen may experience a period of rejection or even resentment.

The second method used to identify potential candidates from within the organization involves a careful review of agency personnel records and performance appraisal forms.[10] In this method, both management and the personnel unit work closely together to decide who might be eligible. The employees in question may not even know they are under consideration. This method avoids the sensitivities between supervisors and employees previously mentioned, but runs the risk of overlooking potentially qualified employees.

Since all agencies are under the constraints of EEO legislation, and should want to give every employee a chance to advance, both methods (posting and management review) should be used. To do otherwise places the park, recreation, or leisure services agency in a position where employees, unions, or interested parties could file a discrimination suit with EEOC because a protected minority-group member was denied equal opportunity to prove himself or herself capable of advancement.

The External Search for Employees

During the discussion on recruiting from within the organization, it was suggested that the best recruitment policy is a flexible one whereby the agency (1) taps qualified talent from within its ranks, and (2) searches outside to find new talent. The external search best fulfills the intent of most affirmative action plans because the agency is searching out good candidates within the appropriate labor market, rather than complacently sitting back accepting applications.

There are a number of sources for personnel outside the hiring agency. A U.S. Labor Department study involving approximately 10 million workers found that the most successful method to obtain a job, in descending order, were direct application to an employer, receiving job information from friends and relatives, and answering newspaper ads.[11] The most successful methods for technical and professional employees were advertising, on-campus recruiting, and employment agencies. Minority employees, according to another survey, found the most success from community agencies, present minority employees, and educational institutions.[12]

Whichever method of outside recruitment is used, all job announcements and advertisements must not violate EEO laws. Terms such as "recent college graduate" or "age 25 to 30" would be unlawful. Ads may indicate a preference for college graduates provided that the employer can prove that a college degree is a BFOQ.[13]

Public Employment Agencies

Every state has a state employment service with branches in most large cities of 10,000 or more population.[14] Federal funds are matched with state dollars for the support and operation of these programs. The U.S. Employment and Training Service, a large unit of the U.S. Department of Labor's Manpower Administration, closely monitors the operations of approximately 2,300 local public employment offices.[15] It should be easy for park and recreation agencies to identify and use this source, especially during times of recession and high unemployment, when certain occupations tend to be laid off more readily than others. Construction laborers and unskilled and semiskilled workers are most frequently found registered with state employment services.[16] Public employment agencies have been reasonably successful in placing the unemployed into entry-level positions.[17]

There has been some criticism of public employment services. Employers complain that some of the applicants sent to them for interviews are not serious about wanting to be employed (supposedly because they want to keep receiving their unemployment benefits and must appear for interviews or lose those benefits). Other complaints stem from the enthusiasm of public employment agencies to place veterans, minorities, and the young, perhaps neglecting proper applicant screening procedures.[18] Consequently, many employers do not want to register job vacancies with the public services. In a concentrated effort to overcome these criticisms, the U.S. Employment and Training Service has established a computerized national job bank, has paid more attention recently to placing professionals, and uses more sophisticated techniques to screen applicants.[19]

Private Employment Agencies

The idea of employment agents brokering people—matching worker needs with employer's needs—is not a recent innovation. Over 200 years ago Boston and New York newspapers ran ads for brokers trying to fill domestic service and agricultural job openings.[20] Today, private employment agencies number about 10,000 and are found in most cities in the United States. These agencies are not government supported and must generate operating revenues from fees charged to clients. Clients may be the employing organization or the person seeking a job. In many cases, the employer is willing to pay the fee of the employee hired through such an agency.

Most private firms specialize in a particular field or profession, although there are agencies for special populations such as minorities, women, or older workers. Specialization allows the firm to be more efficient in meeting client's needs. Over 2.5 million Americans each year find employment through private employment agencies.

It is not uncommon for large cities to recruit for executive positions, such as the park and recreation director, through national executive search firms. These so called "head-hunting" firms operate like private employment agencies, but handle only upper management positions. They locate job candidates from those already employed by contacting leaders in the park and recreation and leisure field to assist them in identifying qualified candidates. A select few of the qualified candidates are asked to submit résumés. This practice saves employers, especially public employers, from screening hundreds of applicants for any one job. The executive search firms differ from private employment agencies in one other way; the search firms represent employers only, not job seekers. Their 1,200 agencies fill about 20,000 positions for organizations each year.[21]

All good private employment agencies carefully screen prospective employees, matching the job specifications with the knowledge, skills, and abilities from their pool of prospective employees.

Advertising

Advertising is the most widely used recruiting method for locating personnel because it generates large numbers of job seekers within a few days from the time the ad is placed. Hundreds of millions of dollars are spent annually on this external technique for recruiting, so it must be effective.[22] Advertising offers the employer several advantages as a recruiting method if the employer is selective in choosing the right media. Ads placed in professional, minority, or women's publications target selective groups of potential employees, representing a specific pool of potential labor.

The month or so lead time required in publishing most national magazines or journals is too great to include any ads but those seeking highly specialized talent managers or top executives. For these positions, a nationwide search may be necessary. Regional and state unbound publications, such as state societies or consulting services newsletters, have shorter lead times and can usually accommodate most ads for professional openings. For example, *Western City*, a monthly publication of the League of California Cities, has a section in the back of the magazine titled "Job Opportunities" which lists top professional and administrative job openings. When recruitment time is limited, daily or weekly newspapers will reach the most people in the shortest time period.[23] Help-wanted advertising is usually inexpensive, also.

Ads may attract many unqualified applicants, regardless of how well written the ad is. Entry-level or lower-paid positions, such as laborers and clerks, are usually placed in the classified columns.[24] Prominent display ads often highlight top management, administrative, and professional openings. Prominent display ads also work well just prior to hiring many seasonal employees or just before hiring a number of new employees. Figure 4.5 is an example of an ad placed in a large city newspaper.

Ad writing should reflect a businesslike style together with some creativity, in order to attract and interest a number of good applicants. For nationwide talent searches, advertising agencies will help organizations prepare help-wanted ads and will have them printed in any newspaper or magazine in the country.[25] But organizations pay well for these professional services. Someone within the organization with innovative thinking and good writing skills might better serve the same purpose because that person has firsthand knowledge of the agency.

Ads can be "open" or "blind." Blind ads use a box number and do not reveal the hiring organization. There are several situations where using a box number might prove advantageous. An organization that is always hiring may cause prospective applicants to pause and wonder what could be wrong with the working environment of that organization. Similarly, an organization with a poor image or reputation may use a box number to attract prospective new employees. Some organizations may not want their own employees to know they are hiring at a particular salary level, creating a new position, or filling an already full position.[26] Furthermore, the use of box numbers does reduce the number of telephone calls and drop-in applicants. It also allows the organization to be

SUNDAY NEWS   MARCH 16, 1986

Help Wanted

Recreation Director
Municipal Recreation System

The City of Rockyham is looking for a person with aggressive planning, administrative, and communication skills.   These are vital to a recreation organization that includes community centers, swimming pools, playgrounds, and extensive sports programs.

The necessary qualifications include a degree in parks and recreation plus leadership and supervisory experience for at least five (5) years.

We have a liberal fringe benefits program, including hospitalization, dental coverage, and life insurance.

Salary is negotiable.

Please send résumé and salary history to:
Donald Colmar, Director
Department of Personnel
581 Long Avenue
Rockyham, Nebraska 44114

Closing date for résumés is March 25, 1986.
Equal Opportunity Employer

Figure 4.5   Example of a job advertisement.

less concerned about acknowledging requests for information or résumés since the applicants do not know the organization's name.

From the candidate's point of view, responding to blind ads is risky, especially in the small and personable field of parks, recreation, and leisure services, where every administrator knows every other administrator in the state and even in the region. It would not be long before the candidate's boss hears that his or her employee is looking for another job. Therefore, the hiring organization may be contacted only by people who have nothing to lose because they are not presently employed or feel that they may soon be unemployed. The advantages and disadvantages of using blind ads should be given careful thought. We believe that parks, recreation, and leisure service agencies should identify themselves, even if they choose to use a box number at a newspaper. It does not seem ethical to ask a candidate to send detailed autobiographical information and not know who will be reading or using that information.

Institutional Recruitment

Educational institutions, state professional societies, state park and recreation consulting services, and the National Recreation and Park Association (NRPA) serve the park, recreation, and leisure employer as additional sources of personnel.

College and university placement offices are the focal points on most campuses where the hiring organization can send recruiting materials, schedule interviews with graduating seniors, and give selection tests. This source of recruiting is generally used only by larger organizations that can afford to send interviewers to selective college campuses. Two examples of large organizations that recruit on campuses are the National Park Service (NPS) and Disney World's Magic Kingdom College.

Generally, the primary contact on campus for recruiting park and recreation agencies is not the placement office, but the recreation or leisure services academic department. The faculty and staff of the recreation department are much more likely to be aware of current and former students who are seeking jobs. For example, one faculty member may have as one of her assigned responsibilities the placement of intern, cooperative, or fieldwork students. Another faculty member will assist seniors and graduate students to find permanent positions. Still other faculty members work with local organizations to place student volunteers for a semester or season as those students meet course requirements. Thus the best place on campus to recruit for employees is through the appropriate academic department, where an effective and mutually beneficial relationship has been established.

Although most park, recreation, and leisure service recruiters know whom to contact within these departments, most people in a central personnel unit do not. This means that if a recreation unit depends on a personnel unit to make its recruitment contacts and if the recreation unit does not specify whom to contact at each university, it is very likely that job notices will be sent to the wrong place. This is sometimes a serious problem. Both the job seekers and recreation department end up frustrated. Clearly, this problem could be minimized if the recreation supervisors provided the personnel specialists with more definitive information about whom to contact at each university.

As we know, not all recreation, park, and leisure service academic departments provide the same quality of learning experience for their students. Approximately 292 park and recreation four-year degree programs and 208 two-year degree programs at colleges and universities exist in the United States and Canada.[27] But in 1985 only 41 of these four-year curricula were nationally accredited by the NRPA. Each year the January issue of *Parks and Recreation* magazine prints the updated list of accredited four-year degree programs. Some leisure service organizations have a policy of sending job notices to all nationally accredited curricula as well as to those that are nearby. In theory at least, the students graduating from nationally accredited curricula are graduating from the schools that meet the highest standards of excellence. This is not to say that nonaccredited recreation, park, and leisure programs do not provide an equally good education, but if they have not chosen to seek accreditation, there is no comparable criterion with which to evaluate their programs.

Agency staff often have a close relationship with university faculty. It is not unusual for a faculty member to call an agency to recommend a specific student, someone whom they feel would relate well to the agency's mission or clientele. Similarly, agency recruiters frequently call faculty members to get referrals or recommendations on present or former graduates. The advantages of this close relationship is obvious. The university knows the agency's situation and special requirements and can provide a better student match through recommendations. The agency knows the curriculum and can feel confident that the faculty member would not recommend a person who through personality or inappropriate skills might embarrass the agency or perform poorly on the job.

University student organizations often sponsor employment conferences or "job fairs" in an effort to bring together hiring agencies and job-seeking students and graduates. The North Carolina State University RISE Conference (recreation internship and summer employment) provides a centralized environment for participating agencies to interview students and graduates for permanent, seasonal, and fieldwork positions. It is an excellent opportunity for hiring agencies to develop rapport and communication channels with both faculty and students, as well as to promote an agency's image.

A number of state park and recreation societies offer the hiring organization an opportunity to interview prospective candidates at annual state society meetings. These so-called "job marts" are usually located in the exhibitor's area at convention centers or hotels. Similar opportunities are offered by the National Recreation and Park Association at its regional conferences and at the annual Congress.

The NRPA publishes *Park and Recreation Opportunities,* a national job bulletin service that lists position vacancies by geographic region. It is published biweekly for NRPA members for a nominal service charge. There is no charge to the recruiting organization. A number of state park and recreation consulting services also publish job bulletins. For example, Florida's Office of Recreation Services publishes *Recreation Assistant Program: Position Available.* Also, a number of state professional park and recreation societies, such as Oregon's and Michigan's, list job openings in their newsletters. In California, the NRPA jointly prints a monthly job bulletin with the California Park and Recreation Society (see Figure 4.6).

Internships and Cooperative Studies

It is a common practice for park and recreation employers to hire college students for a specific period in cooperation with a particular university

A Joint Service Program by

PUBLICATION DATE: JANUARY 13, 1984

JOB ANNOUNCEMENT BULLETIN

CPRS/NRPA, 1400 K Street, Suite 302, Sacramento, CA 95814

SUPERVISION

RECREATION SPECIALIST ($1,620 - $1,976/mo.)   Burbank

DESCRIPTION & QUALIFICATIONS: The individual selected will be responsible for
planning, organizing, and conducting group and individual activities requiring
special skills in all types of recreation for varied skill levels and all ages.
This position requires graduation from an accredited college or university with
specialization in recreation or a closely related field and one year equivalent
experience in paid leadership in recreation activities or sports. Additional
qualifying experience may be substituted for the required education on a year '
for year basis, for a maximum of two years. The applicant must possess a
current Red-Cross standard first aid certificate by the time of permanent
appointment. A valid California, Class III driver's license is required at
time of appointment. Resumes will not be accepted in lieu of a City of
Burbank application. APPLY: City of Burbank, Personnel Department, 275 East
Olive Avenue, Burbank, CA 91502. PHONE: (818) 953-9721. CLOSING DATE:
January 27, 1984. EOE M/F

RECREATION SUPERVISOR ($1,749 - $2,244/mo. + benefits)   Brea

DESCRIPTION & QUALIFICATIONS: Provides technical staff assistance to the
Leisure Services Manager and is responsible for day-to-day coordination,
supervision, and scheduling of recreation and leisure services in a
specialized recreation program. APPLY: City of Brea, Number One Civic
Center Circle, Brea, CA 92621. PHONE: (714) 990-7715. CLOSING DATE:
February 9, 1984, 4:00 p.m.

Figure 4.6 Example of a job announcement bulletin.

department. This practice has been labeled internship, cooperative studies, fieldwork, or practicum. This "on-the-job" experience earns college
credits for the students under the aegis of a leisure studies curriculum.
Cooperative study programs may not always offer college credit, but
they do provide opportunities for the employing organization to observe
the students' work habits and performance for a longer period, usually
for twelve months or more. Whatever the program label, period of time
on the job, or college credit earned, these programs give the employing
organization possible candidates for future positions. Because students
are seeking full-time employment upon graduation, often with the internship or coop agency, they are more inclined to be enthusiastic, at-
tentive to assignments, and willing to work longer hours. Generally,
students are willing to please the employer because they need both the
work experience and the college recognition and approval.

Miscellaneous Sources of Personnel

One of the most obvious ways to recruit employees is through people
sources already familiar with the organization. Former employees, pres-

ent staff and volunteers, professional colleagues from other agencies, and even the clientele that the organization serves may all recommend possible candidates for position openings. Usually, these people will recommend candidates that they feel are qualified. To do otherwise would reflect badly on their own judgment. Referrals may therefore, be better qualified than applicants responding from other recruitment sources, such as public employment agencies or advertisements. Referrals should not be the only recruiting source used, however, especially if employees, clients, and colleagues are predominately white males. The hiring organization should always be cognizant of not violating EEO laws.

Most park and recreation organizations receive many unsolicited applicants. This is especially true for those organizations that have good reputations. Although a good number of these applicants may be employable and make good employees, the organization cannot hire all the job seekers. It is a good idea to have every qualified applicant fill out the agency application form, which can then be filed for possible future use. Although it might be tempting to fill entry- or lower-level positions, exclusively from "walk-ons" or "mail-ins," the agency must be careful not to neglect its affirmative action plan, especially if most unsolicited applicants are white males.

Job Announcements

Prior to initiating either the internal or external search for any new employee, the hiring organization must prepare what is known as a "job announcement." This statement serves three objectives. *First, it explains the position that the agency wants to fill* and includes the job title and the job specifications. *Second, it identifies those qualifications necessary to meet the job responsibilities,* including special requirements, education, and related job experience. *Finally, it tells the applicant how and where to apply for the position.* It is necessary to prepare the job announcement in order to know what to include in the magazine, help-wanted, or special display ad. Similarly, the job announcement is the most critical item in contacting employment agencies and educational and professional institutions.

Job ads and job announcements may include the same basic information, although the cost of advertising may dictate a more condensed text for the ad. The following elements are found in most job announcements, and Figure 4.7 is an example of an announcement that includes almost all the elements.

1. *Name of the position.* Every position has a title or classification and applicants want to know this information.
   Examples: Park ranger; secretary; general tradesperson.

JOB ANNOUNCEMENT

Superintendent Enterprise Division

Opening Date to Apply: May 5, 1986   Closing Date: August 15, 1986

Job Description:

The Superintendent is reponsible for the long-range planning,
coordination, and overall organization and operation of various "special
facilities" within the Division of State Parks, so classified because
of their high revenue production. These facilities include lodges,
restaurants, ski operations, golf courses, and two marinas. Reviews and
analyzes individual facility operations for patron service effectiveness
and cost-revenue ratios.

Minimum Qualifications:

Knowledge of business management practices and ability to work
tactfully and harmoniously with the facilities managers and the
public. Skill in analysis investigation and studies. Experience in
managing a leisure revenue-producing facility and supervising employees.

Education and Special Requirements:

A current Western State driver's license. Degree in parks and recreation
or leisure studies from an accredited college or university and four
years' experience managing an enterprise facility. A degree in business
may be substituted with six years' experience.

Salary: $28,000 - $34,000 annually

Benefits:

State vehicle provided and all travel expenses reimbursed. Generous
fringe benefits with major medical, dental, and retirement insurance.

Work Location:

The superintendent will work in Capital City but will also travel to
state park sites as required.

To Apply:

Submit résumé to Personnel Director
Division of State Parks
One Government Circle
Capital City, Western State 987654
For further information, call Lisa Wilson, (619) 222-1000.

WESTERN STATE
Equal Opportunity Employer

Figure 4.7   Model job announcement.

94

2. *Equal opportunity statement.* This phrase does not guarantee every applicant equal treatment, but its message implies that the employer is aware of EEO requirements.
   Example: Equal opportunity/affirmative action employer.
3. *Job in specific terms.* Job titles are often misleading and do not always mean the same thing to every employer or prospective applicant. It is necessary to explain the major duties and responsibilities of the specific job for the applicants.
   Example: Patrols campground and lake area, enforces park regulations, supervises maintenance crew.
4. *Minimum knowledge, skills, and abilities.* This element explains what minimum qualifications the applicants must possess to accomplish the specific job duties or functions.
   Examples: Considerable knowledge of the principles of supervision; basic knowledge of pricing products to increase sales and revenues; ability to operate heavy equipment on mountain slopes.
5. *Education, experience, and special requirements.* Some positions require the applicants to have special education, certification, licenses, or experience. Applicants who do not have these qualifications would not be candidates for the position.
   Examples: master's degree in planning; licensed electrician; current CPR certification; word-processing experience.
6. *Opening and closing dates to apply.* Naturally, the applicants need this information to know when to submit their résumés or when to initiate inquiries about the position.
   Example: Opening date to apply: June 6, 1985.
   Closing date: June 30, 1985.
7. *Where to apply, how to apply, whom to contact.* Employers may choose to have applicants apply at a blind post office box number, at a centralized personnel office, or to a regional or decentralized site location. Some employers prefer to screen applicants first by telephone before sending out application forms. Other employers may want to see how well applicants write and will request résumés with covering letters. Many organizations use different procedures for different positions.
   Examples: Call 919-872-1100 for additional information; applications may be obtained at 48 Park Dr., Room 210; send résumé to Linda Wrenn, Personnel Office, New Park District.
8. *Salary information.* Applicants may not be interested in applying if the pay scale is too low or below what they are already earning.
   Examples: $12,000 to start; $3.75 per hour; salary range $25,000–$30,000; base salary plus commission on sales; GS-7.
9. *Job benefits.* Often the employee or job benefits are more attractive than the salary and serve to attract applicants. Unusual job benefits should be identified.

Examples: Two-bedroom park house provided; excellent opportunity for immediate advancement; full dental benefits.

The following elements are optional, if space permits.

10. *Agency characteristics.*

Examples: Sundale is the oldest park district in the state, established in 1936; Lorton maintains 1,500 park acres, a rose garden and aboretum, one cemetary, and three miles of median strips; Raven YWCA serves 45,000 women in the greater metropolitan area with a full recreation, health, and counseling program.

11. *Work location.* Applicants may be misled into believing that they will work at an organization's main office or in the city in which they apply for the position. For some jobs, the work location may be in another section of the county and the applicant may have no means of traveling to that site. The job announcement should clarify where the employee will be working if the work site is not at the main headquarters.

Example: Example will work at Mill Run Park off Route 410 located seven miles outside township limits.

Application Forms

Every organization should develop its own formal application form which seeks an applicant's qualifications and work background. Sample forms could be purchased at local office supply stores and modified to fit the organization. There are several good resource books which also provide sample forms; or the organization can obtain forms from other leisure service agencies.

Using the same form for every full-time position meets three good recruitment and selection objectives. (1) It enables the organization to standardize its request for factual information so that every applicant has the same opportunity to present the same type of job-related experience. (2) It reduces human errors in subjectively evaluating résumés that are either too cluttered with irrelevant information or present very impressive data in only one area related to the position being sought. (3) It helps ensure that the organization's search for background information is legal under EEO laws.

An application blank is one of the best ways to obtain factual information.[28] A good application blank (see Figure 4.8) will include the following sections:

1. *Equal Opportunity Affirmative Action Employer phrase* printed conspicuously somewhere on the form. Recent forms have expanded on this phrase. "Qualified applicants are considered without regard for

Figure 4.8   Model job application form.

APPLICATION FOR EMPLOYMENT

DIVISION OF STATE PARKS

An Equal Opportunity-Affirmative Action Employer

Box 191, Capital City, Western State 72008

Please print or type your name and address

Position for which you are applying _____Date_____

Name _____Social Security No._____
    (last)   (first)   (middle)

Mailing Address _____
    (street and number)   (city)   (state)   (zip)

Telephone _____ Are you between the ages of 18 and 70? Yes ☐ No ☐
    (Area Code)   If "No," how old are you? _____

Can you legally work in the United States because of American Citizenship _____

               Permanent Resident Visa _____ Other _____

If you are not a U.S. citizen, give your alien registration number. _____

//

Have you ever been in the U.S. Military Service? No ☐ Yes ☐ Branch of Service _____

    Dates of Active Duty _____ Service Number _____

    Reserve/National Guard Status _____

//

Would you accept ☐ Part time work   ☐ Temporary Work   ☐ Seasonal work - Winter

       ☐ Full time work   ☐ Seasonal work - Summer ☐ Weekend & night work

Have you ever worked for Western State before? No ☐ Yes ☐ Dates _____

    Division _____ Position _____

Distance from home that you are willing to travel to work

    ☐ 10 miles or less ☐ 20 miles or less ☐ 50 miles or less ☐ Free to relocate

---

Note: Answers to these questions are necessarily disqualifying. They will be evaluated in
      relation to job duties and responsibilities.

Do you have a valid driver's license? No ☐ Yes ☐ Which state. _____

Have you even been convicted of driving under the influence of alcohol or drugs? No ☐ Yes ☐

Has your driver's license ever been suspended, revoked or on probations? No ☐ Yes ☐

If yes, state the reason _____

Have you ever been convicted of an unlawful act? (Omit driving violations) No ☐ Yes ☐

If yes, provide details of case _____

Do you have a permanent illness or disability which might interfere with satisfactorily

performing those job duties for which you applied? No ☐ Yes ☐

If yes, explain _____

(continued)

Figure 4.8 (*continued*)

School	Name	City	State	Circle Highest Year Completed	Are you now attending school?
Elementary				1 2 3 4 5 6	Yes ☐ No ☐ Part time ☐ Full time ☐
Jr. High				7 8 9	Courses, Major, Degree
High School				10 11 12	
Business or					
Trade				1 2 3 4	
College				1 2 3 4 5 6 7	

//

EMPLOYMENT DATA

Begin with your present or most recent employer and list all positions held for the past 15 years. Include military, part time, summer and significant volunteer work if these positions relate in any way to the position for which you are applying. Experience gained more than 15 years ago may be summarized in one block if applicable to position.

*Job Title _____ Dates from _____ to _____ | Full time _____

Employer's Name _____ | Part time _____

Address _____ Telephone_____ | No. hours per week _____

Description of duties, responsibilities _____

_____

Number of employes supervised by you _____. May we contact present employer _____

Reason for leaving_____

*Previous title _____ Dates from _____ to _____ | Full time _____

Employer's Name _____ | Part time _____

Address _____ Telephone _____ | No. hours per week _____

Description of duties, responsibilities _____

_____

Number of employees supervised by you _____. Name of immediate supervisor _____

Reason for leaving _____

*Previous title _____ Dates from _____ to _____ | Full time _____

Employer's Name _____ | Part time _____

Address _____ Telephone _____ | No. hours per week _____

Description of duties, responsibilities _____

_____

Number of employees supervised by you _____. Name of immediate supervisor _____

Reason for leaving _____

		Full time _____
*Previous title _____Dates from _____to _____		Part time _____
Employer's Name _____		No. hours per week ___
Address _____		
Description of duties, responsibilities _____		

Number of employess supervised by you _____. Name of immediate supervisor _____

Reason for leaving _____

Other name under which school or employment records are filed. _____

If additional space is needed, ask for a continuation sheet, or use a sheet of paper.

SKILLS/ABILITIES: Check the following skills in which you are qualified. If you are applying
 for full time or seasonal recreational positions, please ask for skills inventory sheet.

TYPING WPM _____SHORTHAND WPM _____WORD PROCESSOR _____

List office equipment operated _____

List specialized types of equipment which you are qualified to operate such as bulldozer,

drillpress, dumptruck _____

Indicate special skills, accomplishments, training, publications or certification you have which

are relevant to the position for which you are applying. Please indicate if you can read,

write or speak a foreign language, and which language(s)._____

//

References (Not relatives or employers previously listed)   Years

Name	Title	Address	Known
1.			
2.			

//

Please read the following statements before signing the application.

 *I understand that employment is subject to evidence of satisfactorily passing a physical
 examination.

 *I authorize the State to make educational, employment and personal reference inquiries of
 my background.

 *I authorize the State to conduct a police and court records investigation of my background
 if such information is relevant to the position I seek.

 *I authorize former educational institutions which I attended and former employers to give
 any information regarding my academic or work performance.

 *I understand that if employed, I will be on probation for six months, and during that time
 I may be discharged for any reason.

(continued)

Figure 4.8 (*continued*)

I certify that all statements made on this application are true and complete to the best of my knowledge, and that any false information will result in employment disqualification or dismissal.

_____

Signature of Applicant

This application will be kept on file for six months.

THANK YOU FOR YOUR INTEREST IN THE DIVISION OF STATE PARKS

for race, color, religion, sex, national origin, age, marital status, or non-job-related handicap."

2. *Current status questions* concerning date of application, position for which applicants are applying, applicant's name, current address, Social Security number, and telephone number where the applicant can be reached. This section might also ask a question about whether the applicant can legally work in the United States with respect to American citizenship, permanent resident visa, or other legal category. Often, the employer needs to know if the applicant has served in the U.S. military service in order to satisfy veterans' preference laws.

3. *Agency policies and job-related questions* usually ask the applicants to identify whether they are seeking full-time, part-time, temporary, or seasonal work. Some forms also ask how far the applicant is willing to travel to work or if they are free to relocate. Most forms inquire about a current driver's or chauffeur's license. If the job requires driving vehicles owned by the organization, questions may also include whether or not the applicant has been involved in recent traffic accidents for which they were responsible; especially convictions while driving under the influence of alcohol or drugs that resulted in the driver's license being suspended or revoked.

Application questions asking the applicant if they have ever been convicted for breaking the law are not appropriate. Many agencies continue the practice, however, because a prior conviction record would be considered a good reason for not hiring an applicant, provided that the conviction was related to the position. Law enforcement positions, jobs requiring high security, and job responsibilities that include handling large sums of money fall into this category. Depending on the nature of the offense, conviction information may be used to screen out applicants who the employer feels are security or safety risks. Agencies that seek conviction information from the applicant on an application blank often use disclaimer statements similar to the ones typed inside the box in Figure 4.8.

Answers to the questions are not necessarily disqualifying. They will be evaluated in relation to the job duties and responsibilities of the position for which you are applying.

Employers who use disclaimer statements believe that they can ask sensitive "business-necessity" or job-related questions which are ordinarily considered discriminatory. In recent years, EEOC officials have cautioned that the use of disclaimers on application forms carries no protection from future charges of discrimination. In one instance EEOC ruled that when criminal records are available from local police sources, the request for such information on job applications is unnecessary, arbitrary, and unlawful.[29]

Some organizations have policies against nepotism—hiring close relatives within the same organizational unit. Questions may seek information about relatives employed by the organization, nature of the relationship, position held, and in which department. This practice has been questioned, also, as potentially sensitive. In the event that the applicant is not hired, he or she could claim discrimination based on biased information known about the relative.

It is also not uncommon to find questions asking if the applicant has previously worked for or applied for a position with the organization. This enables the employer to search its own records for information about the applicants.

4. *Educational questions* that seek information pertaining to job-related duties and responsibilities. The nature of these questions is important. Requesting the type of institution and education attained would be appropriate if the position requires documentation of minimal competency in a professional or skilled occupation.

5. *Employment data* seeking the applicant's employment history, beginning with the present and most recent employer. Some organizations require all job-related experience back to the first job, including part-time, summer, military, and significant volunteer work. Other organizations are interested only in full-time work experience for a designated period of time, such as ten years. The detail requested on every job might be extensive, such as description of duties, responsibilities, accomplishments, salary, number of employees supervised, budgetary responsibilities, and reason for leaving. Other forms simply ask for employer's name, address, dates of employment, and job title.

6. *Skills or abilities inventory* requesting the applicant to check or indicate present skill levels. These may include ability to teach or coach recreational articles, such as scuba diving, sailing, softball, volleyball, orienteering, and so on.

   More frequently, this section seeks information on typing or shorthand skills, ability to operate office equipment or word-processing computers, or ability to operate specialized pieces of equipment such as bulldozers or drill presses.

7. *Certification or special recognition* section, probing for unusual training, accomplishments, or publications which the employer feels are relevant to certain positions. Someone applying for a position requiring good writing skills might list news features or scholarly articles that were published. Certification in lifesaving, rescue and water safety, handling of small firearms, or sports officiating would also be identified for the employer in this section.

8. *Reference information* is usually requested near the end of the application form, asking for the names and addresses of persons who have knowledge of the applicant's work but are not related to the applicant.

9. *Authorization, certification statement, and signature* from the applicant that all information provided is complete and true to the best of the applicant's knowledge. This section may include statements or insert affidavits, such as the following:

   (a) I understand that employment is subject to satisfactory examination by a physician.

   (b) I understand that a condition of employment is residency within the county limits within (time period) of employment.

   (c) I authorize former educational institutions which I have attended to provide any academic information to (name of organization).

   (d) I authorize my former employers to give any information regarding my employment.

   (e) I authorize (the organization name) to conduct a police and court records investigation of my background.

   (f) I understand that, if employed, I will be on probation for a period of (number of months), and during that time, I am subject to being discharged for any reason.

10. *Applicant control sheets* are also becoming more useful to the employer. As EEOC and the courts mandate more detailed documentation on the hiring practices of minority and protected groups, organizations must obtain better data from each member of a protected group. For that information not to be used to discriminate against a minority group member by those employees screening or interviewing, most of that information should *not* be requested directly on the application form. An additional sheet is placed loosely with the application form and is referred to as an applicant control sheet. The completed sheet is immediately removed from the application blank upon submission by the applicant.

    Applicant control sheets state that the information requested regarding national origin, race, sex, age, marital status, and number of dependents is being collected to comply with certain federal regulations and will *not* be used to determine an applicant's suitability for employment. Some sheets ask questions pertaining to how the applicant first learned about the vacant position. This assists the organization in evaluating the effectiveness of different recruitment methods in reaching women and minorities.

Appendix E offers a good example of an application form. It is used by the City of Greensboro, North Carolina, and includes an applicant control sheet and an acknowledgment of residency requirements.

Most of the application sections previously mentioned are included in an application form to determine how successful the applicant might be on the job based on the information provided or subsequently obtained by the employer. Some sections help the organization keep track of which applicants have applied for which positions and which are willing to work under existing organizational policies and practices. Every question in every section, as well as the entire tone of the application blank, should tell applicants that screening and selection decisions are based on job-related qualifications and conditions and are not, therefore, subject to illegal discrimination.

Weighted Application Forms

Some organizations are attempting to improve the effectiveness of application blanks by focusing on the fact that certain types of specific information about employees can serve as an excellent predictor of future job success. For example, if an organization can demonstrate that high school graduates are better workers in a certain job than workers with an eighth-grade education or a college degree, high school graduates would receive a higher application blank evaluation score. In other words, specific information from the application form is evaluated in order to derive a score for each applicant which predicts how well the applicant would perform on the job. At the current time, a number of organizations are conducting research to determine what types of information about people are useful predictors. Information that is not a good predictor is dropped from the application blank.

Weighted application forms have been shown to be one of the most valid selection devices associated with their use. Application blank information must be validated for each specific job, and this can be expensive and time consuming. Also, the information used to predict must not violate equal employment opportunity legislation. For example, age, sex, and race would very rarely be acceptable predictors. Finally, it is frequently difficult to establish the criterion for successful performance. Should "success" be measured by qualities of stability and long-term performance, or by the amount of work performed, or by the quality of the work? In spite of these problems, we predict that more research will be done and more and more organizations will begin using weighted application forms in the future.

Falsification of Information

One other consideration needs to be mentioned about application blanks. Do not assume that all the information provided is accurate. Occasionally, one reads a story such as that about the college professor who held down three full-time teaching jobs simultaneously under three different names within a driving radius of his home. More common are those applicants who claim to have college degrees, but in fact lack a few hours for graduation. In one study, one-fourth of the applicants for the position of nurses' aides offered different information about why they left their former jobs than the information obtained through reference checks. Over half of the same applicants lied about former salaries received and the length of time they with previous employers.[30] Thus, although an application blank is an excellent technique to obtain factual information, it should not be the only method used to screen or select prospective employees.

Recruitment Evaluation

If recruitment is effective, it should match organization needs with the knowledge and abilities of the right people at the time when the organization needs those abilities. Periodically, it is important to determine how effective the recruitment techniques and sources of personnel are in attracting employees. Schuler suggests three stages when recruitment evaluation criteria should be applied.

1. During the *preentry* state the employer examines how many qualified applicants are attracted by the various recruitment techniques utilized by the organization. Are ads more effective than internships for certain types of jobs? Which institutional resource is the most effective for professional positions? Which technique attracts more women and minorities?
2. At the *entry* stage, the criteria shift to the new employees. The evaluation criteria focus on the employees' initial expectations about the agency and whether the employees feel that the agency is meeting

their needs. Were working conditions represented fairly? Are resources to do the job readily available? Is the working environment friendly?

3. The *last* stage, according to Schuler, is the postentry period. In this stage measurements cover a longer period of time and try to evaluate the effectiveness of the match of organizational needs and employee abilities and needs.[31] Organizational needs are met when employees perform well on the job and remain with the agency. The evaluation criteria should examine quality of job performance, employee commitment to the job, employee thoughts about quitting, and rates of resignations and discharges. Employee needs are met when the employee is satisfied with his or her job and feels that the organization challenges his or her abilities. Evaluation criteria should examine those conditions in the work environment which led to employee satisfaction. It is not easy to evaluate the last stage, but recruitment is effective only if both agency and employee are satisfied.

Summary and Recommendations

1. The primary purpose of recruitment is to attract a sufficient number of qualified people, either from within or from outside the organization, to apply for position vacancies. See Figure 4.9 for a summary of the various personnel sources.
2. Contracting out work, paying existing employees overtime, and using temporary employees can sometimes be effective alternatives to the traditional pattern of hiring additional full-time, permanent personnel.
3. Affirmative action plans, which most park and recreation agencies have chosen to adopt, greatly affect recruitment policies and procedures.
4. An effective hiring policy for most agencies is one of filling most positions from within, when qualified employees are available, but going outside when talent is not available.
5. External recruitment is usually a better method of fulfilling the intent of most affirmative action plans (see Figure 4.9).
6. The job specifications and job qualifications that are developed during the planning phase of the staffing process are an essential part of all job announcements and advertisements.
7. Application forms are an effective means of gathering factual information about candidates.
8. Applicant control sheets collect information that is used to ensure compliance with equal employment opportunity legislation but *not* used to make screening selection decisions.

Figure 4.9 Comparison of various recruitment methods.

Sources of Personnel	Advantages	Disadvantages
1. Internal		
(a) Posting/circulating job announcement	Agency knows applicants Good for morale Applicant knows agency Provide career ladder Little cost to employer	No outside talent Fewer applicants Limited affirmative action Infighting for promotions
(b) Management review	Reduces internal sensitivities Few applicants to process	May eliminate qualified employees Voids EEO efforts May be illegal
2. External		
(a) Employment agencies, public	Ready pool of workers Free to employer	Limited knowledge, skills, abilities Not always employable
(b) Professional meetings	Saves travel expenses Face-to-face screening opportunity	Limited to professional positions Many applicants cannot afford to attend
(c) Professional job bulletins	Reaches select market Free	May not reach all possible candidates Many applicants to screen
(d) Internships/coops	Applicant knows agency Agency knows applicants No recruitment costs Enthusiastic workers	Limited to professional positions Awkward if not hired

	Advantages	Disadvantages
(e) Miscellaneous referrals	Higher caliber Promotes goodwill	May violate EEO May establish cliques
(f) Employment agencies, private	Identifies potential applicants Selective screening Efficient; confidential Offers guidance	Service fee required Limited position types
(g) Advertising	Reaches target groups Meets EEO objectives Reaches applicants quickly	Many applicants to screen
(h) Educational institutions	Measurable standard of knowledge and intellect Known amount of education Reaches enthusiastic applicants Hiring agency known by faculty Saves time; efficient	Competitive for better students Limited to professional positions Limited work history of applicants Requires time to develop rapport Recruiter must be very good
(i) Unsolicited	Inexpensive Speed in hiring	No affirmative action Too many applicants Yields less qualified applicants
(j) Raiding	Identifies best qualified	Raiding not ethical

9. Every question in every section, as well as the entire tone of an application-blank, should tell applicants that screening and selection decisions are based solely on merit and the job-related qualifications.
10. Weighted application forms not only gather factual information but also give special importance to the information that is proven to be the best indicator of successful job performance.
11. The recruitment process should include certain evaluation procedures to ensure that it is successfully meeting organizational needs.

Discussion Topics

1. What procedure would you follow if you were a first-line supervisor in a local public park and recreation agency and you wished to fill a full-time permanent position that was now open?
2. What items should be addressed in a personnel requisition form?
3. We do not always have to hire full-time, permanent employees to accomplish our work load. What are some of our alternatives and what are their advantages and disadvantages?
4. Affirmative action plans are mandated by law or court order in two situations. What are these two situations?
5. What are the major elements of an affirmative action plan?
6. What are the advantages and disadvantages of (a) continually hiring from within, and (b) continually hiring from outside the organization?
7. What is the best way of recruiting internally?
8. Assume that you are the director of a racquet club in the geographic area in which you now live. You would like to hire more minority employees at your club. What specific methods and sources would you use to recruit minorities?
9. Assume that you are responsible for recruiting more women in your county park system. Your operation is located in a western mountain state. What specific methods and sources would you use to recruit women?

Notes

1. Wendell French, *The Personnel Management Process*, 4th ed. (Boston: Houghton Mifflin Company, 1978), p. 214.
2. Wayne Mondy and Robert Noe, *Personnel: The Management of Human Resources* (Boston: Allyn and Bacon, Inc., 1981), p. 128.
3. Arthur Sloane, *Personnel: Managing Human Resources* (Englewood Cliffs, N.J.: Prentice-Hall, Inc., 1983), p. 116.
4. Randall Schuler, *Personnel and Human Resource Management* (St. Paul, Minn.: West Publishing Co., 1981), p. 185.

5. Sloane, *Personnel*, p. 85.
6. Schuler, *Personnel and Human Resource Management*, p. 185.
7. Robert Calvert, *Affirmative Action: A Comprehensive Recruitment Manual* (Garrett Park, Md.: Garrett Park Press, 1979), p. 251.
8. Sloane, *Personnel*, p. 101.
9. Edwin Flippo, *Personnel Management* (New York: McGraw-Hill Book Company, 1980), p. 133.
10. Dale Beach, *Personnel: The Management of People at Work* (New York: Macmillan Publishing Company, 1975), p. 233.
11. French, *Personnel Management Process*, p. 215.
12. Bureau of National Affairs, "An Equal Employment Opportunity: Programs and Results," *Personnel Policies Forum*, Survey No. 112 (March 1976): 3.
13. French, *Personnel Management Process*, p. 216.
14. Beach, *Personnel*, p. 233.
15. Sloane, *Personnel*, p. 106.
16. Beach, *Personnel*, p. 233.
17. Sloane, *Personnel*, p. 106.
18. Ibid.
19. Ibid.
20. Ibid., p. 105.
21. Ibid., p. 110.
22. Ibid., p. 103.
23. Flippo, *Personnel Management*, p. 133.
24. Erwin Stanton, *Successful Personnel Recruiting and Selection* (New York: AMACOM Book Division, 1977), p. 55.
25. Ibid., p. 56.
26. Ibid., p. 32.
27. Richard Gitelson and Donald Henkel, "The Accelerating Decline of Enrollment," in *Parks and Recreation*, The 1982 SPRE Survey (Alexandria, Va.: National Recreation and Park Association, August 1983), p. 59.
28. Flippo, *Personnel Management*, p. 139.
29. Staff Recommendations, *Preemployment Screening: Latest Guidelines* (New York: Research Institute of America, 1980), p. 17.
30. Flippo, *Personnel Management*, p. 139.
31. Schuler, *Personnel and Human Resource Management*, p. 136.

5
Employee Selection

Most leisure service managers will make numerous employee selection decisions throughout their careers. Many of these decisions; involving part-time and seasonal employees and volunteers as well as full-time, permanent personnel; might be critical and affect the organization for many years. These decisions should reflect a knowledge of selection procedures as well as an understanding of the fundamental philosophical issues related to selection. The purpose of this chapter is to present park and recreation managers and students with both a philosophical background and a working knowledge of employee selection.

Hopefully, a recruitment effort such as the one described in Chapter 4 will provide a pool of applicants from which position vacancies can be filled. Of course, it is possible that none of the applicants meets minimum qualifications. If this occurs, the agency has three options: lower minimum qualification standards, continue to recruit externally, or search internally for someone to train for the position. Typically, however, recruitment and internal staffing efforts are successful and produce a pool of applicants in which some are not qualified, others are qualified, but some of those qualified applicants are more qualified than others.

The objective of the selection process is to screen out all unqualified persons and then choose the most appropriate person from the pool of qualified applicants. Specifically, *selection is the process of (1) collecting information on each job applicant, (2) using that information to screen out unqualified applicants and predict the future performance of each qualified applicant, and (3) determining the best person for the position to be filled.*

Job Relatedness

With this chapter, we complete our discussion of the staffing process. One concept fundamental to an understanding of human resource management in general and the staffing process in particular is job relatedness: the notion that any employment-related decisions should be based on a person's capacity to perform the duties and responsibilities of the position and not on age, sex, race, appearance or anything else that is not job related.

Job relatedness has been determined to be the appropriate basis for employment decision for two reasons. First, it minimizes unfair discrimination. If employment decisions are based on each person's capacity to perform the requirements of the position, discrimination against certain classes of people, namely women and minorities, will be eliminated. Second, employment decisions based on job relatedness have been determined to be very effective in terms of assembling and maintaining an effective work force.

To ensure job relatedness, decisions should be based on the information contained in job descriptions. Once a position vacancy is identified, a job description is either prepared (job formulation) or brought up to date (job analysis). The job description not only explains what the employee is expected to do and how he or she is to do it (job specifications), but also summarizes the qualities and capabilities a person needs in order to perform the job (job qualifications). Thus *job descriptions, because they provide a clear and accurate description of the position, serve as the starting point for all decisions that need to be job related.*

As explained in Chapter 4, job description information is used in the preparation of job announcements needed for recruitment. As we will discuss in the following section, job description information also serves as the starting point for the selection process.

Selection Process

The seven steps of the employee selection process are as follows:

1. Understand the job. Know what will be expected of a person to perform the job successfully.
2. Establish the criteria to be used to predict candidates' future job success.
3. Recruit.
4. Obtain information about the persons seeking the position.

5. Use the specific information related to education, experience, and special requirements to screen out candidates who do not meet minimum qualifications.
6. Evaluate the information obtained on each qualified candidate in terms of the established criteria.
7. Choose the candidate who best meets the criteria and offer the position.

With the exception of step 3, which was covered in Chapter 4, and step 7, which is self-explanatory, each step is discussed in detail in the remaining sections of this chapter.

Understanding the Job

It is not uncommon for managers to overlook the importance of this first step in the selection process. To illustrate, a community in the southwest recently advertised for the position of supervisor of revenue-producing facilities. The director of parks and recreation did not carefully formulate a job description for the position before it was announced. In fact, the job announcement was prepared from the description of a similar position in a nearby county agency. Six candidates submitted their applications. Two candidates had park and recreation degrees and experience in facility management. One candidate had an M.B.A. degree, another had a strong marketing background, another had a background in financial management, and the sixth had an accounting degree. The director of parks and recreation admitted to being confused. Since he did not clearly understand the job to be performed, he did not know what qualifications to look for in the job candidates.

A manager can use several methods to become knowledgeable about a job. In fact, if the manager has previously held the position to be filled and if the responsibilities of the position have not changed greatly, he or she may already be knowledgeable about the job. It is probable that a manager will gain some understanding of a position just because he or she supervises the person who holds that position. But this situation does not always ensure accurate and complete knowledge about the position. For example, many secretaries might argue that their supervisors are not really knowledgeable about all the work associated with being a secretary.

Perhaps the best way to gain a thorough understanding of a position is to perform a job analysis. It is our opinion that managers should perform a job analysis whenever they do not completely understand the duties and responsibilities of a position being filled.

Establishing the Selection Criteria

The second step of the selection process involves identifying the criteria to be used to predict each candidate's future job success. This is not an easy task. As we pointed out earlier, the criteria must be job related. Also, a certain amount of subjective judgment will always remain in the selection process.

It would be illogical and inappropriate to select people on a set of objective criteria because no suitable criteria have ever been developed— and are not likely to be.[1] Objective criteria such as test scores, years of training, grade-point average, interview score, and work record do not themselves predict which candidate will perform most successfully on the job. But if these quantitative measures are job-related, properly obtained, and valid predictors, they can be very helpful. They can provide a logical basis for making judgmental decisions.

Although the job qualifications listed in a job description are usually job related, they are frequently too vague to serve as effective criteria. For example, a job specification might be "conduct programs within adopted budget guidelines," and the related qualifications might be "knowledge of basic management functions" and "a bachelor's degree in parks and recreation." Even if a candidate "met" these vague qualifications, we still would not have a clear understanding if he or she could "conduct programs under adopted budget guidelines." What is needed is more definitive set of criteria than job qualifications.

Predicting Future Behavior.   A great deal of research has allowed social scientists to determine that the best predictor of near-future behavior is recent-past behavior.

> Knowing what people have done in their past is not an absolutely accurate indication of what they will do in the future. Nevertheless, in making selection decisions it is best to assume that past behavior is the best predictor of how an individual will perform in the future.[2]

Using the job specification that we discussed earlier, the best criterion probably would be:

- Recent past performance in which the candidate successfully operated within adopted budget guidelines.

But what if the candidate is young or new to the field and lacks budget administration experience? Should he or she automatically be rejected for the position? No, an equally valid criterion might be:

- A demonstrated knowledge of the importance of working within adopted budget guidelines and a knowledge of the basic skills needed to successfully perform this duty.

Thus an inexperienced person might have written a term paper on the problems and procedures of budget administration, successfully completed the Revenue Sources Management School in Wheeling, West Virginia, or scored high on a test of budget procedures. If the applicant has also demonstrated a general ability to apply his or her knowledge and skills successfully to actual work situations, it would be reasonable to assume that he or she could successfully "conduct programs within adopted budget guidelines" if given that responsibility.

It is easy to see that the criteria we developed for our hypothetical situation are job related, but how can we be sure that they accurately predict successful future performance? For example, how can we be sure that a high score on a test of budget procedures accurately predicts success on the job? The EEO guidelines discussed in Chapter 1 state that any technique used to make employment decisions must be valid. This means that an organization that uses a particular technique must be able to demonstrate that that technique successfully predicts job performance a high percentage of the time. A technique that fails to do this is not valid and should not be used. The actual task of validating a technique is usually the responsibility of a personnel specialist, not a job for the supervisor.

In an actual work situation, the supervisor, perhaps with the counsel of personnel specialists and colleagues, will need to establish at least one criterion for each major duty or responsibility. As we mentioned earlier, the job qualifications are usually much too vague to serve as criteria themselves, but they can serve as useful guidelines for the supervisor as he or she prepares more detailed criteria.

As information is gathered about each job candidate, it will be used to determine if the candidate meets the predetermined criteria. We suggest that an applicant profile form such as the one presented in Figure 5.1 be used to list the criteria and the information related to these criteria.

One more factor plays an important part in the selection of a job candidate: motivation. Although it is not usually written into a job description, managers want to hire people who will perform with the appropriate level of motivation. Thus motivation is also usually translated into a criterion such as the following:

• Has demonstrated the ability to put in long hours during peak seasons, including work on weekends and holidays.

Throughout this discussion we have avoided the use of such vague terms as "loyalty," "character," "friendliness," and "stable" as selection

Figure 5.1 Sample applicant profile form.

Applicant	A. Rouse					
		Applicant Profile Form			**Date** 1/10/85	
		Position Title	Maintenance Supervisor	Evaluator D. MacLaughlin		
Selection Criteria	Weight*	Evidence of Meeting Criterion		Evidence of Not Meeting Criterion	Rating†	Subtotal (Wt. × Rating)
1 Has the ability to prepare written technical reports.	3	• Received an A in a technical writing course at State College. • Has prepared several reports—very well done.		Has limited experience in the field (three months).	3	9
2 Is willing to take part in manual labor as well as supervise others.	2	None		Expressed the opinion during interview that "managers lose the respect of workers when they stoop to doing manual work."	0	0
3 Has the ability to interpret and prepare maintenance plans.	3	• Prepared a maintenance plan for a class project. • Stated her belief in the importance of proper maintenance plans during interview.		Has never prepared a maintenance plan in the field.	2	6
4 Has the knowledge and skill to administer horticultural chemicals.	1	• Used chemicals while working on a golf course. • Expressed a desire to become certified.		Reference check indicated that her use of chemicals at golf course was very limited.	1	1

*Weighting scale for selection criteria: 3, very important; 2, important; 1, marginally important.

†Rating Scale: 4, clearly meets selection criterion; 3, meets selection criterion to a substantial degree but not totally; 2, partially meets selection criterion; 1, meets selection criterion only slightly; 0, does not meet selection criterion.

criteria. Some managers might say, "I want a person who is friendly and likable." Friendliness is a very vague trait, however. Since it is so vague, it would have different meaning to different people. How could we possibly measure such a trait? How could we ensure that it was job related? It is best not to use such vague terms as criteria. Instead, develop criteria that are concise, measurable, and clearly necessary for the successful performance of the duties and responsibilities of the position.

Obviously, step 2 in our seven-step model is not easily handled, but it is undoubtedly very critical. If the hiring supervisor does not have a clear set of selection criteria established, the rest of the steps will be laborious and the final outcome could be disastrous.

Recruiting

The third step in the selection process is recruitment. Now that the supervisor has a clear understanding of what the job entails (step 1) and has identified the criteria to be used to predict the future job success of each candidate (step 2), he or she is in a position to begin to recruit or explain to the personnel unit how to proceed to recruit. We strongly advocate that the hiring supervisor always retain responsibility for directing the recruitment efforts of support staff. Since recruitment is such a significant staffing area and was allocated an entire chapter (Chapter 4) in this book, it will not be elaborated on here.

Obtaining Information

The next step is to obtain information that will enable the supervisor to judge the extent to which each candidate meets the selection criteria. Leisure service managers will usually want to receive information from five sources:

1. Application forms.
2. Reference checks.
3. Tests.
4. Interviews.
5. Medical examinations.

The information obtained from these sources will be used to complete the applicant profile form presented in Figure 5.1. As information relevant to each criteria is obtained, it is placed in either box 3 or 4. Logically, the manager will discard any irrelevant, non-job-related information. Thus this form, filled out for each candidate, will allow the supervisor to assemble in one place all the information needed to judge each candidate.

The amount of information gathered on candidates will vary according to the position being filled. Since data gathering can be expensive, organizations do not want to spend an inordinate amount of time and money collecting information that is not needed. To illustrate, minimal information is needed for positions such as maintenance laborers, dishwashers, and bellhops because few knowledge, skills, and abilities are needed to perform those jobs. Much more information is needed to make informed decisions about the applicants for positions such as museum curator, camp director, conference organizer, or computer analyst.

Each of the five information sources will now be discussed in more detail. Because professional and managerial positions require more sophisticated information, we will focus our discussion and examples on these types of positions.

Application Forms.   As a first step in gathering information on candidates, almost all employers require that application forms be filled out. In Chapter 4 we discussed the design and content of application forms. These forms can be a valuable hiring tool for several reasons.

First, the information can be used to screen out unqualified applicants early in the selection process. Second, application forms provide a source of verifiable information. If an applicant indicates that he or she received a degree in recreation from Hood College in 1984, it is easy to contact Hood College and verify the accuracy of this information. Finally, application forms, if properly designed, can allow for careful examination of work history. Keeping in mind that past performance is the best predictor of future performance, it is obvious that managers will want to carefully review a candidate's work history. Specifically, managers will want to look for such things as unexplained gaps in the work history, a pattern of increasing responsibility over time, and length of service with each organization.

Reference Checks.   Employers should check the backgrounds of perspective employees for two reasons: to verify the accuracy of the information that has been gathered, and to determine if significant information has not been reported. Again, keep in mind that reference checks should be concerned only with information that is job related.

Sometimes employers ask applicants to submit letters of recommendation. These letters are usually quite useless because applicants request letters only from persons who are sure to write a glowing response. Unless the letters contain negative information about the applicant, managers usually disregard them.[3]

Another way of checking references is to utilize a standardized rating form. The person receiving the form is asked to evaluate the extent to which a candidate possesses certain skills and traits. Most research, however, has found very little relationship between these rating forms and subsequent work behavior.[4]

Standardized reference forms sometimes request that former employers comment on a candidate's previous work record. Because of a court decision (*Rutherford* v. *American Bank of Commerce*) in 1976, many former employers are reluctant to say anything negative about a candidate in writing. In this case the court ruled that the organization had unlawfully retaliated against the employee because she had exercised her legal rights and filed a sex-discrimination charge against the company.[5]

Unfortunately, many people have overreacted to this decision. Former employers should have no fear of telling the truth about a person if that information is verifiable, provided without malice, and job related. Former employers usually provide much more valuable information than character references provided by the applicant. All relevant information gathered from reference checks should be added to the applicant's profile form.

Tests.   Tests serve as an objective measure of a person's knowledge, skills, personality, characteristics, aptitude, interests, or ability. When properly administered, tests can yield results that accurately predict performance. Normally, a park and recreation manager will not be involved in the selection, validation, or administration of tests. This work is usually left to personnel specialists. In addition, managers will need to rely on the personnel specialists for a clear explanation of exactly what the test measures and how the results should be interpreted.

Interviews.   From time to time, most leisure service managers will need to conduct interviews. Actually, there are five different types of interviews that a manager may need to conduct: *selection, performance appraisal, counseling, disciplinary,* and *exit.* Although each type of interview is in some way unique, certain basic principles apply to all types of interviews. Later in this chapter we focus on selection interviews, but first we present basic principles related to planning and conducting any type of employment-related interview. In later chapters we discuss the specifics of the other types of interviews.

PLANNING AN INTERVIEW.   Many interviews fail because the interviewer fails to take the time or lacks the knowledge to plan it properly. Goodale suggests a five-step sequence for planning each interview.

1. Determine the type of interview that is going to take place.
2. Establish specific objectives (e.g., collect specific information about an accident that occurred).

3. Decide what interview style is most appropriate (e.g., highly structured).
4. Establish the specific format to be followed (e.g., first, establish rapport; second, set the agenda; and so on).
5. Decide what topics will be covered (e.g., explanation of agency benefits, the procedure for processing purchase orders).[6]

It is important that these steps be followed in order. For example, the objectives must be decided on before the style can be determined.

THE INTERVIEW ENVIRONMENT.   Because interviews are usually rather serious, it is necessary that they be conducted in an atmosphere that in no way detracts from the discourse between the participants. The site chosen should be quiet and attractive. If it is an office, it should be clean and uncluttered.

Much disagreement exists as to what is the most appropriate seating arrangement. Some managers and personnel specialists feel that any physical barriers produce psychological barriers. They recommend that interview participants sit in two chairs facing each other with no desk or table between. Other people feel that a table or desk between participants provides a convenient prop and allows people to be more comfortable. Generally, people do agree that seating arrangements should not make the interviewee feel inferior or uncomfortable, should permit direct eye contact, and should allow at least 3½ feet between participants.[7]

Interruptions and distractions should be avoided. Once again, advance planning is essential. The secretary should be informed that you will be conducting an interview; hold all telephone calls and stop all visitors. Also, let the secretary know approximately how long the interview will take.

CONDUCTING AN INTERVIEW.   The supervisor's first responsibility in conducting an interview is to make the person feel at ease. Usually, this involves offering the person a cup of coffee or other drink and engaging in casual conversation. This idle chitchat helps to "communicate humanness and interest."[8] Once the person is settled down and acclimated to the surroundings, it is appropriate for the supervisor, calmly and professionally, to lay out the direction for the interview. Goodale states: "It's your interview, and you have the responsibility of establishing and maintaining control from the beginning. It is helpful to summarize the purpose of the interview and to set an agenda."[9]

Most interviews have a dual purpose; the interviewer wants to gather information and to give information. The information gathering tends to be much more difficult; it requires certain special skills, a good deal of concentration, and careful listening. Usually, it is more effective to devote an entire section of the interview to information gathering. In this way, the thoughts of the interviewee are not interrupted. Any extended period of information giving should occur earlier or later but not during this information-gathering phase.

For interviewers, the normal sequence for the information-gathering phase is (1) asking questions, (2) listening, (3) focusing, (4) listening, (5) probing, and (6) listening. Open-ended questions are particularly useful because they help to get the interviewee talking. Focusing remarks help to keep the interviewee's discussion directed toward the specific topics the interviewer wants to cover. For example, the interviewer might say: "I find some of your comments about our work order system very interesting. Could we go back to that topic for a few minutes?" Probing is aimed toward gaining depth and completeness in the interviewee's responses. Probing questions usually pursue such areas as "how," "why," and "to what extent."

INTERVIEWING SKILLS.   A successful interviewer needs to employ certain skills and techniques in order to promote smooth information flow between participants. In this section we discuss briefly seven of these skills and techniques. Keep in mind that their use should not be indiscriminate or excessive.

1. *Using name and eye contact.* Using a person's name occasionally and maintaining eye contact about 25 percent of the time can assist in building professional support.[10]
2. *Summarizing.* This technique not only helps clarify what has been said but also helps to make smooth transitions from one topic area to another.
3. *Affirming understanding.* Occasionally, people need to be reassured that the listener is interested and understands what is being said. A simple nod of the head, "I see," or "um huh" can encourage people to say more.[11]
4. *Reflecting ideas.* This involves paraphrasing: a restatement of the interviewer's message in your own words. This technique has four values. First, it helps to confirm that the interviewer clearly understands the message. Second, it helps the interviewee clarify in his or her own mind the message that was sent. Third, it indicates empathy and concern for what is being said. Fourth, it usually leads to further comments by the interviewee.
5. *Reflecting feelings.* Goodale writes:

   Every spoken thought has two components: an idea and the speaker's feelings about that idea. Often the feeling component is indifference, but in some interviews very strong feelings can be expressed. It is crucial that the interviewer detect and acknowledge the respondent's feelings rather than trying to ignore them. This is particularly important in counseling, exit, and performance appraisal interviews. The emotions of the respondent must be put on the table and dealt with as a part of solving problems and making changes.[12]

6. *Pausing.* A brief moment of silence, four to six seconds, can serve to stimulate further comments from a reluctant interviewee.
7. *Being friendly.* Sometimes, in the process of concentrating on the intense task at hand, we forget to relax, smile, and be friendly. In most interview situations, a balance between friendliness and professional control works most effectively.

THE SELECTION INTERVIEW.   The selection interview is one of the most important single functions of a manager. Of all the techniques used for evaluating job applicants, the selection interview is most widely used. Unfortunately, the selection interview is not usually well done; and when it is not conducted properly, it is virtually worthless. Dozens of research studies have shown that the typical selection interview is neither valid nor reliable. This is because the typical selection interview is usually a poorly planned, loosely structured conversation that never really addresses the central purpose for any selection device; that is, to predict how well the candidate would perform the duties and responsibilities of the position.

We recommend an interview approach that is more carefully planned and structured than that which is typically used. Research has shown that interviews that follow a semi-structured format and employ an interview guide, a list of all relevant questions to be asked of each candidate, tend to have a reasonable degree of validity and reliability.[13] In addition, semistructured interviews avoid major omissions and minimize shallow coverage of important topics.

PLANNING THE SELECTION INTERVIEW.   It is to the organization's advantage to see that applicants receive information about the job and organization in advance of the interview. Not only does this allow the candidate to relate better to the activities of the job and the organization during the interview, but it provides the candidate with an opportunity to assess whether his or her needs and interests match those of the organization. The material sent to candidates varies according to the job and the nature of the agency. For example, a state-operated facility for juvenile offenders seeking a recreation activities specialist might send the job description, the organization chart, the previous year's activity calendar, the facility's master plan, the recreation budget, and a map of the area.

For job candidates who are outside the organization, special plans need to be made for their visit. We recommend that a detailed itinerary be developed and copies sent to everyone involved including the candidate. Keeping in mind that the visit for a lower-level, nonprofessional position might be much less elaborate, the itinerary illustrated in Figure 5.2 reflects the type of planning that needs to be done.

It is not uncommon for an applicant to be interviewed by more than one person. An applicant for the position of office manager for an outdoor

Time	Activity
8:30 a.m.	Candidate arrives
8:30–8:45	Greeted by hiring supervisor; introduced to staff; coffee; move to office of hiring supervisor
8:45–10:45	Interview with hiring supervisor
10:45–11:00	Break
11:00–noon	Tour of facility; meet employees
Noon–1:30	Lunch with key staff
1:30–2:30	Tour of surrounding community
2:30–3:30	Interview with department head
3:30–3:45	Break
3:45–4:15	Interview with key staff member
4:15–4:45	Interview with key staff member
4:45–5:00	Closing remarks with hiring supervisor

Figure 5.2   Itinerary for a job candidate's visit.

adventure company might be interviewed by the owner, the site manager, and the business manager. These interviews should take place separately. Group interviews are usually very ineffective in that none of the interviewers really gets to question, probe, and focus the way they would like. Ultimately, most group interviews are effective only for determining how well candidates react under a lot of pressure, and this approach would be appropriate only if coping with stress were a job-related factor.

Each person who is going to interview a candidate should study the material on the candidate prior to the interview. This material, usually placed in a file folder, might include a résumé, an application form, notes on reference checks, and test scores.

The last step, but probably the most important in preparing for the interview, is the development of an interview guide. An interview guide is a list of questions that gives the interview structure; it allows the interviewer to gather efficiently the information that he or she needs in order to fill out the applicant profile form and make a judgment about the applicant. "The overwhelming majority of managers who do not use a thorough, structured interview guide are unable to gain some very important insights into people because they never asked the questions!"[14] The interview guide usually consists of a list of questions with several inches of space between each question for note taking. Each candidate is asked the same set of questions.

QUESTIONS NOT TO ASK.   Obviously, it is inappropriate to ask any question that does not reflect a bona fide occupational qualification for the specific job being filled. Smart lists twenty-six such areas; six of the most important are listed below:

- Do not ask marital status or questions about names and ages of dependents.
- Do not ask spouse's name.
- Do not attempt to ascertain the lineage, ancestry, or national origin of an applicant.
- Do not ask if an applicant is pregnant or if the applicant plans to have children.
- Do not ask the applicant's race or any questions that directly or indirectly indicate race or color.
- Do not ask an applicant's age (unless you suspect that the applicant is a minor).[15]

If the manager has any doubts about the legitimacy of any of the questions in the interview guide, he or she should seek advice from a personnel specialist.

CONDUCTING THE SELECTION INTERVIEW.   The interviewer should follow the same basic interview steps that we discussed earlier, that is,

1. Begin the interview with a brief period of small talk.
2. Tell the applicant what the format for the interview will be.
3. Provide the applicant with information about the job. Explain such things as the duties of the job, salaries, benefits, the amount of autonomy granted the person in the position, and the undesirable aspects of the job.
4. Ask questions and gather information from the interviewee.
5. Allow the applicant a chance to ask questions.
6. Close the interview. This involves explaining what happens next in the selection process, when a decision will be made, and when the applicant will hear from you.

Note taking during an interview is sometimes a controversial point. Some people feel that note taking is a distraction for both the interviewer and interviewee and should not take place. On the other hand, if the interviewer does not take notes, a good possibility exists that he or she will forget important information even if they try to write down their mental notes immediately after the interview.

We suggest that interviewers take short, abbreviated notes during the interview. This note taking should be done in a manner that minimizes disruptions in the communications between the participants. It is the interviewee that is all-important, not the note taking. After the interview is over, the brief notes should be expanded and written in such a way so that they can be understood at a later date.

Although the selection interview is very useful for gathering and verifying information, we need to keep in mind that it should not be relied on too heavily as a selection tool. As we stated earlier, selection interviews, particularly the typical unstructured interviews, have questionable validity and reliability. We know from research studies that many interviewers are influenced by contrast effects—the tendency to rate people higher or lower due to a comparison with the previous candidate. For example, a person of average qualifications tends to be rated higher if he or she has been preceded by a poor candidate. Research also indicates that interviewers tend to establish stereotypes. Candidates who do not match with the interviewer's "ideal employee" stereotype are unconsciously rated lower. Interviewers also tend to come to a decision about applicants too quickly. Within the first several minutes of the interview, managers make their evaluations based on superficial first impressions.[16]

In spite of the problems associated with the selection interview, we believe that it will continue to be used extensively. To minimize its weaknesses, we suggest that interviewers attempt to do the following:

• Use a semistructured format and interview guide.
• Take quick notes during the interview. Elaborate on those notes later.
• Do not rate applicants during the interview. Transfer the information gathered at the interview to the applicant profile form. Evaluate and rate candidates after all the necessary information has been assembled on all the candidates.

Medical Examinations.   Most organizations will need to establish a policy regarding the medical examination of potential employees. Since a complete physical exam can be expensive, some organizations have chosen to examine only the top candidate for a position. If the candidate passes the exam successfully, they are formally offered the position. If an organization chooses to hire personnel without a physical exam, the results may ultimately cost much more than if they had provided exams. For example, if an employee with a weak back is assigned to a maintenance position, the organization runs the risk of an injury that creates higher insurance costs or substantial benefits payments.

Screening

Continuing our discussion of the selection process, the fifth step is to screen out unqualified applicants. This step, usually performed by nonprofessional staff personnel, is designed to eliminate unqualified applicants from continuing on to the final steps of the selection process. Thus the screening process can save busy managers the undesirable task of reviewing the material of unqualified applicants.

The key to a successful screening process is to have properly written screening criteria that nonprofessional staff can easily compare to each candidate's qualifications. If the job qualifications for a position have been stated in concise, measurable terms and expressed as minimums, they can effectively serve as screening criteria. Consider these two examples.

- At least twelve months of recreation programming experience in full-time or seasonal positions.
- A score of at least 250 on the outdoor skills tests.

Although these two focus on education and skills, just about any job qualification can be used as a screening criterion if it is expressed in this way. If criteria are not written in measurable terms and expressed as minimums, the nonprofessional staff will have no basis for accepting or rejecting applicants other than their own judgment. Park and recreation managers would be very wise not to let this happen.

For example, if the staff person responsible for screening had a very different idea of the qualities and capabilities needed to perform a recreation job, the manager might find that the best candidates for the position were eliminated in the screening process. Too many times managers fail to meet their responsibilities in this area. Not only should managers make sure that screening criteria are written properly; they should also make sure that staff personnel clearly understand what decisions they are and are not expected to make.

Evaluating the Information

The sixth step in the selection process is to evaluate the information on each candidate who has progressed to the final stages of the process. All information on each candidate should have been assembled in one place—the applicant profile form. Hopefully, the manager has not formed a premature opinion on any of the candidates. It is now time to evaluate the candidates to determine the extent to which they have met the selection criteria. If each step in the process has been performed carefully, it is reasonable to expect that the candidate who most closely meets the criteria will perform most effectively on the job.

The evaluated information can be scored on a five-point rating scale in the following way:

4 Clearly meets selection criteria.
3 Meets selection criteria to a substantial degree but not totally.
2 Partially meets selection criteria.
1 Meets selection criteria only slightly.
0 Does not meet selection criteria.

The numbers are totaled for all criteria. A comparison of candidate scores should indicate the person best suited for the position.

Orientation

The new person in a position, even if he or she is hired from within the organization, cannot be expected to understand instantly all the responsibilities of his or her job and how to carry them out. Although the person should have a general understanding of the job because of the information provided during the hiring process, a proper orientation is needed if the person is to understand all the intricacies of a new job.

The purpose of a job orientation is to help new employees learn more about their job, the organization, and the people with whom they will work. It should be understood that job orientation is not the same as job training. If a person lacks certain critical knowledge, skills, or abilities, he or she should be provided with some type of training to overcome these weaknesses. An orientation program, however, should be provided to all new employees regardless of whether they require additional training. In Chapter 10 we discuss job training and development.

Some evidence seems to indicate that an effective orientation program can significantly increase employee satisfaction and reduce turnover.[17] An orientation can also present the new employee with a more favorable impression of the organization. Given the high cost of recruiting and hiring new employees, it is logical that we would want to assist the new employee in making a smooth transition into their new position. Ultimately, a proper orientation is good for the employee, the supervisor, and the organization.

The personnel unit and the immediate supervisor of the position usually share the responsibility for orientation. Usually, the personnel unit will supply information about organization-wide personnel policies, benefits, and compensation arrangements. Handbooks, keys, manuals, uniforms, and equipment may also be provided by the personnel unit.

The supervisor generally has four responsibilities regarding orientation: *prepare an orientation checklist, discuss expectations with the new employee, inform the new employee abut the particulars of the job, and establish a checkback system.*[18] A short example of an orientation checklist is presented in Figure 5.3. Its purpose is to coordinate all the orientation activities and reduce the likelihood of serious omissions.

Orientation Checklist
Division of Cultural Services

Name of New Employee ___A. Hassan_____

Orientation Activity	When to Be Done	Person Responsible
Arrange first-day meeting with personnel unit	Prior to 6/5	Supervisor
Inform and prepare colleagues for arrival	Prior to 6/6	Supervisor
Arrange for first-day lunch with colleagues	Prior to 6/6	Supervisor
Clean office and provide office supplies	Prior to 6/14	Office manager
Nameplate on door	Prior to 6/14	Office manager
Greet in front office	June 14- 8:00 a.m.	Supervisor
Tour museum complex and meet coworkers	8:15-10:00 a.m.	Supervisor
Coffee break with office staff	10:00-10:15 a.m.	Supervisor
Meet with personnel unit	10:15-12:20 p.m.	Supervisor
Lunch with city administrator	12:30-2:00 p.m.	Department head
Discuss expectations with department head	2:00-3:00 p.m.	Department head
Discuss expectations with supervisor	3:00-4:00 p.m.	Supervisor
Review policy manual	4:00-5:00 p.m.	Supervisor
Discuss specific duties and responsibilities of the position	June 15- 8:00-10:00 a.m.	Supervisor

Prepared by _____A. Powell_____ Date _____6/1_____

Approved by _____S. Khorram_____ Date _____6/2_____

Figure 5.3 Sample orientation checklist.

It is very important that a supervisor clearly describe his or her expectations to a new employee. For example, if the employee is expected to volunteer for overtime, work on weekends, or attend all social functions, it should be clearly explained. At the same time, employees should have a chance to express their own expectations. If the employee expects to be given access to a word processor, for instance, he or she needs to convey that message clearly to the supervisor. Requests cannot always be accommodated, but to reduce misunderstandings they need to be expressed openly early in the employee–employer relationship.

Sometimes we overlook the vast number of details associated with the performance of any job. Such things as the location of office supplies, the arrangements for work breaks, the checkout procedure for vehicles, the idiosyncrasies of the secretarial operation, the location of rest rooms, key contacts in outside organizations, and procedures for dealing with the media need to be explained to new employees. In addition, newcomers need to be introduced to everyone they will be working with and given a tour of the areas and facilities with which they will need to be familiar.

Finally, the supervisor needs to establish a check-back arrangement. At periodic intervals the supervisor will need to check with the new employee and discuss any problems or questions that may have arisen. Although a close supervisor–employee relationship is desirable under most circumstances, it is particularly important during the first months after an employee is hired. To ensure that these discussions take place, we recommend that supervisors set aside a definite time and place for these conferences. In sum, employee orientation is important and should not be taken lightly. Although our comments have been directed toward the orientation of full-time, permanent employees, an orientation program should also be provided to volunteers, seasonal personnel, and part-time personnel.

Summary and Recommendations

1. The objective of the selection process is to screen out all unqualified job candidates and then find the most appropriate person from the group of qualified candidates.
2. Selection decisions should be based on the concept of job relatedness. The best way to ensure job relatedness is to base selection decisions on the information contained in accurate and complete job descriptions.
3. A set of selection criteria needs to be established for each position to be filled. Each candidate's background and record will be compared to these criteria. If the criteria have been properly established, the candidate who best matches the cirteria is best qualified for the position.
4. Selection criteria should be (a) as specific as possible, (b) valid predictors of successful performance, and (c) based on the qualifications needed to perform the job.
5. Vague terms such as "positive attitude," "mature," and "hardworking" make very poor selection criteria.
6. Recent past performance is the best predictor of near-term future performance.
7. Application forms, reference checks, tests, interviews, and medical exams all provide information that will allow a supervisor to judge the extent to which each candidate meets the selection criteria. A combination of sources is more desirable than relying on just one source.
8. Managers are frequently required to conduct interviews. Five common types of interviews for managers are selection, performance appraisal, counseling, disciplinary, and exit.

9. Although selection interviews are a common practice, many research studies have found them to be invalid and unreliable because of the way they are typically done. Proper planning, the use of an interview guide, and a semistructured format can improve the reliability and validity of selection interviews.

10. All the information gathered from all sources on each job candidate should be collected in one place—on the applicant profile form—before any final selection decision is made.

11. The screening process is not usually handled by leisure service line managers but rather by staff personnel. This means that the manager must communicate effectively his or her needs and desires to this staff person.

12. All new personnel, including volunteers, seasonal personnel, and part-time personnel, should be provided with a proper orientation.

13. The park and recreation manager is usually responsible for (a) developing an orientation checklist, (b) discussing expectations with the new employee, (c) informing the new employee with the particulars of the job, and (d) establishing a check-back arrangement.

Discussion Topics

1. Sometimes a recruitment effort fails to find a person who meets minimum qualifications. One option is to hire someone who does not meet minimum standards and then provide training for them. What are the advantages and disadvantages of this option?

2. Why should screening and selection decisions be based on the notion of job relatedness?

3. Should an organization make its selection decisions solely on the basis of objective criteria such as test scores, years of experience, and grade-point average? Why?

4. What is a selection criterion? What is its purpose? On what should selection criteria be based? How should they be written?

5. Develop at least five selection criteria for the "position" of college student in the curriculum you are now in.

6. Why do managers do a very poor job of developing a definitive and accurate set of selection criteria for the positions they have to fill?

7. Should an organization attempt to *sell job candidates on the advantages* of working with that organization, or should it *present candidates with a realistic scenerio of both the advantages and disadvantages* of working with that organization?

8. Why is information from former employers usually more valuable than information provided by character references?

9. Briefly sketch the design of an office space that you feel would be

an effective arrangement for an interview. Indicate by an X (interviewer) and a Y (interviewee) the seating location of the participants.
10. What is an applicant profile form? What is its purpose? How is it used?
11. What are the advantags and disadvantages of taking notes during an interview?
12. Develop an orientation checklist for a new student entering your curriculum? Be sure that you indicate who is responsible for these activities and when they should be done.

Notes

1. Arthur A. Sloane, *Personnel: Managing Human Resources* (Englewood Cliffs, N.J.: Prentice-Hall, Inc., 1983), p. 156.
2. David J. Cherrington, *Personnel Management: The Management of Human Resources* (Dubuque, Iowa: Wm. C. Brown Company, 1983), p. 201.
3. Ibid., p. 205.
4. Richard D. Avery, *Fairness in Selecting Employees* (Reading, Mass.: Addison-Wesley Publishing Co., Inc., 1979), p. 216.
5. Ibid.
6. James G. Goodale, *The Fine Art of Interviewing* (Englewood Cliffs, N.J.: Prentice-Hall, Inc., 1982), p. 8.
7. Bradford D. Smart, *Selection Interviewing* (New York: John Wiley & Sons, Inc., 1983), p. 66.
8. Ibid., p. 71.
9. Goodale, *The Fine Art of Interviewing*, p. 11.
10. Smart, *Selection Interviewing*, p. 75.
11. Goodale, *The Fine Art of Interviewing*, p. 14.
12. Ibid.
13. Smart, *Selection Interviewing*, p. 63.
14. Ibid., p. 61.
15. Ibid., pp. 107–114.
16. Cherrington, *Personnel Management*, p. 224.
17. William H. Holley and Kenneth M. Jennings, *Personnel Management: Functions and Issues* (Hinsdale, Ill.: Dryden Press, 1983), p. 262.
18. International City Management Association, *Effective Supervisory Practices* (Washington, D.C.: International City Management Association, 1978), pp. 80–81.

6

Directing Human Resources

In the Introduction, we pointed out that managers of organizations perform five basic functions related to the human resources of their organization. First they plan and organize, then staff, then direct, and finally they control. In the preceding three chapters, we discussed the functions of planning, organizing, and staffing. This chapter focuses on *directing:* the process of *influencing human resources toward the achievement of goals desirable to the organization*. The terms *leading* and *supervising* are often used synonymously with the term *directing*.

In a way, all that we have discussed in this book so far has been in preparation for the main event: doing the work of the organization. We have prepared for and assembled our human and nonhuman resources; we are now ready to act.

Directing the day-to-day actions of the work group involves a myriad of activities. Decisions need to be made, schedules need to be prepared, communications must take place, and tasks need to be assigned. But a supervisor and his or her work group do not function in isolation. A number of the laws and court decisions presented in Chapters 1 and 2 greatly affect the activities of both the manager and the work group. In addition, the manager is responsible to his or her immediate supervisor. This superior may choose to be intimately involved in the day-to-day activities of the supervisor and the work group. Also, organizational policies and procedures exist to guide the overall operation of the organization as well as many of the day-to-day activities. Finally, a complex set of formal and informal relationships exist among people as they perform their various roles in the operation of the organization.

In this chapter we do not attempt to cover all the aspects of directing personnel but focus on five areas that we feel are of primary importance: (1) the leadership role of the manager, (2) the dynamics that occur within a work group, (3) the essential aspect of communications, (4) the delegation and assignment of work, and (5) personnel policies.

Leadership

Through the years researchers have tried to discern just what it is that makes a good and effective leader. At first, much attention was given to personal qualities or characteristics of the people who occupied leadership positions in the work force. This approach led only to vague and confusing definitions. Although personal characteristics certainly cannot be ignored, they are only one part of the picture. Perhaps leadership can be best understood if it is viewed in light of the leadership style that a supervisor chooses to use in directing the work unit. There are two components of leadership style that are basic to this concept.

The first component is the relationship between the manager and his or her work group. Some managers are very worker oriented and some are very task oriented. A manager who is worker oriented is concerned with relationships within the work group as well as the relationship that he or she has with the work group. The task-oriented manager is concerned primarily with getting the job done regardless of the feelings that group members have toward other members or toward him or her as the supervisor. Relationships are secondary to the work tasks of the group.

The second component of leadership style is the degree to which the work unit participates in the decision-making process. The continuum of manager–nonmanager behavior developed by Tannenbaum and Schmidt has become a classic. This model, shown in Figure 6.1, depicts graphically the range of managerial behaviors and the associated degree of involvement by nonmanagers in the decision-making process. (Tannenbaum and Schmidt use the term *nonmanager* to describe all members of the work group other than the manager.)[1]

The patterns that are seen on the continuum can be categorized into three broad styles. The first is the autocratic style of leadership, which can be seen on the left. It is characterized by low nonmanagerial freedom and high managerial control. The manager either acts as the decision maker or passes down orders from his or her supervisor. The center of the line depicts a more democratic approach to management. Here employees participate in various degrees in the decision-making process. The manager sets the controls for group participation and then informs the group of the limits. The manager may or may not act as a member

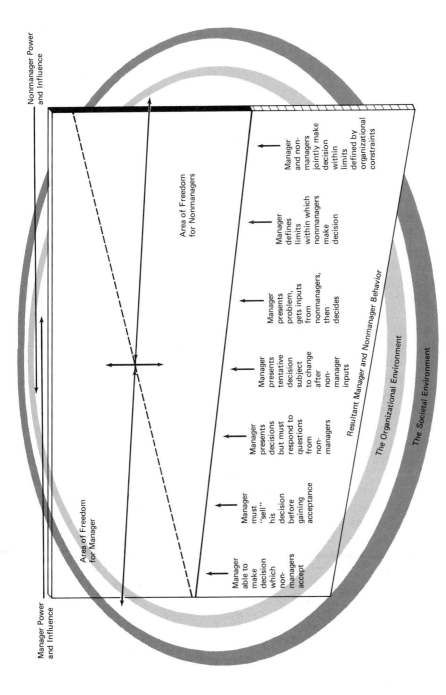

Figure 6.1 Continuum of manager–nonmanager behavior.

133

of the group, but the key factor here is that there is controlled participation by the work unit. On the right end of the continuum lies the laissez-faire style of management. The work unit has a high degree of freedom, with the manager contributing as an equal participant, or if he or she chooses, does not participate at all. As you have noticed the continuum is not closed because there are no "pure" styles of management. There is no style that is without some form of participation and there is no style without some limit on participation.

Another reason for depicting managerial styles on a continuum is to show that managers are not locked into one style. There is no good or bad style of management, only appropriate or inappropriate styles. The next questions would logically be: "What is an appropriate style?" and "What factors determine whether any particular style is appropriate or inappropriate?" Continue to examine the continuum of manager–nonmanager behavior. You can see that there is an interplay of four major forces that should be examined by the manager. After assessing and analyzing these forces, the manager must choose the style of leadership that best matches the needs of the situation. Let us examine these forces individually.

1. *The manager.* There are forces within the supervisor's own personality that direct him or her toward a particular style. People are just naturally more comfortable existing within the boundaries of their own value system. For example, some people feel that they were hired to make decisions and to make sure they are carried out. This person would have a natural inclination toward the autocratic style of leadership. On the other hand, some people feel uncomfortable handing down decisions and feel strongly that workers should have a right to participate in making decisions that affect them. Having this value system would create a propensity toward a democratic leadership style. Also, the degree of security needed in making decisions influences the manager in a certain direction along the continuum. A person who is more tolerant of ambiguous situations is more likely to allow participation by the group in the decision-making process.
2. *The subordinate.* Each person within the work group has predispositions toward certain behaviors and it is important for the manager to know the people in the work unit. (This is discussed in more detail later in the chapter.) The following are aspects of the work group that a manager should consider before choosing a leadership style.
   (a) The independence of the group: the degree to which they are able and desire to work apart from the control of the manager.
   (b) The amount of decision-making responsibility the group is ready to assume. Some employees are motivated by added responsibilities, whereas others are resentful at having to perform some of the duties they see as belonging to the manager.

(c) Just as the manager has a certain degree of tolerance for ambiguity, so do group members. This must be taken into account.

(d) The degree of interest the group shows in solving the problem at hand.

(e) The degree to which the workers share the goals of the organization.

(f) The amount of experience and expertise employees have in performing their duties.

(g) The degree of freedom that workers expect to have in making decisions.

3. *The organizational environment.* The organization also sets policies and limitations on how far a manager can move along the managerial continuum and in which direction. Through such things as job descriptions, policy manuals, and informal verbal discussions, the administrative staff of an organization informs the manager how he or she should behave in the leadership capacity. Other organization factors include size of the organization and size of the individual work units, geographical distribution, and the types of problems to be solved (or goals to be met). The time frame in which problems must be solved also has a great affect on the amount of involvement the work unit can have in decision making.

4. *The societal (external) environment.* Increasingly, society is gaining an enhanced awareness and concern for the quality of work life for the employee. There is also a greater demand for equal opportunity for employment and less sexual and racial discrimination in everyday work practices. Organizations are also affected by the overall economic picture and the degree of competitiveness with other organizations for success.[2]

Because none of these forces are static, they must be assessed continually and adjustments to these changes made as smoothly and as efficiently as possible. The need therefore is "for the manager who is insightful in assessing relevant forces within himself, others, and the situation, and who can be flexible in responding to these forces."[3]

To understand better the need for flexibility and to demonstrate that the best style of leadership is a result of the interplay of these forces, look at your own family situation as it resembles an organization. The style of leadership your parents used when you were two or three years of age was autocratic. You were told what to do and you had no say in the matter. Your opportunities to make decisions were certainly limited and your experiences were so few that you had not yet learned to think through problems. Think about your parent's managerial style at the present time and you will probably see that gradually, as you gained more knowledge and experience, you were able to participate more in making decisions that affected you. If your parents remained autocratic, chances are you rebelled against this authority because you felt that your personal needs were not met.

Group Dynamics

Early human beings recognized that their goals could be accomplished more efficiently when working with others who shared the same goals. For a manager to fulfill successfully his or her responsibilities as a group leader, it is necessary that the person understand the dynamics of a group. In the preceding section we looked at the various styles of leadership. Now we look more closely at the group as one of the factors influencing the style of leadership used in directing the work force.

Group dynamics is a term that indicates change. There are external and internal forces at work in every group, some of which are obvious and some more subtle. The available information on group dynamics "ideally does not say, 'Do this or that,' but rather 'If you do so under certain conditions, such and such is likely to happen.' "[4]

Individual Behavior and Needs

To understand the dynamics of a group, it is helpful to understand something about the behavior of individuals. What is a group but the people who belong to it? This is the first step that a manager can take in organizing a cohesive work group—get to know each member as an individual. The following is a guide for managers to use in understanding the people in his or her group.

1. Early group experiences. The first group experience a person has is within the family. As individuals grow they become involved with other groups, and the experience gained from interacting with different people leads to the development of a dominant personality type. Four personality predispositions have been identified as "fight, flight, pairing, and dependency."[5] Each of us possess each of these tendencies to some degree, but one personality type is dominant. The predepositon to fight would indicate a tendency toward hostility against other group members. A predisposition toward flight indicates a tendency to avoid interacting with other members of a group. To have a predisposition toward pairing is to show support and warmth and to form close relationships with other group members. Finally, the predisposition toward dependency indicates a need for individual support and direction.
2. Psychological needs. In Chapter 7 we look at Maslow's hierarchy of

needs. But there are other less understood and less defined needs which we as individuals bring to the group situation. "Although these needs are often given varying labels, they include such ideas as the need for security, the need for affection or response, the need for status or recognition, for belonging, for new experience, and so on."[6] These needs are often misunderstood because they not only vary from person to person but they vary from moment to moment within each person. These needs may also be expressed differently by each person, and as a result can be difficult to recognize. It is important for the manager to recognize that these needs are legitimate and must be accepted for what they are. These needs must be met and not rejected or ignored or the person may try to get his or her needs met through inappropriate behavior.

3. *Associational forces.* As stated earlier, people belong to a number of groups, some well organized and well defined such as the YMCA or a particular civic club, and some vaguely defined, such as one of the social classes. To some extent a person's behavior is determined by all the reference groups to which he or she belongs, and the expectations from each group could create a conflicting behavior pattern.

4. *Forces from goals and ideologies.* Johnson and Johnson call these "hidden agendas".[7] These are the forces, values, and goals that make each person a unique individual. When individuals find themselves in a situation filled with stress and conflict, they may very well be influenced by these personal goals over the organizational goals. Johnson and Johnson have made five suggestions for creating group cohesiveness when hidden agendas are causing problems for a work unit. First, as a manager, thoroughly discuss the organizational goals and make sure that each employee understands them. By doing this, employees have an opportunity to resolve any personal conflicts they may be feeling. Second, a supervisor should always recognize the presence of hidden agendas. Everyone has them. The members of the work unit are constantly working toward both the achievement of organizational goals and the satisfaction of personal goals. Third, the manager has to decide whether to bring hidden agendas before the group, deal with them on a one-to-one basis with the individual, or whether to bring them up at all. Fourth, hidden agendas should be accepted as a legitimate part of the person, as they are for everyone. Fifth, the manager must be able to evaluate the group's abilities to deal with hidden agendas. With immature groups, the probability that hidden agendas will create conflicts is greater and their ability to handle them is less.

5. *Internal processes.* It is now widely accepted that people do have control over their behavior and personality development. A person's behavior is indicative of the direction of growth that he or she has chosen.[8]

Group Behavior

Now that we have talked about the individual within a group, let us turn our attention to the group as a collective unit. The first thing we need to do is to define a group. There is some disagreement about all the aspects that define a group, but Knowles and Knowles have identified six qualities generally accepted as group identifiers (see Figure 6.2).

There are certain properties of a group that enable it to work together as a unit to accomplish its goals. The degree to which these properties are developed can indicate whether the group is functioning at its greatest potential.

1. *Background.* The members of a group always need the time and opportunity to get to know one another. Each member needs to know what he or she can expect from all the other members. Also, the goals and objectives of the group must be clear to everyone. Take as an example a class of park and recreation students who have been divided into small work groups by the instructor in order to complete a class project. The amount of time needed to work out group tasks and roles depends on the homogeneity of the group. This time is needed even if the work objectives of the group are clear and precise.
2. *Participation pattern.* As discussed in the first section of this chapter, the degree of group participation in making decisions depends on which leadership style is being used: autocratic, democratic, or laissez-faire. One pattern may be used consistently, but generally the patterns will vary based on such things as goals, group members, and group maturity. To illustrate this, let us continue with the example of the group of park and recreation students. If an informal leader surfaces from the group, a democratic style of participation

---

QUALITIES THAT DEFINE A GROUP

1. *Definable membership.* There must be at least two people who can be identified by name.
2. *Group consciousness.* The group membership feels a bond and can identify with one another.
3. *Sense of shared purpose.* There are common goals toward which all group members work.
4. *Interdependence in satisfaction of needs.* The goals can be accomplished only through the interaction and cooperation of the group members.
5. *Interaction.* There is give and take among members of the group.
6. *Ability to act in a unitary manner.* The group acts as a cohesive unit to assure the accomplishments of its goals.[9]

Figure 6.2

might develop. Should no one emerge from the group relatively quickly to assume the leadership role, chances are that the group would flounder until someone decides to take charge. This frustrated person might function as an autocratic leader, assigning tasks and giving orders.

3. *Communication.* This is closely related to the participation pattern, but principally is concerned with how well members are understanding the ideas being expressed. It does not matter if the organization embraces a democratic or an autocratic style of management; communication is an important property. This is discussed in more detail in a later section of this chapter.

4. *Cohesion.* This property is concerned with how well the group is able to identify with each other and the goals they are able to accomplish as a group. If workers do not form this identify with their work group, they are more likely to form outside groups or factions, which have the potential to undermine the goals of the work unit.

5. *Atmosphere.* Although this is a somewhat abstract term to define, the atmosphere in which a group works can usually be felt. It can be defined as friendly or hostile, warm or cold, formal or informal, just to name a few.

6. *Standards.* The group usually sets its own standards or delineates acceptable behavior. These standards are sometimes vague and difficult for new members to adjust to. Members of a group, including the manager, could have a difficult time if standards are ignored.

7. *Sociometric pattern.* The relationships established within a work group have a great deal of influence on how efficiently the activities of a group are performed. New employees may have difficulty fitting into established patterns. These patterns may be so strong that members who do not conform are ostracized.

8. *Structure and organization.* This is generally seen in a group on two levels. One is the formal structure that is established by the organization. The other is the informal structure established by the group members. These two levels can be very compatible with each other and one may even enhance the other. Again, there is a potential for conflict. If the individual's needs are rejected in the formal structure, the informal structure can become strong enough to interfere with the accomplishment of organizational goals.

9. *Procedures.* This property refers to the way things get done within a group and the methods by which decisions are made. Procedures can be very rigid and directly affect other properties of the group. For example, the work unit responsible for the Mom's Day Out Program at the YWCA is trying to decide on task assignments for the summer. The manager, trying to take into consideration such things as worker vacations, asks for assistance from the workers in choosing

times that they can work. The procedure used to make these as-signments directly influences such things as participation pattern, communication, and cohesion.

10. *Goals.* Goals are the motivating force in the behavior of group mem-bers."[10] It is why the work unit is in existence to begin with. There are usually long-range goals and short-range goals. Of utmost im-portance is that the group be thoroughly knowledgeable about the goals of the organization. It is also important that the goals be at-tainable and that the group know when a goal has been accom-plished.[11]

11. *Roles.* Within the group, individuals play different roles. Beal, Boh-len, and Raudabaugh identified three broad categories of roles that group members play.[12] The first category is group task roles. These roles are crucial in goal setting and goal accomplishment. The second category is group building roles. These roles help to build and main-tain cohesive relationships within the group. You can find specific examples of these two broad categories in Figure 6.3. The third broad category of group roles comprises the nonfunctional roles. These behaviors interfere with the group's attempts to reach set goals, but they are played out to satisfy a personal need within the individual. Figure 6.4 lists examples of nonfunctional roles.

It must be pointed out that a person may fill one or more roles during the same group meeting. For example, a person may fulfill the group task role of information giver one minute and later perform the group building role of the harmonizer. The person's role or roles within the group may change, also, depending upon the task to be completed and roles performed by other members of the group. The various types of roles that are played also influence the style of management needed to make or maintain a productive work unit. For example, a work unit with strong supportive group maintenance roles can probably function more productively under a dramatic style of management, whereas a work unit with strong nonfunctional roles may require an autocratic style of management to keep tasks of the organization as a primary objective.

Communication

There are many skills that a supervisor uses in directing a work unit, but probably the most important skill is communication. The supervisor provides that all-important link of communication between the upper management of the organization and the work force. This means that a good supervisor will provide a channel of communication that moves both upward and downward. It is not enough, however, to provide the

GROUP TASK ROLES

1. *Initiator-contributor.* This person is the one who usually presents new ideas for either goal setting or goal accomplishments.
2. *Information seeker.* This person seeks to clarify the issues by asking for facts.
3. *Opinion seeker.* This person is not necessarily concerned with facts but is more interested in the values involved in a situation.
4. *Elaborator.* This person is able to expound on the ideas and suggestions made and how they will affect the goals to be accomplished by the group.
5. *Summarizer.* This person keeps the group straight as to the issues and ideas presented by other group members.
6. *Coordinator-integrator.* This person tries to deduce and present the relationship between suggestions and ideas and the goals of the group.

GROUP BUILDING ROLES

1. *Encourager.* This person takes a positive approach toward praising other members for this contribution. He or she is warm, friendly, and supportive.
2. *Harmonizer.* This person will step into the middle of conflict and attempt to provide harmony and reconciliation to the group.
3. *Gatekeeper.* This person attempts to give everyone the opportunity to contribute.
4. *Standard setter.* This is the person who states and clarifies how the group will proceed with whatever task is at hand.
5. *Follower.* This person is passive in accepting whatever decisions the groups makes. He or she provides an audience for those who express ideas or factual information.

Figure 6.3   Group task and group building roles.

NONFUNCTIONAL ROLES

1. *Aggressor.* This person shows hostility toward the ideas of other members and attacks their motives and confidence.
2. *Recognition seeker.* This is usually the loud talkative person who does not present sound constructive ideas.
3. *Blocker.* This person is negative in his attitude and stubborn in his willingness to be constructive. He interferes with the progress of the group by refusing to accept decisions that have already been made.
4. *Dominator.* This person is overbearing in his attitude and is manipulative in his relationships with other members. He has to have center stage at all times.
5. *Help seeker.* Attempts to focus the attention of the group on himself and his own personal needs.

Figure 6.4

opportunity for communication. There must be *feedback* from the receiver to assure that the message being communicated has been accurately understood.

In any organization there are basically two methods of communication. One is the formal structure, which will be the focus of this chapter. The other is the informal structure, commonly referred to as the "grapevine." The supervisor should always use the methods in the formal structure, to avoid exaggerations and misrepresentations of the information being disseminated. There is no way to stop grapevine communication, but by consistently using the appropriate channels, workers learn where they can go for reliable information.

Chase provides a list of six of the most common problems in providing clear communication within an organization.

1. *Misinterpretation of words.* People interpret words and phrases in different ways and what we think we are communicating sometimes is interpreted to mean something entirely different.
2. *Careless use of abstract words.* Here again, you may run into the problem of misinterpretation of words. We may talk about a "quality" recreational experience, but *quality* may mean different things to different people, and so it helps to provide specific information about what we mean by quality.
3. *Confusion of facts with personal opinions.* This is often the essence of grapevine communication. The manager should attempt to provide factual information instead of allowing rumors or exaggerated misinformation to run rampant.
4. *Judging people and events in terms of black and white.* There are usually gray areas in any issue. Things are seldom at opposite ends of a spectrum without a continuum of degrees between them. This way of thinking is typical of an "either–or" way of thinking.
5. *False identity based on words.* By not being careful to describe accurately, people may get false impressions about what we are saying.
6. *Gobbledegook.* It does no good to write fancy memos using obscure words if no one is going to understand what is being said. Simplicity and clarity are more effective in communicating thoughts and ideas.[13]

The American Management Association has come up with "Ten Commandments of Good Communication." Regardless of the form of communication, these rules should be followed to assure clarity and understanding.

1. *Clarify your ideas before communicating.* We must make sure that we know what we are trying to communicate before we attempt to pres-

ent our ideas to others. This is a planning exercise that could eliminate confusion and ambiguity.

2. *Examine the true purpose of each communication.* It is just as important to know why you are communicating an ideas as to plan how you are going to communicate. For example, there is a difference between gathering information and attempting to persuade someone to change his or her mind.
3. *Consider the total physical and human setting whenever you communicate.* This can make the difference between your ideas being accepted or rejected.
4. *Consult with others, where appropriate, in planning communication.* This will help clarify areas that are vague and go a long way to assure that you are saying what you are really trying to communicate. By bringing others into the planning stage, you may gain valuable support for your ideas.
5. *Be mindful, while you communicate, of the overtones as well as the basic content of your message.* The attitude expressed in both oral and written communication could make the difference between acceptance or rejection of your idea.
6. *Take the opportunity, when it arises, to convey something of help or value to the receiver.* This is a positive approach to communication and lets the receiver know that his or her ideas, opinions, and feelings are important.
7. *Follow up your communication.* This is the only way we have of knowing if we have been understood. This involves allowing two-way communication and a real listening attitude.
8. *Communicate for tomorrow as well as today.* Even immediate objectives are related to long-term goals and objectives. What we communicate at present must relate to the long-range plans of the organization.
9. *Be sure that your actions support your communications.* This is a must if trust is to be established between the manager and the work unit. Without trust, no amount of communication will eliminate problems and reduce friction that can interfere with the accomplishment of duties.
10. *Seek not only to be understood, but to understand—be a good listener.* This, too, is necessary for effective two-way communication. This is the essence of all good communication.[14]

Delegation

To direct the work group toward the accomplishment of agency goals, the supervisor must become skilled in delegating authority and responsibilities to the group. Delegation is not a matter of a supervisor saying to an employee: "We need a program developed for the elderly in Grove View Terrace Housing Project. Now I'd like for you to do it." This could cause a great deal of anger and frustration for the employee if the supervisor stops with that.

There are three aspects of delegation:

1. *Communication.* The supervisor makes this assignment and provides the employee with as much information as is available. The supervisor uses the techniques of good communication discussed previously.
2. *Authority.* The supervisor should grant the employee authority to make certain decisions that must be made in order to carry out the responsibility that has been assigned. For instance, for the employee to establish a program for the elderly, he or she must be given authority to spend money on necessary equipment or other items.
3. *Responsibility.* Although the supervisor is held accountable ultimately for the end results, the employee should share in the responsibilities of the task. An employee who does not accept the responsibility of completing the task will usually not do a satisfactory job of performing the task.

If delegation is to be successful, there are certain things that a manager must do first.

1. Provide necessary information. Without proper and complete information, there is no way that an employee can successfully carry out newly assigned duties. Also inform the employee how much you will be available to assist him.
2. Let everyone who will be involved know what is being delegated and to whom responsibility is being entrusted. The employee with new responsibilities will need the support of the supervisor to carry through with his or her duties.
3. Let the employee know why he or she is being chosen to receive these new responsibilities. Not only could this be a boost to the person's confidence but can also avoid confusion and the feeling that things are being pushed off onto him or her.
4. There are certain responsibilities that should not be delegated because they are not important to the performance of duties in accomplishing organizational goals and objectives.
   (a) Never delegate the overall planning for the work unit. Only the supervisor has the necessary overview and understanding of the agency policies. Workers can plan the specifics of "when" and "how" within the framework of concepts and policies.

(b) Resolution of problems with immediate subordinates should never be delegated. Only those in a supervisory position should ever handle moral problems, discipline, train staff for the future, or counsel or evaluate employees.

(c) Interwork unit relations should never be delegated. When departmental differences emerge, only a supervisor should undertake to resolve them. The supervisor is the official representative of the unit.

(d) When a supervisor is unable to supply complete and adequate information on delegated duties, the duties should not be delegated. If secret or privileged information is involved, the duties should not be delegated to an employee. Incomplete assignments are some of the most desirous tasks to delegate, but the supervisor should never succomb to the desire to pass the buck.

(e) Personal projects should never be delegated. Do not ask subordinates to write speeches for non-work-related presentations. Do not ask secretaries to run to the bank or call for vacation reservations. Be cautious about asking subordinates to drive you to the airport, fetch you coffee, or buy your lunch and bring it back to the office.

Getting the job done through the most efficient use of human resources is the responsibility of the supervisor, and only by delegating can the organization achieve its goal and can workers reach their potential.

Finally, it is important for the workers to know how they are being led and the extent to which they are allowed to participate in the decision-making process. Not knowing or being misled could cause a great deal of confusion, resentment, and conflict, which would naturally lead to a less productive work force. The manager is ultimately held responsible for the performance level of the work unit; therefore, it behooves the manager to avoid these types of avoidable conflicts.

Personnel Policies

One of the most effective ways to provide employees with direction is to develop a clear, concise set of policies. If employees know and understand these policies, they will have a pretty good idea of what is expected of them by management.

Policies are guidelines for action. They outline the strategies to be used in achieving organizational goals. They direct the organization's provision of services as well as the organization's internal operation. Our discussion will focus on policies related to the management of human resources, but keep in mind that most park and recreation organizations find it necessary to have policies covering a wide range of matters, such as fees and charges, facility and program operations, land acquisition, solicitation by persons outside the organization, conduct by spectators, and relations with outside groups. Some organizations compile all these policies into one document, usually called a *policy manual*. The Northbrook Park District of Northbrook, Illinois, has prepared a very complete policy manual that is over 200 pages long.

Some organizations choose to separate their personnel policies from all other policies and place them in their own document, generally called a *personnel policy manual* or an *employees' handbook*. Copies of this personnel policies document are given to all employees and reviewed as part of their orientation.

Although some leisure service organizations have virtually no written personnel policies and others have policies that are out of date and seldom referred to, we feel that clearly written, up-to-date personnel policies are very necessary in most organizations. A true story may help to illustrate this point.

The director of parks and recreation in a midwestern community did not believe in written personnel policies. Instead, all questions of policy were to be brought directly to him. Needless to say, a number of problems arose. First, supervisors found it difficult to solve problems and make decisions. Whenever questions arose, the supervisor would usually have to say, "I'll check with the director and see what he wants to do." Second, when the director was not there, decisions were usually delayed until he returned, but sometimes supervisors were forced to make decisions based on their best guess of what the unwritten policy was. Third, many employees were concerned about the fairness of the director's decisions. Some of the male employees felt that the female employees, especially the "better-looking" ones, were usually given favored treatment when it came to such things as leaves of absence, vacation time, and work scheduling. Some of the female employees felt that they were underpaid for the work they were doing. As a result of all of this, productivity and morale in this organization were low, turnover was high, and services were less than what they should have been.

The purpose of personnel policies is as follows:

- *To provide direction.* Guidance is necessary not just for first-line employees but for everyone in the organization.
- *To serve as a basis for decision making.* Arbitrary and capricious decision making can be reduced or eliminated.
- *To provide fair and consistent treatment to employees.* Failure in this area could lead to charges of discrimination.

Procedures

Sometimes the term "procedures" is used in association with the term "policies." These terms are not synonymous. *Procedures are the specific actions needed to carry out policies.* Because each unit in the organization will have certain procedures unique to itself, procedures should not be incorporated into the organization's policy manual.[15] Instead, each unit should incorporate its procedures into its own operating manual. *An operating manual is a document that includes all the detailed information needed to function in a specific work unit.*

For example, a personnel policy may be as follows:

Employees are entitled to a fifteen-minute work break during each half-day (four-hour) shift.

The maintenance unit's operating manual may address this policy with the following:

Maintenance employees will normally take their morning work break from 10:00 to 10:15 and their afternoon break from 2:00 to 2:15. There will be occasions, however, when these times will be inappropriate, and employees are asked to use their good judgment. For example, if an employee is working at a recreation center at 10:00 a.m. and his or her immediate assistance is required by the recreation personnel, the employee should help the recreation staff until a more convenient time presents itself for a break.

Policy Development and Implementation

Figure 6.5 presents a list of topics normally included in a personnel policy manual. Because the park, recreation, and leisure service field is so diverse, it is difficult to discuss specifics regarding how policies are developed and who develops them. For example, policies for federal employees emanate from the Office of Personnel Management and are based primarily on the Civil Service Reform Act of 1978. In the private sector, policies may be developed at a particular site or may come from a corporation's central office. Local governments utilize various arrangements to develop their policies. In any case, it is important that employees have a chance to provide input as policies are developed. Also, policies should be officially approved by the policymaking group or person. Not only should policies be explained to new employees, but it is in everyone's best interest if veteran employees are reminded periodically of the organization's policies.

Keep in mind that policies are only guidelines. From time to time, it will be necessary to bypass a policy. Usually, upper-level managers are granted the authority to make exceptions to official policy when the circumstances warrant such action.

KEY TOPICS COVERED IN A TYPICAL PERSONNEL POLICY MANUAL

   I. General regulations related to the adoption, implementation, and enforcement of this manual.
  II. Classification plan
 III. Definitions
 IV. Provisions related to employment
    1. Application
    2. Recruitment and selection
    3. Policy on nondiscrimination
    4. Appointment
    5. Probation
    6. Performance evaluation
    7. Promotions
    8. Assignment and transfer
    9. Disciplinary actions
   10. Separation and resignation
   11. Reinstatement
  V. Hours of work
    1. Workweek
    2. Full time, seasonal
    3. Inclement weather
 VI. Compensation and benefits
    1. Pay periods
    2. Deductions
    3. Holidays
    4. Overtime
    5. Vacations
    6. Insurance
    7. Retirement
    8. Credit union
 VII. Absences and leaves
    1. Absences with or without compensation
    2. Sick leave
    3. Paternity leave
    4. Military leave
    5. Jury duty
VIII. Travel and vehicle use
 IX. Training and development
  X. Rules of conduct
    1. Telephone use
    2. Personal appearance
    3. Use of agency property
    4. Keys
    5. Outside employment
 XI. Relations between employees, department, and community
    1. Nepotism
    2. Gifts
    3. Solicitation of funds
    4. Handling of public complaints
    5. Complaints and grievances

Figure 6.5

Summary and Recommendations

1. The focus of this chapter is directing: the process of influencing human resources toward the achievement of goals desirable to the organization.
2. Researchers have learned that leadership is more than personal qualities or characteristics. Leadership can best be understood as a *style* that a person uses in the process of influencing others. Style is based on two components: (a) relationship between the supervisor and the work group, and (b) the degree to which employees participate in the decision-making process.
3. Leadership can be depicted on a continuum with three broad style choices: (a) autocratic, (b) democratic, and (c) laissez-faire.
4. By examining four major forces the supervisor must decide which style of leadership best matches the situation. These four forces are:
   (a) *The manager.* The tendencies within the manager which direct him or her toward a particular style.
   (b) *The subordinate.* Individuals within the work unit have predispositions toward certain behaviors; therefore, the manager should know each person within the work unit.
   (c) *The organizational environment.* The organization sets policies and limitations on how far and in which direction managers can move on the managerial continuum.
   (d) *The societal (external) environment.* There is an increased awareness and concern for the quality of work life of the employee.
5. Often, goals are more easily accomplished by working together as a group. The group process is described by the term "group dynamics," which indicates change.
6. To understand group dynamics, it is necessary to understand individual behavior. There are five guidelines for understanding the individual: (a) early group experiences, (b) psychological needs, (c) associational forces, (d) forces from goals and ideologies, and (e) internal processes.
7. There are eleven properties of a group which enable it to work together as a unit to accomplish its goals. They are: (a) background, (b) participation pattern, (c) communication, (d) cohesion, (e) atmosphere, (f) standards, (g) sociometric pattern, (h) structure and organization, (i) procedures, (j) goals, and (k) roles.
8. Communication is probably the most important skill that a supervisor can have in directing the work unit. The supervisor should provide for both upward and downward communications. There must also be *feedback* from the receiver to assure that what has been communicated has been understood.
9. The formal lines of communication are the ones sanctioned by the

organization. The informal method of communication is the *grapevine* and is often characterized by rumors and exaggerations. Normally, the supervisor should use the formal lines of communication.

10. Six common problems of "miscommunication" are: (a) the misinterpretation of words, (b) the careless use of abstract words, (c) the confusion of facts with personal opinions, (d) judging people and events in terms of black and white, (e) false identity based on words, and (f) gobbledegook.

11. Delegation is another skill of supervision that deals with handing out authority and responsibility to the work group.

12. Personnel policies are established for three purposes: (a) to provide direction, (b) to serve as a basis for decision making, and (c) to provide fair and consistent treatment to employers. With the possible exception of very new and very small operations, all organizations should develop and maintain clearly written, up-to-date personnel policies.

13. Procedures are the specific actions needed to carry out policies. They should be incorporated into an operating manual, a document that includes all the detailed information needed to function in a specific work unit.

Discussion Topics

1. Name three people whom you consider to be effective leaders. What do you consider to be their major style of leadership?

2. Consider your own family and relate it to an organizational work unit. Refer to Figure 6.1 and discuss your family as a work unit in terms of the four major forces depicted: (a) the leader, (b) the subordinate, (c) the organizational environment, and (d) societal forces.

3. You have been hired to work at a camp for the summer. You are responsible for supervising the counselors, helping them to work as a group to ensure a quality experience for all the campers. Using the eleven group properties listed in this chapter, explain briefly how you would go about building a unified work group.

4. You are the supervisor of an outreach recreation program in one of the small outlying communities in the county. The management of the agency is located twenty miles away in a downtown office complex. What will you do as supervisor to assure two-way communications?

5. Delegation is sometimes confused with "passing the buck." Discuss the differences and why delegation is a superior method of handling the assignment of responsibilities.

6. Develop a policy for recreation majors on the subject of class attendance. Next, develop a procedure that would be appropriate for this policy.

Notes

1. Robert Tannenbaum and Warren H. Schmidt, "How to Choose a Leadership Pattern," *Harvard Business Review* (May–June 1973): 167.
2. Robert Tannenbaum and Warren H. Schmidt, "How to Choose a Leadership Pattern," *Harvard Business Review* (March–April 1958): 98–101.
3. Tannenbaum and Schmidt, "How to Choose a Leadership Pattern" (May–June 1973): 166.
4. Malcolm Knowles and Hulda Knowles, *Introduction to Group Dynamics* (New York: Association Press, 1972), p. 16.
5. Ibid., p. 33.
6. Ibid., p. 34.
7. David W. Johnson and Frank P. Johnson, *Joining Together: Group Theory and Group Skills* (Englewood Cliffs, N.J.: Prentice-Hall, Inc., 1975), p. 92.
8. Knowles and Knowles, *Introduction to Group Dynamics*, pp. 34–37.
9. Ibid., pp. 40–41.
10. Johnson and Johnson, *Joining Together*, p. 88.
11. Knowles and Knowles, *Introduction to Group Dynamics*, pp. 42–50.
12. George M. Beal, Joe M. Bohlen, and J. Neil Raudabaugh, *Leadership and Dynamic Group Action* (Ames, Iowa: Iowa State University Press, 1962), pp. 103–109.
13. Stuart Chase, "Executive Communications: Breaking the Semantic Barrier," in *Dimensions in Modern Management*, ed. Patrick E. Connor (Boston: Houghton Mifflin Company, 1974), pp. 356–362.
14. American Management Association, "Ten Commandments of Good Communication," in *Dimensions in Modern Management*, ed. Patrick E. Connor (Boston: Houghton Mifflin Company, 1974), pp. 369–371.
15. Jerry Jensen, *Basic Guide to Salary Management* (Los Angeles: The Grantsmanship Center, 1979), p. 2.

7

Motivation*

"My biggest problem is getting my subordinates to do what I want them to do. No one around here seems to want to work anymore. I've tried everything, but nothing seems to light a fire under them."

The problem of employees working less than they are capable of is not new. In the nineteenth century, a study found that hourly workers could keep jobs by using only 20 to 30 percent of their ability. But the study also found that other workers in the same job situations were working up to 80 to 90 percent of their ability levels.[1] Why the differences? What can you do to influence the level at which a worker performs?

This chapter and Chapter 6 both address the general area of influencing the actions of park and recreation employees. Whereas Chapter 6 presented some basic approaches and techniques that any manager will find useful in his or her day-to-day operation, this chapter presents a more theoretical discussion of the psychology and sociology of people in the work group. This chapter moves beyond the basic fundamentals of directing people and challenges the reader to understand better why people function the way they do.

A number of people have developed theories that attempt to answer the question, "What motivates my employees?" Each theory adds to our understanding of human behavior in the workplace. We will review these theories and present a model that combines the best of these theories.

*This chapter was written by Richard Gitelson, who is a member of the Recreation Curriculum faculty at the University of North Carolina–Chapel Hill.

We will also see that these theories provide suggestions as to what supervisors can do to influence the actions of others.

What Is Motivation?

Why are you reading this chapter? Something has provided you with a reason, or motive, to read this instead of watching television, going to your favorite meeting place, or engaging in some other activity. Motivation theory is concerned with why you chose one behavior over another. Although there are many different views of what motivation involves, most definitions include three essential components.

The first is the *effort* itself. Although everyone in your class may read this chapter, the amount of effort that is applied will probably vary a great deal among the various students. Some will simply skim the chapter, figuring that it will be enough to get the main points. Others will read the chapter carefully and will perhaps even prepare an outline of the main points.

The second component deals with the *persistence of this effort*. Some students will maintain a high level of effort throughout their reading of this chapter, whereas others may start off with a good effort, but end up skimming the last few pages.

The last component of motivation involves the *direction of the effort*. We all know of people who expend great effort toward a questionable goal instead of toward a more appropriate goal. For example, a student may direct his or her effort toward getting a good grade and completely fail to understand the basic concepts and principles inherent in the assignment.

Putting these three components into an organizational context, *motivation is the extent to which persistent effort is directed toward desirable organizational outcomes*. These outcomes could include such things as productivity, decreased absenteeism, or better communication among employees.

Extrinsic and Intrinsic Rewards

Researchers have found that the anticipation of rewards serves as a strong motivating force. To understand motivation, it is important to understand the two types of rewards we can receive: intrinsic and extrinsic.

Intrinsic rewards stem from the work itself. Examples include the feeling of accomplishment after a job has been completed, the challenge of a task that stretches our capabilities to the limit, or the pride one takes from a job well done.

The second type, extrinsic rewards, comes from the work environment, is external to the task, and is usually determined by someone other than the person being motivated. Examples are salary levels, fringe benefits, promotions, and encouragement. Although the second type appears to be more useful to a manager, there are things that management can do to increase the intrinsic motivation levels of employees.

Theories of Motivation

What can you do, either directly or indirectly, to increase the motivation levels of people who work for you? Each of the following theories provides some clues to that answer. The first three theories are based on the assumption that we have certain needs that must be satisfied and that our behavior is directed toward satisfying these needs. In an organizational setting, the goal for management would be to provide conditions for the employees that would help the employees meet these needs in a manner useful to the organization.

Maslow's Hierarchy of Needs[2]

Based on clinical observations and intuition, A. H. Maslow, a psychologist, came up with the idea that we have five types of needs that motivate our actions. He further concluded that these needs formed a hierarchy; that is, the lower-level needs had to be satisfied before the higher-level needs would begin to motivate us. Maslow felt that a person would not be concerned with a higher-level need until the needs below it had been satisfied. He also felt that once a level of needs was satisfied, it would no longer tend to motivate us. The only exception to this is that of the needs in the highest level, which would tend to get stronger. The five types of needs in ascending order of importance according to Maslow are as follows:

1. *Physiological needs.* These involve the basic necessities that we need to survive, such as food, water, and shelter.
2. *Safety needs.* These needs include our desire to feel safe and to be free from anxiety.
3. *Social needs.* These include our desire to belong to groups and include our need for interaction, affection, and love.
4. *Esteem needs.* These needs relate to how we feel about ourselves and include such feelings as self-confidence, adequacy, and competence.
5. *Self-actualization needs.* Maslow's highest level of needs involved the

notion that once we had satisfied everything else, we would strive to reach our full potential as human beings. Although the notion is somewhat hazy, this level would drive us to understand ourselves better, including what we are capable of doing.

Although there has been no empirical support for this theory, it has been an important step in developing a model to explain organizational behavior. The main problems seem to have been (1) the assumption that all of us would be motivated in the same fashion, and (2) the failure to recognize that our situations might change, which might reactivate a lower-level need that had supposedly been satisfied. For example, although our pay may be adequate when we are single, it might not be enough to support a family.

Alderfer's ERG Theory[3]

Another psychologist, C. P. Alderfer, has modified Maslow's theory to overcome some of its shortcomings. First, the five needs were reduced to the following three levels:

1. *Existence needs.* This level combines Maslow's physiological and safety needs.
2. *Relatedness needs.* This level combines Maslow's social and esteem needs. One other difference at this level is in the way that these needs can be met. Although Maslow felt that these needs were best met by positive feedback, Alderfer feels that critical feedback could also satisfy these needs if the feedback was perceived as open and honest.
3. *Growth needs.* This stage combined some of Maslow's esteem needs and what Maslow referred to as self-actualization needs. Both felt that as these needs were met, they would actually become stronger and would never be fully satisfied.

There are some other very important differences between how Alderfer and Maslow perceived human behavior. Alderfer recognized that we may be motivated by higher-level needs even though the lower-level needs had not been satisfied. Also, he felt that if the upper-level needs were not met, the lower-level needs would be intensified. For example, if a worker did not find a particular job rewarding, he or she might ask for more pay as a form of compensation, even though the current level of pay was adequate to satisfy his or her basic existence needs. Finally, Alderfer felt that all three levels of needs could be operative at the same time.

Herzberg's Two-Factor Theory[4]

To find out what motivates people in the workplace, F. Herzberg interviewed 203 accountants and engineers. All were asked to describe a time when they felt exceptionally good about their work and a time when they felt exceptionally bad about their job. Based on the answers to these questions, Herzberg proposed that there are two sets of factors that influence us in the workplace.

Herzberg found that nearly all the favorable responses were associated with work-related factors such as achievement, responsibility, and recognition. He called these factors motivators since they seemed to be associated with job satisfaction, which he assumed lead to increased productivity.

Those factors that Herzberg found related to unfavorable feelings about the job appeared to be more closely tied to the work environment, and included such items as company policy, pay, work conditions, and the relationship between the employee and their supervisors. Herzberg called these maintenance factors because he felt they could lead to an employee's dissatisfaction, but would not tend to motivate.

If Herzberg's theory is correct, it indicates that providing intrinsic kinds of motivation would have the greatest affect on productivity. Alternatively, according to this theory, extrinsic rewards such as pay might influence someone to work for you, but would not influence that person's level of work.

Herzberg's methodology and findings have found mixed support since he introduced his theory in the 1950s. Researchers have found it difficult to replicate his findings, especially with other types of workers. It also seems that the methodology may have biased the responses. For example, people have a tendency to attribute good feelings to things over which they have control, in this case job-related factors.

The biggest problem with this theory seems to be with the assumption that job satisfaction leads to increased productivity or other desirable outcomes for the organization. Although this seems to be a sensible conclusion, there has been little empirical evidence to support it. In fact, the relationship may actually be the reverse, as we shall see later.

The foregoing theories have focused on what *motivates our behavior* rather than on *how these influencing factors actually affect what we do*. The remainder of the theories we will look at deal with why we are motivated to do one thing rather than another.

Expectancy Theory[5]

This theory, developed by V. H. Vroom, recognizes the importance of an individual's perceptions of possible outcomes in determining motivation levels and subsequent behavior. It starts with the premise that we will engage in those activities that we find attractive and that we feel we can accomplish. The attractiveness depends on how valuable we feel the rewards will be for accomplishing the activities.

Thus the amount of effort that a person will expend is based on the following: (1) the probability that he or she associates with achieving a certain level of performance, (2) the valence (or value) that he or she places on various rewards for outcomes associated with certain perform- ance levels, and (3) the probability that a certain level of performance can be achieved.

But do people really think in these terms? Intuitively, the theory makes sense, but it assumes a rational thought process that is probably not followed by many of us. Since it is based on individual perceptions, the theory would be extremely difficult to prove or disprove. But the premise is generally accepted by experts in motivational theory.

What are the implications for you as a manager? You would have to find out what outcomes were valued by each of your subordinates. Then you would have to make sure that the achievement of these rewards were tied directly to the activities that you and the organization wanted the employee to accomplish. Finally, you would have to be able to con- vince the person that he or she could accomplish that task and that the effort would lead to the desired reward.

Sounds good on paper, doesn't it? But how often have you been given an assignment that is not very specific? How often have you felt that the possible reward was not worth the effort, or that the reward was not really tied to the effort anyway? This last question is extremely im- portant, considering how difficult it is to do an effective performance evaluation (which is one good reason for a careful study of Chapter 8).

Reinforcement Theory

The principal proponents of this theory are F. Luthans and R. Kreitner,[6] who based their work on that of B. F. Skinner.[7] The basic assumption is that you can isolate specific behaviors and work from there (such as getting a mouse to run down a specific maze). Four methods of rein- forcement have implications for you as a leisure service manager.

1. *Positive Reinforcement.* This is based on the notion that we will continue a particular behavior as long as it results in a positive outcome or what is considered a positive reinforcer. In the workplace, the positive reinforcer might be praise, attention, or recognition of certain types of effort. Thus, if we wanted to positively reinforce promptness, we would praise a person each time that he or she arrived on time.
2. *Punishment.* This assumes that we will discontinue a particular be-

havior if we receive an adverse stimulus or outcome immediately after we have exhibited the behavior. For example, when you arrive late for class, the teacher stops class, stares at you, and makes a comment to the effect that people who are late are very thoughtless.

3. *Negative reinforcement.* This is based on the notion that a particular behavior will be promoted if the behavior results in the immediate removal of an unwanted stimulus. For example, the supervisor stops nagging when the job is completed on time. This assumes that the worker will thus want to do future jobs on time to avoid the nagging.

4. *Extinction.* This type of reinforcement is based on the assumption that withholding rewards will influence behavior. For example, an increase in pay will not be given until the employee stops being late to work. The problem is that this may not only cause the extinction of the undesired behavior, but may also extinguish other desirable behaviors. Thus the employee may feel that it is no longer worth it to come to work at all on certain days when he or she might be a few minutes late.

The major problem with this theory is that it does not account for individual differences. For example, although it is assumed that most of us like attention and praise (sometimes called "stroking"), not everyone will respond positively to this technique.

Equity Theory[8]

The assumption underlying this theory is that we compare what happens to us with what happens to others in similar situations. Thus people in a workplace would compare what they did and the subsequent outcomes with similar efforts of other workers and their rewards. If the comparisons show inequities, the worker would act accordingly. For example, if a worker thought that he or she was being paid less than another worker even though the efforts were perceived as equal, the result might be less productivity, increased absenteeism, or some other undesirable organizational outcome.

This undesirable outcome might even occur if the inequity were seen in the other direction. For example, an employee who thought that he or she was getting too much in comparison to others might work less, so as to reduce the ill feelings of other employees.

Most of the research based on this theory has been related to the perceived equity of economic outcomes. However, this is a hard theory to study because it deals with social comparisons that are individually perceived.

The theory does suggest another factor that you as a supervisor must consider in attempting to motivate others. You will have to consider what effect your efforts to motivate one employee will have on the motivational level of others.

The Porter–Lawler Model

One model that seems to incorporate many of the preceding theories has been proposed by L. W. Porter and E. E. Lawler[9] (see Figure 7.1). It is extremely useful for us, as it focuses specifically on performance. These authors define performance as a broad range of specific workplace behaviors that relate to the nature of the job and the accomplishment of its assigned responsibilities and duties. The model attempts to explain what affects this performance.

The model shows that effort is directly affected by how valuable a person perceives the potential rewards to be and how likely the person feels that these rewards are actually tied to his or her effort. The value placed on potential rewards will be affected by the person's perceived needs and wants. These are affected by the person's value system, age, current life-style situation (whether or not the person is married, has children, etc.) and current economic condition, health, and a host of other factors. What is important to note here is that no two people will have exactly the same set of needs and wants, and that these needs and wants will change over time (sometimes very quickly) for any particular person.

The level of effort put forth by a person influences his or her performance. However, as noted earlier, performance is influenced by a number of other factors, such as the person's ability to do a particular task, to learn needed skills, to communicate with others, and by the person's understanding of his or her role in the organization.

Rewards and Satisfaction.   Performance is seen as having a more direct effect on intrinsic rewards than on extrinsic rewards. This is due to the nature of how we get these rewards. We determine the level of any intrinsic rewards we give ourselves. For example, a recreation therapist, after setting up a program that helps a patient recover more quickly than had been expected, will probably feel a sense of pride. On the other hand, extrinsic rewards, such as a promotion or pay raise, are controlled by others. In fact, these extrinsic rewards may not even be controlled by our supervisors or by our organization. For example, even if the recreation therapist's performance was highly valued by the hospital, pay raises might be determined by the state legislature, as in the case of state-supported hospitals.

The model indicates that satisfaction is a function not only of the re-

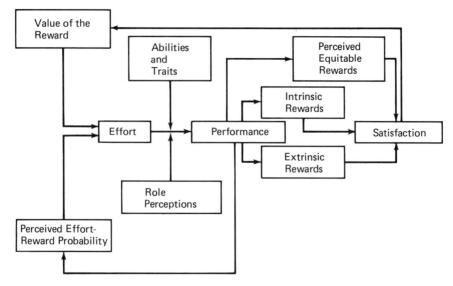

Figure 7.1 Porter–Lawler model.

wards we receive, but how equitable these rewards are perceived to be in terms of our performance and how others in the organization are rewarded for their performance. Studies have indicated in the past that this perception is at least as important as the actual rewards. For example, "even if I do not get promotions as quickly as I would like, this would tend to have less of an effect on my level of satisfaction if I perceived the promotion process to be administered in the same manner for others doing the same type of work."

Also affecting a person's level of satisfaction is the worth placed on different types of rewards by different types of people. A study by Chapman and Otteman[10] indicates that sex, age, marital status, the number of dependents, and years of service affect the types of rewards that are most desirable.

It is important to note here that current research supports the notion that increased job satisfaction does not necessarily lead to increased job productivity, as once thought. In fact, it appears that the reverse is more likely to be true; that is *job performance, when tied to a reward system that recognizes the increase in productivity, is likely to result in an increase in job satisfaction.*[11]

Finally, the model shows that this process does not work in a vacuum. What happens to us in our work, that is, how we are rewarded for certain types of behavior, will obviously have an effect on future efforts as we better understand the reward process in our organization. For example, if we see that extra effort does not lead to any significant increase in those rewards that we value, we are likely not to put forth that extra effort in the future.

Other Effects on Performance

Our level of motivation is only one factor that will influence our behavior. As Maslow stated: "Motivations are only one class of the determinants of behavior. While behavior is almost always motivated, it is almost always biologically, culturally, and situationally determined as well."[12]

What does account for a poor performance by a seemingly highly motivated person, or for that matter, a good performance by someone who does not seem at all motivated? Although the following list is not conclusive, it should indicate some of the possible reasons (see Figure 7.2).

First, our level of ability is rather stable over the short term. Thus a person may simply not be able to become more productive in the short run, regardless of the incentives. For example, we may offer a promotion to someone if they will use a microcomputer in their work. Although productivity may go up in the future, it will probably take the worker a great deal of time to become proficient with the new technology.

The worker must also understand what is expected. Although this has been mentioned before, it deserves mention again. Some jobs are more easily understood than others. For example, the way to line a ballfield may be completely clear. But the goal of increasing attendance at the community center may not be such a clear task, and could involve several approaches, some of which might involve overall negative outcomes.

In addition, a worker's performance is quite often affected by environmental factors outside his or her control. For example, a highly motivated worker may simply not be given the required resources to accomplish a certain goal. Although this seems an easily correctable situation, it may not be possible—even if the situation is recognized by management—due to a budget limitation. Another environmental factor is the dynamics of the work group, which may be out of the control of the worker. Thus, although the worker may be extremely motivated, his or her work group may undermine that person's efforts.

The influence of the work group cannot be overemphasized. Few of us will ever work in complete isolation from others. In addition, although our own needs are important, group needs and pressures may be a much stronger influence on our behavior. Thus, although I may get paid more (which I desire), the group pressure to maintain the status quo may be a much stronger influence, especially if I value the social support of the other group members.

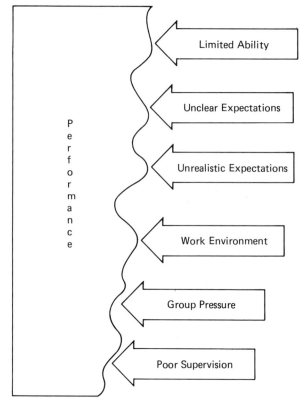

Figure 7.2   Other factors affecting performance.

Other factors that can affect a worker's performance are unclear department policies, inadequate time frames, poor supervision, and to a certain degree, luck. Although it has often been said that we make our own breaks, simply being in the right place at the right time may have more to do with our looking good than the amount of effort we have expended.

Although we would like to believe that we know it "all," keep in mind that much is still being learned about the process that determines why we act in a particular way. We will probably never fully understand why two seemingly similar people facing similar situations can act in such diametrically opposite ways, or why the same person will respond differently to the same motivation techniques from one day to the next. However, what we can do is to apply what we do know and hope that we can minimize these fluctuations, while encouraging our subordinates to perform in such a way that the subordinate, ourselves, and the organization benefit.

Summary and Recommendations

1. Ultimately, a manager should strive to create a work climate in which the group members can achieve individual objectives while contributing to the achievement of the organization's goals and objectives.
2. Success at motivating subordinates is made difficult due to some elements partially or completely outside the control of the manager.
3. Intrinsic rewards are those that are inherent within an activity itself. In other words, the feelings that we derive from certain kinds of activity serve as a reward to us. Intrinsic rewards come from within us; they do not come from an outside source.
4. Extrinsic rewards such as pay, promotions, and recognition from our peers come from external sources.
5. The anticipation of both intrinsic and extrinsic rewards can serve as strong motivators.
6. The following theories were described, which attempt to explain how we chose a particular behavior.
   (a) *Maslow's hierarchy of needs.* Five types of needs, the lowest being physiological needs and the highest being self-actualization needs, affect our level of motivation. According to Maslow, lower needs have to be met before we are motivated by a higher level.
   (b) *Alderfer's ERG theory.* Alderfer reduced Maslow's hierarchy to three types of needs, and recognized that more than one level could affect behavior at the same time. Also, he felt that one could be motivated by a higher-level need before the lower needs were satisfied.
   (c) *Herzberg's two-factor theory.* Herzberg felt one set of job factors could motivate us while another set would only tend to dissatisfy us. This theory has not found much support, because it suggests that job satisfaction directly influences performance.
   (d) *Expectancy theory.* The emphasis in this theory is on our perception of possible outcomes as the primary source of motivation for job performance. A major obstacle that must be overcome in this theory is that rewards must be valued and the achievement of those rewards must be tied directly to performance.
   (e) *Reinforcement theory.* This is based primarily on the work of Skinner and concludes that we will act in a particular way if that action is reinforced in some manner (whether positively or negatively).
   (f) *Equity theory.* The underlying assumption here is that we view the rewards we receive in terms of how others in similar situations are rewarded. As long as the reward system is considered equitable, we would remain motivated.
7. The Porter–Lawler model combines many of the best points of the

previous theories and provides a valuable explanation of behavior within organizations.

8. High job satisfaction does not cause high job productivity. However, successful job performance, when tied to an equitable reward system that recognizes an increase in productivity, is likely to result in an increase in job satisfaction.

9. Needs and wants strongly influence behavior, but group needs and pressures may be an even stronger influence on individual behavior.

10. There are a number of other factors that can thwart the desire of an employee to improve performance. These include, but are not limited to, the employee's skill or ability level, unclear or unrealistic expectations from management, conditions in the work environment, and poor supervision.

11. There is no single formula for motivating all workers in every situation every day, but the conscientious supervisor will learn all he or she can about the psychology and sociology of people interacting in the workplace.

12. Motivation is already inside us. The task of the supervisor is to release and channel that motivation by controlling as many conditions as possible in the work environment and by making jobs more interesting and challenging.

Discussion Topics

1. Define intrinsic and extrinsic motivation. Give several examples of each.

2. Do you feel that Maslow's hierarchy of needs is valid? Do you agree with Alderfer's modifications of Maslow's theory?

3. According to the expectancy theory, what factors influence our level of effort?

4. Give an example of positive reinforcement, punishment, negative reinforcement, and extinction. What is the major problem with reinforcement theory? How can a manager try to minimize this problem?

5. Do you feel that the Porter–Lawler model accurately predicts human behavior in an organization? What changes or modifications would you make to this model?

6. What factors influence a person's level of job satisfaction? Explain the relationship between these factors and job satisfaction.

7. What environmental factors influence an employee's performance? Which of these factors can a manager control? Which can he or she not control?

8. What can a supervisor do to motivate subordinates?

Notes

1. Cited in Paul Hersey and Kenneth H. Blanchard, *Management of Organization Behavior*, 2nd ed. (Englewood Cliffs, N.J.: Prentice-Hall, Inc., 1972), p. 5.
2. A. H. Maslow, *Motivation and Personality*, 2nd ed. (New York: Harper & Row, Publishers, Inc., 1970).
3. C. P. Alderfer, "An Empirical Test of a New Theory of Human Needs," *Organizational Behavior and Human Performance* 4(1969): 142–175.
4. F. Herzberg, B. Mausner, and B. B. Snyderman, *The Motivation to Work*, 2nd ed. (New York: John Wiley & Sons, Inc., 1959).
5. V. H. Vroom, *Work and Motivation* (New York: John Wiley & Sons, Inc., 1964).
6. F. Luthans and R. Kreitner, "The Role of Punishment in Organizational Behavior Modification," *Public Personnel Management* 2(1973): 156–161.
7. B. F. Skinner, *Beyond Freedom and Dignity* (New York: Alfred A. Knopf, Inc., 1971).
8. J. S. Adams, "Toward an Understanding of Inequity," *Journal of Abnormal and Social Psychology* 76(1963): 422–436.
9. L. W. Porter and E. E. Lawler III, *Managerial Attitudes and Performance* (Homewood, Ill.: Richard D. Irwin, Inc., 1968).
10. J. Brad Chapman and Robert Otteman, "Employee Preferences for Various Compensation Options," *The Personnel Administrator* (November 1975): 34.
11. Charles N. Greene, "The Satisfaction–Performance Controversy," *Business Horizons* (October 1972): 31.
12. A. H. Maslow, *Motivation and Personality* (New York: Harper & Brothers, 1954), p. 91.

8

Performance Appraisal

Just as many students and professors dislike grades, many managers and employees dislike performance appraisal. Nevertheless, one of the most important aspect of managing leisure service employees is the task of appraising their on-the-job performance. Without an effective system by which to appraise employee performance, management decisions regarding compensation, motivation, promotion, training needs, and employee development are difficult, if not impossible. Henderson states:

> When appraisal is done poorly, or even done well under unsatisfactory operating conditions, it may lead to increased employee anxiety and hostility, resulting in poor use of both human and nonhuman resources, increased costs, and declining productivity.[1]

In this chapter we define performance appraisal, explain the various objectives that it attempts to achieve, review the alternative components of a performance appraisal system, and present a list of recommended practices and procedures for effective performance appraisal in leisure service organizations.

Performance Appraisal Defined

> Performance appraisal is a formal structured system of measuring and evaluating an employee's job-related behavior and outcomes to discover how and why the employee is presently performing on the job and how the employee can perform more effectively in the future so that the employee, the organization, and society all benefit.[2]

We like Schuler's definition for several reasons. For one thing, it clearly states that performance appraisal is "a formal, structured system." It is an error to think of performance appraisal as just a single activity—the appraisal of a person's performance at the end of some predetermined time period. It is an ongoing process that involves the sequential steps and subcomponents presented in Figure 8.1. This process takes the form of a system in which all parts must work together effectively.

Also, Schuler's definition focuses on the employee's on-the-job performance. It does not mention the employee's personality, age, experience, past legal record, looks, or any number of other personal factors. We are not evaluating the employee, but rather, the *performance* of the employee.[3] Obviously, personal factors may play a definite role in how well employees perform their work, but these factors are not themselves the focus of our evaluation.

In most cases, the appraisal focuses on the employee's job-related behaviors. On occasion, however, off-the-job behavior may affect on-the-job performance and must be dealt with in the appraisal. For example, a person's late-night social habits may cause him or her to perform lethargically on the job. Clearly, this problem cannot be ignored just because it stems from off-the-job behavior.

Finally, Schuler's definition points out the need to understand how the employee can change. It is not enough to know how the employee is currently performing; it is also necessary to understand how the employee can improve and what specific actions can be taken to facilitate that improvement.

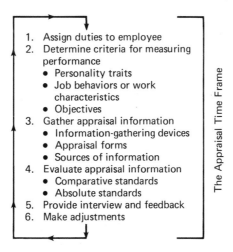

Figure 8.1 Components of a formal performance appraisal system.

Purpose of Performance Appraisal

Essentially, employee performance is evaluated to determine the extent to which employees are achieving their assigned responsibilities. Beyond this, the appraisal process can achieve a number of more specific objectives.

1. Provide *feedback* to the employee by identifying successful performance that should be continued and weak performance areas that need to be strengthened.
2. Establish the relative value of an employee's contribution to the organization so that he or she may receive appropriate *compensation*.
3. Determine specific *training* and *development* needs of each employee.
4. Identify employees who have potential for *promotion*.
5. Enhance *communications* between superior and subordinate.
6. Improve understanding of *personal goals* and *career* concerns of employees.

In addition, appraisals can be used to make decisions regarding discipline, transfers, layoffs, terminations, and a person's move from probationary to regular status.[4] It should be clearly understood that performance appraisal does not exist in isolation from other management responsibilities. The information generated from this process is used to make decisions in numerous areas of human management.

Why Study Performance Appraisal?

Given the great diversity among leisure service jobs and the many levels of responsibility among those jobs, not all professionals have the same involvement in performance appraisal. The extent of involvement customarily takes one of three possible forms.

First, there is no doubt that all leisure service personnel *are evaluated by others in the organization.* This may take the form of a highly subjective, informal evaluation, or of a more objective, formal evaluation specifically designed to meet the organization's appraisal needs. In any case, employees are continually evaluated by superiors, peers, and subordinates.

Second, many leisure service professionals are in positions which require that *they evaluate others.* Usually, they are given brief instructions from their immediate superiors or the personnel department on how to conduct these evaluations, the forms they are to use, and the timetable they are to follow. It is not likely that they are given comprehensive training that explains the purpose of performance appraisal, its relationship to other management responsibility, the problems that might occur, the interview process, the importance of feedback, and the like.[5] In other words, these professionals are asked to implement a performance appraisal system, but frequently they have only minimal knowledge about the process.

Third, some leisure service professionals are actually *responsible for developing and designing an entire appraisal system*. This is especially likely for professionals who own or manage a private operation and for professionals who direct an independent public agency. Although in some cases, these top administrators have the assistance of outside consultants, they must understand performance appraisal in great depth. For example, at High Hampton Inn, a private resort near Cashiers, North Carolina, the owner assumes primary responsibility for developing and administering the appraisal process. In the Palatine Park District in Palatine, Illinois, an autonomous governmental agency, the recreation-trained administrators have this responsibility.

We feel that it is essential for leisure service personnel in management positions to have at least a basic knowledge of performance appraisal. Not only will this enable them to carry out this function more effectively, but it will allow them to provide either better system design or better assistance to others who design the system.

Components of a Performance Appraisal System

Over the past three decades, a great deal of effort has gone into the search for workable techniques and approaches to performance appraisal. Unfortunately, this search has had marginal success. Lazer and Wikstrom explain:

> The history of performance appraisal in this country is characterized by the development and implementation of some new appraisal mechanism, a period of initial enthusiasm for it, followed by a period of deepening disillusionment as its problems became evident, and finally the development of some new mechanisms that was supposed to solve the problems experienced with the old one. That process appears still to be underway.[6]

In this section we present the steps in the formal appraisal system (see Figure 8.1) and discuss the various approaches and techniques that have been tried in the past. In doing this, we describe the advantages and disadvantages associated with each technique and discuss its current or potential usefulness to the leisure service field. Since no single best system of appraisal exists, leisure service managers should understand the various alternatives and put together a system that works well for their situation or organization. A system that works well in a large special recreation district may not, for example, be suited to a ski resort or small park operation.

Criteria for Measuring the Effectiveness of Performance

As we discussed in Chapter 3, it is the job analysis that determines the specific tasks associated with each job. These specific tasks should be spelled out in each position's job description, and it is these specific tasks that serve as the basis for performance appraisal. In other words, it is the goal of performance appraisal to measure the degree to which an employee is effectively performing the specific tasks for which they are responsible. Therefore, *the first step in the system is to ensure that the appraiser and appraisee have mutually reviewed and agreed on the specific tasks assigned to the appraisee.*

The second step is to develop the criteria for measuring whether the subordinate has successfully performed her or his assigned tasks. Be warned that this step is quite difficult, and frequently an entire system flounders because of unclear or inappropriate criteria.[7]

Criteria are the basis or standard on which decisions or judgments are made. Customarily, three types of criteria (see Figure 8.2) are used to measure performance: (1) personality traits required to perform the assigned work (what the employee is), (2) job behaviors and work characteristics (what the employee does), and (3) outcomes or results expressed in terms of the achievement of predetermined objectives (what the employee achieves). Edginton and Williams state:

> Performance appraisal techniques can be seen as existing on a continuum that runs from those emphasizing an individual's personality traits (inputs rather than outputs) to those which stress result-oriented performance (outputs rather than inputs). The latter is concerned with measuring what an employee produces, and the former focuses on identifying what the employee brings to the job in terms of personality. The trend in performance appraisal is clearly shifting from approaches used to measure personality traits to result-oriented appraisal mechanisms.[8]

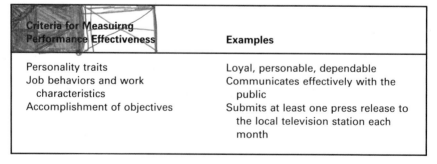

Criteria for Measuirng Performance Effectiveness	Examples
Personality traits	Loyal, personable, dependable
Job behaviors and work characteristics	Communicates effectively with the public
Accomplishment of objectives	Submits at least one press release to the local television station each month

Figure 8.2 Three types of performance criteria.

Personality traits have been used as criteria for a number of years. A quick perusal of performance appraisal forms currently in use by leisure service agencies reveals such traits as leadership, approachability, initiative, dependability, attitude, loyalty, enthusiasm, and neatness. The use of these traits as criteria for measuring performance is a very simple process; the appraiser assesses the appraisee's efforts and determines the degree to which these traits have been demonstrated. Although the process is simple and expedient, it has several very serious weaknesses.

First, the general, vague nature of these terms makes this process highly subjective. Might not five different supervisors have five different opinions as to the meaning of *leadership* or *approachability?* Second, we must ask, "Are these personality traits really relevant to the successful completion of assigned tasks?" Might not two different employees with completely different personality traits perform the same assigned tasks equally well? The U.S. Supreme Court has ruled on these two points.

Wade v. Mississippi Cooperative Extension Service (1974). The court held that the extension service had the burden of demonstrating that an evaluation instrument used to appraise the performance of county professional workers was job related and served legitimate employment needs. Wade maintained that it discriminated against black employees; the court stated that this claim must be negated "by clear and convincing evidence." One key criterion used for determining promotion was an "objective appraisal of job performance." Finding against the extension service, the court concluded that this "objective" appraisal evaluated such general characteristics as leadership, attitude, appearance, personal conduct, outlook on life, ethical habits, resourcefulness, capacity for growth, mental alertness, and loyalty, which are susceptible to partiality and the whim or fancy of the evaluator.[9]

Not only are there problems concerning interpretation and job relatedness, but the personality trait approach puts the appraiser in a position of having to judge the human nature of a fellow employee. As McGregor stated in a frequently quoted article, this puts the appraiser in the position of "playing God," a situation that both the receiver and giver of this kind of information find very disconcerting.[10]

This does not mean that agencies should never use personality traits to evaluate performance. Some professionals feel that personality traits are important criteria for some positions, such as receptionist, concession stand operator, park ranger, and playground supervisor. To operate on a sound legal and rational basis, however, agencies who use personality traits for evaluative criteria must (1) be able to demonstrate that the traits are clearly job related, and (2) take measures to explain and define the traits so that vagueness and subjective interpretation are minimized. These requirements, however, are extremely difficult to accomplish. In our opinion, the problems associated with the use of personality traits far exceed their benefits. Better alternatives are available.

The second type of criteria relates to *job behaviors and work characteristics*. Currently used leisure service evaluation forms reveal such behavior and characteristics as effectiveness in planning, compliance with instructions, skill level, safety habits, analytical ability, job knowledge, communication skills, management of resources, relationship with public, planning and follow-through, and supervisory control. It is apparent that most of these job behaviors and characteristics, like the personal traits, are very vague and subject to a wide variety of interpretations. Therefore, agencies must be very sure to instruct appraisers in the specific meaning of the terms. In addition, it is highly advisable to break down broad categories of behavior into specific activities. This process is illustrated in the following section. The big advantage that job behaviors and work characteristics have over personality traits is that they focus on what employees *do* rather than what they *are*.

The third type of criteria involves the measurement of outcomes or results expressed in terms of *objectives*. In brief, this approach involves the superior and subordinate developing a set of measurable objectives for the subordinate based on the subordinate's assigned job tasks. The criteria for measuring effectiveness is the degree to which the subordinate has achieved the mutually determined objectives. If this approach is properly used, it inhances objectivity and eliminates the total reliance on subjective judgment, is very job related, provides subordinates with clear feedback, and encourages communications between superior and subordinate. An entire section later in this chapter is devoted to the process of goal setting.

Gathering Appraisal Information

Once the manager and employee have clarified the employee's job responsibilities (step 1) and agreed mutually on criteria for evaluating performance (step 2), the employee is ready to tackle his or her assigned tasks. As needed and appropriate, the manager will from time to time informally discuss with the employee specific performance and various aspects of the job. This type of informal evaluation and feedback is absolutely necessary and should not be omitted just because formal reviews are undertaken periodically. In many cases, feedback should be provided daily.

After a predetermined interval, however, the next step in the formal performance appraisal process is to pull together the informal assessment that has been ongoing and put it on an appraisal form. Although form filling is not appraising, it forces the manager to organize his or her assessment and record it for all to see. Thus *step 3 involves gathering the appraisal information.*

Rating Factor	Excellent	Good	Average	Below Average	Poor	No Basis for Judgment
Dependability						
Adaptability						

Figure 8.3   Simple rating scale.

Information-Gathering Devices.   Typically, six devices have been used by leisure service agencies to record appraisal information: rating scales, checklists, rankings, critical incident recording, essay, and comparison of the results produced by an employee with preset objectives.

RATING SCALES.   A number of different versions of the traditional rating scale exist. In most cases, the scales are laid out in the form of a matrix with the criteria for measuring performance listed on the left and the degrees of achievement in a row across the top. Degrees of achievement might run from "excellent" to "poor" (see Figure 8.3).

A major problem with this approach is that words such as "dependability," "adaptability," "excellent," "average," and "poor" are interpreted differently by different people. Because of this, the reliability of rating scales is very questionable.[11] One modificaton that tries to minimize this problem employs the use of descriptive statements to indicate the rating factor and degree of achievement (see Figure 8.4).

WEIGHTED CHECKLIST.   This device lists various behaviors that an employee might demonstrate on the job. The appraiser simply checks off those items that best describe the employee's performance. The Office of Recreation and Park Resources study in Illinois indicated that checklists were the most popular device used to record the appraisal of part-time and seasonal personnel.[12] An example of a weighted checklist is given in Figure 8.5.

RANKINGS.   In using the ranking method of performance appraisal, the manager ranks all members of the work group on various job behaviors and characteristics; the best employee receives a ranking of 1 and the poorest receives the lowest ranking. The rankings for each individual can be averaged to get an overall appraisal for that employee. The appraiser faces a dilemma, however, if a number of employees demonstrate comparable levels of performance. In addition, the appraisal is heavily based on the subjective judgment of the supervisor. Some research has shown, however, that rankings can be very useful for making promotion decisions (see Figure 8.6).

Figure 8.4 Descriptive rating scale.

Rating Factor	Outstanding			Satisfactory				Unsatisfactory		
	1	2	3	4	5	6	7	8	9	10	11	12
Dependability: accepts assigned responsibilities and effectively accomplishes duties in approved manner within time established	Employee is unusually self-motivated and reliable; far exceeds expectations regarding initiative and work habits				Employee requires the usual amount of supervision; usually has good work habits and is on time				Employee cannot be relied on; must be closely supervised; frequently late or absent		

Item	Weighted Value
___ Turns in weekly inventory on time	1.0
___ Daily cash balance is usually very accurate	3.0
___ Work area and counters are clean and neat when not in use	2.0
___ Prices are properly posted	1.5
___ Occasionally runs a sale or special promotion	1.5
___ Checks all delivered products before accepting order	2.0
___ Counter displays are clean, attractive, and eye-catching	1.5

Figure 8.5 Example of a weighted checklist for a concession operator.

CRITICAL INCIDENT RECORDING. One problem with most appraisal devices is that they require the manager to recall someone's performance for a rather long period of time, perhaps six months or a year. Too often, appraisals tend to focus on performance over the several weeks just prior to the evaluation. The critical incident approach alleviates this problem.

This format requires that appraisers keep an ongoing record of the specific actions of subordinates, both positive and negative, that are con-

---

RATING-RANKING SCALE

Consider all those on your list in terms of their (quality). Cross out the names of any that you cannot rate on this quality. Then select the one that you would regard as having most of the quality. Put his or her name in column I below, on the first line, numbered 1. Cross out his or her name on your list. Consult the list again and pick out the person having least of this quality. Put this person's name at the bottom of column II, on line 20. Cross out his or her name. Now, from the remaining names on your list, select the person having most of the quality. Put his or her name in the first column on line 2. Keep up this process until all names have been placed in the scale.

Column I (Most)	Column II (Least)
1. _____	11. _____
2. _____	12. _____
3. _____	13. _____
4. _____	14. _____
5. _____	15. _____
6. _____	16. _____
7. _____	17. _____
8. _____	18. _____
9. _____	19. _____
10. _____	20. _____

Figure 8.6

Evaluation category: Ability to perform assigned tasks with available resources.		
Critical Incidents	**Date of Incident**	**Date of Discussion with Employee**
1. Worked late into the night to repair flail mower and return it to operation	Monday, May 4	Tuesday, May 5
2. Set up bleachers for soccer tournament on short notice	Wednesday, June 7	Friday, June 9
3. Failed to call repair service to fix Lee St. Park security lighting—three week delay	June	Friday, June 25

Figure 8.7 Example of the critical incident method for a maintenance supervisor.

sidered critical to the operation of the organization. When the formal appraisal takes place, the manager has a rather complete and specific record of on-the-job performance for the entire appraisal period. Figure 8.7 gives an example.

ESSAY. This approach requires the appraiser to describe, usually in summary form, the performance of an employee as it relates to the responsibilities of the position. The appraiser is allowed a great deal of flexibility with this approach; the appraisal can focus on the particular job situation unique to the appraisee. The disadvantage is that it requires the appraiser to write skillfully, a talent all appraisers may not have.

COMPARISON OF RESULTS. If the manager and employee are working together to establish specific, measurable objectives for the employee, evaluating performance involves comparing actual results with predetermined objectives. For various reasons, this comparison may not give a clear-cut assessment of performance. For example, a civic auditorium manager's objective was to decrease operating costs by 5 percent, but an unforeseen electric utility rate hike occurred during the appraisal period, causing the operating costs to increase by 2 percent. Clearly, a strict comparison of the objective and the actual result would lead to an erroneous conclusion about the manager's performance. Because of these types of problems, this comparison method is usually supplemented with some type of rating scale. More about this approach is presented later in the section on goal setting.

The Appraisal Form. Typically, agencies prepare forms to document the actual appraisal. Some forms may utilize only one of the previously discussed information-gathering devices, but more commonly, forms incorporate two or perhaps three approaches. This is a controversial issue. Some people feel that it is impossible to devise one form that effectively collects data for multiple purposes. Such forms tend to be too long, too complicated, and too general to be practical; it is better to have one specific form for each use.[13] On the other hand, some small leisure service agencies might find a multipurpose form acceptable. Each agency will have to make its own decision. A sample performance appraisal form is presented in Figure 8.8. The reader will notice that this sample form attempts to be multipurpose, and this may be construed by some as a limitation.

Sources of Appraisal Information.   Each organization must decide who will have responsibility for formally appraising various members of its work force. In most cases, it will be either supervisors, the employees themselves, peers, subordinates, or a combination of these.

SUPERVISOR'S APPRAISAL.   In most cases in leisure services, the employee is evaluated by his or her *immediate supervisor*. This is logical in that the supervisor is not only in an excellent position to observe an employee's performance, but also probably knows the employee's capabilities better than anyone else.[14] On the other hand, since the person who does the appraising has a great deal of power for rewarding and punishing, employees may feel threatened or intimidated if they know they will be evaluated by their supervisor.[15] Also, managers and employees sometimes have trouble relating and communicating with each other. Because of these potential problems, organizations sometimes invite other people to share in the appraisal process.

SELF-APPRAISALS.   Self-appraisals have the benefit of getting employees thinking about their own work efforts, their level of productivity, skills they have that might be underutilized, and additional skills they need to have to function more productively. Given an opportunity for self-appraisal, employees are in an excellent position to recommend their own training and development needs. Research, however, has found that self-appraisals are not effective as a basis for management decisions related to such things as compensation and promotion. As might be expected, employees in these situations tend to be less critical of themselves and try to project a favorable image.[16]

PEER APPRAISALS.   Although some research indicates that peer appraisals can be useful, especially when assessing promotion potential, they are not often used in leisure services. Peer evaluations can be especially useful if managers are not able to observe some aspects of an employee's performance. The validity of peer appraisals is reduced somewhat if (1) the appraisal is tied directly to compensation, (2) the work group is highly competitive, and (3) a low level of trust exists among

Figure 8.8

PERFORMANCE APPRAISAL FORM

Name _____ Job Title _____ Date _____

Section A: Performance of Assigned Duties

Evaluate the employee's performance in terms of the specific responsibilities listed in his or her job description (the first column in the table below). Mark the appropriate numeric rating in the second column.

4 = outstanding	Performance is far above the standard expected of a competent person in the position.
3 = above average	Performance frequently exceeds the standard for a competent employee; sometimes slightly above, sometimes far above.
2 = average	Performance usually meets the standard expected of a competent employee.
1 = below average	Performance is frequently below the standard for a competent employee; sometimes slightly below, sometimes far below.
0 = unsatisfactory	Performance is far below the standard expected of a competent person in this position.

Specific Responsibility Number	Numeric Rating	Specific Examples That Support Appraisal Rating
1		
2		
3		
4		
5		
6		
7		
8		
9		

Section B: Performance Task

Following are listed four categories of tasks that relate to job performance. Under each category, add tasks specific to this job position. Rate the employee on each applicable factor. If a printed task does not apply, skip it and go on to the next one. Cite specific examples of employee performance and/or lack of performance

Knows the Job	Outstanding	Competent	Marginal
Demonstrates knowledge of job requirements, skills, procedures, techniques, and principles.			
Keeps current on changes in technical knowledge.			
Expands knowledge of the job and how it relates to other jobs.			
Other:			

Examples of "Knows the Job" that describe your ratings:

Relates to People on the Job	Outstanding	Competent	Marginal
Develops subordinates.			
Acts as part of a team.			
Practices two-way communications.			
Motivates subordinates to accomplish their goals.			
Leads by example.			
Other:			

(continued)

Figure 8.8   (*continued*)

Examples of "Relates to People on the Job" that describe your ratings:			
Manages the Job	**Outstanding**	**Competent**	**Marginal**
Recognizes problems.			
Analyzes causes of problems.			
Generates alternative approaches.			
Sets realistic goals.			
Establishes work priorities.			
Organizes people and materials to reach goals.			
Handles pressure.			
Evaluates results.			
Operates within affirmative action plans.			
Other:			
Examples of "Manages the Job" that describe your ratings:			
Gets the Job Done	**Outstanding**	**Competent**	**Marginal**
Initiates solutions.			
Follows through.			
Meets deadlines.			
Achieves balance between work quality and quantity.			

Takes responsibility for actions.			
Other:			

Examples of "Gets the Job Done" that describe your ratings:

Section C: Summary

Name of Employee		Position	
Unit		Location	
Years with Company	Years in Present Position		Years Under Your Supervision

Comments on Strengths and Accomplishments

Identify the two or three most significant strengths and accomplishments.

(1)

(2)

(3)

(*continued*)

Figure 8.8 (*continued*)

Comments on Areas Requiring Development

Identify two or three areas where this employee needs to improve (set new goals).

(1)

(2)

(3)

Performance Assessment

Overall Rating (check one)

Outstanding ☐　　　　　Competent ☐　　　　　Marginal ☐

Previous Rating	Previous Rating by	Date of Previous Rating

If there is a change in rating, state the major reason for that change.

Employee Coments (Use additional paper, if necessary)

Performance Review and Communication

Prepared by _____ Date _____

Reviewed with employee _____ Date _____

---

employees.[17] Brademas, Lowrey, and Beaman found that only 13.7 percent of the agencies surveyed allow employees to evaluate fellow employees.[18]

SUBORDINATE APPRAISALS.   This study also found that more than four out of ten agencies (42.1 percent) allowed subordinates to evaluate supervisors.[19] Many agencies have found that subordinate appraisals can make managers more aware of the effect they are having on their work force. Even bosses like to get feedback on how they are doing. It is usually necessary to conduct this process in such a way that subordinates are able to remain anonymous. Otherwise, results may be inflated by intimidated employees.

COMBINATIONS.   Generally speaking, it has been found that management decisions about compensating, promoting, retaining, dismissing, training, and disciplining employees must be heavily weighted in an appraisal of the immediate superior. This is because superiors have the primary responsibility for overseeing the efficiency and effectiveness of their work force and must have the authority to carry out this responsibility. However, managers who understand the importance of a participative approach to management will want to take into account the expertise and opinion of others. By utilizing a combination of sources for gathering appraisal information, greater insight into a person's actual performance may be achieved. This is especially important with regard to decisions about employee training and development needs.

For example, an athletic supervisor may be evaluated by her immediate superior with regard to all aspects of her work performance. This appraisal would serve as a basis for a recommendation regarding a merit salary increase. In addition to this evaluation, a second evaluation is done to determine promotion potential and training needs. In the second evaluation, peers and subordinates are asked to assess interpersonal relationship skills, communication skills, cooperative behavior, leadership skills, the ability to give direction, and organizational ability. Finally, in a third evaluation, the supervisor would evaluate her own skills and abilities to help determine what areas need enhancement through further training and development.

Evaluating the Appraisal Information

Although informal evaluating occurs constantly, *the formal process of eval-uating the appraisal information is a specific step, the fourth in our overall system* (see Figure 8.1). Observing and recording performance information is not enough; those data only have meaning if based on some standard. If during a week an interpretive naturalist makes sixty-three contacts with park visitors, has he or she performed the task poorly, very well, or somewhere in between? A standard is needed. If an employee's per-formance is compared to the performance of other employees, a *com-parative standard* is being used. If an employee's performance is compared to a predetermined figured based on historical data, expert opinion, or empirical research, it is said to be an *absolute standard*. Also, there is the question of whether performance should be measured on (1) raw output, (2) improvement on performance, or (3) both. Our interpreter may have improved his or her performance by twenty contacts compared to the previous week, but may still be far short of the average number of con-tacts made by all interpretors in the park. Should he or she be rewarded for this improvement or criticized for failing to meet the group's standard?

Throughout our discussion of the performance appraisal process, we have emphasized the need to be as objective as possible as we direct, observe, and record individual performance. Given the diversity of peo-ple in the work forces and the complicated relationships that can exist between managers and employees, this is not an easy task. Ultimately, however, the information that has been gathered and recorded must be judged subjectively by the manager.

> Subjectivity can be reduced but never completely eliminated from the eval-uation process. All judgments are to some degree subjective. It is important, however, that those judgments be made on dimensions which more perfectly represent the elements of successful performance.[20]

Perhaps the best advice we can give to the appraiser for carrying out this step is to (1) retreat to a solitary place where you will not be disturbed, (2) allow yourself sufficient time to think through all the information, and (3) develop a clear and strong rationale for the decisions you make or recommend. In most cases, the manager will not be the final step in the decision-making process; the manager's immediate superior will usually review recommendations and make the final decision.

The Appraisal Interview and Feedback

The fifth step in the performance appraisal process is *an interview involving the manager and the employee.* These interviews are not always pleasant, and many managers avoid them like the plague. This is unfortunate. Even worse, many managers conduct these interviews very poorly, primarily because they have never received proper training.

> It is very unfortunate that so few [managers] receive any training in how to conduct these interviews. This is not a skill that many bosses can afford to pick up by trial and error. The trials are very trying, and the errors are exceedingly costly.[21]

We contend that the performance appraisal interview does not have to be a bad experience. If managers have a positive, open relationship with their employees; the organization supports its management personnel with reasonable salaries and clearly defined policies and procedures; managers have proper training in conducting interviews; and feedback is given on a regular basis and not just at appraisal time; the interview can be a less painful and more meaningful experience for both parties.

An interview will usually have one of two purposes: (1) present to the employee management's decision regarding salary, promotions, or the like, or (2) discuss employee training and development matters. General agreement exists that an interview should not attempt to deal with these two purposes at the same meeting. They inherently conflict.[22] If a person's salary is discussed, he or she will tend to focus on this aspect of the interview and give less attention to matters related to improved performance and personal development. Therefore, these interviews should be held separately.

After the manager has determined the purpose of the interview, the next step is planning and preparation. Prior to an interview to explain salaries, the manager needs to have his or her rationale clearly in mind. A vague explanation concerning the size of someone's future income will frequently create a concerned response. Obviously, if the appraisal process follows the appropriate procedures discussed previously in this chapter, the manager's task of justifying the salary decision will be made much easier.

If the purpose of the interview is employee development, a different type of format is followed. The following steps are suggested for the manager.

- Encourage employees to prepare for the interview by thinking about (1) how well they performed in the previous appraisal period, and (2) their work and career goals for the next appraisal period.
- Begin the interview by clearly restating the purpose of the interview.
- Get the employee talking about his or her work performance. Ask open-ended questions, listen carefully, probe for specifics, and note points on which you wish to follow up later.

- Provide employees with feedback. React to their comments. Show them the performance appraisal form that was filled out previously.
- Set mutually agreed on, specific goals. Put these in writing with a final copy given to both persons.[23]

Also, every effort should be made to focus on *specific behavior;* avoid criticizing personality traits or basic character.[24] For example, if an employee has had a difficult time motivating the seasonal personnel in her charge, the interviewer should not say, "Your supervisory skills are really weak and should be improved." A better response might be, "If your summer staff is unsure of what is expected of them, you may have to prepare written work orders for each job assignment." This type of feedback is much more likely to result in changed behavior and improved performance.

Avoid belaboring what went wrong in the past; keep the interview directed toward planning for future improvement. Managers, concerned about improving performance, sometimes spend an inordinate amount of time discussing negative aspects of performance. Positive work performance also needs elucidation. Once again, specific examples are far more meaningful to the employee than are vague statements.

It is inappropriate for the manager to surprise the employee with past incidents that displeased the manager. This type of behavior by the manager usually indicates poor communications, an uneasy relationship, or both. For example, if the incident had never been discussed previously, it would be inappropriate to state, "Last spring, you were late in sending out job notices for lifeguards." It would have been proper for the manager to discuss this incident at the time it occurred. If the matter is referred to in the interview, it should only be for the purpose of clarifying goals and improving future performance. A more in-depth discussion of the principles of interviewing was given in Chapter 5.

Adjustments

The sixth and last step in the formal performance appraisal process is making adjustments. These adjustments could involve the employee, the manager, or the organization. For example, the appraisal process might lead to the development of a set of specific objectives for the employee. A maintenance supervisor might resolve to:

- Allocate three hours each Wednesday and Friday afternoons to inspect parks and observe crews.
- Develop on Friday morning each week a list of projects to be started the following week.

- Take a course at the community college: Planning and Scheduling for Results.

Perhaps the appraisal process revealed that the manager needed to make some changes. He or she might resolve to:

- Provide the maintenance supervisor with more direction by (1) reviewing the weekly list of new projects each Friday afternoon, (2) meeting with the supervisor each Monday morning at 10:00 a.m., and (3) making at least two park inspection tours with the supervisor each month.

Finally, the organization might be in need of some changes. Following the appraisal, the manager might contact his or her immediate supervisor and the personnel department about reviewing and revising the job description for the maintenance supervisor. The appraisal process might have revealed that the work activities of the supervisor were not accurately reflected in the job description.

Goal setting is extremely useful, regardless of whether it is tied to performance appraisal. In the next section we discuss the concept and process of goal setting as well as the very commonly discussed formal system of goal setting known as management by objectives (MBO).

Goal Setting

In their text *Financing, Managing and Marketing Recreation and Park Resources,* Howard and Crompton present a complete step-by-step model of a management-by-objectives program.

> The three primary steps in our MBO model are: (1) Establishing Overall Agency Objectives, (2) Establishing Unit and Individual Performance Targets, and (3) Measuring and Evaluating Objective Achievement.[25]

Therefore, one aspect of Howard and Crompton's model involves establishing objectives for employees and assessing the degree to which those objectives are achieved. However, it is possible to provide goals and objectives for employees without actually having a complete, formal MBO system for the entire operation. In fact, although the notion of goal setting is widely accepted, relatively few agencies have adopted formal MBO systems.

It is not our purpose to present a complete description of MBO.[26] We wish only to discuss the concept of goal setting as it relates to performance appraisal. For our purposes, goals will be defined as broad guidelines that provide overall direction.[27] Objectives are specific targets that focus on the achievement of goals. The use of goals can be very simple or complex. Some agencies ask the supervisor and employee to establish jointly goals and objectives for the employee at the culmination of the appraisal interview. For example, a goal might be to "improve work habits" and an objective might be "to increase the number of hours per week that is actually spent working on assigned responsibilities by 10 percent. Other agencies develop *work plans* for each evaluation period or assigned project. The work plan spells out in detail the objectives of each person involved. In addition, a work plan usually specifies organizational or project objectives, allocates resources, indicates procedures to be used, sets a time table, indicates key contacts and relationships, and incorporates an evaluation procedure.

Whether the use of goals and objectives is a simple or complex effort, it usually involves four steps.[28] First, supervisors and employees work together to establish broad goals and specific, measurable objectives. The development of specific, measurable objectives is a difficult process that sometimes requires a considerable effort and a series of meetings. Clegg offers an explicit step-by-step procedure.

1. The objective starts with the word "to," followed by an action or accomplishment verb.
   "To reduce the response time. . . ."
2. The objective specifies a single key result to be accomplished.
   "To reduce the response time to routine work order requests. . . ."
3. The objective is as specific and quantitative (and hence measurable and verifiable) as possible.
   "To reduce the response time to routine work order requests by 20 percent. . . ."
4. The objective specifies a target date for its accomplishment.
   "To reduce the response time to routine work order requests by 20 percent by July 1, 1978. . . ."
5. The objective specifies maximum cost factors. The cost factors may be expressed in dollars, labor hours, or both.
   "To reduce the response time to routine work order requests by 20 percent by July 1, 1978, at a cost not to exceed 40 labor hours and $100."[29]

Once goals and objectives are finalized, the employee should know *what* (outcomes) he or she is expected to accomplish. The question of *how* (means) he or she is to accomplish these outcomes may or may not be addressed.

The second step involves the employee completing the assigned task. The degree to which the manager oversees an employee's efforts *is variable* and dependent on a number of factors, such as the nature of the work and the level of motivation of the subordinate.[30] In the third step, the manager and employee attempt to determine to what extent the employee actually achieved (outcomes) what it was mutually agreed would be achieved (objectives). In addition, to determine *why* objectives may or may not have been achieved, it is necessary to look at (1) the means that were used, and (2) the external factors that were beyond the control of the employee. For example, an employee may not achieve his or her objective, but the primary cause may be insufficient resources, insufficient time, or poor weather conditions. Another employee may accomplish his or her objective but use inappropriate means, waste resources, or be aided by outside factors that he or she did not influence. In the fourth and final step, new goals and objectives are devised and, possibly, new means for achieving those objectives are developed.

Regardless of whether a formal MBO system exists, the goals of the employee should coincide with organizational and departmental goals. In fact, the goals of the employee lie at the base of a hierarchical arrangement; employee goals are directed toward the achievement of departmental goals, departmental goals are directed toward organizational goals, and the organizational goals strive to accomplish the mission of the agency.

In summary, goal setting can be an effective method of measuring productivity. Its strength is that it focuses the employee on the accomplishment of desired goals; however, its weakness is that it provides very little feedback to employees as to the effectiveness of their day-to-day behavior in achieving those goals. *We strongly recommend a comprehensive performance appraisal system that integrates a goal setting approach* (what employees achieve) *with an approach that evaluates behavioral effectiveness* (what employees do). In the following section we explain the design and implementation of a comprehensive, integrated system.

Implementing a System

The following example demonstrates a comprehensive appraisal system. Assume that you are the new employee who has just been hired. Your formal appraisals follow this hypothetical pattern.

January 10	You are hired and begin your ninety-day probationary period.
April 1	You are evaluated by your supervisor. A rating scale format is used to evaluate your job behavior and work characteristics.
April 10	Congratulations. You are changed to full-time permanent status.

July 1	You meet with your supervisor, who explains the importance of goal setting, goal-setting procedures, and the forms to be used in drafting your goals.
July 1–10	Both you and your supervisor draft possible goals and objectives for your next twelve months.
July 10	In a meeting you and your supervisor mutually agree on your goals and objectives after discussion and respectful debate.
January 1 (second year)	Your supervisor evaluates your past year's performance using a rating scale format. Based on this appraisal your next year's salary is determined by your supervisor and her immediate supervisor.
July (second year)	Your actual results are compared to your first year's goals and objectives. New goals and objectives are developed. This process will take place every July each year.
January (third year)	Your performance is evaluated by your superiors and your salary is determined for the following year. This process will take place every subsequent January and might follow a step-by-step procedure similar to the one presented in Figure 8.9.

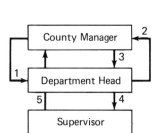

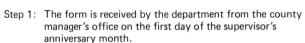

Step 1: The form is received by the department from the county manager's office on the first day of the supervisor's anniversary month.

Step 2: The department head completes the form and the county manager reviews and approves.

Step 3: The county manager returns the form to the department head.

Step 4: The department head presents the evaluation to the supervisor.

Step 5: The supervisor signs the evaluation and receives a copy. The original evaluation is returned to county manager's office through the department head.

Figure 8.9 Step-by-step procedure for the evaluation of a supervisory-level person. (Courtesy of Lee County Parks and Recreation, Sanford, N.C.)

This example describes a system that has several advantages. First, it separates appraisals and interviews for salaries and promotions from appraisals and interviews for training and development needs. Second, two separate evaluation forms, designed for their separate purposes, are used, thus eliminating the problems created by one long, multipurpose form.

Once a system is in place, the formal appraisals are carried out on a routine basis. Figure 8.9 describes the step-by-step procedure for supervisory personnel followed by Lee County, North Carolina. Note that Lee County's system was developed by Ron Ferris, director of parks and recreation, as ordered by the county manager.

Summary and Recommendations

Based on the latest research findings and information available, the following recommendations are tenable.

1. Leisure service managers at all levels should be knowledgeable about the theory and practice of performance appraisal. In addition, they should have the opportunity to provide input as to how the system is operated.
2. In most circumstances, performance appraisal systems should focus on specific job-related behavior, the achievement of objectives, or preferably, both. These approaches are far superior to evaluating personality traits or vague work characteristics.
3. Employee responsibilities should be delineated at the beginning of each rating period so that workers know what is expected of them.[31] Furthermore, employees should understand what criteria will be used to evaluate their performance.
4. The purpose of the appraisal dictates how it should be conducted, the type of instrument used, and the type of information gathered. First, determine the purpose of the appraisal, then put together the appropriate system.
5. Personnel need to be trained to use a performance appraisal system. Either have the personnel department provide this training or contract with an outside consultant.
6. Matters related to improving performance and personal development conflict with matters related to administrative decision making and should not be discussed at the same appraisal interview session.[32]
7. By supplementing the evaluations of immediate supervisors with evaluations from the appraisee, peers, and subordinates, valuable insights from different perspectives can be achieved.

8. By recording and keeping on file important incidences related to performance, the problem of trying to recall all these incidences at the end of the appraisal period will be considerably reduced.
9. Periodic, formal evaluations do not eliminate or reduce the need for regular, continuous feedback on both positive and negative aspects of performance.
10. The overall appraisal process should be a formal, standardized system that allows subjective judgments to be made on an objective foundation of information.
11. Busy managers, caught up in routine day-to-day work, should never underestimate the importance of allocating sufficient time to performance appraisal and feedback.

Discussion Topics

1. Define the term *criteria*. What criteria might your instructor use to evaluate class assignments? Should all criteria be given the same weight? Explain.
2. Explain how performance appraisal aids management in making decisions that affect both the employee and the organization. Explain how performance appraisal aids the employee.
3. Why are immediate supervisors most frequently the ones who evaluate the performance of employees? Why might it be important to involve other periodically in the appraisal process?
4. Under what circumstances might the validity of peer appraisals be reduced?
5. What are some of the problems that might develop when subordinates are asked to appraise their superiors?
6. Describe some of the characteristics of a well-designed performance appraisal form.
7. Explain the concepts of comparative and absolute standards. Do you feel that your instructor should use a comparative standard or an absolute standard when determining your course grade?
8. To what extent do you agree with the statement, "We must be as objective as possible as we evaluate performance?"
9. Why should a manager not attempt to discuss employee training and development matters at the same appraisal interview when a management decision about compensation or promotion is explained?
10. When providing feedback, why is it important that managers refer to specific behavior rather than make vague, general statements?
11. Discuss some ways that managers might want to adjust their behavior based on the results of an effective appraisal interview.

12. Many supervisors and employees dislike performance appraisal, especially the interview and feedback component. Identify some of the aspects of the process that can be disconcerting and suggest ways to minimize or eliminate these problems.
13. How does performance appraisal differ in the public and private leisure service sectors?
14. The formal performance appraisal process is made of six components. Assume that you are a supervisor in a leisure service agency with the responsibility of appraising employee performance. Develop a hypothetical situation in which you would go through these steps to appraise an employee. Discuss each step as it relates to your specific situation.

Notes

1. Richard I. Henderson, *Compensation Management: Rewarding Performance*, 3rd ed. (Reston, Va.: Reston Publishing Co., Inc., 1979), p. 382.
2. Randall S. Schuler, *Personnel and Human Resource Management* (St. Paul, Minn.: West Publishing Co., 1981), p. 221.
3. Sometimes in parks and recreation, the term *employee evaluation* is used instead of *performance appraisal*. We feel the latter term is far more appropriate because it emphasizes the notion of focusing on performance.
4. Richard G. Kraus, Gay Carpenter, and Barbara J. Bates, *Recreation Leadership and Supervision.* 2nd ed. (Philadelphia: Saunders College Publishing, 1981), p. 296.
5. D. James Brademas, George A. Lowrey, and John Beaman, *Personnel Performance Appraisal Practices in Leisure Service Agencies* (Urbana-Champaign, Ill.: University of Illinois, 1981), p. 19.
6. Robert I. Lazer and Walter S. Wikstrom, *Appraising Managerial Performance: Current Practices and Future Directions* (New York: The Conference Board, Inc., 1977), p. 1.
7. J. M. McFillen and P. G. Decker, "Building Meaning into Performance Appraisal," *Personnel Administrator* (June 1978): 76.
8. Christopher R. Edginton and John G. Williams, *Productive Management of Leisure Service Organizations: A Behavioral Approach* (New York: John Wiley & Sons, Inc., 1978), p. 383.
9. Richard F. Olson, *Performance Appraisal: A Guide to Greater Productivity* (New York: John Wiley & Sons, Inc., 1981), p. 91.
10. Douglas McGregor, "An Uneasy Look at Performance Appraisal," *Harvard Business Review* 35 (May–June 1957): 90.
11. James G. Goodale, "Behaviorally-Based Rating Scales: Toward an Integrated Approach to Performance Appraisal," in *Contemporary Problems in Personnel*, ed. W. Clay Hammer and Frank L. Schmidt (Chicago: St. Clair Press, 1977), p. 247.
12. Brademas, Lowrey, and Beaman, *Personnel Performance Appraisal Practices*, p. 16.

13. Lazer and Wikstrom, *Appraising Managerial Performance*, p. 17.
14. R. Wayne Mondy and Robert M. Noe III, *Personnel: The Management of Human Resources* (Boston: Allyn and Bacon, Inc., 1981), p. 258.
15. Schuler, *Personnel and Human Resource Management*, p. 236.
16. Graig E. Schneier, "Multiple Rater Groups and Performance Appraisal," *Public Personnel Management* 6 (January–February 1977): 15.
17. L. L. Cummings and D. Schwab, *Performance in Organizations* (Glenview, Ill.: Scott, Foresman and Company, 1973).
18. Brademas, Lowrey, and Beaman, *Personnel Performance Appraisal Practices*, p. 16.
19. Ibid, p. 17.
20. J. M. McFillen and P. G. Decker, "Building Meaning into Performance Appraisal," *Personnel Administrator* (June 1978): 76.
21. James G. Goodale, *The Fine Art of Interviewing* (Englewood Cliffs, N.J.: Prentice-Hall, Inc., 1982), p. 66.
22. Regina B. Glover and Jim Glover, "Appraising Performance: Some Alternatives to the Sandwich Approach," *Parks and Recreation* (November 1981): 27–28.
23. Goodale, *The Fine Art of Interviewing*, pp. 89–95.
24. Ibid., pp. 80–81.
25. Dennis R. Howard and John L. Crompton, *Financing, Managing and Marketing Recreation and Park Resources* (Dubuque, Iowa: Wm. C. Brown, Company, 1980), p. 273.
26. For a comprehensive discussion of MBO in leisure services, see Howard and Crompton, *Financing*, pp. 250–274, and Charles C. Clegg, *Implementing a Management by Objectives System Within Recreation and Park Departments* (Athens, Ga.: University of Georgia, 1977), pp. 1–27.
27. Monica Nolan, *Program Evaluation Procedure for Leisure Service Agencies* (Urbana-Champaign, Ill.: University of Illinois, 1981), pp. 8–9.
28. Schuler, *Personnel and Human Resource Management*, p. 231.
29. Charles C. Clegg, *Implementing a Management by Objectives System Within Recreation and Park Departments* (Athens, Ga.: University of Georgia, 1977), pp. 5–6.
30. Howard and Crompton, *Financing*, pp. 198–199.
31. Olson, *Performance Appraisal*, p. 70.
32. Glover and Glover, "Appraising Performance," p. 27–28.

Compensation

Compensation is a part of the exchange arrangement between employees and employers. In exchange for making their time and talent available to the organization, employees receive compensation.[1] In this text, *compensation is defined as all the monetary rewards, both direct and indirect, provided to employees.* Direct monetary rewards include wages and salaries, incentive pay, paid vacations, holidays, retirement benefits, relocation reimbursement, and paid sick leave. Indirect monetary rewards include such things as an automobile, free access to recreation facilities, free medical examinations, low-cost health and life insurance, and free or low-cost day care services.

For most of us, employment and its associated compensation is a very important part of our lives. Few of us would bother to show up for work if we were suddenly told that from now on we would receive no compensation for our efforts. Because most people have strong feelings on the matter of the size and form of their compensation, this topic can be the source of conflict in any leisure service operation. Unfortunately, middle- and lower-level managers tend to get caught in the center of these conflict situations.

In most cases, park, recreation, and leisure service managers are not responsible for designing a compensation program or determining the policies and practices for the operation of that program. However, managers are usually involved in the specific decisions regarding the compensation of their subordinates. In addition, managers play a critical communications role. The more they understand the compensation program, the better they will be able to communicate compensation matters both up and down in the organization structure. In summary, leisure service managers will be more effective if they have a basic understanding of the primary aspects of compensation.

In earlier chapters we discussed the various processes and principles related to *planning, organizing, staffing,* and *directing*. The manager's fifth basic function is *controlling*. Performance appraisal, discussed in Chapter 8, and compensation are closely linked, and both are important aspects of control.

In many cases a person's compensation level is based on an appraisal of his or her performance. By maximizing compensation for good performance and minimizing compensation for weak performance, organizations have a reward mechanism that serves as a tool for controlling the work activities of its employees. In addition, some people desire greater levels of compensation and are willing to increase their output in order to get it. Thus an organization is able to exert considerable control over some members of its work force by promising more compensation for more output.

Organizations establish compensation programs to achieve three basic purposes.

1. Attract and retain employees.
2. Reward individuals for their past performance and longevity.
3. Serve as an incentive for increased or improved future performance.[2]

On the surface, the notion of compensation is deceptively simple. It seems that all we have to do is (1) measure each person's level of performance, and (2) allocate the correct level of compensation. This simplistic view does not take into account the many factors that affect the compensation system. In the first major section of this chapter we assess some of these factors. In another section we discuss designing and administering a compensation system. In the third major section we discuss the various forms of compensation. Although compensation can take many forms, most of us equate compensation with wages and salaries (base pay). Most experts agree that base pay is the most important form of compensation, but it is not the only form. Other forms of compensation (usually called *benefits*) are also important factors in the employee–employer exchange relationship.

Factors Influencing Compensation

Organizations often have less control over the wages and benefits they pay than many people realize. *Legislation, labor unions,* and *market forces* all influence what a leisure service employer can compensate its employees. A fourth factor, *compensation philosophy,* also influences wages and benefits, but it is one that we do control.

Legislation

Chapter 1 pointed out several pieces of legislation that affect compensation. The 1964 Civil Rights Act, the Age Discrimination in Employment Act of 1967, and the Equal Pay Act of 1963 all require organizations to take steps to ensure that certain people are not singled out and paid unfair wages and salaries because of their race, color, religion, national origin, age or sex.

In addition, the Fair Labor Standards Act, passed in 1938, requires that employers pay (1) a minimum wage, and (2) an increased wage for overtime work. Agencies must make cash payment at time and one-half times the employees' regular rate of pay for all hours worked in excess of 40 hours in a work period of seven consecutive days.[3] The law prohibits compensating for overtime hours in excess of 40 hours in the form of compensatory time, that is, giving the employees time off from work equal to the number of hours worked overtime.

For example, if a grounds maintenance foreman knowingly allows a laborer to volunteer five hours of his time and work 45 hours in week one, he cannot allow the laborer to work only 35 hours in week two. The foreman must compensate the laborer at the regular rate of pay for 75 hours and five hours at time and one-half. Work that the employer does not request but permits is considered work time and must be counted as hours worked for pay. The law does not permit averaging of hours over two or more weeks. The only exceptions are law enforcement and fire protection employees. Their work period may be calculated from seven to 28 days.

In 1974 Congress passed an amendment to the Fair Labor Standards Act that extended its coverage to all state and local government employees, but in 1976 the Supreme Court ruled this legislation unconstitutional.[4] For nine years government employees were not covered by this act. In February 1985 the Supreme Court reversed its earlier decision, and now all government park and recreation agencies must follow the law.[5] Many states have enacted legislation to cover intrastate employees, and obviously, other employees in our field would be covered by these state laws. Currently, thirty-nine states have minimum-wage laws for intrastate employees.[6] Executives, administrators, and professionals, however, are exempt from the Fair Labor Standards Act. This means that any leisure service employee who falls in one of these three classifications does not have to be paid extra for the hours that he or she works in excess of forty hours per week.

Labor Unions

It is not at all uncommon for a leisure service organization to have all or some of its employees in a collective bargaining unit represented by a union or employee association. In Chapter 13 we present a detailed discussion of organized labor in parks and recreation. Leisure service employees covered by a labor contract will have the general level of their compensation covered by negotiated agreement. For example, the base pay of all Recreation Supervisor IIIs in a city recreation department falls within salary range 9, which is from $22,000 to 28,000. Although the boss of these supervisors can still evaluate their performance and establish their salaries at any point within this range that he or she feels is justified, the range itself is established by the negotiated contract. In addition, the union will probably scrutinize the performance appraisals very closely and push hard for the supervisors to get $28,000—the high end of the salary range. Unions tend to be very skeptical of performance appraisals and merit systems; they generally feel that length of service (seniority) is a more appropriate basis for salary determination.[7]

The general level of compensation that an organization provides its employees in an organized labor situation depends largely on that organization's power relative to the union or employee association. For example, if an organization faces a powerful union, it may end up paying very high wages and salaries.

In fact, the threat of a union may itself cause organizations to increase compensation levels. For example, an agency without an organized work force may compensate its employees generously to reduce the need for those employees to join a union. Some park and recreation agencies have chosen to pay their employees not covered by a union contract at higher rates than those which were negotiated by their organized employees. Although such tactics may be questionable with regard to certain labor laws, it clearly illustrates that either the presence or potential presence of organized labor can greatly affect the amount of compensation an organization will pay its employees.

Market Forces

The economic law of supply and demand has a great deal to do with the compensation level paid by park and recreation organizations. Although numerous new jobs have opened up in the field over the last several decades, the supply of people wanting recreation jobs is high relative to the demand. In other words, even though demand has been good, supply has been even greater. Since the leisure field tends to provide its professionals with numerous noncompensation-related rewards, both intrinsic and extrinsic, it is attractive to many people. This over-supply has helped to keep salaries relatively low. The Bureau of Labor Statistics reports that the average beginning salary of a recreation program leader with a bachelor's degree is about $11,500. This figure is lower than the entry-level salary paid in similar fields, such as social work, secondary school teaching, personnel and labor relations, and landscape architecture.[8]

Many professionals who were in the field in the 1960s remember when the supply of recreation-trained professionals was very low compared to the demand. Recreation curricula could not turn out graduates fast enough. But as many of us can recall, recreation salaries were low. Why did the high demand–low supply situation not drive salaries up? Recreation and park managers did *not* compete for the limited number of recreation-trained professionals by offering higher salaries. Instead, they frequently hired nontrained personnel.

Many leisure service managers at that time and many today do not feel that formal training in recreation and parks is needed in order to work in the field. Thus, in recreation, supply is not equal to the number of trained park and recreation persons available for employment; it is equal to the total number of persons that managers feel can provide leisure services—regardless of their professional training. As long as managers substitute non-recreation-trained people for recreation-trained people, it is extremely unlikely that salaries will increase significantly.

Several additional points need to be made before leaving this section. First, we do not mean to imply (1) that park, recreation, and leisure service agencies should not hire non-recreation-trained personnel, or (2) that non-recreation-trained people are not competent. Many non-recreation-trained employees have proved to be very effective. A few have risen to leadership positions in their agencies and in the profession.

Up to this point, our discussion has focused on the recreation field in general. A few areas, such as recreation therapy, are more specialized and, therefore, employers are less willing to substitute nonprofessional people. In some cases, certification requirements prohibit the hiring of noncertified recreation therapists. Our earlier generalizations would not apply to these special areas.

Finally, some leisure service operators are not sufficiently aware of the recreation field and, therefore, the laws of supply and demand are restricted. This point is frequently illustrated in the commercial recreation sector. Assume that a wealthy person decides to build a marina complex with a restaurant, lounge, and boutique. This entrepreneur might entrust the management of the facility to a friend or relative. Perhaps he or she would hire a local person with a business background. If the entrepreneur is not aware of the recreation field or the advantages of hiring a recreation-trained professional, it may be that the field has not marketed itself effectively. In any case, the economic forces that control the labor market are bypassed because the uninformed entrepreneur is not aware of the supply of human resources available.

Compensation Philosophy

In any community, people will be paid various salary levels for various kinds of work. For example, assume that five different companies in the Portland, Oregon, area have hired one or more recreation specialists. The total compensation packages for these people range from a high of $27,000 to a low of $12,200. Even though these jobs may vary somewhat and other noncompensation rewards may differ, a compensation differential of $14,800 exists. In the next section we focus on the individual differences among employees, such as longevity, experience, and performance, which might account for this differential. But let us assume that each of the industrial recreation specialists is about 26 years of age, has about the same education and experience, and that each is performing effectively. These salary differences could reflect each company's philosophy toward compensation.

Some organizations have chosen to pay salaries that are equal to or greater than those paid by other organizations. In this way, the agency puts itself in a better position to attract and keep the best people in the area. Higher salaries can help to reduce turnover, and therefore the work force remains more stable over the long run.

For a number of reasons, other leisure service organizations choose to pay lower salaries than those that prevail for comparable jobs in the local area. In a few cases, these agencies legitimately may not be able to afford higher salaries. In most cases, however, these agencies have chosen to pay lower salaries. These managers rationalize low salaries in various ways. For one thing, the labor market of our capitalistic system allows it. As we pointed out earlier, the recreation labor supply currently exceeds the demand. Thus these managers are using the same rationale that many capitalist managers have used for several centuries: Get the most from employees but pay the least possible salary.

A second rationale used to justify low salaries is that it stretches the budget. By paying low salaries, an agency can employ more people. A large staff looks more impressive to some people than a small staff. However, a large staff does not necessarily translate into greater productivity or higher-quality services.

Another rationale for low salaries used by some managers in governmental operations is that it saves the money for the taxpayers. Finally, another rationale for low salaries is that it almost ensures a steady supply of fresh people. One park and recreation director has stated that he does not mind if his staff members leave because of low salaries; he can always find an enthusiastic, new college graduate who will be willing to fill the position at the same salary. Unfortunately for this person, he has not read Chapter 12 and probably does not understand the enormous costs associated with a high turnover rate.

Obviously, not all managers agree with the philosophy of keeping salaries low. Some have worked diligently for salary increases but failed to convince higher-level decision makers. In any case, the problem of low salaries may be a critical issue for the field in the years ahead. Based on our discussions with professionals who have recently left the field, low salaries were definitely a factor in many cases. In addition, some very good students are also avoiding recreation curricula because they have heard about our low salaries. All these factors together could lead to a general decline in the recreation profession in the years ahead.

Finally, compensation levels are also affected by one additional factor that needs to be mentioned: working conditions. Some jobs are less desirable than others because of adverse working conditions. In these situations, employers frequently choose to increase the level of compensation to remain competitive in the labor market. For example, the receptionist position in a local public park and recreation department might be very demanding and stressful. Unless the department provides higher compensation to its receptionists, it may find them leaving for comparable or even lower-paying jobs in less hectic organizations.

Designing a Base Pay Program

Up to this point, we have looked at several factors that affect the level of compensation paid to recreation employees. Next, we will focus on the design of a pay program. *A pay program consists of the policies and procedures related to the allocation of base pay (wages and salaries) to the people performing the various jobs in an organization.*

Alternative Base Pay Arrangements

Since the park, recreation, and leisure service field is so éxtremely diverse, a wide range of pay programs exist. As depicted in Figure 9.1, most programs can be placed on a continuum ranging from very informal and arbitrary on one end to very formal systems based on the notion of comparable worth on the other end. In between are those programs that informally attempt to make pay decisions based on comparable worth.

To illustrate the informal, arbitrary system depicted on the left end of the continuum, we offer the following scenario of a hypothetical private nonprofit recreation organization in a small city.

Informal, arbitrary	Informal, comparable worth	Formal, comparable worth

Figure 9.1   Three alternative base pay arrangements expressed on a continuum.

As the budget is prepared each year for Organization XYZ, supervisors are asked to submit recommendations regarding their subordinates' salaries. Together with each recommendation is a performance appraisal or written statement which supports that recommendation. Typically, the performance appraisal is not well done, and the written statement is an undocumented, vaguely written opinion. The chief executive of Organization XYZ, a white male, reviews the recommendations and makes the final decisions. The chief executive has had very little training in compensation administration. He bases his decisions on his subordinates recommendations but also takes into consideration labor market factors related to supply and demand. Since some jobs are hard to fill, the people in those positions are paid more. People in easy-to-fill jobs are paid less. He decides to keep raises pretty low this year in order to add on several new programs.

Although flexible, easy to establish, and easy to administer; an informal, arbitrary pay program usually leads to favoritism, discrimination, unfair politicing, and game playing. The only people who like this kind of system are usually (1) the chief executive, and (2) people who benefit from the system because they have learned to manipulate it.

In the middle of our continuum is the informal, comparable-worth situation. Although this system is informally established and administered, it attempts to base pay decisions on the notion of comparable worth. *The idea of comparable worth is that pay should be allocated based on each position's relative worth compared to other positions.* Jobs that are more difficult and more important are generally worth more. For example, if the position of food services director is worth more to the organization than the position of cashier, the position of food services director should be allocated a higher level of pay.

To determine the comparable worth of each position, a careful analysis is made of each position's (1) duties and responsibilities, and (2) the job. This analysis is called a *job evaluation*. Based on this job evaluation, positions are ranked, and based on the rankings, salary ranges are established. We discuss this process in more detail in the next section.

The informal, comparable-worth situation (the middle of our continuum in Figure 9.1) is common in the recreation field. Typically, the organization tries to rise above the arbitrary system we described earlier but falls short of the formal system we describe in the next section. In most cases, a formal system based on the notion of comparable worth is the most desirable pay program arrangement. Although such a system takes more time to design and administer, it eliminates many of the problems created by the informal systems previously discussed.

Formal Base Pay System

The design of a formal system usually entails four steps:

1. Conduct a job evaluation.
2. Establish a classification system.
3. Establish pay rates for each position.
4. Determine each person's salary based on an appraisal of his or her performance.

Job Evaluation. *Job evaluation is a systematic way of determining the relative worth of jobs within an organization.*[9] In Chapter 3 we said that a job description should be prepared for each position. Job evaluation involves analyzing and comparing all the job descriptions for an entire organization. Each job description is examined for three things:

1. The relative importance of the job.
2. The relative qualifications needed to perform the job.
3. The difficulty of each job versus other jobs.[11]

Since World War II personnel specialists have worked hard to develop methods for performing job evaluations. Obviously, no method can be completely objective, but a number of systematic methods have been developed to improve the subjective decision that ultimately has to be made. These methods differ considerably and each has advantages and disadvantages. We will not present a detailed discussion of these methods, primarily because recreation managers will seldom be required to perform job evaluations. But it is important that recreation professionals understand that each method will ultimately produce an overall ranking of positions as they compare to one another.

Unlike job analyses, which should be performed whenever there is any confusion about the content of a particular job, job evaluations performed very infrequently. Once the basic classification system is established, it usually needs only minor modifications from time to time. As new positions are developed, they are evaluated and inserted into the appropriate job class.[11]

Job Classification. After a job evaluation, the next step is to group the jobs that are ranked close together. Each grouping is generally re-

Figure 9.2 Sample job classification plan.

Job Class	Administrative Division	Parks Division	Recreation Division
12	Executive Director		
11		Deputy Director of Parks	Deputy Director of Recreation
10	Planning Director		
9		Design and Construction Coordinator	Special Facilities Manager
8	Chief of Security	Supervisor of Operations	
7	Office Manager	Horticulturalist II	Center Director II
6	Personnel Director	Park Foreman	Program Supervisor
	Administrative Assistant	Horticulturalist I	Pool Manager
5	Security Officer II	Crew Chief	Center Director I
	Secretary II		
4	Security Officer I	Park Maintenance II	Senior Lifeguard
	Secretary I		
	Bookkeeper III		
3	Bookkeeper II	Park Maintenance I	Recreation Leader III
			Recreation Instructor III
			Lifeguard II
2	Receptionist II	Park Laborer II	Recreation Leader II
	Bookkeeper I	Stockroom Attendant	Recreation Instructor II
			Lifeguard I
1	Receptionist I	Park Laborer I	Equipment Room Attendant
	Switchboard Operator		Recreation Leader I
			Recreation Instructor I

ferred to as a job class. Jobs of comparable worth are grouped together even though they may be quite different. For example, the manager of a tree nursery may be placed in the same classification with a supervisor of programs for the visually impaired. Figure 9.2 presents a typical classification plan for a small local public park and recreation department.

Pay Structure.   The next step in the design of a compensation program is to establish a pay level for each job class. In some cases, one salary is established for all positions in a class, but more frequently, each class is represented by a salary range. The document that explains the pay structure for an organization is usually called a salary schedule (see Figure 9.3). Note that each grade in a salary schedule corresponds to a job class in the job classification plan. Both the salary schedule and the job classification plan reflect organizational policy and therefore must be officially approved by the appropriate policymaking group or person.

The U.S. government has a pay schedule with which many people are familiar. The General Schedule contains eighteen grades, ranging from GS-1 (least difficult position) to GS-18 (most difficult). GS-18 has only one pay rate. All the others have ranges: ten rates each in GS-1 through 15, nine in GS-16, and five in GS-17.

Figure 9.4 visually shows two interesting aspects of a typical pay schedule. Notice how the pay ranges overlap. This means that an experienced person who performs effectively can move to the top of his or her grade and receive greater compensation than an inexperienced person in the next-higher grade. Also, the ranges get wider as the grades get higher. This allows policymakers a great deal of flexibility when determining the salary of top management.

Pay Grade	Minimum Rate	Midpoint Rate	Maximum Rate
12	$26,500	$31,900	$37,300
11	22,800	28,500	34,200
10	19,700	24,400	29,100
9	17,000	20,800	24,600
8	15,000	17,600	20,200
7	13,400	15,400	17,400
6	12,200	13,500	14,800
5	11,100	12,300	13,500
4	10,200	11,000	11,800
3	9,500	10,100	10,700
2	8,800	9,300	9,800
1	8,200	8,600	9,000

Figure 9.3   Sample pay schedule.

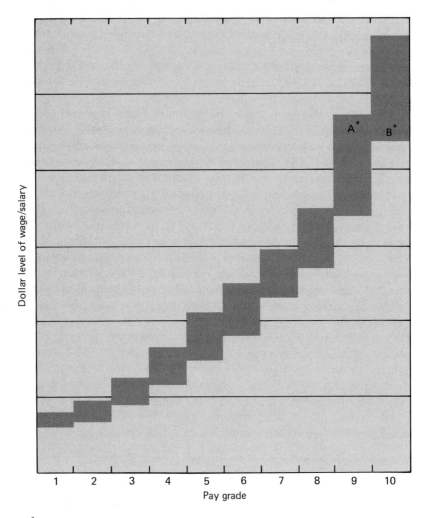

*The salary of employee A is greater than the salary of employee B even though A is in a lower rate range than B.

Figure 9.4   Sample wage/salary structure.

The salary range within each pay grade is usually divided into a series of steps. Usually, a person begins employment at or near the bottom step of the pay grade. If a person performs well, he or she advances to the next-higher step. People whose work does not meet acceptable standards usually remain in their step. (In a few organizations, they may actually drop down in steps.)

At this point the reader should clearly understand the connection between performance appraisals and compensation. Under a merit system, a person's salary may increase only if his or her performance receives a positive appraisal. Some organizations modify the merit system and automatically advance people who are performing acceptably to the next-higher step within the grade after a certain amount of time on the job. For example, if a person is performing acceptably, he or she might automatically advance one step within their grade for each fifty-two weeks of service. The automatic progression arrangement is used in the federal government and is common in many local and state governmental operations. Critics charge that automatic advances are unfair and demoralizing to the best employees, who work hard to earn their increases. Jensen states:

> Government employers have not dealt with this problem effectively because they use automatic-progression pay systems that advance individuals on a predetermined schedule, regardless of work quality or quantity. Moreover, they provide the marginal performer with job security through cumbersome procedures that all but eliminate the possibility of being fired for inadequate performance.[12]

It is not uncommon for employees to reach the top of their pay grade. This creates another problem, because these people cannot receive any further advance, regardless of how well they may perform. If these people want to continue to advance, they may have to retrain for a new position.

During the inflationary years of the 1970s and early 1980s, cost-of-living increases became very popular. Organizations gave all employees across-the-board increases to offset the effects of inflation. Many organizations found that cost-of-living increases greatly undermined merit systems. After getting these increases for a period of years, employees grew to expect them regardless of their individual levels of performance.

Finally, we need to address the question of how monetary values, such as the ones depicted in Figure 9.3, are established for each pay grade. This is usually done through a *salary survey*. Each agency gathers information about wages paid by other organizations in their local area. The average wage paid by other organizations usually becomes the midpoint or middle step for that particular grade.

Other Forms of Compensation

Benefits are forms of compensation, in addition to basic wages and salaries, given to employees as a reward for their service to an organization. At the current time, benefits make up about 30 to 40 percent of the total cost of compensation for many recreation employers. Taking it from the employees' perspective, if a person earns $13,650 in basic wages and receives benefits at a rate of 35 percent of her total compensation, her

Figure 9.5 Examples of different benefits.

Required Security	Voluntary Security	Time-Off Related	Insurance	Financial	Social and Recreational	Retirement Related
1. Workers' compensation	1. Severance pay	1. Birthdays	1. Medical	1. Credit union	1. Tennis courts	1. Social security
2. Unemployment compensation	2. Supplemental unemployment benefits	2. Vacation time	2. Dental	2. Cash profit-sharing	2. Bowling league	2. Pension fund
3. Old age, survivors' and disability insurance	3. Leave of absence	3. Company subsidized travel	3. Survivor benefits	3. Company-provided housing or car	3. Company Newsletter	3. Early retirement
4. State disability insurance		4. Holidays	4. Accidental dismemberment insurance	4. Legal services	4. Professional memberships	4. Preretirement counseling
5. Medicare hospital benefits		5. Sick pay	5. Travel accident insurance	5. Purchase discounts	5. Club memberships	5. Retirement gratuity
		6. Military reserve	6. HMO fees	6. Stock plans	6. Counseling	6. Retirement annuity plan
		7. Election day	7. Group insurance rates	7. Financial counseling	7. Company-sponsored events	7. "In kind" benefits for retired employees
		8. Social-service sabbatical	8. Disability insurance	8. Moving expenses	8. Child care services	8. Disability retirement benefits
			9. Life insurance	9. Tuition assistance	9. Cafeteria	
			10. Cancer insurance		10. Season tickets	
					11. Service award jewelry	

total compensation is $21,000. As a portion of total compensation, benefits have been increasing over the past several decades at a much faster rate than wages and salaries.[13]

Ironically, many employees do not place a high value on their benefits.[14] Most employees, especially younger ones, are far more concerned about the level of their base pay.

Figure 9.5 groups benefits into seven different areas and gives examples of each. Certain benefit areas, such as insurance, workers' compensation, and retirement programs are relatively technical. In these areas, leisure service managers will probably not be directly involved in the administration of the benefits and will only need to refer employees to the specialists in the personnel unit. Other areas, such as rest breaks, sick leave, counseling, and vacations, will affect the manager, especially in the areas of scheduling and record keeping.

The provision of benefits is a policy matter. Therefore, all benefit arrangements are officially approved by the policymakers and usually discussed in the organization's personnel manual.

As we pointed out earlier, many employees are not fully aware of the value of the benefits they are provided. Since the cost of benefits can be considerable, it is to the organization's advantage to make employees more aware of the value of their benefits. Some leisure service organizations hold periodic meetings and prepare special literature describing their benefit packages.

In general, the line manager's primary responsibility related to benefits will be as a referral person, information provider, and record keeper. Good communications with the personnel specialists is highly desirable.

Summary and Recommendations

1. Compensation is all the monetary rewards, both direct and indirect, provided to employees.
2. Compensation levels are influenced by state and federal legislation, labor unions, market forces, and compensation philosophy.
3. Park, recreation, and leisure employees are generally paid rather low wages and salaries.
4. A pay program consists of all the policies and procedures related to the allocation of base pay to the people in an organization.
5. Comparable worth is the notion that pay should be allocated based on each position's relative worth compared to other positions.
6. Job evaluation is a systematic way of determining the relative worth of jobs within an organization.
7. Based on the results of a job evaluation, jobs are grouped together into classes. This is called job classification.

8. A pay schedule is a document that describes the pay grades and salary levels paid by an organization.
9. Benefits are forms of compensation, in addition to basic wages and salaries, given to employees as reward for their service to the organization.

Discussion Topics

1. Which of the following would not be covered by the Fair Labor Standards Act: a U.S. Forest Service ranger, a ride operator at a major amusement park, the manager of a country club, and/or the supervisor of a municipal recreation center?
2. Why do labor unions generally feel that seniority is the most appropriate basis for salary determination?
3. Do you think that the compensation levels paid to recreation professionals would significantly increase if the supply of recreation trained professionals dropped below the level of demand? Explain.
4. If you were the manager of a leisure service operation, would you prefer to have several fewer employees but pay them a higher-than-average wage, or would you prefer to have several more employees but pay them less than the average wage?
5. If park, recreation, and leisure employers continue to pay rather low wages to their employees, what might be the long-term effects?
6. What are the potential problems associated with an informally organized, arbitrarily administered pay program?
7. Should base pay be determined by the notion of comparable worth, or should pay be established based on the market force of supply and demand?
8. Do you agree or disagree with a pay program that automatically advances people who are performing acceptably to higher pay levels after a certain amount of time on the job? What are the arguments for and against this arrangement?
9. Why do you think many employees tend to place a low value on benefits?

Notes

1. Marc J. Wallace, Jr., N. Frederic Crandall, and Charles H. Fay, *Administering Human Resources: An Introduction to the Profession* (New York: Random House, Inc., 1982), p. 331.
2. Ibid., p. 339.
3. Arthur A. Sloane, *Personnel: Managing Human Resources* (Englewood Cliffs, N.J.: Prentice-Hall, Inc., 1983), p. 263.

4. Randall S. Schuler, *Effective Personnel Management* (St. Paul, Minn.: West Publishing Co., 1983), p. 335.

5. John Libert, Daniel Cassidy, and Larry Frierson, *Implementing the Fair Labor Standards Act: A Guide for Public Agencies,* prepared for the League of Arizona Cities and Towns (Los Angeles: Law Offices of Libert, Cassidy, and Frierson), p. 2.

6. Schuler, *Effective Personnel Management,* p. 336.

7. Richard I. Henderson, *Compensation Management: Rewarding Performance,* 3rd ed. (Reston, Va.: Reston Publishing Co., Inc., 1979), pp. 103–105.

8. U.S. Department of Labor, Bureau of Labor Statistics, *Occupational Outlook Handbook,* Bulletin 2200 (Washington, D.C.: U.S. Government Printing Office, April 1982).

9. Robert L. Mathis and John H. Jackson, *Personnel: Contemporary Perspectives and Applications,* 3rd ed. (St. Paul, Minn.: West Publishing Co., 1982), p. 325.

10. Ibid., p. 326.

11. Jerry Jensen, *Basic Guide to Salary Management* (Los Angeles: The Grants-manship Center, 1979), p. 5.

12. Ibid., p. 3.

13. Wallace, Crandall, and Fay, *Administering Human Resources,* p. 384.

14. William H. Holley and Kenneth M. Jennings, *Personnel Management: Functions and Issues* (Hinsdale, Ill.: Dryden Press, 1983), p. 369.

10
Training and Development

Americans in recent decades have experienced unprecedented changes in life-styles, leisure behavior, new technologies, and federal legislation. Societal changes also have had an impact on the park and recreation field. Employees are having to adapt to new equipment and operating policies, changes in fiscal and personnel management practices, and shifting populations and recreational needs.

Adapting to these changes influences the productivity level of leisure organizations. As recreation services and equipment become obsolete, worker competency levels drop and organizational effectiveness declines.

There are two ways in which organizations can respond to change and its negative effect on productivity. New employees with new knowledge and new skills can be hired, or current employees can be retrained. It has already been stated in Chapter 4 that recruiting new employees is a time-consuming and costly procedure. It would not be cost-effective for an employer to fire employees and hire new workers every time the organization had to react to external changes. The alternative is to provide training and development programs to improve employee competency levels.

Training and development is becoming an important and necessary function of human resource management. It is also expensive. According to the American Society for Training and Development, businesses in the United States spend approximately $30 billion a year—or about half of the total cost of higher education in America—on employee training and development.[1] Because it is both costly and important, leisure organizations should strive to make every dollar invested produce desired results. Organizations must train the right employees to meet the right objectives.

What Is Training and What Is Development?

Training and development together comprise the employer's efforts through employee learning to improve present work performance and to ensure that future human resource requirements are met. This broad definition serves two distinctly different purposes.

Development is an educational process that may include training but which is broader in scope. It concentrates on preparing the employee to meet objectives for a future job or responsibility. This definition serves the needs of both the organization and the employee. The employer is prepared for the future and the employee's need for growth is satisfied. People want more from the job than a paycheck and fringe benefits. They want greater responsibility, greater opportunity to use personal abilities, and they want to feel that they are being recognized for their efforts by "getting somewhere."[2] Abraham Maslow might call these employee aspirations "finding self-actualization."

Purpose and Importance of Training and Development

Sometimes it becomes necessary to convince the big boss or those who make budgetary decisions that training and development are important. They know that these programs can be expensive, and there is no guarantee that organizational productivity or park patron satisfaction will improve because an employee was involved in a training activity. If the training is successful, there is no guarantee that the employee will not accept a better job with another park and recreation agency. The following discussion provides five sound reasons why training and development programs are important.

1. *Training leads to improved job performance.* Productivity usually improves when employees receive training in new work methods and new technologies. For example, user complaints may decrease after seasonal workers have been trained in effective public relations techniques and good interpersonal communications. It has also been documented that training reduces accidents, absenteeism, the need for discipline, and grievances.[3]

2. *Self-improvement leads to improved work attitudes.* Self-improvement leads to self-confidence, and these two conditions lead to a desire to maintain a high level of performance in order to maintain success and a positive self-image.

Employee attitudes are improved if they perceive that the work environment assists and encourages them toward achieving all they are capable of becoming.[4] Today, young people join leisure organizations with high expectations of job satisfaction and self-fulfillment. Helping these young employees expand their abilities increases their cooperation and loyalty toward the organization.

3. *Training and development meet affirmative action objectives.* Employers have an obligation to meet three affirmative action objectives in conducting training and development programs.

(a) Programs must be monitored to ensure against systematic and adverse impact discrimination (illegal practices are discussed in detail in Chapter 1).
(b) Training must be designed to eliminate those employee performance deficiencies which were recognized and accepted at hiring by the employing organization.
(c) Development programs must include women and minorities so that these protected groups have equal opportunities for future promotion.

The first objective prohibits the practice of intentionally not including women and minorities in training and development programs, as well as unintentionally using non-job-related criteria for entry into or successful completion of a training program. For example, passing an exam written in English would not be a fair criterion to determine if a Spanish-speaking laborer knows how to identify the diseases of palm trees.

The second objective ensures that training opportunities will be provided to help an employee eliminate those performance deficiencies predicted at hiring as a result of not meeting the desired qualifications stated in the job description. If, for example, desired qualifications include experience in tree removal, trimming, spraying, and root cutting and the applicant was hired without that experience, the employer must provide some type of training to meet that particular job requirement. In the last decade or so, federal funds hve been available to states, local units of government, and private organizations to train economically disadvantaged workers.[5]

The third objective focuses on the organization's commitment to affirmative action. To meet established affirmative action goals at all organizational levels, it may be more economical to develop and promote employees from within the organization than to recruit and hire new employees.

4. *Training and development attracts new personnel and retrains competent employees to meet future human resource needs.* Adaptability not only means training or retraining employees to meet today's changes in society, it

also means planning ahead to meet future needs. Anticipated organizational expansion, new program directions, and planned retirements place future demands on the employer. Good employee development programs serve as an attraction for prospective employees and an incentive for current employees to stay with an organization. When organizations reimburse employees for tuition and books or send employees to executive development or management schools, it becomes a more attractive place in which to work.

5. *Training reduces turnover and saves money.* The percentage of wage and salary employees who quit their jobs has increased steadily since 1975. During the same period the productivity level has dropped significantly.[6] According to the Bureau of Labor Statistics, American workers are unwilling or unable to increase productivity and are increasingly willing to quit their jobs for whatever reason. Lower productivity and higher turnover rates cost money.

Organizations are becoming increasingly more interested in designing development programs, such as the one shown in Figure 10.1, which focus on long-term benefits for the agency. Keeping good employees

---

Actions That Meet Employees' Immediate Needs

1. Expand preretirement planning to include leisure counseling.
2. Provide information on appropriate referrals for family and personal crisis situations.
3. Begin tuition reimbursement for job-related continuing education and degree programs.
4. Initiate flexibility in work scheduling and organizing work tasks.

Actions That Meet Employer and Employee Needs

1. Begin long-range planning for in-house job and career development.
2. Identify and publicize career and job mobility paths within the organization.
3. Initiate diagnostic health activities, such as heart and blood tests.
4. Establish on-site physical exercise activities.
5. Institute personal and technical development continuing education programs for supervisors and managers.

Actions That Meet Primarily Organizational Goals

1. Initiate management and supervisory team building.
2. Ensure that recruiting and hiring practices are designed to obtain the best match of person with position and to communicate realistic expectations of the employer.
3. Revise compensation and performance appraisal procedures for all supervisors so that they become accountable for employee development.
4. Develop ethnic, aging, and racial sensitivity training programs.

Figure 10.1 Sample employee development program that seeks to retain good employees.

happy means planning ahead for their future needs and matching their emerging interests and abilities with new job responsibilities. Unfortunately, the hierarchical structure in most organizations adversely influences promotion opportunities for all good employees. Progression up the organizational ladder is limited to a few outstanding employees. But upward mobility is not the only path to success.

To satisfy those good employees who will not reach the top, employers are providing career profiles that reward performance and offer intrinsic rewards of success. If doctors and lawyers find a lifetime of happiness in one steady-state career profile, so can park and recreation employees. Lateral transfers, job rotation, job enrichment, and in some cases, job enlargement are mechanisms to keep the good employee. Employee development is mandatory if the employee is to experience more than one job within the same organization.[7]

Training and Development Process

The training and development process is ongoing. It is not a one-time operation which has a beginning and an end. Every work unit should have a well-organized program that includes every employee. On occasion, management may decide that training is needed for the entire organization, or it may focus on targeted groups. Special training may be necessary for people in order to solve problems caused by their poor performance. If training and development is to be effective throughout the organization, it requires someone or some unit to assume the responsibility for the entire process as it is displayed in Figure 10.2.

Determining Training and Development Needs

In most organizations the function of determining training and development needs is a complex process and requires the overall guidance of trained staff in a personnel department. The supervisor who conducts a job analysis and performance appraisal may identify specific training needs for a given employee. But organizational assessments must also be made and the average supervisor does not have the skills or the time to perform those tasks.

Organizational Needs Analysis.   Personnel specialists are best able to conduct an organizational needs analysis. This study includes examining long-range and short-range objectives for human resource needs; reviewing efficiency indexes; and determining the organizational climate by studying patterns of absenteeism, turnover, grievances, accident rates,

Figure 10.2 Training and development process.

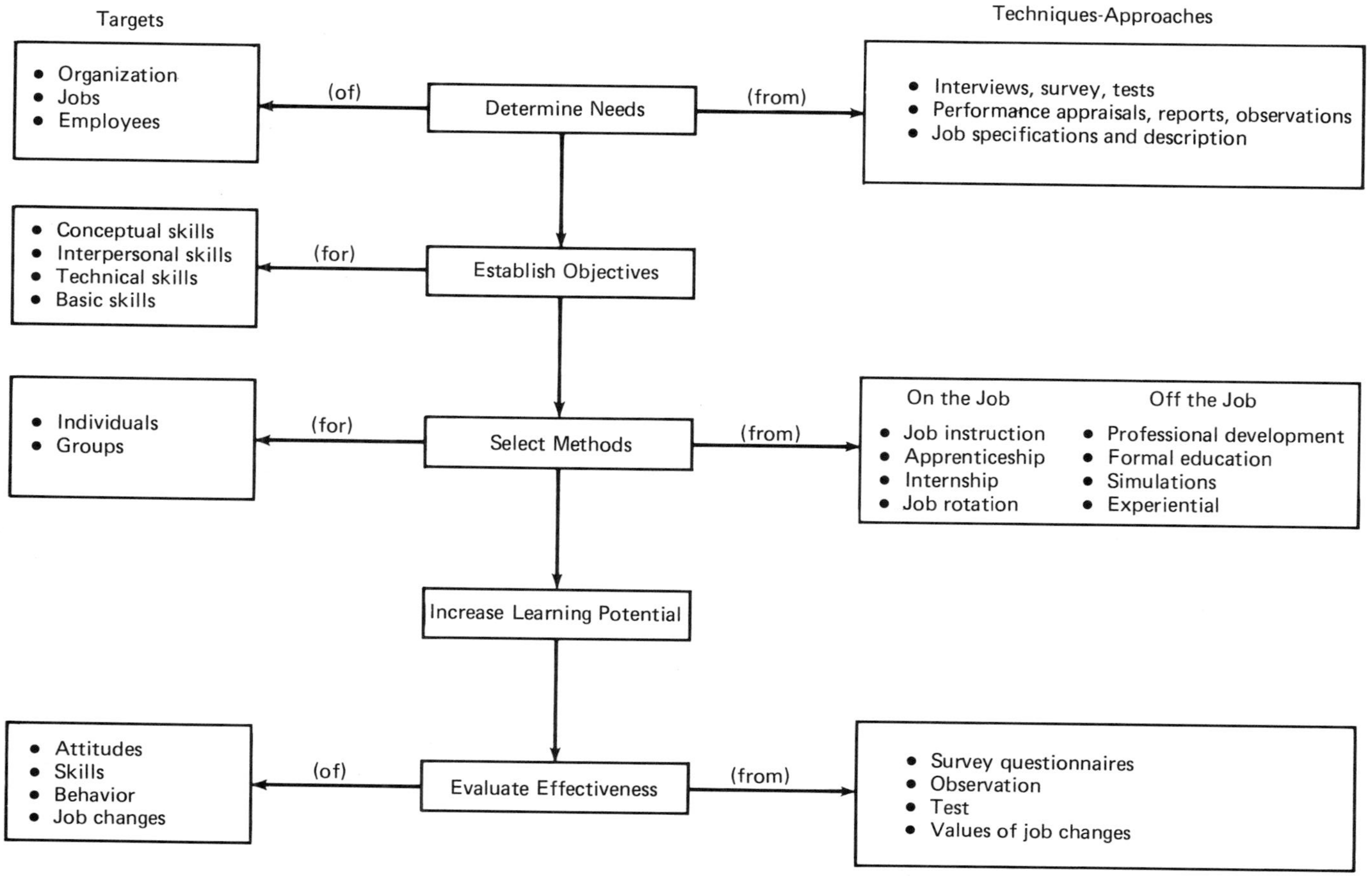

Techniques-Approaches

- Interviews, survey, tests
- Performance appraisals, reports, observations
- Job specifications and description

Off the Job
- Professional development
- Formal education
- Simulations
- Experiential

On the Job
- Job instruction
- Apprenticeship
- Internship
- Job rotation

- Survey questionnaires
- Observation
- Test
- Values of job changes

Determine Needs

(from)

Establish Objectives

Select Methods

(from)

Increase Learning Potential

Evaluate Effectiveness

(from)

Targets

(of)
- Organization
- Jobs
- Employees

(for)
- Conceptual skills
- Interpersonal skills
- Technical skills
- Basic skills

(for)
- Individuals
- Groups

(of)
- Attitudes
- Skills
- Behavior
- Job changes

and general attitudes of employees. These data are indicators of problems, but the problems may not be training related. Although it is not difficult to recognize an increase in on-the-job accidents or a decline in sales volume, it may be difficult to determine the actual cause of these changes and still more difficult to determine whether employee training will solve the problem. A decline in food and beverage sales may be a problem caused by indifferent or unpleasant employees interacting with the public. Public relations training might solve the problem, but a decline in sales might be caused by a change in the quality of food products. In that case, public relations training would not solve the problem of declining food sales.

Job Needs Analysis.   Job needs analyses are vital to determining training needs for specific jobs. Job descriptions and specifications must be reviewed to gain an understanding of those tasks performed in each job and the skills necessary to perform those tasks. Again, personnel specialists in partnership with the supervisor are important in this function.

Employee Needs Analysis.   Employee needs analysis is the third type of review that is essential in determining training and development needs. Two questions are asked: (1) Can the employee do the present job satisfactorily? (2) Can the employee do some new assignment in the future?

Employee needs analyses rely heavily on supervisor's performance appraisals and day-to-day observations. Employee self-assessment is also used. This technique involves the employee in identifying present needs and those which the employee perceives to be necessary for future promotions.

It is the pooling of all the information obtained from the three needs analyses—organization, job, and employee—that gives the composite picture of organizational training and development needs. Personnel and training specialists assist the supervisor by conducting interviews, gathering performance data, analyzing job tasks for each position, testing for job knowledge and skills, and conducting employee surveys. The composite then leads to the recommendations and design of training and development programs that improve employee skill levels, reduce noted deficiencies in performance, and meet future human resource needs.

Major Skill Categories.   Most training and development needs fall into one of four major skill development categories:

1. *Conceptual skills* such as planning, policy development, and adapting to rapidly changing environments are most often needed by middle- or top-level management employees.
2. *Interpersonal skills* such as leadership, communications, and human relations are needed by all employees, but more specifically by first-line supervisors, recreation leaders, volunteer coordinators, and those employees who interact with the public and with other employees on a regular basis.
3. *Technical skills* such as how to organize and schedule tournaments, repair machinery, write bid specifications, or propagate plants are needed to perform successfully in specific jobs.
4. *Basic skills* such as reading, writing, listening, or figuring are necessary to meet at least minimum standards of competency in every job. Good listening skills are essential for all supervisors, and speed-reading skills are vital to most middle- and top-level managers.

It is the job needs analysis that identifies the skills necessary for every job in the organization. It is the employee needs analysis that determines which workers need additional training to satisfy one or more of the four major skills required for the job. It is the organizational needs analysis that helps to determine the priority of training efforts in relationship to their relative value to the organization.

What Training Is Most Needed?   Training specialists have methods for calculating the costs of training, the cost of alternatives to training, the cost of substandard performance, and the costs and benefits for individual development.[8] This information helps to set priorities as to which training is the most cost-effective for the organization. If one training endeavor must be sacrificed for financial reasons, the organization needs to know where the cutbacks will hurt the least. The authors of this book believe that the supervisor should always be included in the process to prioritize training needs because the supervisor knows the standards of performance for each job and recognizes the performance deficiencies of subordinates.

Deming suggests four steps in determining what training is most needed:

1. *Compute and rank the cost of each training program.*
2. *Prioritize each program according to its perceived potential value to the organization.* If hard data are not available, key personnel need to pool their opinions.
3. *Judge the overall effectiveness of each training program by interviewing or polling trainees and their supervisors.*

(a) Have you (they) used the training on the job?

(b) Could (you) (they) become proficient in a short time without the training?

4. *Fix the cost of evaluation.* Some upward mobility development programs may require years of evaluation, running costs into thousands of dollars.[9]

Look at Figure 10.3. Let us assume that nine training and development activities had been supported for several years until the agency experienced a 20 percent budget reduction. The value of some of these programs is being questioned and a worksheet is prepared to help answer the question: What training is most valuable and needed?

Entry-level technical training is clearly the most expensive program, costing $4,000, but its value to the park agency is ranked second by key personnel. Employees taking the training and their supervisors rate technical training to be effective. Since the cost to evaluate this program is only 4 percent of its total cost, this program should *not* be eliminated. The reverse seems to be true, for formal education, which costs $3,000, is only ranked eighth and its overall effectiveness is unclear. This program would probably be considered for elimination, together with facility manager and program supervisor training at state and regional conferences. Although this simple technique includes subjective data input, it does provide some evidence from which to support the most cost-effective and/or needed training and development programs.

Establishing Objectives

Once training and development needs have been identified, concrete, measurable objectives must be established for each training and development program. Let us take the example of the previously identified problem "decline in food and beverage sales." The job needs analysis indicates that one of the most important tasks of snack bar attendants is to serve customers in a pleasant manner. But employee needs analyses from performance appraisals reveals poor-to-mediocre public relations skills for most snack bar attendants. This suggests the need for public relations training. Or does it? What if 30 percent of the snack bar attendants are Hispanics? Should their training be oriented toward public relations, conversational English, or a combination? Hispanics may be trained to smile when approached by customers, but they will not be able to respond satisfactorily to customer questions if they cannot speak good English. What type of training is appropriate for the non-Hispanic attendants? Training objectives to meet both of these immediate needs might look like this:

Figure 10.3 Four-step process to determine which training activity is the most needed.

Program	Cost	Value Rank	Overall Effectiveness	Evaluation Cost as Percent of Training Cost
1. Executive/manager development	$1,200	4	Effective	28
2. Equal opportunity training	2,000	5	Unclear	17
3. Facility manager training[a]	1,500	7	Ineffective	5
4. Program supervisor training[a]	1,500	6	Ineffective	6
5. Formal education	3,000	8	Unclear	15
6. Entry-level technical training	4,000	2	Effective	4
7. Orientation	500	1	Unclear	7
7. Recreation internship	800	7	Ineffective	8
9. Preseason training	1,300	3	Effective	3.5

[a]Attendance at state and regional conferences and a few professional development schools.

221

1. Develop employee interpersonal skills to demonstrate promptness, enthusiasm, friendliness, and courteousness in responding to customer questions or requests for service.
2. Train employees on the proper approach and technique to serve customers, handle complaints, and answer questions about other park activities.
3. Teach conversation English to Hispanic employees, focusing attention on the questions asked most frequently.

If the Hispanics are full-time employees, long-range employee development objectives for this group of employees might be stated this way:

1. Teach basic oral communication skills in English until the employees can understand and respond to complex job-related instructions and explain their job tasks to English-speaking employees.
2. Teach basic written communication skills in English until the employee can prepare correspondence and written reports and read employee policy and procedure handbooks in English.

These long-range development objectives may take several years to accomplish, but they are aimed at developing present workers into fully productive employees who have a competitive chance for promotion within the organization in the future.

Training and development objectives should be simple, easily understood, and should specifically identify which new behavior or skills the employee is to demonstrate after completing the training or development program. Objectives should be kept within the experience and understanding of each individual employee in order to provide a focus for both the trainer and the employee. Evaluating training and development is also made easier because the success of the program is dependent on whether or not the specific objectives were met.

Selecting Training Methods and Learning Techniques

After determining which behavior, attitudes, or knowledge need adjusting, the next step in the process is to select the right training and development methods. There are advantages and disadvantages to every method, depending on the nature of the subject matter, the number of employees to be taught, and the organization's financial or training resources.

On-the-Job Training.   On-the-job training (OJT) is the most common form of training and developing employees because it is relatively inexpensive, because it provides "hands-on" experience which facilitates learning transfer, because it does not require separate classrooms or special techniques for training and development, and because the employee can be productive for the employer while learning the job skills. There are also disadvantages to OJT. These include costly mistakes, damage to equipment, frustration for both the supervisor and the immediate employee, customer dissatisfaction, and the loss of considerable time as the supervisor spends many hours training or developing employees to master a new technique or assignment.[10]

SUPERVISORY ASSISTANCE. The most informal approach to OJT is supervisory assistance through day-to-day observation, coaching, and counseling. This technique is effective only if the supervisor provides immediate feedback, takes the time to create feelings of employee self-confidence, and delegates more and more responsibility as the employee is able to handle it.

JOB INSTRUCTION. This method is used to train employees in specific tasks which can be completed in a logical sequence of steps. It breaks a single task down into smaller steps and is useful in training employees in the care and operation of equipment or where safety is a consideration. It ties up the use of equipment, however, and interferes with productivity until the tasks are learned.

EMPLOYEE SHARING. In larger departments a committee of employees may be charged to investigate a particular problem by gathering pertinent data. When they report back with their findings, other employees benefit from the report by listening at staff meetings. Similarly, field trips encourage information sharing. Employees are taken to other organizations to observe programs or functional operations, such as an ice rink, a wave pool, or specialized maintenance procedures.

JOB ROTATION. Another common form of OJT is job rotation in which the employee is moved from job to job at planned intervals as either an observer or worker. It is expected that the employee will eventually assume some supervisory or management position. This program does not give the employee full responsibility in any of the jobs because the stay in any one job is too short. Some employees may be given special assignments to gain firsthand experience in budgeting, long-range planning, problem solving, or coordinating a project.

ASSISTANTSHIPS. These may be formal or informal arrangements where the employees work closely with a superintendent or manager to learn a wide range of jobs. This approach ensures the employer of trained employees to assume key positions in the future.

Several methods combine both OJT and off-the-job training in order to realize the advantage of both environments. Apprenticeships and internships fall into this area of training and development.

APPRENTICESHIPS.   This training combines on-the-job training under the supervision of an experienced journeyman, with related classroom instruction. This learning method is mandatory for more than 700 occupations, such as the culinary arts, electronics, carpentry, and plumbing.[11] There are approximately 48,000 skilled trades apprenticeship programs in this country, with the average training period lasting four years.[12] The apprenticeship involves a cooperative relationship between unions, employers, and vocational schools. These programs are formally defined by the U.S. Department of Labor's Bureau of Apprenticeship and Training.

INTERNSHIPS.   From a national perspective, internship programs (also referred to as fieldwork practicums) are less formalized than apprenticeships, but they do involve an agreement between employers and colleges and universities. This type of OJT is more frequently found in park, recreation, and leisure settings. Interns receive close supervision from both the employer and the university, and the work schedule is usually varied and carefully planned to provide learning opportunities in all functions within the organization. Interns are usually paid less than full-time employees, and many internships are voluntary.

Off-the-Job Training.   Off-the-job training and development methods include a number of different formal program structures, such as workshops, conferences, and classrooms, and techniques such as role playing, case studies, and simulations. Many of the learning techniques may be used in conjunction with different formal program structures and with different media approaches, such as video taping or film recording. The possible combinations are as numerous as the training officer's imagination and the available financial resources. In addition, formal course methods may be self-directed (such as programmed instruction) or they may involve large groups in seminars or formal classrooms.

Self-directed learning is cumulative. Facts or problems are presented in a workbook, on a video tape, or on a computer. The trainee responds and feedback is provided on the accuracy of the response. Information is divided into segments to allow the employee to learn at her or his own pace, thereby reducing the risk of repeated mistakes. When knowledge such as interpersonal skills cannot be taught through self-directed methods, group learning structures must be utilized.

Metropolitan Dade County Park and Recreation Department offers excellent examples of group learning structures which are developed by a full-time staff of training specialists. Approximately 860 Dade County park and recreation employees and supervisors and twelve participating local agencies are served by dozens of work-related educational workshops, seminars, lecture series, and demonstrations. Attendance is voluntary and all participation is recorded on an individual employee training record. Departmental certificates of completion are also provided.

To avoid conflicts, the training specialists prepare an annual calendar of offerings which is sent to 200 supervisors and section heads (see Figure 10.4). This enables supervisors to assign employees logically to appropriate training classes. The diverse nature of the programs involves many job skills, ranging from zookeeper to stock clerk and computer programmer to tree trimmer.

Approximately 26 percent of the training is provided by a unique on-the-road mobile program which uses a van equipped with audiovisual equipment. This popular training effort takes the information out in the field right to the worker.

Professional Development Programs. Development programs for supervisors, managers, administrators, and executives are found in many fields of endeavor. They may be offered by colleges and universities, private companies, or professional associations such as the American Management Association (AMA), the American Society for Training and Development, and the National Recreation and Park Association (NRPA). Management development is important because promotion from within is a major source of talent. According to Dessler, 90 percent of supervisors, 73 percent of middle-level managers, and 51 percent of all executives are promoted from within the organization.[13] Management development programs prepare employees to assume higher-level positions by teaching them those skills needed at each level of management.

NRPA, through its Division of Professional Services, publishes a very detailed calendar each year on scores of state society and regional conferences, workshops, forums, and schools offering development opportunities in recreation, park, and leisure services. Many of these NRPA educational programs offer continuing education units (CEUs). A CEU represents ten hours of participation in an organized continuing education program under responsible sponsorship and qualified instruction. The CEU is a nationally recognized criterion of participation in professional development education programs. More than 1,000 colleges keep records on CEUs earned from their training and development programs. The NRPA and most state societies also keep records for participation at recognized CEU professional development sessions. Although CEUs cannot be used to obtain degree-granting credit at most universities, they are required by state park and recreation societies that have adopted the NRPA Certification Plan discussed in Appendix F. It is becoming increasingly important for professionals and technicians working in recreation, park, or leisure services to participate in those training and development programs that offer CEUs.

Figure 10.4 One-month excerpt from Dade County's calendar of training and development programs. (Courtesy of Metro-Dade Park & Recreation—Personnel Development.)

PRESENTED BY

PARK & RECREATION — PERSONNEL DEVELOPMENT
CALL 258-3103

SEPTEMBER

SUNDAY	MONDAY	TUESDAY	WEDNESDAY	THURSDAY	FRIDAY	SATURDAY
	"On-The-Road" - Basic Building Care You Choose The Time And Day Call 258-3103			1	2	Next Month's Program Safety On The Job
4	5 Labor Day	6 Tool and Equipment Control	7 Roger's-On-The-Green "Creative Decision Making"	8 Time Management Purchasing Procedure North Division	9 Slide Production Program	Successful Communication Continued Building Maintenance Finance Review & Interpretation
11	12	13 P.E.R.T. Planning Workshop	14 Tool and Equipment Control	15 Time Management	16	Heavy Equipment Safety Roger's-On-The Green "Team Of Two"
18	19 Successful Communication For Career Employees	20 READ THE LABEL STOP BEFORE USING PESTICIDES	21 New Hire Orientation Tool and Equipment Control	22	23	Dealing With The Public Landscape Supervisors' Luncheon Horticulture Film Festival
25	26 Supervisor Training Successful Communication Continued	27 Pesticide Certification	28 Landscape Supervisors' Luncheon	29 Supervisors' Meeting	30	New Hire Orientation Performance Evaluation Workshop

PLEASE NOTE: This schedule is tentative, consult the flyers sent each month for details or call 258-3103

When employees are given leave to return to high school or college to attend classes, it is referred to as formal education. Employees may be reimbursed for tuition, books, and transportation costs. These benefits serve as an inducement to continue formal education.

There are distinct disadvantages to all formal group methods of learning. (1) They require participants to be absent from their jobs, which can be costly for the employer and reduce or delay productivity. (2) Participants must also be able to make the learning transition from off-the-job to on-the-job. (3) It is difficult to hold the interest and attention of participants in larger groups, for which the lecture is a very popular teaching technique. (4) Most of the formal education methods of learning require good verbal and written skills.

Simulation Training.   Simulation is a teaching technique preferred to the lecture. It presents participants with equipment or situations that are similar to those of real job conditions. Games, case studies, role playing, and behavior modeling training are simulation techniques in which participants solve real-life management problems. Simulation is particularly necessary where on-the-job training is too expensive or dangerous. Law enforcement, cardiopulmonary resuscitation, and water safety instruction are examples of situations which require that employees learn through simulation before applying knowledge or skills on the job.

Films, closed-circuit television or video tapes are excellent media for simulation techniques. Employees can observe how a specific operation should be handled as many times as necessary before actually doing it on the job. Audiovisuals are more expensive than case studies but greatly enhance simulation training.

CASE STUDIES.   This technique presents specific scenarios in writing to a group of employees. Participants utilize group discussion to analyze and test their ideas. Feedback is immediate. Real-life situations with real-life personalities make the learning more interesting. For example, a supervisor may have to decide on which of several corrective disciplinary actions are appropriate for a disruptive subordinate.

ROLE PLAYING.   In role playing, employees assume the characteristics of specific persons in a given situation in order to act out a real-life scenario. Role players must respond with their own personalities, however, as they explore leadership, delegation, disciplinary, or other supervisory or decision-making skills. Some employees do not learn well from this technique because they feel childish in acting roles. They see the exercise as a waste of time.

BEHAVIOR MODELING.   Behavior modeling training may utilize both role playing and videotapes in giving simulation participants an opportunity to handle day-to-day situations such as those on the job. Courses may be conducted over a long period of time where the leader encourages participants to use observed skills in practice sessions. This technique tries to get employees to choose unconsciously the ideal way to handle any one situation.[14] Videotaping interview role plays, for example, is a good way for employees to see their strengths and weaknesses, gaining helpful insight into interview techniques.

COMPUTER AND BOARD GAMES. These media techniques provide simulated markets and environments where employees must compete with each other for limited resources or for a target population's leisure dollars. Complex decisions are required in advertising, capital development, pricing, staffing, purchasing, and program offerings. The employees must get actively involved, and active involvement enhances learning. Games are usually interesting because of their realism and competitiveness and are good for developing problem-solving skills and controlling multiple units of data and information overload.

IN-BASKET EXERCISES. In contrast, an in-basket exercise is a more solitary activity where the employee works through a stack of papers of the type that would be found on the average manager or director's desk. The trainee must prioritize the importance of each paper, recommend solutions to problems, and take whatever action is necessary. Management games and in-basket exercises are good training techniques and have proven useful in identifying employees for potential promotion and additional development in the future.[15]

EXPERIENTIAL LEARNING. Experiential learning techniques focus on getting participants to interact with one another and to express their feelings. There is no attempt to learn new skills or to solve management problems. The emphasis is on solving human relations problems and on discovering what motivates people and how to deal with time more effectively. A number of human relations training techniques may be used, but most of them require the direction of trained psychologists. Sometimes these techniques can backfire unless highly specialized leaders know how to bring a group together successfully.[16]

Experiential methods explore ways to establish more open and harmonious working environments. They are designed to change employee values, behaviors, and attitudes so that they can become more responsive and adaptable to organizational and societal changes. Some of these methods actually aim at developing a group of employees into highly functional working teams which can identify problems, gather and interpret data, and plan solutions.

Sensitivity training, psychodrama, transactional analysis, assertiveness training, and *team building* are all experiential methods which advocate learning about the self in order to bring about behavior changes. New self-perceptions are supposed to help employees develop new behaviors.

Increasing Learning Potential

Selecting the right training method and techniques to meet stated training objectives does not ensure the success of the training and development effort. Success also depends on the presence of an appropriate learning environment. Such an environment incudes the application of learning principles by knowledgeable, sensitive supervisors or trainers; and instilling in the worker before the program the desire to learn.

Learning Environment

Every person who has ever sat for several hours in a hot room on an uncomfortable chair knows that the learning environment can enhance or distract from the learning experience. A room that introduces too many interruptions makes it equally difficult for the learner to give full attention to the subject. Any program format that requires intense mental concentration for more than six hours in one day is designed to be counterproductive to its purpose. Similarly, if the employees are isolated for several days and nights in a new environment, special consideration should be given to their "off-duty" needs. If the only recreation option is a bar that serves alcoholic beverages, the trainers can expect to see a few tired, hungover employees the next morning unable to maximize learning opportunities. Leisure professionals should be able to offer a few recreation and exercise alternatives to television or drinking.

Learning Principles

The application of learning principles should be consciously planned into every training activity. Figure 10.5 offers the reader nine learning principles, simply stated. One of the most important principles is to reinforce a person for learning something new. Without some kind of reinforcement, a word of encouragement, for example, people find it difficult to sustain a high level of motivation.[17] The reward of success and a sense of achievement also have a great transfer value back to the regular job assignment.

Since individuals are motivated to repeat newly learned behavior if they experience some type of success, training should be short in duration and teaching should impart smaller units of information. In this way the learner receives immediate feedback and reinforcement (reward or praise) for demonstrating the new skill or applying new knowledge.

Nine Learning Principles

1. We learn best when we receive immediate feedback on our progress and reinforcement that we are learning.
2. A reward for desired behavior stimulates us to repeat the behavior.
3. We learn best when we are highly motivated to want to learn.
4. We learn faster those things that give us the most satisfaction.
5. We learn by doing.
6. We learn best those things that are related to our past experience.
7. If the content of learning is simple, it is best to learn the entire unit at once. But if the operation is complex, learning the tasks in sequential order is best because we learn best when we learned in the preceding step.
8. We learn faster and can better apply the information if we know why the information or new technique is important.
9. We learn best when instruction uses most of our senses—hearing, seeing, touching, smelling.

Figure 10.5

Shorter learning blocks also help to reduce frustration and discouragement, emotions that interfere with learning.

Once the employee has learned the new work method, he or she needs time to practice. We learn best by doing. This is especially important in the development of skills. The supervisor can teach the worker how to line a ball field, but practice will make the worker proficient at it. Several of you are asking "How can we practice theories and concepts?" A number of training methods were discussed under the third step of the training and development process, which facilitates the learning of concepts. These included, among others, case studies, simulations, and role plays.

Another important learning principle involves participation planning. Workers are more likely to be enthusiastic and supportive of a training activity if they are involved in helping to identify the training need, establishing the training objectives, and perhaps even planning the program. Autocratic management can lead to resentment, another emotion that does not facilitate learning.

Preparing the Worker to Learn

Most people will learn only enough to satisfy their own personal objectives. When learning satisfies short-term needs, the supervisor may have to prepare the employee to extend himself or herself to learn material that meets long-term objectives. The following true story illustrates this point.

An older employee asked to attend a half-day maintenance workshop offered locally because he wanted to get the latest information on pesticides. The supervisor thought it was in the best interest of the organization to send the employee away for a six-day maintenance management school. The well-meaning supervisor ordered the employee to go but made no attempt to shape the attitude or thinking of the employee to want to attend the longer program. Resentful (and afraid of failing the exam given at the end of the school), the older employee attended the six-day school in another state, but he sat in his room every evening and made no attempt to make new contacts or gain knowledge outside the classroom. Suffice it to say, the learning opportunities were not maximized for either the employer or the employee. In this situation, the supervisor should have remembered that each employee approaches a learning experience with different motives and needs different words of encouragement. The right preparation would have made the difference between a motivated employee gaining much from the maintenance school or the fearful, resentful employee who learned little.

Older workers are generally stable, careful, and reliable; characteristics that usually produce good-quality work and loyalty for the employing agency. These are good reasons to invest in training or retraining the older worker. But the supervisor needs to recognize that the older worker may experience special anxieties about failure. "Am I too old to learn new habits or new techniques?" This anxiety could be an asset for the supervisor if it is channeled toward giving the older worker self-confidence before the training program begins. This is not difficult to do because the older worker has already proven his or her ability. The supervisor is only asking the worker to transfer that ability into a new area of operation because the worker is a valuable resource for the organization.

Whether training is aimed at an older worker or a younger worker, the supervisor needs to recognize into which of three types of categories the worker falls:

1. The employee is not performing because she does not know what is expected in terms of standards.
2. The employee is not performing because she does not care and does not want to perform better.
3. The employee is not performing because she is hindered by some physical or mental impediment, or because she was put into the wrong job in the first place.

Willing Learner.   The easiest type of employee to prepare is the employee who wants to learn about new equipment or wants to try new methods in order to perform better. Training an eager, experienced worker is much like teaching a new employee except that the trainer may not have to begin instruction at the very beginning. A simple explanation about why the training is necessary to improve the quality of work or to reduce effort should be the only introduction needed to put the worker at ease and in a good frame of mind to learn.

Unwilling Learner.   It is the worker who has no interest in learning something new or seems unwilling to cooperate that presents a real challenge to the supervisor. It is not a matter of putting him at ease, but a problem of gaining his cooperation. This employee may be on the defensive because he feels that the supervisor is critical of him as a person or critical of his present level of work. Even if he knows that he is below performance standards, he will resist any attempt at retraining. In this situation the supervisor will want to try an indirect approach such as: "Your job must be frustrating having to make all those calls for information. We want to try and make it easier on you by placing a computer terminal and monitor on your work desk." Another indirect approach might include transferring the blame onto earlier training: "I did not do a very good job explaining that procedure last year, so I would like you to listen to an expert for a few hours next week." This approaches enable the employee to save face and correct performance.

Other employees appear lazy and do not seem to want to make the effort to learn something new. This poses the problem of how to motivate them to want to change. The solution might be as simple as giving the employee more recognition and generous praise, or it might require lengthy counseling sessions. The supervisor should also recognize that training may not be the answer for every employee. Training may be seen as a waste of time by those employees who are not interested in doing their job satisfactorily. The answer for these employees may lay in changing jobs, transfer, or termination.

Special Considerations.   The third training category into which workers might fall is one in which workers are not performing because they were either placed in the wrong job initially or are experiencing a recent physical or mental impediment. If vehicular equipment was designed to be operated by 5 foot 8 inch males, a 4 foot 11 inch female may experience difficulty in controlling the clutch or brakes while trying to see where to maneuver the vehicle. Training will not reduce her number of accidents. If the equipment cannot be modified to enable the short worker to perform better, the short worker should be trained for other duties without being made to feel incompetent.

If the work impediment did not exist at the time of hiring, the worker may be worrying about the problem and not able to keep her mind on her work. She may be irritable with the public or her coworkers. These conditions impede concentration and motivation and make training less effective. If lower productivity is a result of heart trouble or back pains, the supervisor needs to determine if the problem is temporary or permanent. The worker may have to be reassigned responsibilities where the impediment is not an obstacle to good performance.

In all situations relating to this third category of employees, the supervisor needs to address two questions: (1) Do they have the capability to successfully perform in their present positions? (2) Would they benefit from training or retraining? If the answer to both questions is "yes," here are some important points for the supervisor to remember.

1. Make the employee feel wanted. Stress that training is good business, not charity. Build self-confidence by being tactful.
2. Encourage the employee to work at her own pace. Emphasize that speed in learning is not as important as learning the new material. Do not push the employee during training. She may feel she is being reprimanded for being slower than other trainees.
3. Be patient in correcting mistakes. Repeat practice sessions as often as possible, giving additional encouragement.
4. Do not forget about the employee after the training has been completed. Observe behavior and performance. Offer suggestions if necessary and be generous in praise for improved performance.

The supervisor who knows his or her employees will be able to utilize the best approach in each case when introducing and preparing the worker for retraining or training opportunities. A well-planned training program to meet the most practical objectives is doomed to failure if the participating employees have not been prepared for the learning experience.

Evaluating the Effectiveness of Training and Development

If training and development costs represent major investments for employers, how does management know if these investments achieve any results? Is it possible to measure the degree of success of training and development efforts? Unfortunately, few organizations take the time to measure training and development results, except informally, through supervisor observations and performance appraisals.[18] It is not uncommon for an organization to send four employees each year to a nationally recognized development program, at a total cost of $2,400. But it is most unlikely that any attempt is made to determine how much the four employees learned, or if more information could have been attained at less expense from a different program, or whether the knowledge gained was ever transferred into better work performance once the employees returned to work. Most decision makers accept training and development programs at face value because they do not understand the importance of evaluation or because they do not understand the methods of evaluation.[19]

It is important to determine how well a program achieves its objectives and whether any changes in employee behavior or other measurement criteria occurred because of a specific training program. There are a number of assessment techniques which can be used to evaluate the effectiveness of training and development, but not all of them are reliable or useful. In fact, there appears to be some correlation between ease in administering an evaluation technique and the usefulness of the evaluation results. In other words, the simpler the evaluation technique, the less reliable may be the results in determining the success of a particular training program.[20]

Survey Questionnaire and Interview.   The most common evaluation technique has been the survey questionnaire distributed to trainees or program participants at the completion of the program. Employees are asked for their reactions to three things: (1) What is the value of what you learned to your present or future job? (2) How effective were the presentors or trainers? (3) How appropriate was the learning environment and teaching technique? Sometimes opinions are sought through interviews once the employees have returned to work. Whichever approach is used, there is no guarantee that an employee's performance will change just because he or she has a favorable impression about a particular training experience. Conferences may be fun and intellectually stimulating, but once the employee returns to work, nothing may change. This is not to say that conferences are not valuable educational experiences, but it is difficult to evaluate the effectiveness of those programs through survey instruments that seek to measure opinions and not learning or behavioral changes.

Tests.   Some training methods, such as formal education programs, apprenticeships, internships, and simulations, use tests as a means of evaluating learning. Students are tested to determine if they learned those principles, facts, or skills they were supposed to learn. It is not easy to develop a written test which time after time actually measures those things for which it is intended to measure. But assuming that a good test measures that which it purports to evaluate, there is no guarantee, again, that learning will transfer to job application and performance improvement once the employee is back on the job. Learning does not always mean behavioral change.

Observations. If the main purpose of training is to cause a change in employee behavior in order to improve the effectiveness of the organization, training and developing evaluation should really measure employee behavior on the job, rather than their reactions to the training program. In the absence of surveys or tests, the comparison of employee performance before and after instruction is the technique used by most organizations. The supervisors look for improvement in work performance when the employee returns to his or her job and may even document improvement on performance appraisals records.

This technique also has its weaknesses. Although performance may have improved, can the training specialist and supervisor know for sure that it was the training that caused the behavior to change? If employee morale seems improved and productivity levels increase, can these changes be attributed to a successful training program; or did morale improve because of the change in routine or because employees had a chance to spend time together in a learning situation?

Measuring the Value of Job Changes. The evaluation method that has the most potential for effectively evaluating training and development is one that measures results.[21] This means that the evaluation technique tries to determine whether or not (or to which degree) training brought about the desired change in those criteria that measured organizational climate or productivity. If the program's objective was to improve job skills, the evaluation criterion might be a measurable decrease in the number of accidents. If the objective was to improve public relations, the evaluation criterion would be a reduction in park user complaints, or perhaps vandalism. This "result" technique can become very complicated and needs input from training and personnel specialists. Measuring the dollar value of absenteeism or productivity requires the application of complex models, formulas, and statistical interpretations.

Once the decision is made on what criteria should be measured in the evaluation process—opinions, behavior, skills, knowledge, or job results—the next step is to design the evaluation procedures. The best procedure, of course, would be a training program that involves controlled experimentation. This means that the employer would randomly select some employees to receive training, while other employees, representing the control group, would receive no training. Measurements of the evaluation criteria would be taken before and after training in both groups. This would enable the evaluators to demonstrate better the extent any changes in the trained group of employees occurred because of the training rather than some other cause, such as change in routine.

Controlled experimentation procedures are not commonly used for training and development evaluation.[22] Their use not only increases the

---

PLANNING FORMAT FOR A TRAINING PROGRAM ON SELECTION INTERVIEWS

Purpose: To train all supervisors in appropriate interview techniques to ensure compliance with all EEO legislation and the hiring of qualified employees.
Target group: All recreation program supervisors and specialists.
Objectives:
    (a) Determine the best sources from which to gather information on each candidate
    (b) Establish a format and appropriate questions for interviewing.
    (c) Develop selection criteria and evaluation procedure.
    (d) Create best interview environment.
Training program content: Topics covered will include the interview planning and preparation process; establishing rapport and maintaining open dialogue; selecting the appropriate interview technique; the importance of the interview environment; review of illegal questions and topics of conversation; and developing appropriate interview questions and interview evaluation criteria. Participants will role play several different interview situations and later observe their behavior on videotape. Consultant will guide discussion.
Program structure: Workshop, three hours.
Learning technique: Brief lecture, question-and-answer period, and simulation role play utilizing videotape recording and play back.
Instructor: Consultant from University of Akron, Ohio: professor and author Candace Faulk.
Participant preparation: Each supervisor and specialist will be given four brief scenarios which require their review before the workshop. Scenarios are designed to be provocative and raise questions.
Evaluation technique: Survey questionnaire and monitoring for one year the rate of EEO interview complaints, early "quits," and number of "turn-downs" after job offer.

Figure 10.6

cost of the training program, but most organizations would have difficulty randomly assigning employees to training and development activities. Smaller park and recreation agencies do not have the numbers of employees in each job category; therefore, everyone is trained. This procedure would also tend to impact negatively on the affirmative action commitment to improve job skills of minorities and women.

So what is the answer to evaluation if every technique has its weaknesses and the best designed evaluation procedure cannot be utilized in most organizations? The answer to those questions continues to challenge supervisors and training specialists and probably explains why so many organizations without training specialists do not even bother to evaluate their training efforts formally except through observation, testing, or attitude surveys. But the importance of evaluation is not diminished because current evaluation methodologies contain flaws. Evaluating the effectiveness of training and development is a critical step in the total process. Conscientious attention must be given to measuring tangible benefits from training. The position that training and development is important to the employer and not just an employee fringe benefit cannot be defended if it cannot be demonstrated that there is a positive relationship between training and improved job performance. See Figure 10.6 for an example of the format needed for planning a training program.

Summary and Recommendations

1. Training teaches employees specific job-related skills, techniques, or information necessary to perform satisfactorily in their present jobs. Development concentrates on preparing the employee to meet the work objectives of some future job responsibility.
2. Training and development (T/D) not only improve job performance and attitudes toward work, but they serve to further affirmative action objectives, retain and atrract good employees, and reduce turnover. It has been documented that T/D is cost effective.
3. Effective T/D involves a five-step process. First, training and development needs must be determined. Second, objectives must be established that identify which types of skills the employee is to learn. Next, the appropriate program structure and learning technique must be developed and the right instructor or facilitator identified. Fourth, the supervisor is responsible for ensuring that maximum learning take place by preparing the worker for training and development. Last, the T/D program must be evaluated to learn whether or not the objectives established in step 2 were met. Figure 10.6 offers the reader a planning format that utilizes all the steps in the training and development process.
4. The function of determining T/D needs and designing an effective program is complex. It requires the input and cooperation of the supervisor, training specialists, and the support of management. Some individual or unit must provide the overall guidance and assume the responsibility for the entire process.
5. Job needs analysis identifies which skills at which competency level are necessary to perform each job. Employee needs analysis determines who needs additional training to satisfy those skill requirements. Organizational needs analysis helps to determine the priority of training efforts in relationship to their value to the organization.
6. There are many on-the-job and off-the-job T/D methods and techniques, each with its own advantages and disadvantages. On-the-job training is the most popular because it is inexpensive and facilitates learning transfer by giving the worker hands-on experience.

7. It is becoming increasingly important that recreation, park, and leisure professionals and technicians attend T/D programs that offer CEUs. Most state societies and the NRPA require that nationally certified employees earn two CEUs every two years in order to maintain their professional certification on the National Roster.

8. There are several disadvantages of formal group methods of learning, but these can be minimized if the learning technique of simulation training is used rather than the traditional lecture approach. Simulation presents the learners with situations that are similar to their real job conditions and involves them in skill building, knowledge application, or problem solving.

9. Successful T/D also depends on the selection of a good learning environment free from distractions and the application of recognized learning principles. Employees will learn best when they are motivated to want to learn, when they receive immediate feedback and reinforcement, and when they understand why the learning is important.

10. If the organization is to continue to fund training and development, managers must be able to see changes in employee behavior that result in increased productivity or client/patron satisfaction.

11. The most common evaluation technique has been to ask the learners if they liked the training and development program and if they can use the learned material back on the job. But this technique does not measure behavioral changes or changes in services to the public.

12. The best evaluation procedure is one that measures results and not learner opinions or skill development. Although "result"-oriented procedures are complicated and need the input from training specialist, conscientious attention must be given to measuring tangible benefits from training and development programs.

Discussion Topics

1. Why is training and development so important to organizations? What are the benefits to the organizations?

2. What role should the federal government play in training people so that they are able to work?

3. How is training and development related to EEO and other personnel functions such as recruitment?

4. Why is it so important to do an analysis of the organization in order to determine training needs? How is this type of analysis related to job analysis and employee analysis?

5. Why is it important to try to increase the learning potential of trainees? How might we accomplish that?

6. Why are the principles of learning important to employee training and development?
7. What are some of the disadvantages of off-the-job training and development?
8. What are CEUs and why have they become important in recent years to the recreation, park resources, and leisure services field?
9. What are the major steps in the training and development process?
10. Why do organizations overlook or lack proper evaluation of employee training and development programs?

Notes

1. Randall Schuler, *Personnel and Human Resource Management*, 2nd ed. (St. Paul, Minn.: West Publishing Co., 1984), p. 385.
2. William Kent and Fred Otte, "Career Management: The Ultimate Incentive" *Advanced Management Journal* (Spring 1982): 9.
3. Dale Beach, *Personnel: The Management of People at Work*, 4th ed. (New York: Macmillan Publishing Company, 1980) p. 359.
4. Paul Preston and Thomas Zimmer, *Management for Supervisors*, 2nd ed. (Englewood Cliffs, N.J.: Prentice-Hall, Inc., 1983), p. 197.
5. Schuler, *Personnel and Human Resource Management*, 2nd ed., p. 394.
6. Kent and Otte, "Career Management," p. 11.
7. Meryl Louis, "Managing Career Transition: A Missing Link in Career Development," *Organizational Dynamics* (New York: AMACOM, Periodicals Division, American Management Association, Spring 1982), p. 70.
8. Basil Deming, *Evaluating Job Related Training* (Washington, D.C.: American Society for Training and Development, 1982), p. 117.
9. Ibid., p. 123.
10. Schuler, *Personnel and Human Resource Management*, 2nd ed., p. 406.
11. Ibid.
12. Wendell French, *The Personnel Management Process*, 4th ed. (Boston: Houghton Mifflin Company, 1978), p. 337.
13. Gary Dessler, *Personnel Management: Modern Concepts and Techniques* (Reston, Va.: Reston Publishing Co., Inc., 1984), p. 257.
14. Jack Halloran, *Supervision: The Art of Management* (Englewood Cliffs, N.J.: Prentice-Hall, Inc., 1981), p. 150.
15. Schuler, *Personnel and Human Resource Management*, 2nd ed., p. 408.
16. Halloran, *Supervision*, p. 150.
17. Lawrence Steinmetz and Ralph Todd, *First Line Management: Approaching Supervision Effectively* (Plano, Tex.: Business Publications, Inc., 1979), p. 273.
18. Dessler, *Personnel Management*, p. 248.
19. Randall Schuler, *Personnel and Human Resource Management* (St. Paul, Minn.: West Publishing, Co., 1981), p. 348.
20. Beach, *Personnel*, p. 377.
21. Dessler, *Personnel Management*, p. 249.
22. Schuler, *Personnel and Human Resource Management*, 2nd ed., p. 414.

11

Discipline and Grievances

Prior to the era of collective bargaining and federal, state, and local labor laws, managers could discipline employees as arbitrarily, inconsistently, and harshly as they chose. Through the years this posture has changed. Employers have exercised more care in demonstrating fair treatment in disciplining workers and listening to their complaints. There is some evidence that management has actually seen the wisdom of establishing and administering a fair disciplinary policy and a sound grievance procedure because it thwarts efforts to unionize workers.[1] Employees have little need for union protection if management is fair in administering discipline and in handling grievances. Management has also been careful in recent years because it is not uncommon for disgruntled employees to appeal to the courts if they believe management acted unfairly out of bias.

Nature of Discipline on the Job

Historically, discipline has had a punative connotation in the work environment. It represented punishment for misconduct or for failure to perform according to established standards. The threat of punishment was often used by employers to keep employees on the job producing goods and services. Fear of punishment was expected to deter employees from misconduct. This approach to discipline is negative. It does not focus on worker cooperation to enforce rules and creates an "us" versus "them" atmosphere.

The word *discipline* comes from the word *disciple*. A disciple is a person who willingly follows the teachings and examples of a respected leader. If this definition is applied on the job, employees become willing disciples who respect and follow the leadership of their supervisors. This more positive definition implies "self-discipline," where workers cooperate and behave in relative harmony.

Discipline can be either negative or positive. Negative discipline eliminates undesirable behavior by punishing or hurting employees. Positive discipline encourages self-control. This chapter adopts the positive definition of discipline whereby supervisors take only those actions necessary to correct misconduct. Employees accept standards of behavior because it makes the work environment a better place to work for everyone. *Positive discipline involves creating an organizational climate where employees exercise self-control and willingly conform to recognized rules of behavior in order to maintain a better working environment for everyone.*

When employees do not exercise self-discipline, they violate rules of behavior and jeopardize the harmony of the work place. When this happens, it is the responsibility of the supervisor to take corrective action for the benefit of all the employees. *Disciplinary action is the process that addresses employee misconduct by administering corrective action and thereby serves to maintain a safe, harmonious, and productive working environment.* The supervisor's job is to manage his or her work group by inspiration, not repression.

Establishing Guidelines

The maintenance of discipline in any organization is both the obligation and responsibility of management. Unions, the courts, and employees all agree that management has the right to decide what constitutes appropriate employee conduct. With this right goes the obligation to maintain reasonable standards of behavior by using good judgment. Most labor contracts express these sentiments in words such as "management may issue and promulgate such directives that are reasonable." Most employees are used to conforming to laws of the land which they believe are reasonable, are established in their best interests, and are fairly enforced.

To achieve a healthy state of discipline throughout the organization, management must decide what kind of behavior it expects from its employees, how to sustain that behavior and how to maintain consistency in subsequent disciplinary action. Management decisions should be formulated in written guidelines or rules. These guidelines should be a part of the personnel policy manual discussed in Chapter 6.

Elements of Disciplinary Guidelines

Guidelines should be easy to understand and reasonable in number. To satisfy the definition of positive discipline, guidelines should focus on self-discipline, preventive and rehabilitative measures, and not stress punishment in the form of many penalties. The following elements should be incorporated into all disciplinary guidelines. They are summarized in Figure 11.1.

Necessary. Rules must be aimed at furthering the interests of both the employer and employees, ensuring their collective health, safety, and welfare. Where behavior is unrelated to the success of the organization, there should be no rules to restrict such behavior. For example, it would be arbitrary for an organization to ban all background music from every workstation. What might be necessary is a rule restricting employees from wearing headphones in the workplace, because then they could not hear questions, instructions, or possible danger signals.

Reasonable. Every employee should be able to abide by every rule. Employees have different job requirements, abilities, and needs. It would be unreasonable to require that employees only visit the rest room on their scheduled breaks, require a doctor's statement as proof of illness for one day's absence, or demand that summer playground leaders wear the same clothing attire as workers in an air-conditioned office.

Enforceable. Another test for appropriateness is whether or not a rule can be enforced by the supervisor. It weakens the disciplinary action process if some rules cannot be enforced because they strive to control behavior beyond the jurisdiction of the supervisor. A rule forbidding

---

Ten Essential Elements of Disciplinary Guidelines

1.	Necessary	For the successful operation of the organization
2.	Reasonable	For employees to follow
3.	Enforceable	For the supervisors to administer
4.	Communicated	To every employee
5.	Consistent	Interpretation and application to all employees
6.	Flexible	For considering mitigating circumstances
7.	Timely	Due process in response to accusations
8.	Proof	Of "just cause"
9.	Penalties	Appropriate to the misconduct
10.	Progressive	In severity of corrective actions

Figure 11.1

nonrelated verbal communications on the job would be difficult to enforce because a supervisor cannot monitor every subordinate eight hours a day.

Communicated.   All rules, reasons for the rules, and the procedure to enforce those rules should be in written form, distributed throughout the organization, and explained to every employee by the supervisor. Arbitrators have ruled that employees cannot be expected to comply with regulations they do not know.[2] It is the responsibility of management to make known all disciplinary policies and rules. This can be done in pay envelopes, union contracts, memoranda and employee handbooks, on bulletin boards, at hiring interviews, during orientation, informally, and at staff meetings.

Some illegal or immoral acts are considered so obviously wrong that a specific rule may not be thought to be needed. Falsifying official documents and stealing valuables from dressing room lockers is so reprehensible that most employees should not have to be told that such behavior is unacceptable. But the employee still needs to know *what* will happen if such misconduct occurs.

Disciplinary policies and rules should be written so that every employee can understand them. A rule is not preventative if the supervisor interprets it one way and the grounds maintenance workers interpret it another way. It may be necessary to ask a sampling of employees in different work settings, in different positions, and with different educational backgrounds, for their interpretation of written rules. If the answers are very different, the written rules were not clearly stated and should be rewritten.

Consistent.   All supervisors should be consistent in their interpretation and application of written guidelines. Inconsistency or arbitrary application of the rules reduces employee respect for leadership. Policies quickly lose effectiveness if some rules are enforced, but not others, or if certain supervisors strictly enforce rules while others supervisors remain lax, or if harsher penalties are imposed on one employee for rule infraction but not for similar misconduct by other employees. Every employee should be treated with the same standards of conduct and judged by the same rules. Otherwise, employees will not be able to distinguish between acceptable and unacceptable conduct in the workplace.

Consistent application does not always mean equal application. Equal application implies identical treatment for breaking the same rule. Management must address each rule violation with equal seriousness, and employees must be approached every time they violate a rule. But the background and circumstances of each case may require different corrective action.

Flexible. Although consistent application of the guidelines means taking action each time a rule is violated, supervisors also need the flexibility to consider the mitigating circumstances that may have led to the rule infraction.

How should a park employee be disciplined in this situation? On Christmas Eve an employee drives a public vehicle into a neighborhood convenience store to make a purchase for the annual departmental Christmas party. The rules state that under no circumstances will government employees use public vehicles for personal reasons, but the employee remembered at the last minute that he had left his contribution to the party at home. When he went to the store to purchase the drinks, he was reported by a government official. The employee's supervisor was told to reprimand the employee for the rule violation. The supervisor chose to delay action until after Christmas. Was this action appropriate?

A flexible disciplinary policy will enable supervisors to consider all extenuating circumstances as well as the past record of the employee and the length of service with the organization. The effect the rule violation has on coworkers or program participants is another important consideration. Reprimanding the park employee on Christmas Eve might have demoralized the entire staff.

In some instances, the organization itself is guilty of perpetuating a working environment that leads to rule violation. If a policy prohibits the use of auxiliary space heaters or fans in offices, but maintains temperature controls beyond the normal range of comfort, employees have no choice but to be absent from work on very hot or cold days, or utilize auxiliary electrical appliances in order to function without discomfort. It is important that employees see corrective action as being both consistent and fair, but no set rules can identify in advance how different circumstances should be handled.

Timely Due Process. When rules are believed to have been violated, corrective action should be taken immediately. Union contracts usually stipulate three to five scheduled workdays for management to initiate discipline against an employee for rule infraction.[3] The reason for this clause is to prevent supervisors from initiating corrective action long after the incident has taken place and to minimize the time an employee must live under suspicion or accusation without the right to trial through due process. The anxiety associated with accusation can emotionally and physically hurt the employee and the employee's family. Employees are entitled to a timely impartial hearing or a discipline interview where guilt or innocence can be determined.

Another reason for prompt corrective action is to ensure that the penalty will be associated with the rule violation and to reduce the likelihood that the offense will be repeated in the future. Timely due process meets the objectives of positive discipline because an employee is more likely to reform if corrective action occurs right after the misconduct.[4]

Timeliness is also important in collecting "just cause" evidence to support the case for corrective action. Memories of what happened will fade with time and testimonies are weakened. It is possible that over a period of time peer pressure will influence witnesses not to give written or oral testimony.

Organizational guidelines should include a specific time period in which disciplinary action can be brought against an employee for misconduct. Timely action does not mean handing out penalties on the spot without investigation, but if supervisors do or say nothing when misconduct occurs, they appear to condone the violation.

Proof of "Just Cause."   In today's legal climate, where employees have the right to challenge any rule that deprives them of their rights, management has begun to require proof of misconduct from supervisors. Our society dictates that an accused person is presumed to be innocent until proven guilty by the accusor. Disciplinary guidelines should reflect this same principle of placing the burden of proof on the organization that accuses an employee of wrongdoing. Since the supervisor initiates disciplinary action, supervisors must demonstrate substantive reasons why corrective action is necessary. This is known as proving cause for discipline, or "just cause."

What is just cause? This is a difficult question to answer even for representatives of management, unions, and third-party arbitrators. There is no standardized definition, except that the employer must not react arbitrarily, unreasonably, or in bad faith (promising one thing and reacting differently later).

It is not necessary that the evidence of wrongdoing be conclusive or "beyond reasonable doubt," except where the behavior is criminal, might damage the employee's reputation, or prevent future employment.[5] If the just cause criterion is met, most arbitrators and courts will support the decision for corrective actions.

Penalties.   What is an appropriate penalty for breaking a rule? Is a verbal warning sufficient for a recreation aide who leaves preschool-aged children unattended for thirty minutes to visit with a friend? Is discharge appropriate for the laborer who falls asleep under a tree on a hot, humid day?

Disciplinary guidelines usually include a comprehensive list of rules that, if broken, will result in corrective action. There are differences of opinion about whether or not the guidelines should also include a uniform scale of penalties for each rule violation. Those opposed to such lists argue that each situation is different and must be evaluated according to extenuating circumstances. Those who favor such lists of rule violations and penalties argue the case of consistency, that a published list adds credibility to management's efforts to maintain discipline.

Almost all authorities agree that certain behaviors are so unacceptable and so serious that discharge is the only appropriate penalty. Sabotage of company equipment, gross insubordination, and flagrant sexual mis-

Figure 11.2   Four suggested classes of disciplinary action.

Suggested Disciplinary Action - Class 1		
Offense	**First Offense**	**Second Offense**
Absenteeism	Verbal warning	Warning and letter on record
Altering doctor's certificate	1-day or 3-day suspension	3-day or 7-day suspension
Dual employment	No action taken unless employee is falling down on job or a protest is entered by another employee. Employee must choose one employer	
Excessive personal or lunch time	Verbal warning	Letter on record
Failure to exert reasonable effort - loafing	Verbal warning	Letter on record
Forging supervisor's signature	Discipline would depend upon seriousness of offense, which could be considerable	
Leaving job early	Verbal warning	Letter on record
Outside activities	Verbal warning on first offense followed by progressive suspensions	
Sleeping on the job	Verbal warning	3-day or 7-day suspension
Tardiness	Verbal warning	Letter on record
Violation of conditions of leave	Verbal warning	Warning and letter on record
Loafing outside department	Verbal warning	1-day or 3-day suspension

Suggested Disciplinary Action - Class 2		
Offense	**First Offense**	**Second Offense**
Carelessness resulting in personal injury or damage to equipment	Letter on record	1-day or 3-day suspension
Defective work	Verbal warning	Letter on record
Insubordination - refusal to work	3-day suspension	7-day suspension
Poor attitude and lack of cooperation	Counseling and warning	Letter on record
Poor performance	Counseling and warning	Letter on record
Poor work habits	Counseling and warning	Letter on record
Reporting for work under influence	Verbal warning	Letter on record

Suggested Disciplinary Action - Class 3		
Offense	First Offense	Second Offense
Drinking on company premises	Letter on record	7-day suspension or discharge
Encouraging or instigating a work stoppage	Letter on record and 7-day suspension	Discharge
Fighting or assault upon another employee	3-day or 7-day suspension	7-day suspension or discharge
Gambling - bookmaking	Letter on record and 3-day suspension	7-day suspension or discharge
Horseplay	Verbal warning	Letter and short suspension
Possession of intoxicating liquor	3-day or 7-day suspension	7-day suspension or discharge
Smoking in unauthorized location	Verbal warning	Letter on record
Threatening a member of supervision	1-day or 3-day suspension	7-day suspension or discharge
Threatening another employee	1-day or 3-day suspension	7-day suspension or discharge
Use of abusive language	Verbal warning	Letter and short suspension
Work stoppage - participation	7-day suspension	Discharge

Suggested Disciplinary Action - Class 4		
Offense	First Offense	Second Offense
Altering specifications	Long suspension or discharge	Discharge
Carrying a dangerous weapon	Call in police department	Long suspension or discharge
Deliberate damage to equipment	Discharge	
Falsifying piece count	3-day suspension or 7-day suspension	Discharge
Forced entry	Discharge	
Ringing another employee's time card	3-day suspension	7-day suspension or discharge
Stealing	Discharge	
Assault on supervisor	Discharge	

conduct are but a few offenses that should rightly result in discharge. Some guidance is needed in order that supervisors fit the severity of the penalty to the seriousness of the misconduct. Each time an employee violates a rule, he or she should be told what penalty will be imposed the next time that same rule is broken. Figure 11.2 provides the reader with an example of what is meant by establishing minimum and maximum penalties for each offense.

Progressive Corrective Action.   Most authorities agree that the most effective policy is one where the application of disciplinary action is progressive in severity. *Progressive discipline attempts to modify behavior by providing for more severe corrective actions each time the employee breaks the same rule.*

Not all disruptive behaviors deserve five chances for reform, but in ascending order of severity, the following progressive corrective actions are most frequently recommended by management in disciplinary policies:

1. Counseling informally to make the employee aware of the violation.
2. Simple oral warning that is usually noted in the employee's personal file.
3. Written warning to the employee with a copy placed in the personal file. Also known as reprimand.
4. Suspension from the job without pay for one day to two weeks.
5. Discharge from the position.

These actions are explained in greater detail later in the chapter. Other types of punitive penalties, such as demotion and fines, are also discussed in the section "Stages of Corrective Action."

Administering the Disciplinary Process

In the preceding sections we discussed two of the four conditions that must exist before an organization can effectively maintain discipline on the job. This section explains the remaining two conditions. These conditions are:

1. Workers must want to exercise self-discipline in order to make the work environment a better place for everyone.
2. Management must establish written rules that set forth what type of behavior the organization expects from its workers.
3. Management must develop a process whereby supervisors know when and how to take corrective action when employees break the rules.
4. The disciplinary action process must include an appeals procedure which allows accused workers to defend themselves against charges of misconduct.

Supervisors must be trained to investigate cases of possible misconduct and then initiate appropriate disciplinary action without feeling guilty when evidence of guilt is found. It is important that supervisors un-

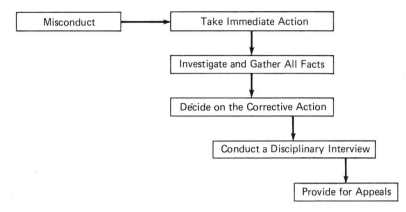

Figure 11.3 Administering the disciplinary process.

derstand that the disciplinary process and the appeals procedure are closely interrelated.

Administering the disciplinary process requires constant vigilance, sensitivity to employee needs and behavior, and regular review of policy for rule changes. The burden of administering the process falls on the supervisor. Figure 11.3 shows the ongoing phases of administering the disciplinary process.

Investigating Allegations of Misconduct

There are two purposes for investigating employee misconduct: to bring to light sufficient, pertinent facts to determine if a rule was violated, and to determine which disciplinary action is appropriate to correct the misconduct. To satisfy these purposes, investigations should be objective and fair. A series of questions serve as guidelines for the investigating supervisor.

1. *Was the rule broken?* Obviously, the best evidence that a rule was broken is admission of guilt—voluntarily given without coercion, threats, or promises of leniency—in writing and in front of a witness. The employee may request the presence of a coworker or a third, union representative during the investigative interview. The presence of this third party is to protect the accused from unfair treatment and to assist the employee in accurately relating the incident being investigated. Employers violate federal labor laws if they refuse an employee the right to bring a fellow worker to an investigative interview.[6]

If management does not want to have a third party present, it does not have to hold an investigation interview and may gather evidence through some other means without interviewing the accused employee.

But the National Relations Labor Board (NRLB) in a 1982 decision held that disciplinary action would be considered illegal if the employer unlawfully denied a request from the accused for a representative at an investigative interview and then later disciplined the employee for misconduct that was the subject of the illegal interview.[7]

Without a confession, the supervisor may rely on his own first hand knowledge of misconduct. If the supervisor did not see the rule violation, witnesses may be sought who observed the incident. Without the testimony of witnesses, other admissible evidence may be used as proof of guilt, such as the physical evidence of a doctor's medical report, official records from time clocks, or cash register audit tapes.

The use of circumstantial evidence or hearsay (secondhand information), is not a good practice because neither the supervisor nor the accused can challenge its accuracy. Arbitrators generally reject hearsay evidence and remain cautious about using circumstantial evidence.[8] The use of affidavits and sworn declarations result in the same problems. The persons giving testimony are not present to be cross-examined.

Naturally, evidence from any source must be relevant or logically related to the case. Past conduct may be considered in determining appropriate penalties, but past conduct should not be a determiner in whether or not the rule was actually broken on the date in question. Supervisors must be careful not to entrap employees into breaking rules in order to provide evidence of wrongdoing. Supervisors should also exercise care in searching employees' personal belongings, including desks, lockers, and files. These actions violate privacy rights and could result in lawsuits, grievance proceedings, or union complaints.

2. *If the rule was broken, did the employee know that he had broken a rule?* Is there adequate physical evidence that the employee had been forewarned about rules pertaining to unacceptable behavior, and that subsequent disciplinary action would follow if the rules were broken? Memoranda, notices, fliers, and written policies are important ways to communicate with employees about disciplinary guidelines, but if an employee cannot read, management must have documented evidence that the employee was told about the rule and resulting penalties for breaking the rules.

3. *If the rule was deliberately broken, were there related extenuating circumstances?* It is not uncommon for an employee to have financial or personal problems outside the job that reflect temporarily in behavior on the job. Workers under stress more quickly lose control and blow up at coworkers, the boss, or the public. In one case, a community center director knowingly disobeyed a directive from the mayor's office to close all public buildings at dark in order to conserve energy. The director was openly insubordinate by keeping his center open until 11:00 p.m. for a scheduled, end-of-season basketball tournament. Two considerations were carefully reviewed before deciding on the appropriate disciplinary action

in this case. First, the scheduled activity had been negotiated through contractual agreement two months previously, and five weeks before the mayor's directive. There was some question about the legality of breaking the contract. Second, the center was in a neighborhood where unemployment was high and residents had always supported the recreation programs and attended all evening events. Canceling the basketball tournament might have had a negative effect on the community's attitude toward the center, the entire park and recreation department, and government in general. Although the rule was broken, the extenuating circumstances played an important part in determining the corrective action—a written reprimand documenting all the details surrounding the incident. The supervisor also included in the employee's file a letter of commendation from a citizen leader in that particular community congratulating the center director for keeping the center open that night when the alternative might have resulted in disruptive, antisocial behavior in the neighborhood.

4. *How did breaking the rule affect the agency's operation, its image to the public, and the morale of other employees?* Rules are important because they help maintain the safe, efficient, and effective operation of a park and recreation agency. On occasion, rule violations may not adversely effect any one of the conditions of safety, efficiency, or effectiveness. Falling asleep in a staff meeting is not as critical as falling asleep in the gate house of a campground on Labor Day weekend. Employees building trails may exchange swear words all day long and not offend anyone, but employees picking up trash and litter at an amusement park would certainly offend most park patrons if they used foul language.

A supervisor may also have to consider whether or not the mistake or misbehavior was solely the fault of the accused worker, of if others were guilty. Is one employee taking the blame or being the scapegoat for everyone else? In one case of deliberate sabotage, the arbitrator ruled that although only one employee deliberately damaged the piece of equipment, five silent coworkers were guilty of conspiring to obstruct the investigation by remaining silent to protect their colleague. They, too, received a five-day suspension.[9]

5. *Does the employee have a history of misconduct?* If discipline is to produce change, how far back should supervisors look in reviewing an employee's work record to establish if the current offense is a continuation of unacceptable behavior or the start of new bad habits? Unions often argue that reference to a worker's past disciplinary record to determine appropriate corrective action actually constitutes double jeopardy, or being punished twice for one offense.[10] If after a reasonable period of time there are no recurring rule violations, the employee should be considered rehabilitated. Misconduct after that period of time should not be evaluated in the shadow of old incidents.

What is considered a reasonable length of time in which to consider past offenses? Labor management groups suggest no more than twelve months for less serious offenses; previous serious misconduct should be considered for eighteen to twenty-four months.[11] Should related offenses be considered in determining appropriate corrective action? One arbitrator of a labor management dispute ruled that disciplinary records of *related offenses* may also be used as a basis for corrective action for a period up to two years.[12]

6. *How have similar incidents been treated in the past?* Does the rule infraction carry a penalty that has been ignored or overlooked in the past? The supervisor who has a bad day, sees a subordinate eating a candy bar, and jumps on him for violating the rule about eating on the job is acting arbitrarily if it is a common practice for employees to eat snacks on the job. When rules are loosely enforced or ignored, a supervisor cannot suddenly enforce the rule without giving some warning to the workers.

7. *What should be the appropriate corrective action?* Four classes of offenses that cover a range of unsatisfactory behavior on the job have been suggested by W. H. Weiss:[13]

(a) Taking advantage of the company.
(b) Improper demeanor and conduct.
(c) Disruptive behavior.
(d) Criminal behavior.

Figure 11.2 lists the offenses in each class and suggests appropriate corrective action for both first and second offenses. These are only suggestions and the reader should remember that the supervisor must decide the right penalty after evaluating all the evidence produced in the investigation.

Stages of Corrective Action

Disciplinary guidelines should include the types of penalties that a supervisor can impose on an employee for misconduct. Labor contracts also outline the steps that management can take in corrective disciplinary action. The following five steps are progressive in severity of discipline and are commonly found in disciplinary policies and labor agreements.

1. *Counseling techniques* may be used by the supervisor or someone else in the organization to learn "why" the misconduct occurred in order to reduce the chances of recurrence. It is a suggested first step in progressive discipline to find out to what extent the misconduct occurred for reasons

of ignorance. An employee cannot be expected to control behavior that he or she did not think was wrong.

Counseling is also a good first step to learn if the misconduct may be caused by something outside the control of the employee. If an employee is late to work because the public transportation system is frequently behind schedule, the rule violation is not intentional. This is not to say that the organization will allow the tardiness to continue. Rather, counseling helps the employee to understand that other arrangements will have to be made to get to work on time.

Counseling is most effective when the employee accepts the fact of guilt and wants to remedy the situation to avoid further corrective action. The supervisor should keep the first counseling session informal, short, and relaxed so that the employee will not become nervous or anxious. With proper sensitivity on the part of the supervisor, the employee should not only change his or her behavior but return to work with a new perspective and a new feeling of loyalty to the organization.

2. *Oral warning* is more formal than counseling, although these steps may be combined. The employee is told that the noted misbehavior must be corrected and what the next penalty will be if the behavior is not corrected. In most cases, oral warning proves sufficient and the employee's behavior changes.[14] Too many warnings can result in a nagging atmosphere and can be just as bad as not giving any warning at all. Once the employee admits guilt and is told what must be done in the future, the warning is over. The employee and supervisor should depart on a friendly note and the supervisor should follow up later with a friendly contact without mentioning the warning. Most organizations recommend that a written note be placed in the employee's file explaining the reason and circumstances of the oral warning.[15]

3. The *reprimand* (or written warning) is a formal record of the disciplinary interview with an employee. Figure 11.4 illustrates how the interview can be documented. This formal report should contain all the major areas discussed in the interviews, such as circumstances and behavior for which the reprimand is given, expected improvement in behavior, and the nature of the reprimand as corrective action. During this interview, the accused is reminded of previous offenses and told that the next rule infraction will probably result in suspension. Everyone present should sign the dated form.

One copy of the warning is given to the employee and another copy is placed in the employee's personnel file. It is always a good idea for the supervisor to give a copy to his or her boss, and if a union contract exists, a copy should go to the steward. Naturally, the supervisor will want to keep a copy.

Many supervisors are requiring that a witness be present at a reprimand interview, just as the accused employee may have requested a

Name _____

Your behavior made it necessary to give you this warning because of the following:

_____ Tardiness	_____ Leaving work without permission
_____ Absence	_____ Fighting
_____ Refusal to obey directions	_____ Failure to work harmoniously with coworkers
_____ Using abusive, vulgar language	_____ Failure to obey agency policies
_____ Abuse of equipment, supplies	_____ Neglecting duties
_____ Unauthorized use of equipment, supplies	_____ Refusing to wear appropriate attire
_____ Violating safety rules	_____ Other reason_____
_____ Disrespect or rudeness to the public	_____ Other reason_____

Evidence of the offense:

Previous penalties, if any, related to this kind of behavior:

Others involved in the incident:

Recommended corrective action:

This warning will be included in your personnel record. The next time this rule is violated, you may expect to receive corrective action in the form of:

Supervisor_____,   Date _____

The offense and corrective action explained above were discussed with me. I understand why corrective action was necessary and what will happen the next time I violate this rule.

Employee_____   Date_____

Comments from Employee:

Witnesses _____

_____

cc: Employee
    Supervisor
    Personnel File
    Steward

Figure 11.4   Sample employee disciplinary action form.

witness at the prior investigation interview.[16] The supervisor does not have to satisfy the request of the guilty employee to have a steward or coworker present when the purpose of the interview is to inform the employee of corrective disciplinary action which has already been determined from an investigation.[17]

Following the reprimand the supervisor will need to follow up with the employee to determine if the corrective behavior was effective, and to reestablish friendly rapport. Regardless of the misconduct, the supervisor and employee must work together in the future.

4. *Suspension* or layoff without pay is the most serious action that an employer can take prior to discharge. When employees do not respond to reprimands, they may recognize the seriousness of their behavior if they lose wages. Suspension is not often used for professionals or so-called white-collar employees. After counseling, employees in these categories are usually discharged.[18] The supervisor must specify when the suspension begins and when it will end. Indefinite suspensions, unless related to the court settlement of a criminal offense, are contrary to the purpose of positive corrective discipline and the amount to dismissal.

Suspensions can hurt others not involved in the misconduct. The loss of pay can become a financial hardship on the employee's dependents, persons not guilty of misconduct. Lengthy suspensions also can cause hardship on coworkers who must perform the suspended worker's tasks during the suspension. Because of the possible negative reaction to this penalty, many organizations require upper management to review cases of suspension before final action is taken.[19] In all cases of suspension, an interview is conducted and the written documentation is similar to the procedure followed for a reprimand.

5. *Discharge* is the most extreme disciplinary action an organization can take, although some authorities consider it more humane than suspension because it allows the employee to start over again somewhere else.[20] Corrective actions prior to discharge may be omitted if the offense is very serious. Frequently, a higher authority within an organization must make the final decision on dismissal. The legal constraints and possible consequences of discharge are discussed in detail in Chapter 12.

Unsatisfactory Penalties. Some approaches to discipline are so punitive or negative that we do not recommend their use as positive corrective actions. These include demotion, transfer, reassignment, giving demerits, imposing cash fines, ignoring or harassing the employee, requiring a public apology, ridiculing or intimidating the employee, or scheduling undesirable work shifts as punishment.

The act of transferring an employee does not always indicate employee misconduct. Many persons request transfers because they feel they would be happier in a different job and under a different supervisor. But transferring an employee with a behavior problem to another unit is passing the buck and not helping the employee develop self-discipline and control. The marginal employee that a supervisor does not want should be counseled, disciplined, and even fired. But he should not be "traded" like a piece of property, unless the transfer is voluntary and serves better to match employee interests and job qualifications with the new position.

A demotion is a type of transfer whereby the employee receives a cut in pay, status, privileges, opportunity, and possible longevity. It may be necessary to demote employees because of staff reductions or reorganization or because the worker was incorrectly assigned in the first place. In some cases, the employee requests demotion for reasons of health or change in interests. Demotion for these reasons is not punitive. But using demotion as a disciplinary penalty defeats the purpose of getting the employee to rehabilitate his or her behavior. The employee who is demoted to a less desirable job will be punished for the remainder of his or her time with the organization. The blow to the person's self-esteem is permanent as long as he or she works in the lesser position. This humiliation creates ill-will and loss of motivation. In most instances it is a waste of human resources.[21] Most management and arbitration boards feel that demotion is an inappropriate penalty because the employee loses too many rights. The penalty does not fit the misconduct.

The practice of placing demerits in an employee's record is seldom used today. It tends to leave permanent marks against the employee, especially for future promotion. A few public agencies such as police departments, still fine their employees for breaking rules.[22] Most organizations, however, consider money penalties too severe for corrective action. Like suspension without pay, the nonguilty families are also punished.

Disciplinary Interview

Supervisors should almost always discipline in private, away from listening ears of other employees. This private meeting is called the disciplinary interview and protects the pride and dignity of the employee being corrected. Embarrassing the guilty worker in front of others focuses attention on the employee as a person receiving a public bawling out and not on why the corrective action is being taken. Do not make a martyr out of the guilty employee. A public reprimand is also unwise because in order to save face, the guilty worker will feel compelled to argue with the supervisor and perhaps even retaliate by embarrassing the supervisor. A public show of feelings and exchanging emotional language does not serve the purpose of positive discipline.

The exception to this rule is when immediate action must be taken for safety reasons to protect agency property, the welfare of coworkers, or the public. The purposes of reprimanding in public is to stop the dangerous behavior immediately.

Each employee has a different personality, some more fragile than others. Every disciplinary incident is also different. Supervisors need to recognize that each situation must be handled differently. Firmness and fairness is always a suitable posture for the supervisor to take, but some employees need a more soft-pedaled approach than others, or their egos will be seriously threatened. If handled poorly, corrective action can erode respect and trust in the leadership of the organization, damage interpersonal relationships, temporarily injure the employee's sense of self-worth, and in extreme cases, precipitate a serious and possibly violent confrontation with the supervisor.[23] If properly handled and executed, this meeting will promote personal responsibility, facilitate communications by clearing up any misunderstandings, and provide a forum for the employee to explain the reasons for the misconduct. The employee should leave the meeting believing that the purpose of discipline is rehabilitation and not punishment.

Preparing for the Interview.   Preparation for the disciplinary interview includes fact gathering and attitude adjusting. All documents, records, and testimony should be organized and reviewed prior to the meeting to learn as much as possible about the background, history of employment, and the personality of the employee. If the supervisor is frustrated or angry, he or she should work to bring these emotions under control, recognizing that the employee could also be feeling the strong emotions of hostility, indignation, or fear. It is more probable that the worker will be feeling guilt or anxiety.

Consideration should be given to the physical location in which the meeting will be held, perhaps a neutral place like someone else's office. This type of environment might help to defuse the potentially hostile and belligerent employee. The more serious the offense, the more formal and structured the meeting and meeting place should be. In this situation, the office of the supervisor's boss might serve the disciplinary interview.

Conducting the Interview.   Once the meeting begins, the supervisor would be advised to restate the purpose of the interview and what the specific charges against the employee are in order to ensure that everyone is addressing the same issue. Rambling or addressing unrelated issues should be avoided. Sometimes an employee knows the purpose of the meeting but does not agree that there has been a rule violation or that a problem exists.

It becomes important that supervisors not overreact. Even if the accused offers contradictory facts and begins to argue, emotions must be kept in check or reasoning and judgment will be clouded. Most employees are sincere and honest. They honestly believe that their version is correct. If the supervisor watches the employee's body language and carefully listens to the spoken words, this phase of the interview can be weathered without too much friction between the participating parties. Only a few employees will insist on being aggressive and dishonest. If the employee insists on being argumentative, the disciplinary interview should be terminated.

In some instances, the investigative and the disciplinary interview may be one and the same. Even if the supervisor has witnessed the misconduct or has another equally conclusive evidence of guilt, the employee should be given an opportunity to tell his side of the story in his own way. The supervisor should listen with an open mind, trying not to interrupt too often to gain additional information. Only after evaluating all the facts should a constructive corrective action be taken. Judgment must not be made until the employee has been heard.

Off-Duty Behavior

Does the employer have the right to discipline employees for misbehavior away from the place of employment? Would such corrective action violate freedom of privacy laws? Is an employee's personal life any of the employer's business? The answers to all three questions are "yes" and "no" depending on the circumstances.

No arbitrator, court of law, or enlightened manager would support a supervisor's decision to discipline a worker for off-duty behavior in the absence of any proof that the behavior had a negative impact on the business. There is equal agreement, however, that discipline for off-duty behavior is appropriate under four conditions:

1. When recognizable harm has been done to the employer.
2. When harm has been done to the program participants or park users.
3. When employee relations have been adversely affected.
4. When off-duty behavior results in the employee's inability to meet job requirements.

Under these conditions the employer has the right to discipline employees, but the circumstances may be more complex than they appear on the surface. Supervisors should seek consultation with someone higher in the organization, with the personnel unit, or with an attorney before taking action on off-duty behavior.

Right of Appeals

What happens when an employee honestly believes that the corrective action was unfair or too harsh? Is there anyone besides the supervisor or the supervisor's boss to whom an aggrieved employee can tell his or her side of the story?

The answer to this question is "yes" if the employer is (1) a party in a collective bargaining agreement, (2) a public agency, or (3) enlightened enough to provide the employees with an internal procedure to appeal disciplinary actions. Collective bargaining agreements and public political jurisdictions offer rights of appeal procedures to the workers, but non-public and nonunion organizations may not have such a procedure.

The procedural mechanisms for rights of appeal may take one of several forms. Individual complaints about disciplinary action might be heard by a hearings or mediation panel composed entirely of employees who are periodically elected to serve on the panel but who convene only when a complaint is filed. An ad hoc body of employees may be appointed by management and elected by fellow workers after a complaint is filed. Sometimes private citizens sit on the appeals body for public agencies. Other organizations provide a formal grievance procedure like the one described in the next section and summarized in Figure 11.5.

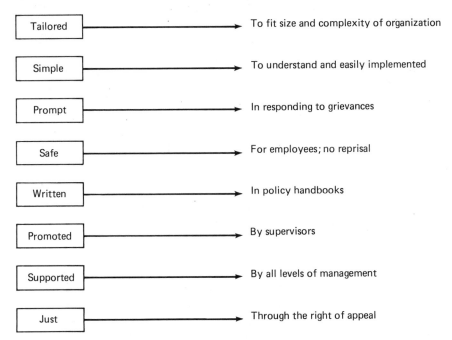

Tailored	To fit size and complexity of organization
Simple	To understand and easily implemented
Prompt	In responding to grievances
Safe	For employees; no reprisal
Written	In policy handbooks
Promoted	By supervisors
Supported	By all levels of management
Just	Through the right of appeal

Figure 11.5 Features of a workable grievance procedure.

Grievance Procedure

While the disciplinary action process provides an avenue for the organization to investigate employee misconduct and impose penalties, the grievance procedure provides a due-process avenue for the employee to receive a fair hearing in appealing perceived unfair treatment. The grievance procedure is a valuable management tool that serves four purposes:

1. It helps to fulfill the employee's need for recognition and belonging. The fact that the employer listens to the employee's problem demonstrates the importance of the individual worker and that somebody "upstairs" cares about working conditions.
2. It establishes an orderly process to ventilate pent-up emotions which might otherwise be turned toward work stoppage, disruptive behavior, or even sabotage. It is generally believed that grievance procedures minimize worker–employer conflicts and thus enhance the nation's overall economy.[24]
3. It reduces abusive supervisory practices. Recent research demonstrates a relationship between the number of grievances filed and the supervisor's behavior. The more considerate supervisor experiences fewer complaints. On the other hand, complaints increase if the supervisor's behavior is autocratic.[25] The grievance procedure can be a yardstick by which the supervisor may measure the effectiveness of his or her leadership.
4. It is interrelated with the process of labor contract negotiation. As complaints are reviewed throughout the steps of the grievance procedure, the contract is also being reviewed and can result in the revision of the contract.[26]

Four terms need to be defined so that the reader may better understand their usage in the following section. These include gripe, complaint, grievance, and grievance procedure.

Gripes are expressions of dissatisfaction where employees simply let off steam. They do not expect anyone to take their griping seriously or to try and change things. They may not even want things changed. Griping is considered a natural condition of employment which relieves the strain of circumstances generally beyond anyone's control.

Complaints are more serious than gripes. They may be real and involve minor incidents on the job, or they may be imaginary and have no actual basis. Real or imaginary, complaints express worker dissatisfaction over a perceived injustice. Supervisors should never ignore complaints because they probably will not go away and can result in a grievance.

Grievances may take on several definitions. Some labor authorities restrict the definition to include only dissatisfactions arising out of violations of the labor agreement. With this narrow definition, employees may complain only about issues specifically spelled out in the labor contract. In general, management tries to restrict the definition, while unions try to make it as broad as possible.[27] A broad definition would include any worker dissatisfaction in connection with employment conditions. In this book we define grievance as *employee dissatisfactions over specific employment conditions that immediate supervisors cannot resolve and which have been brought to the attention of management in writing.*

Grievance procedures are formal processes that are stated in the personnel policies or the union contract. They involve a systematic review and deliberation of an employee's grievance at successively higher levels of management within an organization until the grievance is either denied at the last level or resolved to the employee's satisfaction. The problem may be resolved at any level, but if it is not, the grievance may be submitted to an impartial third party outside the organization called an arbitrator or umpire.

Grievance Procedures in Nonunion Organizations

Between 75 and 80 percent of this country's labor force works for nonunion employers.[28] A number of recent studies indicate that few nonunion and nongovernmental organizations provide any kind of workable mechanism for handling employee grievances. One expert estimated that only a few hundred organizations out of 20,000 companies had adopted formal "employee due-process" grievance procedures.[29] Most of the rest of the organizations have "open-door" policies. This means that management attempts to handle employee complaints by stating that "the door is open to anyone who wants to talk." A few companies have management grievance committees or ombudsmen.[30] Most mechanisms to resolve employee complaints fall into the following categories:

1. Supervisory listening.
2. Personnel counseling.
3. Open-door policy.
4. Ombudsmen.
5. Employee committees.
6. Multistep grievance procedure.

Supervisor. Much emphasis is placed on the supervisor's ability to handle complaints. The theory is to settle the complaint, informally, as close to the problem as possible. This means that the employee should initially tell the supervisor about the problem. This may not be easy because the supervisor's actions may be the problem.

In listening to a dissatisfied subordinate trying to explain a problem, the supervisor is placed in the position of counselor. For example, a new secretary-receptionist complains that she cannot get any work done because her desk is located in the main flow of traffic. She is defensive, argumentative, and insists on a different work site. Upon further questioning, it is learned that the real reason for her dissatisfaction is not her work location, but the fact that she feels insecure about answering questions from the public about the park district. The sensitive supervisor ensures the employee that she is doing a good job and only needs more information about the organization's programs and more time to organize that information for quick and easy access. The supervisor offers to help her gain mastery over the myriad of details about a park and recreation agency.

Sound simple? Sure, if the supervisor is skilled in the use of nondirective interviewing techniques, among other counseling approaches. But most supervisors are doing well if they develop good communications with employees and create an atmosphere in which subordinates feel safe in expressing complaints. Few supervisors are also trained to be counselors and to probe for the unexpressed dissatisfaction or the hidden motive.

Counselor. In some organizations a counselor is hired and attached to the personnel department. This person is better trained to probe for hidden reasons for complaints and may assist the supervisor in determining the real nature of the employee's complaint. Although a counselor may surface the real reason for the complaint, the problem will not go away unless someone resolves the problem at its origin, and that someone is either the supervisor or someone else with authority to effect changes.

Open-Door Policy. An open-door policy means that any worker has the right to go to the office of the chief executive and complain about a work-related matter. These executives are to make themselves available for such purposes and investigate each complaint. This is the most commonly used procedure to handle the complaints of nonunion workers, but in practice, this procedure is not feasible.[31] First, few workers have the courage to walk into the office of the "big boss." Second, few executives have the time to administer an open-door policy for hundreds of employees. Third, if the executive overrules a decision made by a supervisor, the supervisor loses credibility and finds that it becomes difficult to command respect from subordinates. The supervisor may harbor resentment toward both the employee and upper management under this procedure.

Ombudsmen.   Some organizations have modified the open-door policy and offer employees the chance to air their complaints before a neutral official in the organization called an ombudsman. These officials are outside the chain of command but are given the authority to investigate complaints, review official records, and make decisions. This procedure was first used in 1809 by the governments of Finland and Sweden to hear the complaints of citizens.[32] Its popularity in other countries did not catch on until the 1950s. It is still a relatively new concept for nongovernmental employees.

Employee Committees.   Employee committees are sometimes created by the organization to hear grievances on appeal from employees. These committees are composed of nonmanagement employees and may have only "listening" authority. Any recommendations they may make are not binding on the organization.

Multistep Grievance Procedure.   The multistep grievance procedure in nonunionized organizations is very similar to the procedures found in union contracts except that arbitration is rarely included in the final step of nonunion organizations.[33] There are two reasons for this exclusion. First, the individual employee in most cases cannot afford to pay one-half of the arbitrator's fee and the employee does not have an equal chance against management at the hearings unless an attorney helps prepare the case. The second reason is that management rarely chooses to relinquish any authority to an outside party unless forced to do so by union contract.

In many organizations the final step is a panel or board review by neutral parties.[34] In Norfolk, Virginia, for example, if the employee is not satisfied with the park and recreation department head's decision, the employee may request in writing that the director of personnel initiate action for the selection of an employee panel to review the complaint. The panel's decision is final and binding, provided that the opinion rendered falls within the authority of the panel and does not violate city personnel policies or ordinances. Figure 11.6 reflects the typical multistep grievance procedure in nonunion organizations.

Of all the six procedures described previously, only the multistep grievance procedure guarantees employees the right to air their grievances and appeal to successively higher levels of management *without fear of reprisal*. Although this procedure is always printed and distributed to the entire work force like other policies, workers do not take advantage of the procedures for fear of retaliation. There is the perception that an

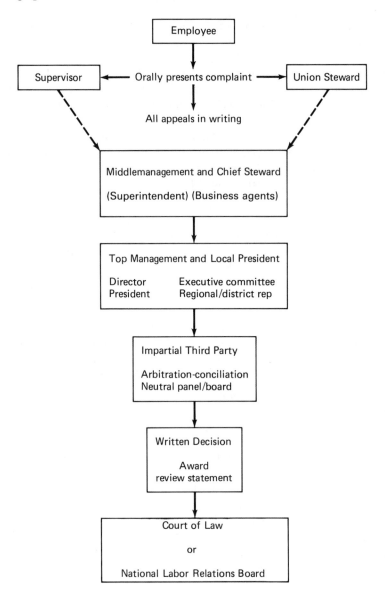

Figure 11.6 Formal grievance procedure.

employee cannot go up against the power of the employer and win. Some higher authority may withhold salary increases and promotions, or assign undesirable jobs. Upper managers and every supervisor must encourage employees to use the formal grievance procedure. To do otherwise is an open invitation to union organizers, who offer employees a better balance of power between the employer and the worker.

Grievance Procedures in Union Organizations

Approximately 99 percent of the union contracts in industry contain grievance procedures which have been standardized in most labor contracts.[35] Like the multistep grievance procedure for nonunion organizations, the basic concept is to settle disputes by moving through successively higher levels of authority until the dispute is settled. The terminal step is arbitration in over 90 percent of U.S. labor agreements.[36] There are usually three to five steps in the entire process from supervisor to arbitration. The actual number of steps depends on the size of the organization.

Preliminary Step in the Grievance Procedure. The role of the supervisor in resolving employee complaints in a union organization is different from that same role in a nonunion agency. In both situations, the employee with a complaint talks first to the immediate supervisor, but many union contracts also allow the employee first to bring the complaint to the union steward.[37] The steward may tell the employee that there is no cause for the grievance and the case should be dropped. If there is probable cause for the complaint, the steward may present the complaint to the supervisor orally or in writing. The supervisor should insist that the employee be present for any discussion of the employee's complaint, but some contracts may stipulate that the aggrieved employee does not have to be present. Approximately 75 percent of the complaints are resolved at the supervisory-steward level.[38]

Frequently, union agreements specify the amount of reasonable time that stewards are to be allowed to spend on the job investigating grievances. Since the amount of time for each case may be different, conflicts may arise over this issue. The commanding officer at one federal military installation believed that the union representative was guilty of stretching the definition of "reasonable time" and set a ceiling on the time to be allowed for future grievance investigations. His decision was upheld by the arbitrator, who concluded that excessive time had been taken by the union official.[39]

The best situation is one where the supervisor and the steward work conscientiously together to resolve legitimate complaints and to discourage union employees from filing weak grievances.

Second Step in the Grievance Procedure. If the supervisor and the employee cannot resolve the problem, the complaint is written out as a formal grievance and submitted to the superintendent or the next level of management, and to either the chief steward or business agent of the union. Once a grievance is filed, it is no longer guided by the aggrieved employee, the supervisor, or the steward. Union officials and management will determine how far the grievance will be pursued. The supervisor may be called on to provide background information or to testify as a witness, but others will make the final decision.

Third Step in the Grievance Procedure.

When union representatives and organization officials at middle-management cannot agree on a solution, the grievance moves to the third step in the process. Depending on the organization or governmental unit, this might be the last opportunity for resolving the problem within the structure of the organization.

In some organizations the grievance procedure may be different for different classifications of employees, depending on the various labor contracts that are negotiated. The city of Wichita, Kansas, negotiates with Local 513 of the AFL-CIO, Local 666 of the International Association of Firefighters, and Lodge 5 of the Fraternal Order of Police. City officials must be familiar with each labor contract and grievance procedure.

Fourth Step: Arbitration/Conciliation.

Almost all grievances are resolved through negotiation between management and union representatives. A few may remain unresolved. About 90 percent of all labor contracts in the private sector and 75 percent of those in the public sector provide for binding arbitration when cases cannot be settled "inhouse."[40] This is the final step in the grievance procedure and should be resorted to only when all other means fail, because arbitration is costly and time consuming. It may take as long as 250 days to resolve an employee's grievance.[41]

Arbitration hearings are quasi-judicial and may be very informal or as formal as a court of law. Both sides, management and the union, are represented by legal counsel. Charges are filed, witnesses and statements are heard, evidence is reviewed, and then the arbitrator renders a decision in writing within thirty days, referred to as an "award." A separate document called the "review of statement" summarizes both sides of the presentation made by the two parties and outlines the reasons for the award. Since both union and management agreed that the arbitrator's decision would be final, the aggrieved employee has no further appeal options, except in the courts. It is most unusual for awards to be set aside by the courts.[42]

On occasion, union agreements will stipulate that conciliation may be used to settle grievances. A conciliator makes no judgment nor renders a final decision. His role is to assist both parties in reaching a mutually satisfying agreement. If conciliation fails, the only recourse is the National Labor Relations Board or the judicial court systems.

Desirable Features of a Grievance Procedure

Whether the organization is union or nonunion, a good grievance procedure should contain some of the same features as the guidelines for discipline discussed earlier in the chapter. The procedure should be written down, the language should be simple to understand, easy to follow, and it should be communicated to every worker by the immediate supervisor. In addition, the grievance procedure and number of appeal steps should be tailored to fit the size and complexity of the organization.

Early settlements should be a clearly stated goal of all procedures and time limits should be established for each appeal step in the process within which management must give its decision. Long, drawn-out affairs are costly in terms of morale and lost work.

Employees must be encouraged to use the grievance procedure and convinced that no one will retaliate against them because of their honesty. If the procedure is to work, employees must believe that all levels of management support its purpose and that someone beyond their supervisor is there to hear their problems and offer relief.

The Supervisor and Early Settlements

The keys to settling complaints before they become formal grievances lay in the attitude and behavior of the supervisor. Trained and experienced supervisors know that wherever people work, there will be gripes and complaints. Seeking out or being confronted by dissatisfied workers and trying to resolve their complaints takes patience, understanding, and much effort. This effort is often frustrating for supervisors because the complaints may be directed at their personal leadership style, on-the-job actions, or perceived injustices to the employee. Supervisors who settle complaints before they become grievance practice the following:

1. *Early detection.* Settling future grievances in the present means recognizing the early symptoms of dissatisfaction and being sensitive to sudden changes in employee attitudes, enthusiasm, interest in the job, and relationships with coworkers. These changes may precede verbal complaints and will need monitoring.

2. *Understand causes of complaints.* Disciplinary actions, work assignments, off-the-job personal problems, physical work conditions, and the relationship with the supervisor or coworkers are all common causes of complaints. Off-the-job problems may cause an employee to express dissatisfaction about working conditions on the job. A sensitive supervisor

will spot a shift in attitude or behavior and suspect personal problems if there is no evidence of on-the-job cause for the complaints.

3. *Listen and observe.* Once the complaint has been verbalized, the supervisor must sincerely want to understand the point of view of the complaining subordinate. Understanding does not mean agreement. The employee should be asked to come into the office to tell his or her side of the story. The supervisor should listen, ask questions to clarify all points, and take notes. It is a good idea to summarize back to the employee what has been said so that both people are sure of the message being sent. The employee should be asked to suggest solutions to the problem.

4. *Gather the facts.* If it is necessary, the supervisor should talk to other employees and other supervisors to check on past practices and records. They will also need to review the personnel policies or union contract.

5. *Document.* All discussions and investigations should be recorded. Federal, state, and local laws require the maintenance of accurate records. Supervisors may need to defend decisions to union stewards, upper management, governmental agencies, and arbitrators.

6. *Make a decision.* A list should be developed that compares the advantages and disadvantages of each alternative decision and the possible consequences. Decisions should best satisfy all conditions, be fair to everyone concerned, be consistent with past decisions, and not infringe adversely on future decisions. The supervisor's boss or the labor relation's specialist in the personnel department may have to be consulted prior to announcing the decision.

7. *Take action.* The decision must be concisely explained in writing, particularly if the complaint is being denied by the supervisor. Next, the grievance procedure should be explained to the employee and what the employee can do next if he or she does not agree with the supervisor's decision. If, however, the complaint is legitimate, there is no disgrace in being honest and admitting fault.

8. *Follow through.* The entire work force expects promises and commitments to be kept. This means getting back in touch with the employee to ensure that everything is all right. If the complaint was denied, the decision needs to be referred to others in the organization.

9. *Do not be offended.* Should the employee choose to follow the supervisor's advice and appeal the decision to the next step in the grievance procedure, the supervisor should not become defensive toward the employee. The appeal process without reprisal is a guaranteed right and what grievance procedures are all about. The supervisor cannot always settle every complaint, for several reasons. He or she may lack the authority to take the required action to solve the problem. The supervisor may not have developed the necessary human relations and counseling skills to help the worker defuse the gripe. The supervisor may even

agree that the complaint is legitimate but knows from past experience that upper management will not be receptive to changing anything. Some supervisors even suppress complaints, thinking that it looks better for them.[43] When supervisors cannot satisfactorily resolve problems leading to complaints, a formal grievance system is necessary to bring employees' dissatisfaction to the attention of the highest authorities within the organization.

Summary and Recommendations

1. Management's concept of positive discipline today is very different from former practices when employers punished workers as arbitrarily, harshly, and inconsistently as they chose.
2. The organization, the supervisor, and the employee benefit from a positive, disciplined work environment that encourages employees to want to abide by rules and exercise self-control.
3. Management has the responsibility and the obligation to establish appropriate rules of conduct on the job as long as those rules are necessary, reasonable, and fairly enforced.
4. Rules of conduct must be communicated in such a way that every employee understands them and knows what disciplinary action will be taken each time a rule is broken.
5. Every employee should be treated with the same standard of conduct and judged by the same rules, but consistent application does not always mean equal application. Supervision must consider all extenuating circumstances as well as the past record of the employee before deciding on the appropriate, corrective action.
6. Before taking any disciplinary action the supervisor should become familiar with the organization's disciplinary guidelines, the union contract (if appropriate), and the organization's past practices in disciplining employees.
7. A thorough investigation of any misconduct must be made prior to administering discipline in order to prove "just cause" reasons why corrective action is necessary.
8. The most effective disciplinary policy is one where the penalties are progressively more severe each time the rule is broken. The most frequently used penalties include informal counseling, oral warning, written reprimand, suspension, and discharge.
9. All supervisors should be trained to enforce the rules, and their disciplinary actions should be monitored, at least for a given time period, until they develop proficiency in responding to situations that require corrective action.

10. Employees should be disciplined in private by the immediate supervisor unless immediate action is necessary to protect property, the employee, coworkers, or the public. If handled poorly, discipline can damage respect for the employer and the supervisor and injure the employee's sense of self-worth.
11. The grievance procedure provides due process for the employee to receive a fair hearing in appealing perceived unfair treatment.
12. Grievance procedures involve a systematic review and deliberation of an employee's grievance at successively higher levels of management until it is either denied at the last level or resolved to the worker's satisfaction.
13. A good grievance procedure should be written in handbooks, promoted by the supervisor, and supported by all levels of management. Employees should be encouraged to use the procedure and be convinced that no one will retaliate against them.
14. The attitudes and understanding of the supervisor are very important in settling work complaints before they become grievances.

Discussion Topics

1. What is the difference between positive discipline and punitive discipline? Which one is the most effective in the workplace? Why?
2. Outline the steps in a progressive disciplinary procedure.
3. How much proof must be assembled by the supervisor to satisfy the "just cause" criterion for disciplining an employee?
4. When might an employer have the right to discipline an employee for off-duty behavior?
5. What is the difference between a complaint, a gripe, and a grievance?
6. Explain the successive steps in a formal grievance procedure. What is the difference between arbitration and conciliation?
7. What appeal rights does an employee have after the arbitrator gives the award and review statement?
8. The statement "grievance procedures are for troublemakers" has been expressed by some supervisors. Do you agree? Why or why not?

Notes

1. Arthur Sloane, *Personnel: Managing Human Resources* (Englewood Cliffs, N.J.: Prentice-Hall, Inc., 1983), p. 401.
2. Dale Beach, *Personnel: The Management of People at Work*, 4th ed. (New York: Macmillan Publishing Company, 1980), p. 528.
3. Louis Imundo, *Employee Discipline: How to Do It Right* (Oakland County, Mich., Managers and Supervisor's Seminar, September 1983), p. 10.

4. Sloane, *Personnel*, p. 406.
5. Bruce Stickler, "Limitations on an Employer's Right to Discipline and Discharge Employees," *Employee Relations Law Journal* 9 (Summer 1983): 70.
6. John Kruchko and Lawrence Dubé, "The Right for Non-union Workers," *Personnel* (November–December 1983): 64.
7. Ibid., p. 63.
8. Walter Baer, *Discipline and Discharge Under Labor Agreement* (New York: American Management Association, Inc., 1972), p. 38.
9. William Lissey, "Circumstantial Evidence and Refusal to Talk," *Supervisor* (April 1983): 19.
10. Baer, *Discipline and Discharge Under Labor Agreement*, p. 54.
11. Imundo, *Employee Discipline*, p. 18.
12. Baer, *Discipline and Discharge Under Labor Agreement*, p. 56.
13. Weiss, W. H., "What Discipline Action Is Proper," *Supervision* (June 1983): 8.
14. Glen Stahl, *Public Personnel Administration*, 8th ed. (New York: Harper & Row, Publishers, Inc., 1983), p. 298.
15. Jack Halloran, *Supervision: The Act of Management* (Englewood Cliffs, N.J.: Prentice-Hall, Inc., 1981), p. 200.
16. International City Managers Association, *Effective Supervisory Practices* (Washington, D.C.: International City Managers Association, 1978), p. 5.
17. Kruchko and Dubé, "The Right for Non-union Workers," p. 62.
18. Sterling Schoen and Douglas Durand, *Supervision: The Management of Organizational Resources* (Englewood Cliffs, N.J.: Prentice-Hall, Inc., 1979), p. 216.
19. International City Managers Association, *Effective Supervisory Practices*, p. 5.
20. Stahl, *Public Personnel Administration*, p. 299.
21. Schoen and Durand, *Supervision*, p. 216.
22. Stahl, *Public Personnel Administration*, p. 300.
23. Imundo, *Employee Discipline*, p. 17.
24. Wendell French, *The Personnel Management Process*, 4th ed. (Boston: Houghton Mifflin Company, 1978), p. 531.
25. Robert Mathis and John Jackson, *Personnel: Contemporary Perspectives and Applications* (St. Paul, Minn.: West Publishing Co., 1982), p. 513.
26. French, *Personnel Management Process*, p. 521.
27. Felix Nigio and Lloyd Nigio, *The New Public Personnel Administration* (Itasca, Ill.: F. E. Peacock Publishers, Inc., 1976), p. 258.
28. Schoen and Durand, *Supervision*, p. 295.
29. Mathis and Jackson, *Personnel*, p. 507.
30. Beach, *Personnel*, p. 548.
31. Robert Eckles, Ronald Carmichael, and Bernard Sarchet, *Supervisory Management*, 2nd ed. (New York: John Wiley & Sons, Inc., 1981), p. 427.
32. Beach, *Personnel*, p. 548.
33. Eckles, Carmichael, and Sarchet, *Supervisory Management*, p. 427.
34. Beach, *Personnel*, p. 450.
35. Mathis and Jackson, *Personnel*, p. 507.
36. Eckles, Carmichael, and Sarchet, *Supervisory Management*, p. 424.
37. Schoen and Durand, *Supervision*, p. 294.

38. Eckles, Carmicael, and Sarchet, *Supervisory Management*, p. 432.
39. Nigio and Nigio, *The New Public Personnel Administration*, p. 261.
40. Beach, *Personnel*, p. 544.
41. Wayne Mondy and Robert Noe, *Personnel: The Management of Human Resources* (Boston: Allyn and Bacon, Inc., 1981), p. 452.
42. Eckles, Carmichael, and Sarchet, *Supervisory Management*, p. 431.
43. Beach, *Personnel*, p. 539.

12

Employee Separations

It has already been established in Chapter 10 that Americans are very mobile. Today's worker will change jobs approximately four times during his or her career.[1] This phenomenon of employee turnover—people leaving organizations—has both negative and positive potential consequences for individuals, employers, and society. The park and recreation supervisor needs to understand the events that can lead to turnover and how a supervisor's actions can precipitate those events. The supervisor must also understand the impact that turnover can have on productivity, employee morale, and agency image in order to anticipate and minimize the negative consequences of turnover.

When most authorities in personnel management refer to turnover, termination, or separation, they are referring to *employees who no longer receive monetary compensation from their employers*. This definition does not include those employees who are transferred by the employer to another location or assignment. Because the consequences of transfer can be as potentially negative or positive as other types of separation, we have included transfer in this chapter on employee separation.

Consequences of Separation

Separating an employee from an organization can have a dramatic effect on the remaining workers and on the effectiveness of a particular program to serve the public. Figure 12.1 shows both the negative and positive consequences of employee separation.

Figure 12.1 Negative and positive consequences of separation.

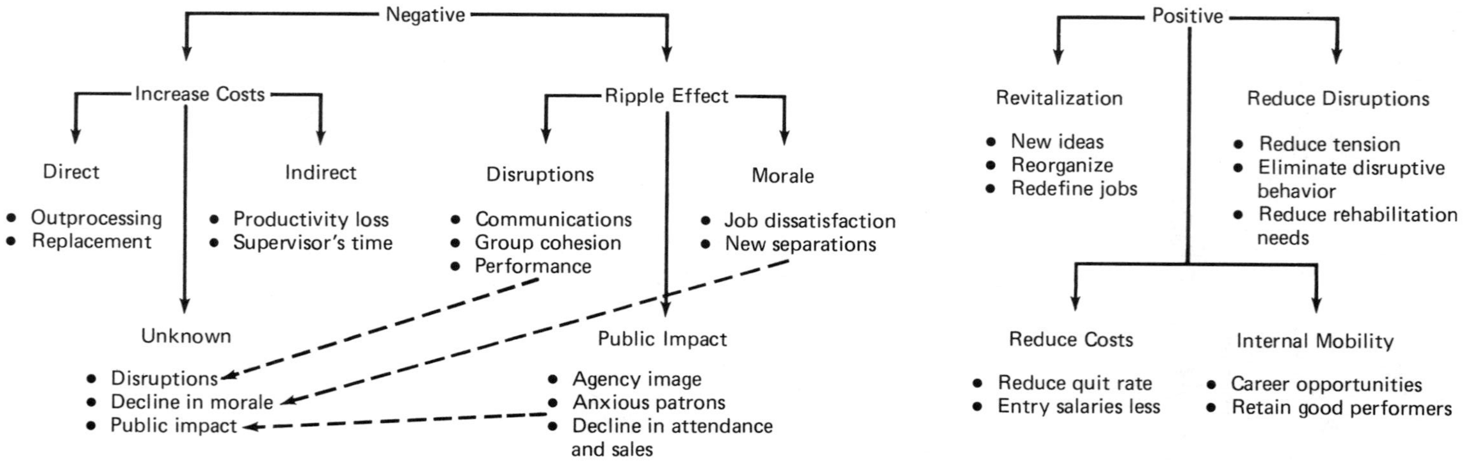

Positive

Revitalization
- New ideas
- Reorganize
- Redefine jobs

Reduce Disruptions
- Reduce tension
- Eliminate disruptive behavior
- Reduce rehabilitation needs

Reduce Costs
- Reduce quit rate
- Entry salaries less

Internal Mobility
- Career opportunities
- Retain good performers

Negative

Increase Costs

Direct
- Outprocessing
- Replacement

Indirect
- Productivity loss
- Supervisor's time

Ripple Effect

Disruptions
- Communications
- Group cohesion
- Performance

Morale
- Job dissatisfaction
- New separations

Unknown
- Disruptions
- Decline in morale
- Public impact

Public Impact
- Agency image
- Anxious patrons
- Decline in attendance and sales

Negative Consequences

Increased Costs. Separation is expensive because of the costs associated with terminating an employee, hiring a replacement, and training the new employee to be as productive as possible. Some of these costs are obvious, such as recruitment expenses and separation pay, while other costs are more difficult to determine. A few studies have focused on the indirect costs of the supervisor's time to orient and train the new employee, as well as the cost of loss of productivity just prior to separation when the separating employee has his or her attention directed toward the future. During the time it takes to find a replacement, the organization loses the investment in idle equipment and empty office space. Once someone is hired there is the loss of efficiency until the replacement is fully productive. What cannot be easily identified are the costs of the ripple effect.

Ripple Effect. The separation of any employee can create a ripple effect on the day-to-day operation of an organization, on the morale of other employees, and even on the public that interacted with the separated employee.[2] Others may temporarily have to perform the duties of the departed worker, placing stress on their own work loads. Some employees play pivotal roles in the agency's communication network and in the cohesiveness of work groups. Their loss can weaken these structures and systems.

The separation of a friend and coworker may sadden those who remain behind. They may begin to question their own job satisfaction, reexamine their work environment, and think about looking for better jobs somewhere else. Decline in morale may be temporary or it may lead to additional separations.

Finally, the ripple effect also reaches the public. In one community a newspaper editorial questioned the 50 percent turnover rate among county park employees, asking whether low salaries alone accounted for the high quit rate. When three more employees resigned before the summer season began, parents became anxious about safety and supervision and withdrew their children from an overnight camping program. Separations for whatever the reason may have an adverse impact on the park patron or program client and seriously jeopardize the agency's image and credibility.

Positive Consequences

Revitalization. It would be misleading to think only of the ripple effect and the costs of separation if the organization is exchanging a poor or disruptive performer for a more qualified employee with new ideas, technical skills, and a fresh outlook. Not only might the organization gain from the infusion of new experiences, but separation provides the opportunity to reorganize, redefine jobs, and break up entrenched pockets of stodgy, mediocre employees who may waste time or resist change. Departing employees during the exit interview often offer suggestions for improvement, which if implemented, could raise morale, decrease costs, and resolve internal conflicts. These internal changes revitalize and increase organizational effectiveness and help reduce the turnover of valued employees.

Reduced Disruptive Behavior.   The departure of disruptive employees usually eases tension among the remaining workers. It is possible that if the employee had not quit or been discharged, poor performance and disruptive behavior would have been manifested in apathy, alcoholism, sabotage, absenteeism, or aggressive, argumentative behavior. These behaviors are always counterproductive for the employer, and the costs associated with rehabilitating a disgruntled worker can be greater than the separation costs.[3]

Internal Mobility.   Turnover creates internal mobility opportunities for remaining workers. Good performers may not be able to advance their career with the employer unless someone leaves. One analysis conducted by a large multidivisional corporation demonstrated that the quit rate was greater among high-performing professional employees than among lower performers.[4] If organizational hiring policies give preference to internal promotion, separation becomes the key to retaining good workers. Whenever an employee resigns or is discharged, an opportunity is created for another employee to be promoted from within.

Reduced Costs.   The potential to reduce costs as a result of separation has already been partially addressed in the earlier sections on reducing disruptive behavior and reducing the quit rate among good performers. A real advantage comes with hiring new employees at entry salary levels. As employees move past the midpoint of their salary range, the remuneration of high salaries and accumulated vested interests in benefits and pension plans may be greater than the employee's increase in productivity. New hires may offer the same ability to perform the job for less pay.[5]

It has also been suggested that it may be less expensive to cope with turnover than to prevent it. The costs of retaining a high performer may outweigh the advantages of keeping that person if the employee expects more benefits, better working conditions, more pay, and expensive training and development for future advancement.[6] Several years ago a southern municipal park and recreation director negotiated a $10,000 salary increase and the opportunity to attend a two-week management development seminar costing $5,000. These negotiated benefits were provided to keep him from leaving his position to accept a better-paying job in another state. The city might have considered letting him go and replacing him with an equally qualified professional for less money.

We have taken the time to explain all the potential consequences of separation so that the reader understands the complex nature of turnover. It is the responsibility of management and the supervisor to provide the appropriate work environment to retain good employees while providing a fair and progressive discipline procedure to terminate poor performers. It is also important to assess the costs and ripple effects in retaining or separating employees.

Involuntary Separation

When the employer elects to terminate the worker's employment, it is referred to as *involuntary separation*. These situations include discharge, political patronage termination, and layoff. Retirement and transfer are discussed separately because they may be either voluntary or involuntary situations.

Discharge

Discharge is a permanent separation from the organization because of unsatisfactory performance or misconduct on the part of the employee or because there is a change in job requirements or political climate over which the worker has no control. Discharge or dismissal is the most severe penalty that an employer can impose on any employee. Some labor authorities liken discharge to capital punishment.

The common practice for the past century was to dismiss employees for any reason the employer chose to give. This is known as "termination at will" and means that the owner of a business has the right to run the business as he or she sees fit. A Tennessee court explained it this way in 1884: "All may dismiss their employee(s) at will, be they few or many, for good cause, for no cause, or even for cause morally wrong without being thereby guilty of legal wrong."[7] It was this decision that helped establish the common law rule "termination at will," viewed as protecting the employer's business investment.

Employers' rights have been modified somewhat in recent years, through legislation, the judicial system, and because of unions and civil service systems. The Civil Rights Act and state fair employment laws prohibit dismissal for reasons of race, age, sex, religion, or national origin (see Chapter 1). Collective bargaining agreements between unions and employers state that workers can be discharged only for "just cause," explained in detail in Chapter 11. When the Federal Civil Service Act of 1883 established the merit system for federal workers, public administrators could no longer fire employees without evidence of wrongdoing and prior warnings to the workers.[8] Due process and appeal rights were also guaranteed federal workers. The Taft–Hartley Act and the National Labor Relations Act further guarantees employees rights from arbitrary discharge due to union involvement.

But in most cases the legal recourse for fired employees depends on the laws in the state in which they work. Despite some federal legislation and contractual guarantees, many workers are still vulnerable to dismissal for reasons that are not job related, or because they challenged company policies or directives. These discharged employees are finding protection in state laws and in state courts that reflect a growing sensitivity to employee rights. It is the state legislatures and court systems that move to curb the power of employers to fire for unfair reasons.[9] The United States is one of the few industrialized nations that does not have a federal law which addresses the right of the employer to fire employees at will.[10]

This shift in "right to hire, right to fire" philosophy has emerged as a result of changes in societal thinking about status, position, and property. Property ownership once denoted status, but our culture has evolved into a society where one's employment is also an important status symbol.[11] This shift in status values translates into the right of the employee to his or her job unless that right is denied for a just reason.

Good-Cause Reasons for Discharge.   With evidence that more and more courts are ruling in favor of discharged employees, with the history of arbitrators reversing discharge decisions more than 50 percent of the time, and after reflecting on a National Labor Relations Board (NLRB) 1979 report which shows back-pay awards totaling $16.5 million to 14,627 workers, it makes good sense to examine those causes for dismissal which have less chance of being reversed at a later date.[12] Figure 12.2 shows the relationship between good-cause and no-cause situations that lead to discharge.

JUST CAUSE.   The following constitute "good cause" reasons for discharge which have been upheld in recent court decisions:[13]

1. Absenteeism (the principal reason given by employers for discipline and discharge.)[14]
2. Incompetence in performance that cannot be corrected by training.
3. Repeated insubordination.
4. Verbal abuse and physical violence.

5. Falsification of records.
6. Drinking on the job.
7. Theft.

As we stated in Chapter 11, discharge should be the last step in a progressive discipline process which documents decisions at each step in the procedure, regardless of the reason given for the discharge.

No-Cause Discharge Situations.   There are discharge situations that clearly could result in lawsuit or arbitration reversal. Employers should not fire workers for the following behavior or activities:

1. Engaging in peaceful and lawful union activity, or for filing unfair labor practices with the National Labor Relations Board.
2. Resisting work orders prohibited by federal or state law.
3. Filing discrimination charges with political units of government such as the EEOC or for complying with a statutory duty.
4. Cooperating in any governmental investigation of employer wrongdoing.

Employees may also have a case for challenging their dismissal based on the following employer behavior and activity:

5. Depriving employees of due process guaranteed under the Fourteenth Amendment to the Constitution.
6. Terminating employment under conditions of implied verbal or written contract.
7. Dismissing employees in "bad faith" in the absence of good or "just causes."

Several of these no-cause situations need explanation. Item 5 jeopardizes the finality of the discharge. One study suggests that 2.2 million employees are terminated each year without the due-process appeals procedures available to government and union employees.[15] Involuntary discharge is undeniably related to the discipline and grievance processes. In the absence of discipline and grievance procedures such as the ones suggested in Chapter 11, the employers stand to be sued in court by the discharged workers. Since many more employees are suing their former employers today and winning, organizations are being forced to reinstate the workers and/or pay back wages.

If it is decided that the reasons for discharge violate a relatively new doctrine called "public policy," the employee may win financial compensation for emotional damages.[16] Violating public policy includes firing a worker for resisting work orders prohibited by law, for filing workers'

Figure 12.2 Good-cause and no-cause reasons for discharge.

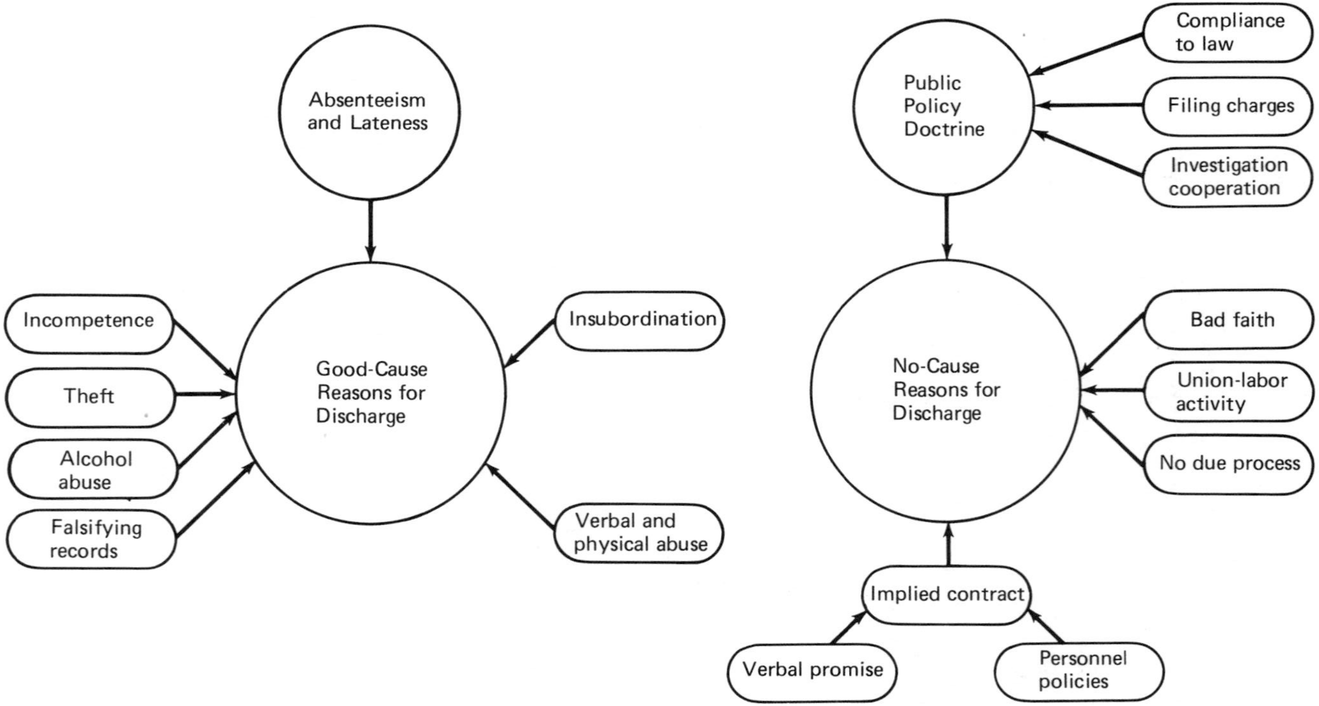

compensation claims or discrimination charges, or for cooperating in the investigation by an authorized governmental agency such as OSHA. Figure 12.2 shows the relationship of these three no-cause reasons for dismissal to public policy.

The doctrine of "implied contract" has been cited in very recent court decisions as another no-cause reason for dismissal.[17] Many employers and supervisors do not realize that when they hire a worker they may verbally insinuate to hire the employee permanently once the probationary period is concluded. It has been suggested that line supervisors should be instructed not to make claims about job security, and all personnel policies and manuals should be reviewed carefully to ensure that they are not implicitly promising the worker something the employer does not want or legally have to give. For example, conversation and documents should not use words such as "permanent employee" but should substitute words such as "regular employee."

General Electric and several other organizations have adopted a system that appears to have merit for park and recreation organizations. It requires disciplined employees to develop their own corrective behavior plans in an attempt to avoid costly lawsuits should the employee ultimately have to be fired. The premise is that a jury would not fault the employer for discharging an employee who fails to meet his or her own improvement plan of action.

Reluctance to Fire.   As a result of increasing judiciary and legislative restrictions on the employers' right to fire, as well as an emerging human rights consciousness, many supervisors and managers are demonstrating an unwillingness to fire employees unless the circumstances are so compelling that no alternative is possible.[18] Most supervisors agree that their most unpleasant job is firing an employee who does not measure up to the job.

Several reasons explain this reluctance to fire subordinates. Separations from the work force are unpleasant events, even when the reasons are impersonal and based on budget cuts or staff reductions. Discharged employees not only lose their wages, but their feelings of identity and self-worth may suffer even greater damage. Added to these negative short-term effects is the stigma that separation carries when the person seeks another job. Adding further insult to injury is the fact that most state unemployment compensation laws will not recognize discharged persons as eligible recipients for unemployment benefits. For all these reasons, few supervisors want to be responsible for causing such hardships on another person.

There are some very selfish reasons why supervisors are reluctant to recommend discharge for poor performance. Supervisors feel that a firing reflects ill on their ability to select, train, and lead employees. Upper management may informally support this position because of the high costs associated with turnover and recruiting new employees, and because other employees may have to take on the discharged person's duties in addition to their own. Not to be ignored is the possibility of a lawsuit filed against the employer alleging slander.

Approaching Discharge. Every supervisor has to face the unpleasant decision of discharge once in awhile. The best course of action is to make it with a minimum of delay and with the action carefully planned in advance. Remember the discussion on disciplinary action in Chapter 11. These four questions must be asked before the supervisor takes action:

1. *Was the employee warned?* If the worker was not warned, the supervisor should reconsider firing and try and salvage the worker. If the worker was warned, are there records documenting the warnings?
2. *Did the employee understand the ultimate consequences of not changing misbehavior or poor performance?* If the supervisor did not advise the worker that the next corrective action would be dismissal, the worker should be given one more chance and the final warning should be in writing to the personnel department, to the employee, and to the supervisor's boss. Furthermore, the employee should be given a period in which performance should improve, or termination will result.
3. *Was the employee given adequate training?* Did the supervisor train the employee, giving him or her all the help possible?
4. *Was the person right for the job in the first place?* If not, what can be learned from this mistake in selecting the replacement?

When all the questions can be answered satisfactorily, the supervisor should proceed with the discharge and call the employee into his or her office. The discharge interview should be kept very short and as painless as possible. Here are a few suggestions:

1. There is no point in wasting amenities. Get to the point immediately. State the purpose for the meeting.
2. Avoid trite expressions such as "this hurts me as much as it does you." This will only make the person angry.
3. Stick to the facts and avoid any discussion of poor attitudes. The task is to fire the person, not to improve his or her character.
4. Do not give advice. The person will not be influenced by anything you say.
5. Accept the fact that the person may place the blame on you, someone else—anything other than accepting it personally. Be charitable. Sit and listen and do not get dragged into emotional or defending verbal exchanges.

Separation Pay.   Separation pay is provided by organizations in lieu of several weeks' notice when a disruptive employee threatens to affect the morale of fellow workers if he or she remains on the job. Length of service is the criterion for determining the severance pay in most firms, with one week of severance pay for each year of service, up to a specified maximum figure.[19] Separation pay is also provided by many large organizations when they terminate employees for reasons other than just cause. For less than five years of service, the pay is typically just two weeks' pay.[20] This rule does not apply for top executives appointed under a political patronage system.

Case Study

POLITICAL PATRONAGE SEPARATION

Ten years ago five new public officials were elected to a County Board of Commissioners. When these men took office on January 1, they immediately held an executive session at 7:30 a.m. and hired a locksmith to change the locks on the office doors of four county department heads and the county executive officer. One of the directors was park and recreation director Ray S. All five employees served at the pleasure of the elected officials and were considered exempt from the employee civil service system.

Ray S. was notified by Mail-Gram that effective January 1, he had been dismissed with three weeks' severance pay. He was instructed to meet a sheriff's deputy at his former office at 8:00 a.m. on the following Monday. The deputy was to let him into the office, accompany him to remove any personal belongings, and receipt the return of his credit cards and the keys to various recreation buildings and the main office. No reason was given for the dismissal other than: "Your services will no longer be needed. The commissioners plan to reorganize the park and recreation department and hire a director supportive of their new plans."

Ray was stunned. He knew that several commissioners before they took office had publicly expressed their lack of support for two park projects, but his previous performance appraisal had been excellent and he had received a 15 percent merit increase in recognition of his outstanding service. The newspaper editor had commended his department for moving so quickly to meet the recreation needs of a rapidly growing county. Feeling betrayed and experiencing deep frustration, Ray S. began the search for another position.

Was Ray's firing legal?

Was it handled appropriately?

Political patronage appointments by newly elected officials are accepted practices of our two-party, representative democracy. Patronage means offering employment rewards to persons who perform the necessary tasks of getting a political candidate elected to office or who perform those tasks necessary to keep a political organization functioning.

Patronage is thought to serve a variety of governmental interests. Elected officials depend on appointees who hold similar views to carry out their policies and administer their programs. Political patronage serves the public interest by facilitating the implementation of policies endorsed by the voters. Patronage is practiced because it is thought that public employees immune to public elections will resist change without suffering job loss or cut in pay.[21] According to Justice Stewart: "The benefits of political patronage and the freedom of voters to structure their representative government justify the selection of certain public officials on the basis of political affiliation. The decision to place these positions in a civil service system should be left to the voters and the elected representatives of the people."[22]

The case study of Ray S. illustrates several points that have been accepted traditionally regarding the nature of patronage appointments in this country.

1. Top executives and even their seconds in command often are excluded from employee classification systems protected in union contracts, civil service systems, or personnel policies. These men and women serve at the whim of elected officials in government and accept this risky condition of employment at the time of hiring. They negotiate higher salaries and better benefits because they lack long-term job security. They often ask for a written contract for a given period. Elected officials have been known to ask for letters of resignations from appointed employees when the employees first report to work. These letters are kept on file until a later date when they may be activated at the pleasure of the "big boss."

   For many professionals in the park, recreation, and leisure field, the uncertainty of employment is worth the higher salary, excellent benefits, and perceived power to accomplish humanitarian goals. But this tenuous employment situation does not excuse the absence of dignity in discharging an employee, even if the separation pay is very generous. Elected officials who treat professional managers so shabbily are operating in another century. Not only do they jeopardize the goodwill of their supportive public, but good executives in all disciplines will soon boycott governmental units that allow such separation practices to continue.

2. There is no disgrace in losing a top-level park and recreation position because elected officials prefer the loyalty of better known political party supporters over persons such as Ray S. who are associated with a previous administration. State park directors have been particularly vulnerable to changes in administration but have not lost their professional image as competent administrators.

3. The voting population can express unhappiness with one administration by voting in a completely new group of legislators or execu-

tives, such as mayors or governors. They expect their elected officials to make reforms. With this challenge it is no wonder that elected officials appoint trusted people to key positions to help them carry out their constituents' desires. Hiring trusted party members means dismissing employees already filling those positions.

This explanation is not intended to excuse sloppy hiring and firing practices. Nor is it intended to defend a system where good administrators who efficiently accomplish the goals of their employers are later discharged for being so competent and loyal. The point of this discussion is to present the facts and arguments that support political patronage.

There are equally sound arguments in support of an employee classification system that includes executives, administrators, and managers who carry the professional credentials from their respective disciplines and who are not permitted to become involved in the arena of politics. An interesting Supreme Court decision in 1980 has given strong support to excluding public employees such as Ray S. from the patronage system (see Figure 12.3).

DISCHARGE FOR POLITICAL BELIEFS

A newly appointed public defender in Rockland County, New York, following a county legislature shift to the Democrats, notified two assistant public defenders that they were dismissed. They brought suit in U.S. District Court to be reinstated on the grounds that they had satisfactorily performed their jobs and had been discharged only because of their political beliefs, in violation of First and Fourteenth Amendments. The District Court, the U.S. Court of Appeals, and the U.S. Supreme Court decided that the public defender could not terminate the assistants' employment because they were neither policymakers nor confidential employees.*

This Supreme Court decision weakened the perogative of elected officials to hire and fire governmental employees on the basis of political affiliation. The First Amendment does not prohibit the use of membership in a national political party as a criterion for discharging public employess, but government officials have to *demonstrate* that a person's private beliefs must conform to those of the hiring authority. It is not a matter of the label "policymaker" or "confidential" fitting a particular position, but whether the hiring authority can prove that political party affiliation is a BFOQ.

*Three judges expressed the view that this decision intrudes into the area of legislative and administrative concerns which have traditionally decided matters concerning governmental practices. They question whether or not executive discretion may now be subject to judicial review and approval. Federal judges could become the final arbitrators, as to whom federal, state, and local government may employ, in violation of the separation of powers set forth in the U.S. Constitution.[23]

Figure 12.3

Layoffs

Layoff is not a termination in the strictest definition because the employer expects the no-work situation to be short term and plans to recall the worker when work is available. It is a separation, though, because the employee no longer receives monetary compensation. Layoff is defined as *an indefinite separation from the employing organization due to factors beyond the employer's and employee's control.*

In recent years it has not been uncommon for both public and private organizations to have to let employees go for financial reasons. Changes in business cycles and governmental administrations and diminished resources have left thousands of workers unemployed. Seniority is usually the determiner of who will continue to work.[24] An employee in one job may be allowed to "bump" or displace a worker in another job, provided that the worker can do the new assignments without additional training.

Layoff in the recreation, park, and leisure field has traditionally been associated with change in the seasons rather than loss of sales or production delays. Although temporary layoffs may become permanent separations, most organizations give preferential consideration to previous employees with good performance records. The National Park Service considers seasonal "rehires" over new employees, as do most resort and public park and recreation agencies. It is not difficult to understand why this is a common practice. Rehiring former employees with known work records reduces the risk of hiring a poorly performing employee and reduces the time and cost associated with orientation and training.

Employers may act to keep laid-off workers from seeking employment elsewhere by giving them noncompensatory benefits. Many laid-off workers continue to accumulate seniority for a certain period of time and claim recall rights. Time spent on layoff may count towards vacation, pension, and sickness benefits.[25] Assistance to employees under union contract often includes supplemental unemployment benefits. With both supplemental unemployment benefits and unemployment compensation payments, employees might receive 90 to 100 percent of their base pay while awaiting recall.[26]

Alternatives to Lay Off. It is not uncommon for organizations and unions to look at alternatives to lay off even in the park and recreation field. Work sharing is provided in many labor agreements. The most common worksharing practice is reduction in hours for many employees so that more employees may continue to work.[27] Labor agreements will usually specify how many hours may be cut back. In some instances, unions have not agreed to reduction in hours even if it means saving positions and employee jobs.

In Cincinnati, for example, Local 1543, Ohio Council No. 8 of the American Federation of State, County and Municipal Employees (AFSCME), filed both a grievance with the Civil Service Commission and a class-action suit in court on behalf of sixty-four community center directors whose positions were abolished on January 29, 1984. On January 30, the directors were given the option to be rehired at the same hourly rate for 30 hours per week for three-fourths of their base salary. The Recreation Department had chosen this course of action after consulting with the personnel department and the solicitor's office. A 20 percent budget reduction had forced the Recreation Department to lay off eighty-two full-time employees.

AFSCME, representing 3,000 city employees, claimed that the layoff violated civil service laws and the union contract, which forbids reducing employee hours except for disciplinary reason. The union lost the grievance with the Civil Service Commission, which said that the layoffs were for economic reasons, which is legal. The city, however, lost the court case and fourteen of the sixty-four center directors lost their jobs. This is one situation in which unions preferred the loss of jobs over work-sharing.

Retirement: Mandatory and Voluntary

Retirement is a relatively new condition in the human life. As recently as the early twentieth century, workers stayed on the job until they became disabled, were forced to leave their jobs by their employers, or died. When the Social Security Act was passed in 1935, it provided some financial security for workers who wanted to retire. Public and private pension plans have also increased the financial incentive to retire. A University of Michigan study estimated that one-third of American heads of households plan to retire before 65, and most of the rest plan to retire between the ages of 65 and 69.[28] This means that working men and women can expect years of retirement life since Americans of both sexes are living longer. The life expectancy of women is now 78 years and that of men is 70 years.

According to Robert N. Butler, Chairman of the Department of Geriatrics, Mount Sinai School of Medicine, New York City, the gap in longevity between men and women is widening, affecting the ability of women to obtain health care services in old age.[29] Retirement for women may be particularly difficult, as they face many more years of living on Social Security and limited pensions. Women will have a 60 percent chance of being destitute in old age because of lower earnings during their working years and because of inequalities in pensions.

Although life after retirement is usually desirable, most employees prior to retirement become apprehensive about not working and about

losing financial independence. They start thinking about what they have
and have not accomplished in life. For others, retirement may be a very
exciting personal adventure, a time to visit children, travel, and pursue
hobbies. In all cases, retirement is an important life change. To help
preretired employees make the mental adjustment through what may
be a difficult time, many employers are establishing a systematic process
of gradual preparation several years before the employees actually retire.[30] This represents an awareness on the part of employers that they
have a responsibility, in part, for an employee's retirement plans.[31] If
the employer cannot afford a structured program, the supervisor should
encourage the preretiree to contact local, state, and federal agencies which
offer preretirement assistance and information.

Retirement Planning

Retirement planning has found increased popularity in recent years.[32]
Employers are conducting retirement counseling sessions to encourage
employees to plan for retirement, both financially and emotionally. It is
an effort to eliminate fear of the future without work and to ease the
transition from worker to nonworker. The older employee, several years
before retirement, is encouraged to think about and make plans for all
the opportunities that lay ahead. Although workers in the recreation,
park resources, and leisure services field may already know about available recreation programs and facilities, they may need to think about
how they are going to use their time and in which activities they may
want to become involved.

Retirement planning also includes helping the employee identify public
and not-for-profit groups which provide services and assistance to older
Americans. The American Association of Retired Persons is a good example of a national organization that offers its members numerous benefits.

Financing preretirement planning is very important for the employee.
Retirement benefits such as Social Security and pension plans should
be thoroughly explained in terms of monthly income and survivor's benefits. Only about one-third of the entire U.S. work force is covered by
private pension programs, although this figure is growing as it becomes
increasingly obvious that Social Security benefits are not sufficient to
provide a comfortable life-style—nor was Social Security ever intended
to be an end-all. Many people do not realize that they have little retirement security until they approach retirement. Telling the employee two
years before her retirement that her income will be cut 50 percent may
be very devastating. Retirement financial planning should begin when
the worker approaches 50, not 60.

Retirement Security

Retirement plans were originally designed to reward good, long-service employees, but employer generosity, federal legislation, and union pressure have expanded retirement plans to cover almost every worker. The average firm spends 5.5 percent of its total payroll costs on private pensions, in addition to Social Security costs.[33]

There are several ways to develop a retirement plan. If the employer pays the entire amount, it is called a noncontributory plan. Contributory plans require contributions from both the employer and the employee. Some plans allow the employee to leave the company or governmental unit and still receive pension benefits if the employee has been "vested." Vesting means that the employee worked a minimum number of years for the employer. Should the employee leave before benefits are vested, the worker may only withdraw his or her own contributions plus a nominal interest rate earned on the employee's contribution to the pension.

Many plans mature before the worker reaches age 65 or 70, allowing the employee to retire early and still receive benefits. Retirement prior to age 65 has normally meant reduced benefits, but many employees are not even aware that early retirement is an option for them. This is why retirement planning is so important. Supervisors and employers have a responsibility to their workers to help them make the emotional, financial, and leisure transition from worker to retired citizen.

Supervisors should be aware of the possible "ripple" effect discussed previously that a retirement might have on other employees and the public. Anticipating any possible negative consequences will help the supervisor minimize the impact of those consequences on the remaining employees and the recreation programs.

Transfer: Involuntary and Voluntary

Transfer means to reassign an employee to another job of similar pay, status, and responsibility. It may be between job families or between geographical locations, or both. It may be initiated by the employer or the employee. Transfer is a separation only in the sense that the employee is separated from the supervisor, coworkers, subordinates, and a known working environment. There is no separation from pay. Demotions (a vertical move downward) and promotions (a vertical move upward in rank, pay, and responsibility) are not transfers. Separation for reasons of transfer may require special attention by the supervisor. If the move is initiated by the employer, it may be viewed with suspicion by the employee. Fewer motivational problems occur if the transfer is initiated by the worker.[34]

Reasons for Transfers

There are many reasons why employees ask to be transferred or why management seeks to move a worker. Employees may request relocation for the following reasons:

1. Unhappiness in the present work environment.
2. Perception that the present work environment offers no opportunity for career advancement.
3. Desire to live in a new location and accept new work challenges.
4. Need to follow a family member who must leave the area.

State park systems, armed forces recreation, the Corps of Engineers, and the National Park Service offer employees a variety of geographical opportunities, each with its own desirable features and advantages. Young and single professional employees often seek out different jobs in different locations, hoping to advance their careers.

Organizations elect to move employees to another work location for an equal number of reasons:

1. To match the personality, attitudes, and interests of an employee, which would be better suited to another location.
2. To correct an initial assignment where work skills and abilities to job responsibilities did not match.
3. To reward a conscientious worker.
4. To utilize outstanding abilities of an employee to solve a problem, initiate new programs, or improve productivity in another location.

Some transfers are only considered temporary, perhaps to fill an unplanned vacancy. Union contracts and civil service positions may restrict transfer by requiring that all job vacancies be posted so that all interested persons may apply. Recent court cases have decided in favor of seniority rights when new positions become available. Employers have to offer the new jobs to qualified senior workers who want to move to the new location.[35]

Resistance to Relocation

Employees appear to be resisting geographical transfers.[36] Women may be the exception to this growing reluctance to relocate. According to one report, career-minded women hoping for future promotion almost never turn down transfers.[37] Although marital and family stability are the reasons given by men for their reluctance to move, studies indicate that nonmobile employees are less satisfied with their marriages and family life than are mobile employees.[38] These apparently contradictory facts should warn employers and supervisors to exercise caution in initiating employee transfers that require geographical relocation.

The important thing to remember about transfers is that these kinds of separations can have the same kinds of traumatic impact on other employees as does discharge, resignation, layoff, or retirement. Similarly, the cohesion of a particular work group may be lessened and communication linkages will be broken.

Voluntary Separation

An employee may initiate termination by voluntarily resigning his or her position from the organization. It should not be assumed that the employee is leaving because another position looks more attractive or promises better pay or benefits. A worker may choose to resign because he knows he is one step away from discharge, because he feels the supervisor's expectations are unrealistic, because he was passed up for promotion, or because he feels he is being "pushed" out deliberately by the supervisor. Internal conflicts should be carefully explored for future resolution during the exit interview (discussed in the next section).

There are many reasons why an employee may seek voluntary separation which do not suggest the need for an internal witchhunt. These reasons should also be explored during and after the exit interview to provide the organization with knowledge about its competition for good employees. Facts on the turnover of talented workers who are getting better salaries and benefits elsewhere may convince decision makers to establish better pay scales with better benefit packages. Since most recreation, leisure services, and park resources organizations do not employ hundreds of employees, much less thousands of employees, it becomes necessary for many employees to resign and look elsewhere for career advancement and better pay. Only a few workers can hope to reach middle and upper levels of management within the organization in which they began their working careers. Add to this condition of employer's size the situation of low salaries at entry levels, and it is not surprising that turnover may seem higher in the leisure field.

Separation Procedures

- How do employees leave a job?
- Do they work up to quitting time, wave goodbye, and disappear without anyone asking why they are leaving or where they may be reached?

- Are discharged employees permitted to return to work for a period of time after being notified that they are being fired?

Supervisors need to know the answers to these questions, as well as understanding which procedures the organization follows for each type of separation, and what responsibilities the immediate supervisor and the supervisor's boss have in any out-processing functions or exit interviews.

Out-Processing

Most of the out-processing functions are conducted by the personnel unit in order to clear the employee for departure. Payroll and accounting records need to be updated, unemployment or retirement benefits explained, severance pay processed, and related documentation completed. The departing employee usually has to sign a final termination form.

The immediate supervisor or some other designated agent of the employer is responsible for securing the departing employee's keys, uniforms, credit cards, documents, badges, weapons, and any other property belonging to the employer. Those forms must also be completed and signed. The immediate supervisor may have to initiate a "notice of termination" form (with an attached letter of resignation, if appropriate) to the personnel unit and to his or her own immediate supervisor which explains why the employee is terminating or being terminated. In addition, the supervisor may be asked to complete a final performance evaluation on the terminated employee, listing job duties and comments on performance characteristics. These would include measurable performance deficiencies, unacceptable behavior, and significant undesirable events. The supervisor will have to recommend whether the employee should be rehired.

The supervisor's report of termination may be very crucial in the payment of unemployment insurance claims, a major cost to the employer. When factual documentation is lacking, the state agency generally accepts the employee's claim even though it might not be accurate. Similarly, the outcome of any future lawsuit of unfair labor practices or complaint of discrimination may depend on final documentation of the employee's performance and reason for leaving.

Exit Interview

An exit interview is a discussion between the departing employee and a representative of the organization to determine conditions within the organization that may be contributing to employee turnover and to learn what other organizations are offering that attracts employees. The following remark has been overhead more than once:

"Why bother with an exit interview? The guy is leaving—so who cares?"

The answer to that question is always the same: "The organization cares!" It is a matter of good business, good public relations, and good professional ethics. (1) Top administrators want to improve the agency's efficiency, public image, and work force morale by improving personnel practices, policies, procedures, benefits, and working conditions. (2) It is a matter of good public relations because the employee has relatives, neighbors, and friends who live in the community, people served by the park and recreation department, the YMCA, or the local country club. The image of the organization is at stake. By defusing any anger during the exit interview, the employee is less likely to hurt the employer. (3) It is a matter of ethics because the organization is a composite of hardworking employees who want to maintain self-respect. Anything that might help a fired employee maintain self-respect helps the remaining workers feel better about themselves.

The exit interview has been the traditional mechanism to find out "what's wrong with us," although many authorities have begun to question the value of asking a departing employee to "level" with the agency.[39] Employees leave, whether voluntarily or involuntarily, with a degree of ambivalence. Feelings are strong at this time. Workers leaving friends and good memories tend to whitewash the organization. If they experience resentment and anger, they may describe nonexisting problems. At best, they are rarely in a frame of mind to be objective. Furthermore, these people may be reluctant to reveal their real reasons for leaving. In spite of these problems, we strongly recommend that exit interview opportunities be made available for separating employees, even if the procedure is optional.

Who Should Conduct the Exit Interview?   There does not seem to be agreement on the answer to this question. Some authorities suggest a neutral person with whom the employee can be open and frank, such as a person trained in counseling in the personnel unit. There are two benefits of having the same person conduct all exit interviews. First, this person can become very skilled in the interview techniques discussed in detail in Chapter 5. Supervisors may understand counseling techniques but have little opportunity to develop skill in applying those techniques. Second, if the same person conducts all exit interviews, he or she may begin to detect patterns of similar complaints, problem areas, or conditions that lead to discharge or cause employees to resign. He or she can keep these statistics on turnover for the entire organization until some conclusions can be documented and recommendations made for changes.

Confidentiality is also important. Many employees will not trust a strange personality in a different work unit or department.[40] They want to talk to a familiar, nonthreatening personality who understands their specific work environment. It is a real dilemma. Although the supervisor best knows the employee, the work environment, and the job responsibilities, the immediate supervisor should not conduct exit interviews. The very closeness of the supervisor–employee relationship poses a built-in handicap.

Familiarity not only reduces the ability of the immediate supervisor to be objective in interpreting critical remarks directed at the organization or the immediate work unit, but familiarity also affects the worker's desire to be open and honest. He or she may see the "boss" as the same irritating and misunderstanding person who formerly controlled many of the resources and rewards of employment.[41] He or she also knows that the immediate supervisor controls the content of future job references. These reasons may also apply for the immediate supervisor's boss if the organization is small and everyone works together in the same location or office.

Nevertheless, we recommend that whenever possible, depending on the established procedures for separation, the supervisor's supervisor conduct an exit interview with every separated employee. This should be coordinated with the personnel unit to make the out-processing and termination experience as smooth and nonthreatening a transition as possible for the employee.

Conducting the Exit Interview. Some organizations claim to hold exit interviews when they administer only impersonal questionnaires such as the one in Figure 12.4 to employees who are resigning. This form limits the employees response and provides no opportunity for two-way conversation, but it is popular because it is safe, unemotional, and brief.[42] No one has to risk his or her real feelings.

Not only does the use of any form in the absence of an interview limit responses, but the answers do not always provide enough information to be meaningful. For example, if the employee checks "the job" and "immediate supervisor" as the two reasons for leaving, management still does not know which job and supervisory characteristics caused the resignation. If a self-conducted questionnaire is completed by the employee during the exit interview, the questions should provide specific information pointing to identifiable problems of weaknesses within the organization. For example, an employee can be asked to rate specific characteristics pertaining to the supervisor and to the job, as follows (where 1 = very dissatisfied and 5 = very satisfied):

Exit Questionnaire

(Completed by the Employee)

Name _____   Social Security Number _____

Work Unit _____

| REASON(S) FOR LEAVING |

Check below the appropriate reason(s) for leaving

| FUTURE PLANS |

Check below your immediate plans

Reasons for Leaving	
Work Related	Personal

• No advancement opportunity _____
 • Inadequate recognition _____
 • Personality conflict
     w/supervisor _____
     w/coworkers _____
 • Poor social climate _____
 • Immediate supervisor _____
 • Upper management _____
 • Work standards _____
 • Benefits _____
 • Working conditions _____
 • Pay _____
 • Nature of work _____
	• Military _____
	 • Maternity _____
	 • Marriage _____
	 • Return to school _____
	 • Family relocation _____
	 • Transportation problems _____
	 • Other_____ _____

Future Plans	
• Accepted new job _____ • Working part-time _____ • Self-employed _____ • Stay at home _____	• Looking for another job _____ • Leaving work force _____ • Return to former job _____ • Care for relative _____
• Other _____	

Figure 12.4 Inappropriate exit questionnaire.

Your Supervisor	*Sample Score*
1. Supervisor's technical competence	5
2. Supervisor's awareness and understanding of employees' problems	3
3. Supervisor's advance planning of job assignments	4
4. Supervisor's interest in employees' career development	2

Your Job

1. Opportunity to use abilities and skills   2
2. Amount of responsibility given   3
3. Opportunity to supervise other people   1

It is a better idea to use a standard form for an exit interview—completed by the person conducting the interview. As the employee supplies the answers to very general questions such as those in Figure 12.5, the interviewer can jot down a few notes and then later summarize the employee's opinions and factual comments onto the form. Although the same form may be used for both voluntary and involuntary exit interviews (resignations and discharges), it is necessary to customize the questions that will be asked during the interview. The following statements give the reader some indication of how exit interviews have to be tailored for the situation.

- *Standard opening for every exit interview.* "Each time a recreation employee leaves our organization an exit interview is conducted. It is a policy of Memorial Hospital's Recreation Department. We hope to learn something about ourselves from your comments, and appreciate your time and help. I personally guarantee that anything you tell me will be kept confidential."
- *Sample for involuntary separation.* "Could you give me some suggestions as to how we might remedy the problems you experienced with us? By learning more about what caused your termination we might make the working situation better here in the recreation department." (Touch on resources, training, procedures, communications, etc.)
- *Sample for voluntary separation.* "Tell me what can be done to make our work unit a better place to work in respect to . . . ." (Touch on play unit, planning, communication feedback, etc.) Would you be interested in working part-time for us on weekends or evenings?"

Figure 12.6 provides a step-by-step procedure to use in planning and conducting an exit interview. The nondirective interview technique described in Chapter 5 is as applicable for the exit interview as it was for the selection interview. Do you remember the steps of the nondirective interview technique? (Initiate, listen, focus, and probe.)

The present section began (see page 291) by asking three questions.

- How do employees leave a job?
- Do they work up to quitting time and disappear?
- Are discharged employees permitted to return to work after being notified that they are fired?

Exit Interview Form

Summary by _____ For _____ On _____
         (Interviewer)   (Employee)   (Date)

| Major Reason for Leaving |

_____

_____

| Exit Interview Results |

The Job (Duties) _____

_____

(Positive aspects) _____

_____

(Negative aspects) _____

_____

Supervisor _____

_____

Coworkers _____

_____

Management Policies, Practices, Communications _____

_____

Working Conditions _____

_____

Personal Problems _____

_____

| Do You Recommend Us as an Employer? | _____

(Why, why not) _____

_____

| Recommended for Rehire? | _____

(Reasons) _____

_____

| What Actions Might Have Retained/Rehabilitated Employee? | ____

_____

| Recommendations | _____

_____

Figure 12.5 Recommended exit interview form.

EXIT INTERVIEW PROCEDURES

Step 1: Plan the Interview

1.1 Select time, neutral location, and notify employee.
1.2 Collect employment data:
   1.21 Performance appraisals.
   1.22 Disciplinary information.
   1.23 Supervisory comments.
   1.24 Review service/benefit package.
1.3 Develop topic areas to be covered:
   1.31 Job characteristics.
   1.32 Supervisor and coworker relationships.
   1.33 Organization's policies, procedures, and benefits.
   1.34 Reasons for leaving, if resignation.
   1.35 Recommendations for improving work unit.
   1.36 Service–benefits package explanations.
1.4 Identify potential problems, employee reactions, and appropriate interviewer responses.

Step 2: Conduct the Interview

2.1 Get to the point and state the purpose of the interview.
2.2 Avoid emotionally loaded statements and responses.
2.3 Stick to facts and avoid personalities.
2.4 Do not give advice or defend the employer.
2.5 Avoid "yes"–"no" questions.
2.6 *Listen, listen, listen,* (80 percent of the time).
2.7 Tell employee what the next step is.
2.8 Keep it short (twenty to forty minutes).

Step 3: Evaluate the Interview Results

3.1 Complete the exit interview summary form.
3.2 Seek additional support information for particularly sensitive issues.
3.3 Look for trends from previous interviews.
3.4 Recommend corrective action, or take such action.

Figure 12.6

The first two questions have been answered indirectly in the preceding discussion. The third question deserves more attention.

Every organization will have its own policy and procedure for discharging employees. Collective bargaining agreements will also stipulate the exact procedure for discharge. Those procedures should be carefully reviewed by the supervisor before any action is initiated toward terminating the employment of a subordinate. We offer a few comments here, based on personal experience and observations, a review of the literature, and discussions with park and recreation managers.

It is not a good practice to return employees to work after they have been notified of their discharge. They should return to their work location, get their belongings, and go home—with pay if it is necessary to make the official termination date several days after the notification.

Arrangements for the out-processing appointment will have to be coordinated and scheduled as soon as possible with the appropriate persons and the employee must understand that all documentation will have to be completed before severance pay and final remuneration can be released. But discharged employees should not be permitted to return to work for even a short period of time.

This practice holds true for employees who did not anticipate layoff. Each set of circumstances is different, but in all situations, the employee is in no frame of mind to complete assignments or function on the job. Distress, anxiety over the future, anger, and resentment are only a few of the emotions that could affect the morale of the remaining work force. Worse yet, sabotage, vandalism, theft, and work stoppage for others are all possible behaviors that might result from involuntary separations.

Summary and Recommendations

1. The problem of employee turnover is complex. It has both negative and positive potential consequences for individuals, employers, and society. Management and supervisors must understand the impact of turnover and provide the right work environment to minimize the negative and costly consequences of employee separations.
2. Often, employee separations result in reducing costs, revitalizing the organization, and creating promotion opportunities for remaining workers.
3. Involuntary separations include discharges, political patronage termination, layoff, and mandatory retirement. Transfer can also be considered a separation because the employee is separated from co-workers and the known working environment. Employees may resign voluntarily for many reasons.
4. Termination at will by the employer with or without just cause was a common management practice until recent years. Legislation, court decisions, unions, and civil service systems have provided some protection from unjust firing, but many workers are still vulnerable to dismissal for reasons that are not job related.
5. Absenteeism heads the list of good-cause reasons why employers fire workers. Other reasons that have been upheld in court include incompetence, insubordination, verbal abuse and physical violence, theft, and drinking on the job.

6. Discharges that could result in a lawsuit include breaking an implied contract for permanent employment, dismissing without good cause or due process procedures or for engaging in union activity, and firing for resisting orders to violate public policy or federal or state laws.

7. Supervisors should not avoid firing an employee because it is an unpleasant experience, or because of the hardships that discharge causes the employee and family, or because of the possibility of a prolonged siege of grievances or lawsuits. If the employee was the right person for the job in the first place, received adequate training, knew the rules and ultimate consequences, and had been warned previously, the supervisor has no alternative but to discharge a worker who will not perform.

8. In the past, political patronage served a variety of governmental and citizen interests in our democratic, representative system. It is still not uncommon for top executives to be excluded from the protection of civil service systems or union contract, and there is no disgrace if they are fired because elected officials change and want their own party supporters in key positions. But political patronage should not excuse sloppy firing practices or the absence of dignity in discharging political appointees.

9. Employers continue to seek alternatives to lay off in order to protect positions and keep good workers. The most common type of work-sharing is reduction in hours for many employees so that more men and women may continue to work.

10. A good retirement planning program should offer employees in their 50s leisure, financial, and emotional counseling to ease the transition from worker to nonworker. Many people do not realize what financial benefits they are entitled to receive until after they retire. Unfortunately, many of these benefits do not provide adequate security. Similarly, many lifelong recreation pursuits will not provide adequate fulfillment after retirement. Employers have a responsibility to their workers to help them plan for retirement.

11. Employers should exercise caution in initiating employee transfers that require geographical relocation. Unless the employee has requested the transfer, it may be viewed with suspicion. Male employees appear to be resisting transfers.

12. The function of out-processing includes updating employee records, explaining entitled benefits, processing separation pay and final compensation, securing property belonging to the employer, and completing final performance evaluations. Factual documentation on why the employee is leaving and comments on performance characteristics are very necessary to meet the requirements of unem-

ployment insurance claims and to provide evidence should lawsuits or complaints be filed in the future.

13. The exit interview is a discussion between the departing employee and a representative of the employer to determine conditions within the organization that led to the separation. Although exit interviews sometimes raise the question of whether or not the information provided is reliable, separating employees should be given an opportunity to express their feelings and observations about the employer. It is good business and good public relations.

14. The supervisor's boss or someone in the personnel unit should conduct the exit interview. The exit interview process should include carefully planning the interview and collecting all available employment data, conducting the interview in twenty to forty minutes, and listening 80 percent of the time, and then evaluating the interview results to take corrective action, if necessary.

Discussion Topics

1. What are the potential positive consequences of separation? What are the negative consequences?
2. What is meant by the concept of "termination at will"? Is it a valid doctrine for today's employment decisions?
3. On what grounds is it unwarranted to fire employees?
4. In your opinion, how much right does the employer have to discharge employees? What considerations are necessary before an employer can terminate employment?
5. Why are managers often reluctant to discharge employees?
6. What is the difference between the discharge interview and the exit interview? What is the difference between exit interview and out-processing?
7. If a man is promoted or transferred and then fails to perform well on the new job, should he be returned to his old job? Demoted? Discharged? What if someone else was hired or promoted into his old job?
8. If a land development corporation after operating a recreation complex for five years completes a planned community and turns over title of all the recreation facilities to the new homeowners' association, what rights to jobs do the recreation personnel have? Should the corporation transfer them to another resortlike site? Should the association retain the employees for a given period of time?
9. Do you agree with the patronage system? Why or why not?
10. Explain the steps in the exit interview process.

Notes

1. Stephen A. Stumpf and Nancy M. Hanrahan, "Designing Organizational Career Management Practices to Fit Strategic Management Objectives," in *Readings in Personnel and Human Resource Management*, 2nd ed., by Randall Schuler and Stuart Youngblood (St. Paul, Minn.: West Publishing Co., 1984), p. 327.
2. William H. Mobley, *Employee Turnover: Causes, Consequences, and Control* (Reading, Mass.: Addison-Wesley Publishing Co., Inc., 1982), p. 20.
3. Mobley, *Employee Turnover*, p. 42.
4. Ibid.
5. Edward Roseman, *Managing Employee Turnover: A Positive Approach* (New York: AMACOM Book Division, 1981), p. 7.
6. Michael Abelson and Barry Baysinger, "Optimal and Dysfunctional Turnover: Toward an Organizational Level Model," in *Readings in Personnel and Human Resource Management*, 2nd ed., by Randall S. Schuler and Stuart Youngblood (St. Paul, Minn.: West Publishing Co., 1984), p. 531.
7. Randall Schuler, *Personnel and Human Resource Management*, 2nd ed. (St. Paul, Minn.: West Publishing Co., 1984), p. 497.
8. Dale Beach, *Personnel: The Management of People at Work*, 4th ed. (New York: Macmillan Publishing Company, 1980), p. 350.
9. Social Issues, "It's Getting Harder to Make a Firing Stick," *Business Week* (June 27, 1983): 104.
10. Gary Dessler, *Personnel Management: Modern Concepts and Techniques*, 3rd ed. (Reston, Va.: Reston Publishing Co., Inc., 1984), p. 514.
11. Social Issues, "It's Getting Harder to Make a Firing Stick," p. 104.
12. Stuart Youngblood and Gary Tidwell, "Termination at Will: Some Changes in the Wind," in *Readings in Personnel and Human Resource Management*, 2nd ed., by Randall Schuler and Stuart Youngblood (St. Paul, Minn.: West Publishing Co., 1984), p. 408.
13. Randall Schuler, *Effective Personnel Management* (St. Paul, Minn.: West Publishing Co., 1983), p. 251.
14. Youngblood and Tidwell, "Termination at Will," p. 406.
15. Social Issues, "It's Getting Harder to Make a Firing Stick," p. 104.
16. Peter Panken, "How to Keep a Firing from Backfiring," *Nation's Business* 71 (June 1983): 74.
17. Ibid.
18. Arthur Sloane, *Personnel: Managing Human Resources* (Englewood Cliffs, N.J.: Prentice-Hall, Inc., 1983), p. 410.
19. Dessler, *Personnel Management*, p. 514.
20. Beach, *Personnel*, p. 674.
21. *U.S. Supreme Court Reports: Lawyers Edition*, (Rochester, N.Y.: The Lawyers Co-operative Publishing Co.), (Vol. 63L, 2nd ed., No. 3, April 30, 1980), p. 590.
22. Ibid.
23. Ibid.
24. Dessler, *Personnel Management*, p. 512.

25. Beach, *Personnel,* p. 346.
26. Marc Wallace, Frederic Crandall, and Charles Fay, *Administering Human Resources* (New York: Random House, Inc., 1982), p. 275.
27. Beach, *Personnel,* p. 347.
28. Wallace, Crandall, and Fay, *Administering Human Resources,* p. 280.
29. Sharon Johnson, "Women Outpacing Men in Life Expectancy," *News and Observer,* Raleigh, N.C. (May 27, 1984): 27A.
30. Robert Mathis and John Jackson, *Personnel: Contemporary Perspectives and Applications* (St. Paul, Minn.: West Publishing Co., 1982), p. 375.
31. Schuler, *Effective Personnel Management,* p. 637.
32. William Werther and Keith Davis, *Personnel Management and Human Resources* (New York: McGraw-Hill Book Company, 1981), p. 308.
33. Ibid, p. 307.
34. Wallace, Crandall, and Fay, *Administering Human Resources,* p. 272.
35. Beach, *Personnel,* p. 345.
36. Dessler, *Personnel Management,* p. 511.
37. Schuler, *Effective Personnel Management,* p. 123.
38. Dessler, *Personnel Management,* p. 511.
39. Robert Baylor, "Exit Interviews of Departing Employees Can Provide Valuable Management Information," *Practical Accountant* 14(June 1981): 66.
40. Roseman, *Managing Employee Turnover,* p. 178.
41. Aaron Sartain and Alton Baker, *The Supervisor and the Job* (New York: McGraw-Hill Book Company, 1978), p. 235.
42. Roseman, *Managing Employee Turnover,* p. 175.

13

Collective Bargaining

Many people would be surprised to know that almost 43 percent of the local public park and recreation agencies in the United States have at least some portion of their employees involved in collective bargaining.[1] Also, about 23 percent of the supervisory personnel in these organizations belong to bargaining units.[2] In some agencies, all full-time park and recreation employees, professionals and nonprofessionals alike, belong to bargaining units.

Organized labor involvement is not confined to local government. Leisure service professionals working in hospitals, at large resorts, on cruise ships, in amusement parks, and cultural arts centers may also find themselves members of a union. Even Smokey the Bear's best friend, the U.S. Forest Service ranger, may be carrying a union card in his or her hip pocket. There can be no doubt; organized labor is a significant element in the working lives of many leisure professionals.

This chapter starts with a brief look at the history and key legislation of the labor movement in the United States. Additional sections help the reader understand how unions are structured, how bargaining units are organized, and the role that a supervisor plays in a collective bargaining situation. A strong effort is made throughout the chapter to relate all material to the leisure service field. The general public often uses terms such as *unionize, union,* and *union movement* in very vague ways. Actually, employees can be organized and bargain collectively but not belong to a union. In this chapter, key terms will be used according to their precise definitions. Figure 13.1 defines various key terms and the reader should be familiar with these terms before reading further.

GLOSSARY OF COMMONLY USED TERMS IN LABOR RELATIONS

Bargaining agent: the formally designated organization, generally a labor union, which represents employees during the process of seeking and administering a labor agreement.

Bargaining unit: a group of employees who are represented by a union or employee association which serves as their bargaining agent.

Collective bargaining: the performance of the mutual obligations of the employer and the exclusive representative of the employees to meet at reasonable times, to confer and negotiate in good faith, and to execute a written agreement with respect to wages, hours, and other terms and conditions of employment, except that by any such obligation neither party will be compelled to agree to a proposal or be required to make a concession.[3]

Employee association: an organization of persons linked together by common job-related interests. May or may not serve as a bargaining agent for its membership.

Lockout: the suspension of work initiated by the employer as the result of a labor dispute. The antithesis of a strike, which is initiated by the employees.

Management's rights: from management's viewpoint, "the right to manage"; the right of management to make certain decisions and take certain actions without notification to, consultation with, or negotiation with the union. Management would usually contend that the rights are nonnegotiable issues.

Negotiable: matters of principle, policy, and practice relating to wages, hours, and other conditions of employment which the parties agree they can discuss and about which they can bargain.[4]

Strike: the concerted failure to report for work or the stoppage of work for the purpose of influencing or coercing a change in the conditions, compensation, privileges, or obligations of employment.

Union: an association of employees organized to further their mutual interest with respect to wages, hours, and working conditions of their employment.

Union steward: a member of the work group who serves as the union's representative and carries out such union duties as handling grievances, collecting dues, and recruiting new members. The steward continues to work at his or her regular job and performs union duties on a part-time basis.

Figure 13.1

Overview of the Private Sector

As the United States moved into the industrial age during the last decades of the eighteenth and early part of the nineteenth centuries, organized labor began to flourish. However, a number of circumstances occurred to make the early organized labor movement a sporadic and sometimes frustrating struggle. The labor movement's growth did not follow a steady, straightforward line of development.

The expanding frontier and improved transportation system made the growing young nation a prominent market for goods and services. Competition for new markets became furious; business owners who were unwilling or unable to reduce costs and maximize productivity lost out to those who did. To survive or, in some cases, take advantage of opportunities for huge profits, employers typically (1) hired women and children at very low wages, (2) cut wages of male workers, (3) increased the hours in the work day, (4) subdivided the work into a series of minute tasks that could be accomplished more efficiently (but were very repetitive and boring), and (5) hired aggressive overseers to strictly enforce tightened work standards.[5]

The first workers to challenge the early capitalists were the skilled tradesmen, such as shoemakers, carpenters, and printers. These groups not only had the most to lose in the new industrial system but also had the most power to exert against employers. Although there was no collective bargaining as we know it today, these workers would sometimes establish a minimum wage or working condition below which they would not work. To achieve their desires, workers would resort to strikes, which were for the most part peaceful and successful.[6]

By 1836, it was estimated that about 300,000 workers, 6.5 percent of the labor force, were union members. The following year brought a severe and long economic depression, however, and the labor movement vanished almost completely.[7] Unions thrived when the economy was strong and struggled when the economy was weak. This phenomenon is still generally true today. Another factor that greatly restricted early union growth was the judicial system and its interpretation of the law. For example, because they banded together to achieve their means, organized employees were defined by the law as conspirators until 1842.[8]

During the 1870s and 1880s the confrontations between labor and industry took on a violent character. During this time period, an aura of hostility and anger was produced that is still reflected in society's view of union–management confrontations today. Employers began utilizing a new series of tactics against organized labor: employees were locked out of their workplaces, spies were hired to infiltrate worker groups, union sympathizers were fired and blacklisted, and strikebreakers were employed. Unions, unable to react through the political and legal systems, retaliated with violence. Federal troops had to be used to quell the violence of rioting workers in Chicago and Pittsburgh during railroad strikes. The infamous Molly Maguires, a secret society of union miners, killed and burned in the coal-mining areas of Pennsylvania.

In 1886, a significant new organization, the American Federation of Labor (AFL), was formed. This organization, more than any other, shaped the cause of organized labor in the United States today. The AFL united a number of labor groups, mostly associated with the trades, into one overall organization. Under the direction of the pragmatic Samuel Gompers, the AFL focused its attention on direct concerns such as the wages and working conditions of its members. It avoided broad, long-term social goals such as land reform and temperance which would supposedly improve the general condition of the entire working class in the United States.[9] Gompers advocated the use of strikes and worked for an effective system of controlling and sustaining strikes. In spite of Gompers and the AFL, union growth was slow and sporadic until the 1930s.

Significant Federal Legislation

The Great Depression, although devastating to millions of American workers, provided great impetus for the organized labor movement. Many people blamed the Depression on business and shifted their sentiment toward the work class.[10] Thus an important piece of legislation, the National Labor Relations Act, was passed in 1935. This act, more commonly referred to as the Wagner Act, was essentially a commitment by the federal government to protect the right of employees to bargain collectively. Although modified by court decisions and amendments, this act serves as the cornerstone of labor–management relations in this country today.

The Wagner Act clearly and specifically restricted certain "unfair labor practices" by management and established the National Labor Relations Board (NLRB), an independent, quasi-judicial agency, to enforce the provisions of the act. The NLRB was charged with investigating unfair labor practices by management and conducting the elections that determine if employee groups wish to bargain collectively. The passage of the National Labor Relations Act had the effect of moving labor–management relations from violence in the streets to negotiations at the bargaining tables. In short, it provided strong federal government support for labor unions.

Thanks to the Wagner Act, union membership rose rapidly after 1935 to 15 million in 1947.[11] Immediately after World War II, unions used their newfound strength in a series of long and controversial strikes. Quickly, public opinion began to turn against organized labor; many Americans felt that the Wagner Act had been too favorable to unions. In 1947, a newly elected Republican-controlled Congress passed the Taft–Hartley Act to amend the Wagner Act. Whereas the Wagner Act had originally been passed to protect unions from management abuses, the Taft-Hartley amendment added protection for management from union abuses. With the passage of Taft-Hartley, the federal government put itself in a position of being the "referee" of union–management relations. In other words, the national government of this country assumed responsibility for establishing the rules of conduct so that (1) both labor

Figure 13.2 The federal government's role as "referee."

308

and management would have the opportunity to function without unfair restraint, and (2) the best interest of the general public would be maintained.

During the 1950s certain union officials were investigated and found to be engaging in unethical and corrupt practices. In addition, individual employees were sometimes being coerced and abused. In response, Congress passed in 1959 the Labor–Management Reporting and Disclosure Act (Landrum–Griffin Act). This act requires extensive reporting on numerous internal union activities, establishes specific ground rules for union elections, and guarantees the rights of union members in certain union relationships.[12] Whereas Taft–Hartley set the rules for labor–management relations, Landrum–Griffin was a serious step by the federal government to force compliance with those rules. In addition, as depicted in Figure 13.2, the federal government also meant to look out for the rights of individual employees.

As we explained earlier, the Wagner Act, as amended by Taft–Hartley and Landrum–Griffin, provides a broad outline of federal labor policy. It is not a national policy, however; it deals only with the major elements of policy for the private sector. It does not apply to either federal employees or state and local public employees. History and legislation specific to public-sector employees are discussed in the next section. Also, the National Labor Relations Act (Wagner Act) has left some specific policy to be determined by the individual states. To illustrate, Taft–Hartley left up to each individual state the matter of allowing or rejecting labor agreements that require union membership as a condition of employment. Much against the wishes of organized labor, twenty states (frequently referred to as "right to work" states) have passed legislation that gives employees the right to determine whether they want to become union members. These states are indicated in Figure 13.3. In most of the remaining states, such as Michigan and Massachusetts, union membership (or at least paying dues in support of the union) is a requirement for employment in any work group represented by a union.

Overview of the Public Sector

Federal Employee Regulations

For decades the total focus of the labor movement in the United States was on the private sector. Public employees, for a number of reasons, did not join private-sector unions or establish their own bargaining units. All of that began to change around 1960. From 1965 to 1975, union membership at the federal level rose from 319,724 to 1,200, 316, a 275 percent increase.[13] The increase in state and local government figures are just as

Figure 13.3 "Right to work" states. (From information provided by The National Right to Work Committee, 8316 Arlington Blvd., Fairfax, VA 22038.)

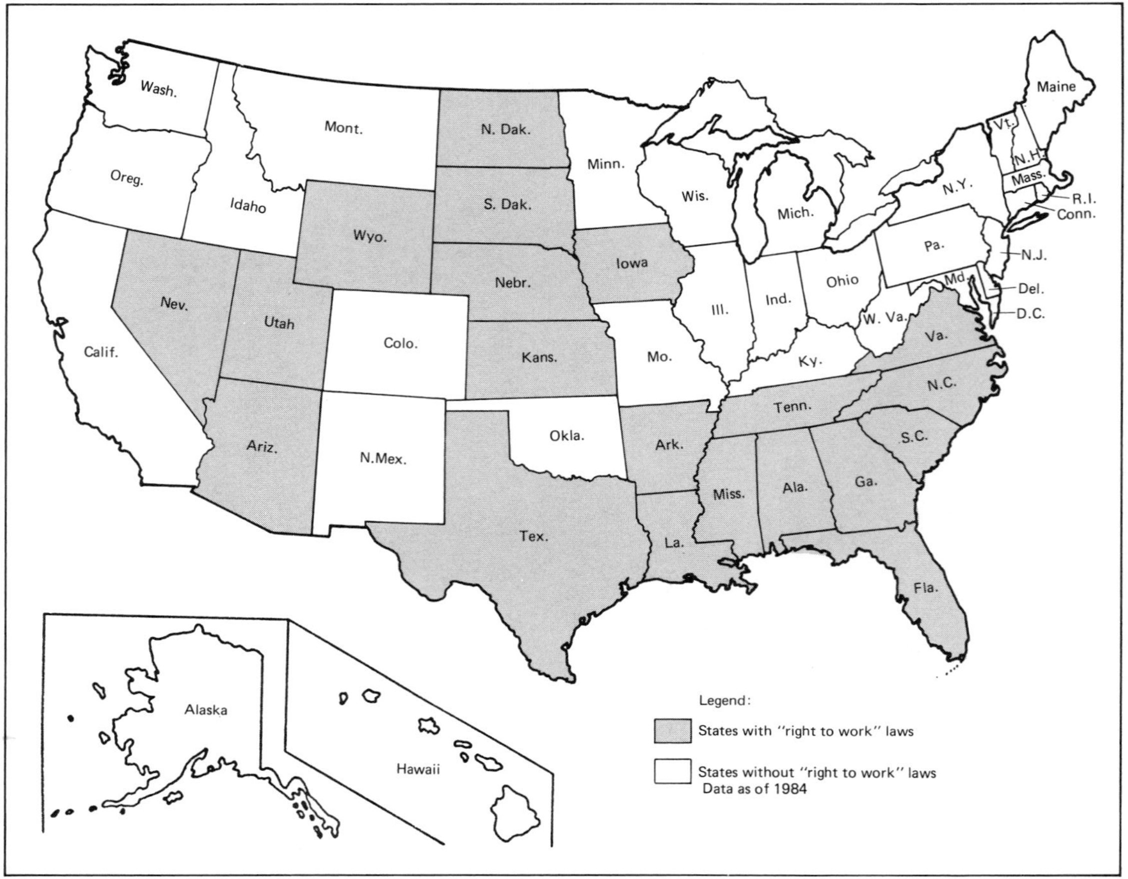

Legend:

States with "right to work" laws

States without "right to work" laws
Data as of 1984

impressive. By October 1980, 5.1 million full-time state and local employees were members of labor organizations. This figure represents 48.8 percent of all state and local employees.[14]

Just as the Wagner Act gave impetus to private-sector growth, legislative enactment helped stimulate public-sector unionization. The first attempt at a policy for collective bargaining between federal employees and management in the executive branch of government came in 1962 when President John Kennedy issued Executive Order 10988. The order stated:

> Employees of the Federal Government shall have, and shall be protected in the exercise of, the right, freely and without fear of penalty or reprisal, to form, join and assist any employee organization or to refrain from any such activity.

Subsequent executive orders expanded on and clarified EO 10988, but the federal sector lacked a comprehensive policy until the passage of the Civil Service Reform Act of 1978. Title VII of this act, the Federal Service Labor–Management Relations Statute, established the Federal Labor Relations Authority (FLRA) as an independent agency within the executive branch.[15] Modeled after the NLRB, FLRA oversees labor practices for agencies, labor groups, and individual employees within the executive branch. Thus any employee of the National Park Service, U.S. Forest Service, or Corps of Engineers would be covered by this piece of legislation. In general, federal employees have about the same bargaining rights as do private-sector employees. The one major exception, however, is that federal employees do not have the right to bargain over salaries or other economic issues.

State and Local Employee Regulations

Local and state collective bargaining arrangements are dependent on state statutes for their legal framework. In 1959, Wisconsin passed the first state law providing for the recognition of public employee unions and granting certain collective bargaining rights to municipal employees. Today, most states permit collective bargaining among state employees and many states allow the same privilege to some or all local employees. Keep in mind that legislation varies widely from state to state. For example, the state of Iowa passed the Public Employment Relations Act in 1977. This act provides that all state and local public employees have the right to negotiate collectively. In addition, the act establishes the Public Employment Relations Board (a mini-NLRB), spells out both employee and employer rights, and specifies the procedure for establishing a bargaining unit.[16] The state of North Carolina, on the other hand, passed an act in 1959 that prohibits the negotiation of any collective agreements. A court decision in 1969 does allow North Carolina's state and local public employees to join labor unions, but any negotiated agreement would have no validity.[17] Park and recreation employees working for a state or local agency would be well advised to ascertain and understand the laws specific to their situation.

Current Status among Leisure Service Personnel

Because of the extreme diversity of the leisure service field, it is very difficult to judge the extent to which leisure service employees have joined organized labor groups. As yet, no research has been done to determine the extent to which private for-profit and private nonprofit employees have joined collective bargaining units.

Public-Sector Involvement

Several definitive studies have looked at the extent of collective bargaining involvement among park and recreation units of local government. Almost 43 percent of these local units have at least some portion of their work force involved in collective bargaining.[18] A National Recreation and Parks Association study in 1975 found that most union activity centered around nonskilled and semiskilled employees, but almost one-fourth of the responding municipalities reported union involvement by professional personnel.[19] A nationwide study of local public park and recreation agencies conducted in 1980 by one of the authors found the following:

- Agencies that serve large populations are much more likely to have employees in collective bargaining than are agencies serving small populations.
- The larger the number of full-time employees, the greater the likelihood of collective bargaining.
- Agencies located along the Pacific coast (71.0 percent) and in the east (64.3 percent) were more likely to have collective bargaining than agencies elsewhere. Agencies in the south (11.1 percent) were least likely to have collective bargaining.
- Special park and recreation districts (23.5 percent) were less likely to have collective bargaining than were county (31.0 percent) or municipal (50.4 percent) departments.[20]

To a large extent the growth pattern of organized labor in local public park and recreation agencies has paralleled the growth pattern of the entire public sector. About 8 percent of local public agencies had their first bargaining unit established prior to 1960. Over 70 percent of the agencies reported their first organized labor units were formed in a twelve-year period from 1966 to 1977. Since 1977, however, very few agencies have experienced their first bargaining unit.[21]

The Structure of Organized Labor

Bargaining Units

The basic unit of organized labor is the bargaining unit: a group of employees who have joined together for the purpose of promoting their collective interests when dealing with management. In some cases, this bargaining unit may take a very informal nonstructured approach when dealing with management and function more like a social club than a union. Often, these less formal worker organizations are referred to as employee associations.

One such bargaining unit exists in a small community in Delaware. All five full-time park and recreation employees belong to this association, as do all the other municipal employees. Each year the association (1) sponsors the annual employee's picnic, and (2) "negotiates" with the city council. The negotiation process consists of the leaders of the association sitting down at a council meeting and explaining what the employees would like in terms of salaries and conditions of employment. The conversation is usually friendly and open. Apparently, the council tries to be as accommodating as possible while maintaining its responsibilities to the entire community. This arrangement seems to work very well for this particular bargaining unit, but this situation is not typical.

Bargaining Agents

Most bargaining units decide not to deal directly with management; they choose an organization to serve as their official representative in matters regarding the employment relationship. This official representative, usually a nationally or internationally affiliated union but possibly an employee association, serves as the unit's bargaining agent. Negotiated arrangements are usually put in writing and called collective bargaining agreements or contracts. The bargaining agent, such as the American Federation of Government Employees or American Federation of State, County, and Municipal Employees, is the exclusive representative of the bargaining unit for the life of the contract. Thus the bargaining agent not only negotiates the contract but also has the responsibility of administering it. Once the contract has expired, the bargaining unit has the privilege of finding a new bargaining agent if it so desires, but in most cases the bargaining agent becomes permanent through endless renewals.

When a bargaining unit arranges to use a bargaining agent, it has the effect of putting the agent squarely between the employees and management. To a large extent, this means that management no longer deals directly with employees on matters of compensation, employment, and working conditions, but works through the employees' bargaining agent. Management retains whatever rights and privileges the contract allows.[22]

Union Structure

Most bargaining agents are unions. According to the U.S. Department of Labor, approximately 63,721 local unions exist and most are affiliated with one of 174 national or international unions.[23] Local unions vary in size from a few members to 20,000 to 30,000 members.[24] National and international unions are composed only of local unions; it is not possible for an employee individually to hold membership in a national union.

Operating funds for the nationals and internationals come from assessment of affiliated local unions based on the membership size of the local. (Local unions get their funds from dues collected from the members of the bargaining unit who have chosen to enlist the services of the union, that is, "join the union.") Some nationals and internationals, such as the American Federation of State, County and Municipal Employees (AFSCME), are composed only of locals that serve public employees. Others, such as the International Brotherhood of Teamsters (Teamsters) and Service Employees International Union (SEIU), draw their membership from both the public and private sectors.

The highest level of union hierarchy is the American Federation of Labor and Congress of Industrial Organizations (AFL–CIO). This loosely knit federation of about 110 national and international unions does not engage in collective bargaining but tries to foster an overall cooperative effort in dealing with the broad goals of organized labor. The major activities of the AFL–CIO are:

- Improving the image of organized labor.
- Extensive lobbying on behalf of labor interests.
- Political education through COPE (Committee on Political Education).
- Resolving disputes through national unions.
- Policing internal affairs of member unions.[25]

Employee Associations

As we mentioned earlier, some bargaining agents call themselves an employee association rather than a union. With only a few exceptions, local employee associations function as independent groups, unaffiliated with state associations, other local associations, or labor unions. Stieber estimated that more than half of their estimated 1970 membership of 300,000 was concentrated in California and the New York City area.[26] In addition to local employee associations, the Bureau of Labor Statistics lists thirty-seven major professional and state employee associations with a total 1978 membership of 2,635,000. The largest of these is the National Education Association, with over 1.6 million members.

Many employee associations came into existence between 1920 and 1950 for the purpose of promoting professional concerns; they tended to be supportive of civil service, antiunion, and only slightly inclined toward collective bargaining. This situation has rapidly changed in recent years. Although not calling themselves unions, many of these employee associations are now functioning very much like unions. According to Mondy and Noe, employee associations negotiated over 12,500 agreements for their members in 1974.[27]

Organized Labor in Parks and Recreation

A 1980 study of local park and recreation agencies that had collective bargaining revealed that almost 60 percent of the agencies had only one bargaining unit.[28] At the other extreme, however, parks and recreation departments in the cities of Seattle and Los Angeles dealt with fifteen and eighteen bargaining units, respectively. Almost two-thirds of the bargaining units organized in park and recreation organizations were affiliated with a national or international union such as AFSCME or the Teamsters. Most of the remaining one-third were employee associations. The union to which most park and recreation employees belong is AFSCME. This union represented almost half (48.8 percent) of the bargaining units in local public parks and recreation. The Teamsters (15.3 percent), the International Union of Operating Engineers (10.7 percent), and Service Employees International Union (9.5 percent) also represented a substantial number of employees.[29]

The Organizing Process

At this point, we need to discuss how a group of employees actually becomes a bargaining unit, achieves recognition from management, and determines which bargaining agent will represent it in negotiations with management. Once again, policies and procedures in the private sector are different from those in the federal sector and the state and local sector. Except where specific details are important, this section will present a broad overview of the typical organizing process.

An employee group can approach management and ask to be recognized for the sake of bargaining collectively. If management chooses to extend this recognition voluntarily, the employee group becomes a bargaining unit. This unit can either do its own negotiation or choose an agent to represent it. Assuming that collective bargaining is allowed by the jurisdictional authority (keep in mind that bargaining is not allowed for some state and local employees), the bargaining process can begin.

In reality, however, things do not usually work this simply. First, except in the federal sector where management must remain neutral and accept whatever decision the work group decides, management does not usually recognize an employee group voluntarily. Second, usually at least some portion of the work group does not want to form a bargaining group at all. Third, the decision as to who will serve as the unit's bargaining agent usually takes place at the same time the decision is made as to whether a unit should be formed. Finally, two or more unions may compete vigorously for the right to serve as bargaining agent (in the public sector, the competition might be between an employee association and one or more unions).

The various stages of the organizing process are shown in Figure 13.4. Perhaps a group of employees are upset with certain arbitrary manage-

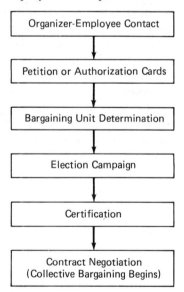

Figure 13.4   Stages of the labor organizing process.

ment decisions affecting their work situation and initiate the contact. On the other hand, union organizers may approach the employees. The process typically begins when contact is made between employees and a potential bargaining agent.

The next step is to determine if a sufficient number of employees want to engage in collective bargaining. Organizers usually ask employees to sign a petition or authorization cards. When a sufficient number have signed (30 percent of the work group is the typical required amount), the organizers can request the appropriate authorized body (NLRB regional office, FLRA, or designated state agency or department) to conduct a representation election.

Prior to the election, the appropriate authorized body determines the employees that will actually make up the bargaining unit. These employees will also be the ones eligible to vote in the election. Every effort is made to make the potential bargaining unit a compatible group of employees. If their needs strongly conflict, professionals and nonprofessionals are not put into the same unit. Also, employees are seldom put in the same bargaining unit with their supervisors. It is easy to understand how the employees, when discussing problems related to their work, might feel intimidated by the presence of their supervisor.

Election Campaign

The election campaign is carefully monitored by the appropriate authorized agency to ensure that participants do not engage in unfair practices. In the private sector and in many of the states that allow collective bargaining at the state and local levels, unfair practices include:

- Management promising pay increases or special favors to employees if they vote against organizing.
- Management spying on union organizing meetings.
- Supervisors asking employees how they intend to vote.
- Union organizers campaigning for votes when employees are scheduled to be working.
- Management discharging or threatening to discharge employees if they vote for organizing.

If any member of management commits an unfair labor practice, it is very likely that the union organizers will complain to the agency overseeing the election. If the organizers can convince the labor agency that a violation did occur, it is not unusual for that agency to cancel the election and certify the union as the exclusive bargaining agent for the employees in the unit.

Federal regulations do not allow federal government management personnel to take any position regarding employee organizing. They must remain neutral throughout the campaign.

The ballot will have one box for checking that indicates "no union." The other box will have the name of the union or employee association. (If there is competition for the right to serve as agent, additional names and boxes will be on the ballot.) If a union or association is chosen by a majority of the voters, it becomes officially certified as the bargaining agent of the unit. In most cases, state or federal law will demand that management recognize this arrangement and proceed to bargain in good faith.

Although it is frequently not mentioned in the literature, employees have the right to cancel their union arrangement. An election is held if 30 percent or more of the employees request it. If a majority so choose, the union or employee association is officially decertified as the bargaining representative. Although the number of decertification elections has increased over the past several decades, these elections involve less than 1 percent of the total union labor force.[30]

Case Study

A CASE OF NO LONGER NEEDING THE UNION

The Cultural Arts Division of a large community in the southwest consisted of sixteen full-time and twenty part-time employees. Although most of the employees genuinely liked their jobs, a general feeling of discontent permeated the entire division. Griping and complaining was common. Many people were frustrated, but no one felt the problems could be solved by going to the division manager.

Randy Owens, the division manager, was a very hardworking, highly structured supervisor. He organized all major activities, established the division's goals and objectives, pushed for increased funding for programming, and made assignments directly to his staff on a day-to-day basis. Randy usually worked 60 to 65 hours a week and scheduled his time very tightly.

Sally Velez, a full-time employee with the division for the last fifteen years, happened to mention her work-related frustrations to one of her husband's friends, Julio Romano. Julio worked for the AFSCME as a labor organizer. After a long discussion, Sally agreed to invite some of her friends from work to her house to hear Julio talk about the benefits of a labor union. The group meeting was successful for Julio; all six people who attended signed union cards and promised to try to persuade their fellow employees to do likewise. Within a week, thirty-two of the thirty-six employees in the division had signed cards. Next, Julio made an appointment to see the city manager and presented him with the facts.

The city manager understood that the city really only had two choices. One, they could officially recognize the employees of the Cultural Arts Division as a bargaining unit and the AFSCME local as their bargaining agent. Two, the city could take no action and force Julio to petition the state's labor board to call an election. During an election campaign, the city's management personnel would

---

have a chance to explain their position regarding the desirability of a union. Since so many of the employees had signed union cards, the city officials decided an election would be hopeless and chose to recognize the union. Both sides immediately began preparation for contract negotiations.

Since the Department of Leisure Services was directly involved in this matter, the director of that department was appointed to serve on management's negotiating team along with the city attorney, the budget director, and the labor relations specialist. As the team began preparing for the negotiations, a very important revelation occurred; the director discovered that her division manager, Randy Owens, was completely unaware of the employment-related concerns of his employees, their professional needs, their interest and backgrounds, and their reasons for wanting a labor agreement. Feeling that the manager was not effectively supervising the human resources of the division, the director decided to move the manager to a different area of responsibility. After many hours of hard negotiating, a contract was drawn up and approved by both the city council and the bargaining unit.

Virginia Wilson, Randy Owens' replacement, quickly realized that major problems existed within the work force. Her first step was to become very familiar with the new contract; she did not want to do anything that would unnecessarily create turmoil among her staff. Next, she began to involve people in the decision making. Open communications began to develop and Virginia spent a lot of time listening to others. Eventually, a feeling of mutual trust and respect was established between the manager and her staff.

Within six months after the arrival of the new manager, the Cultural Arts Division was a beehive of activity. Morale was excellent and productivity was higher than it had ever been. One morning during the coffee break someone remarked that there seemed to be no need for the union these days. Someone else remembered the $325 they had paid in annual union dues. That afternoon several employees contacted the state's labor board and found out a decertification election could be held to sever the relationship with the union. The election was held and the employees voted overwhelmingly in favor of decertification.

Management's Response to an Organizing Effort

The question that many managers face at one point is: "How should I respond if I am confronted by a union organizer?" First of all, do not accept or look at the authorization cards or petition. To do so might be construed as tacitly acknowledging the existence of the union.[31] Ask the union organizer to correspond in writing to the organization's top management. Second, immediately report any knowledge of a union-organizing effort to top management.

It will be top management's responsibility to develop a strategy in response to the organizing effort. If the leisure service agency does not have access to the services of a labor specialist or attorney, it is strongly suggested that such services be quickly obtained. This person's counsel will be invaluable as management investigates the background and tactics of the organizers and prepares its response.

Management has the right to oppose the unionization effort actively as long as it does not violate fair labor practices. For example, managers can point out any untrue or misleading statements made by the organizers and give employees the correct information. Also, managers can tell employees about the disadvantages of belonging to a union, such as the expenses of initiation fees, membership dues, strike assessments, and the restrictions imposed by membership rules.[32] At all times it is important to provide only true information. Management also has the right to assemble and address groups of employees, send out letters, put up posters, and pass out handbills.

Howard and Guadagnolo feel that management's message is most effective when it:

- States that management is not antiunion but does oppose collective bargaining in its own organization because it would hinder the achievement of organization and individual goals.
- States that job security is not created by a union but by the organization's ability to provide effective services to its clientele.
- Offers evidence demonstrating that current wages and benefits compare favorably to other comparable organizations.[33]

Contract Negotiation and Administration

An important part of the overall process of collective bargaining is the period of time when the contract is negotiated. Contracts usually run from one to three years. Slightly over 40 percent of all local public park and recreation contracts are for one year only.[34] Typically, contract negotiations move through six stages.

- *Negotiators chosen.* In most cases today, both sides are represented by a negotiating team. The union side's chief negotiator is usually a well-trained professional provided by the national office. If the organization is large, management may have its own labor relations specialist who serves as chief negotiator. Smaller organizations usually contract for the services of a labor specialist or labor attorney. It sometimes happens that the chief leisure services manager is chosen to serve on the negotiating team.
- *Preparations made.* Both sides take as much as six months to gather information about such things as current prevailing wages and benefits in the geographic area, the current level of management's resources, productivity levels, the nature and number of complaints and grievances, and the rate of absenteeism. Inevitably, park and recreation managers at all levels are involved in this information gathering.
- *Strategy developed.* Both sides identify objectives, set priorities, develop a negotiating plan, and try to anticipate the methods of the other.

- *Initial demands made.* Each side submits to the other their list of proposed arrangements (traditionally called "demands"). At this time, the sides are usually quite far apart.
- *Bargaining takes place.* This is the stage when each side takes its turn listening, speaking, suggesting, and compromising.
- *Settlement reached.* After tentative agreement is reached at the table, each side usually returns to their constituencies to seek final approval.

There are times when the two sides cannot reach agreement through the aforementioned process. If this happens, an impasse is said to have occurred. Employees can respond by going on strike; management can conduct a lockout and shut down its operation. Although these tactics sometimes get a great deal of coverage in the media, their occurrence is relatively rare. According to Mathis and Jackson, the amount of work time lost in this country due to strikes and lockouts is considerably less that in than many other countries.[35] The items that are typically covered in a park and recreation labor contract are presented in Figure 13.5.

Contract administration is a term used to describe the process of carrying out the provisions of the contract. Once the contract is signed,

---

TYPICAL ITEMS COVERED IN A LABOR AGREEMENT FOR LEISURE SERVICE PERSONNEL

- Purpose of the agreement
- A statement that management recognizes the bargaining agent as the sole representative of the bargaining unit for the length of the contract
- A management's-rights clause which specifies certain areas of decision making as the sole right and prerogative of management.
- Wages and salaries
- Hours of work
- Overtime
- Vacation time
- Working conditions
- Sick leave
- Leaves of absence
- Holidays
- No strike–no lockout provision
- Dues check-off system that allows employees to have management take their membership dues out of their paycheck and turn it over to the union or association.
- Seniority
- Retirement benefits
- Insurance
- Grievance procedure and a list of subjects that can be grieved
- Discipline and discharge
- Length of the contract and expiration date

Figure 13.5

both sides usually make a major effort to educate everyone involved. Training sessions and meetings are held to go over every clause of the contract. From management's perspective, it is absolutely critical that supervisors clearly understand what they can and cannot do when dealing with their employees. For example, a supervisor may violate the contract if she asks her subordinates when they would like to take their annual vacation leave. It may be that she must ask the union steward to ascertain this information for her. In fact, in many cases the union must be informed and their ideas and opinions considered before any change can be made if the change involves employment practices or working conditions. To do otherwise would be a contract violation. Chapter 11 deals more specifically with the supervisor's role in administering a union contract.

Problems and Benefits

Hopefully, the reader has noticed that up to this point we have avoided labeling collective bargaining as "good" or "bad." Many people and most writers on the subject usually have very definite feelings about the problems and benefits of organized labor. It is fair to say that like many other aspects of human resource management, the phenomenon of collective bargaining is far too complicated to label as simply "good" or "bad." Some leisure service operations that are totally unionized from the top manager to the part-time personnel are very efficient and effective. Other unionized operations are rather unproductive. In some cases, unionization appears to be a very rational response on the part of employees to employment-related problems. In other cases, unionization seems to have come about for very illogical reasons. Some important research has been done to help clarify our understanding.

One study asked chief administrators of local public park and recreation agencies to assess the impact that collective bargaining has had on their organizations.[36] From their perspective, collective bargaining *did*:

- Improve the welfare of the employees by gaining for them higher salaries and benefits than they would have otherwise received.

On the other hand, collective bargaining *did not*:

- Hurt employee morale.
- Improve the quality of service provided the community.
- Force the organization to reduce the quantity of services it provides for the public.
- Enhance management's ability to hire well-qualified personnel.
- Force the organization to seek alternative revenue sources in order to meet union pressures for greater wages and benefits.

Managers were evenly split as to whether collective bargaining:

- Restricted management's ability to enforce proper conduct and discipline in the work force.

In summary, the administrators felt that the employees benefited economically, and their organizations were not hurt, but that collective bargaining generally made their jobs more difficult.

This same study found that administrator's attitudes toward collective bargaining varied greatly according to which union represented their employees. The International Brotherhood of Teamsters, a very agressive union, generated a much less positive response than AFSCME, a union that has long had highly respected leadership. This factor points out how extremely individualized each specific situation can be. A union–management relationship may be very successful in one situation and provide positive benefits for the employees, the organization, and the consuming public, but in another situation unions may be a disaster for all concerned.

Summary and Recommendations

1. Federal employees, state and local employees, and private-sector employees are all covered by separate labor legislation. Each manager needs to be familiar with the legislation that is relevant to his or her situation.
2. In the "right to work" states, membership in the union is not a requirement for employment in any work group represented by a union. This type of legislation enhances the rights of individual employees but greatly restricts the efforts of organized labor.
3. When a bargaining unit arranges to use a bargaining agent, it has the effect of putting the agent squarely between the employees and management. This situation greatly alters the way management can handle matters related to compensation, employment, and working conditions.
4. During a labor election campaign, it is necessary for managers to know and follow fair labor practices. A violation may cause the government labor agency to cancel the election and certify the union.
5. If leisure service managers find that a union is attempting to organize their work force, they should immediately obtain the services of a labor specialist or attorney.
6. Management has the right to oppose actively any attempt to organize their work force as long as it does not violate fair labor practices.
7. Once a labor agreement has been negotiated and accepted by both sides, it is critical that supervisors be clearly imformed as to what they can or cannot do when dealing with their employees.

8. Leisure service administrators generally feel that although unions have benefited employees economically, unions have made management's job more difficult.

Discussion Topics

1. Discuss how the Great Depression provided impetus to the organized labor movement.
2. What role does the national government play regarding the organized labor in the United States?
3. What labor legislation most affects each of the following groups: federal employees, state and local employees, and private-sector employees?
4. What are "right to work" states?
5. In which areas of the country are leisure service agencies most likely to have collective bargaining? Least likely to have collective bargaining?
6. Explain the difference between an employee association and a union.
7. What is the relationship between a bargaining unit and a bargaining agent?
8. What national union represents more local public park and recreation bargaining units than any other?
9. Explain how bargaining units are organized.
10. How should management respond to an effort to organize employees?
11. Explain the six stages in the contract negotiation process.
12. Discuss the following statement: "Unions serve a useful purpose in that they keep management on their toes."
13. Do you agree with the following? "If managers paid their employees a reasonable salary and treated them fairly, the need for unions would not exist."
14. Just like other organizations, unions can be poorly managed. What alternatives do employees have if they feel that both their union and their agency are poorly managed?

Notes

1. David F. Culkin, "The Extent and Impact of Collective Bargaining on Local Public Park and Recreation Organizations in the United States," Ph.D. dissertation, University of Oregon, 1980, p. 133.
2. Roger A. Lancaster, "Municipal Services," *Parks and Recreation* 11(July 1976): 26.
3. *National Labor Relations Act* (Wagner Act), sec. 8(d), 1935.
4. *Glossary of Labor Relations Terms*, distributed by the Labor Education and Research Center, University of Oregon (original source unknown).

5. Arthur A. Sloane and Fred Witney, *Labor Relations*, 3rd ed. (Englewood Cliffs, N.J.: Prentice-Hall, Inc., 1977), p. 59.
6. Randall S. Schuler, *Personnel and Human Resource Management* (St. Paul, Minn.: West Publishing Co., 1981), p. 392.
7. Sloane and Witney, *Labor Relations*, p. 62.
8. R. Wayne Mondy and Robert M. Noe III, *Personnel: The Management of Human Resources* (Boston: Allyn and Bacon, Inc., 1981), p. 380.
9. Sloane and Witney, *Labor Relations*, p. 69.
10. Mondy and Noe, *Personnel*, p. 382.
11. Sloane and Witney, *Labor Relations*, p. 115.
12. Ibid., p. 89.
13. Jay M. Shafritz et al., *Personnel Management in Government* (New York: Marcel Dekker, Inc., 1978), p. 209.
14. U. S. Department of Commerce, Bureau of the Census, *Labor–Management Relations in State and Local Government* (Washington, D.C.: U.S. Government Printing Office, 1977), pp. 1–2.
15. Henry B. Frazier III, "Labor–Management Relations in the Federal Government," *Labor Law Journal* 30(March 1979): 131.
16. Midwest Center for Public Sector Labor Relations, *Labor Legislation in the Public Sector* (Bloomington, Ind.: Indiana University, School of Public and Environmental Affairs, 1979), pp. 50–51.
17. Ibid., p. 112.
18. Culkin, "Extent and Impact of Collective Bargaining," p. 133.
19. Lancaster, "Municipal Services," p. 26.
20. Culkin, "Extent and Impact of Collective Bargaining," pp. 69–81.
21. David Culkin and Dennis R. Howard, "Collective Bargaining and Recreation and Park Operations," *Parks and Recreation* 17(October 1982): 60.
22. George H. Hildebrand, *American Unionism: An Historical and Analytical Survey* (Reading, Mass.: Addison-Wesley Publishing Co., Inc., 1979), p. 40.
23. U.S. Department of Labor, Bureau of Labor Statistics, *Directory of National Unions and Employee Associations* (Washington, D.C.: U.S. Government Printing Office, 1980), p. 73.
24. Mondy and Noe, *Personnel*, p. 394.
25. Ibid., p. 395.
26. Jack Stieber, *Public Employee Unionism: Structure, Growth, Policy* (Washington, D.C.: The Brookings Institution, 1973), p. 9.
27. Mondy and Noe, *Personnel*, p. 389.
28. Culkin, "Extent and Impact of Collective Bargaining," p. 84.
29. Culkin and Howard, "Collective Bargaining," pp. 60–61.
30. Schuler, *Personnel and Human Resource Management*, p. 400.
31. Dennis R. Howard and Frank B. Guadagnolo, "Labor Relations," *Leisure Today* in *Journal of Physical Education, Recreation and Dance* (April 1982): 50.
32. National Association of Manufacturers, *Some Dos and Don'ts for Supervisors* (Washington, D.C.: Industrial Relations Department), 1–3.
33. Howard and Guadagnolo, "Labor Relations," p. 50.
34. Culkin, "Extent and Impact of Collective Bargaining," p. 109.
35. Robert L. Mathis and John H. Jackson, *Personnel: Contemporary Perspectives and Applications*, 3rd ed. (St. Paul, Minn.: West Publishing Co., 1982), p. 469.
36. Culkin and Howard, "Collective Bargaining," p. 62.

14

Employee Well-Being

Maintaining safety and good health in the workplace is a management imperative. In a society that espouses the free-enterprise system and the profit motive, employee well-being has too often been neglected. Most people would agree that the maintenance of safety and good health in the workplace is clearly justified on moral grounds alone. Human beings simply have no right to jeopardize or impair the lives of their fellow human beings.

But not every individual feels a moral responsibility for the health and safety of his or her work force. For such people, concern for employee well-being can perhaps be justified on legal or economic grounds. Tardiness and absenteeism due to sickness, personal problems, job-related stress, and safety problems can cost the employer more than the maintenance of a work environment that supports good health, safety, and employee peace of mind.[1] In addition, the federal government and all states have established laws that set certain minimum safety and health standards.

In this last chapter, we discuss how the supervisor plays a key role in preventing accidents and injuries and enforcing safety standards. He or she must also identify employee problems that interfere with work performance, detect the problem employee who needs special assistance, and help employees manage job-related stress.

Job-Related Safety and Health

The terms "safety" and "health" are not synonymous. Safety refers to the potential of accidents and injury. Health is related to illness. An accident results in physical injury that is immediate and noticeable. Illness may be neither immediate nor noticeable and can include both physical and mental disorders.

Although substantial progress has been made in the past century in reducing occupational safety and health hazards and their affects, costs are still high. Each year 15,000 American workers are killed and 2 million more are injured on the job.[2] Approximately one out of every eleven workers in the private sector suffers an injury or illness caused by exposure to hazards in the workplace.[3] These casualties result in approximately 2.25 million lost workdays[4] and an estimated aggregate cost of $20 billion.[5]

In their text, Sternloff and Warren report a 1974 study by the National Safety Council (NSC) which indicated that park and recreation employees receive "more than three times the average number of injuries of all industries reporting to the Council."[6] As you might expect, the NSC found that approximately two-thirds of all park and recreation injuries involved maintenance personnel.[7]

Causes of Workplace Accidents

The causes of accidents fall into three categories: (1) unsafe employee behavior, (2) unsafe work environment, and (3) acts of nature (see Figure 14.1). Certain places and certain physical conditions are more likely to produce injuries. In order of decreasing frequency, these include:

1. About one-third of all accidents are caused by improperly moving heavy, awkward materials.
2. The most dangerous machines are metal- and wood-working machines, power saws, and machinery with exposed gears, belts, and chains.
3. Falls are a major source of accidents anytime that workers climb, descend, or walk on narrow and high walkways.
4. Hand tools such as axes, chisels, and pliers cause many injuries.
5. Wherever electricity is used, especially outdoor power lines, a potential hazard exists.[8]

There is much evidence to show that young workers, untrained workers, and newly hired workers experience a substantially higher number of injuries than older workers, trained workers, and more experienced workers.[9] One research study found that age had a much greater influence on accident rates than did time on the job.[10] Thus an organization that maintains a well-trained, older work force is much less likely to have a high rate of accidents.

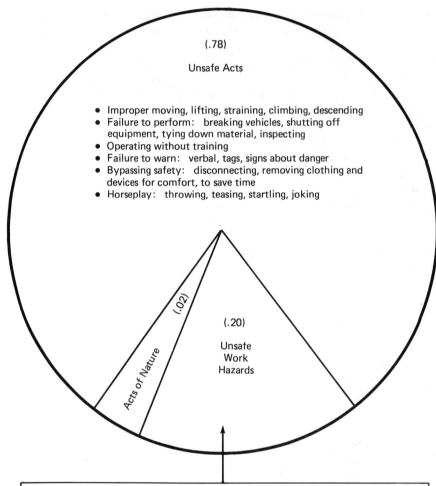

Figure 14.1   Causes of workplace accidents.

Occupational Health Hazards

Occupational health hazards fall into four general categories: (1) *physical conditions,* such as noise, heat, vibration and radiation; (2) *chemicals,* such as dusts, poisonous fumes, gases, toxic metals, and carcinogens; (3) *biological organisms* such as bacteria, fungi, and insects; and (4) *physical or psychological stress.*

It is even more difficult to protect employees from occupational health hazards than it is to safeguard them from injuries. This is because health hazards are frequently hidden and unknown. For example, American industry has produced about 500 new toxic substances each year. About 13,000 known toxic substances are in common use.[11] Fewer than two dozen of these toxic substances are addressed by Occupational Safety and Health Administration (OSHA) regulations. Park and recreation employees involved in maintenance will quite frequently use cleaning solvents, gasoline, paint removers, insecticides, herbicides, fungicides, and the like. The possibility of hidden dangers with the use of these chemicals is very real.

Legal Responsibility for Health and Safety

The most ambitious governmental attempt to improve health and safety in the workplace was the passage of the Occupational Safety and Health Act in 1970. This act, discussed in Chapter 2, primarily protects workers in private industry, but it also requires all states to develop and maintain comprehensive health and safety programs for all public employees. In addition, Executive Order 12196, effective October 1, 1980, requires federal agencies to comply with the same standards required of private industry.[12]

Workers' compensation (WC) laws, which can be found in all fifty states, also deserve mention. WC laws protect employees from economic hardships by providing financial benefits should they experience work related illness or injury. Although WC has no mandates for safety as does OSHA, the laws are designed to provide economic incentives such as lower insurance premiums to employers who want to improve job safety. The amount of each employer's insurance premium depends on the number of annual employee accidents. Fewer accidents mean a financial savings for the employer.

Since every state has a different WC law, the two questions for the manager to ask are: "In my state, who is covered?" and "What are work-related injuries?" Workers' compensation problems most often stem from vague or confusing language in the laws themselves. The standard verbiage "arising out of and in the course of employment" leaves open the question: "What are work-related injuries?"

According to Frakt and Rankin, even injuries resulting from "horse-play" during work and lunch breaks will be compensated since fault or negligence are not normally a consideration in workers' compensation. Injuries that take place during employer-sponsored recreation programs or sports are also covered.[13] The courts have upheld these decisions based on the premise that company-sponsored recreation promotes morale, loyalty, and better productivity, conditions that are of value to the employer.

There are several other interesting points for recreation employers and managers to remember about workers' compensation. Injuries incurred while driving to different work sites or while living on the recreation site are also covered. If a program supervisor stops to check on a playground activity while driving home from work, any injuries sustained during that trip would be compensated. River guides, camp managers, or recreation therapists who must reside at the work site or live at any institution are also covered by WC, especially if their services may be called upon at any time.

Part-time recreation employees and some volunteers are usually covered, even when their pay is limited to meals or expenses, or even if they work for only one event. When the organization provides equipment, uniforms, or supplies to volunteers to help them in fulfilling their job assignments and exercises supervisory control over their duties, these persons will be considered employees under the terms of most WC laws. According to Frakt and Rankin, however, "pure" volunteers such as Little League coaches or managers would not be considered employees and would not, therefore, be covered by workers' compensation.[14]

Health and Safety Programs

Leisure service organizations have a legal obligation to establish an employee's safety and health program. At a minimum, this program should comply with governmental standards. We recommend that the principal components of a safety and health program include those identified in Figure 14.2.

Management Support

The organization must decide how comprehensive a program it wants and adopt safety policies to suit its size, circumstances, and financial resources. Studies indicate that low-accident-rate organizations have greater management commitment and involvement in the implementation of the program.[15] This involvement and sincere concern about safety serves as a motivational force for employees. They perceive that

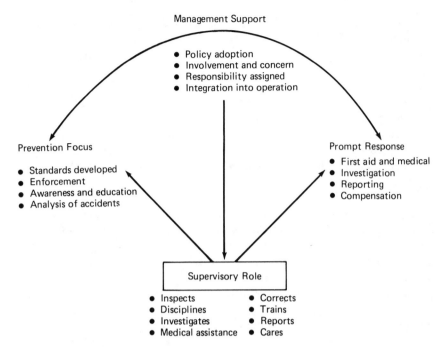

Management Support

- Policy adoption
- Involvement and concern
- Responsibility assigned
- Integration into operation

Prevention Focus

- Standards developed
- Enforcement
- Awareness and education
- Analysis of accidents

Prompt Response

- First aid and medical
- Investigation
- Reporting
- Compensation

Supervisory Role

- Inspects
- Disciplines
- Investigates
- Medical assistance
- Corrects
- Trains
- Reports
- Cares

Figure 14.2 Safety–health program.

management is interested in their well-being as individuals, and those feelings heighten their morale. Employees with higher morale tend to have fewer accidents.[16]

Responsibility for overall agency safety and health must be assigned to one individual, even if the responsibility represents only a portion of that employee's time. Larger organizations call this person the safety director, and it becomes his or her job to organize, advise, collect data, analyze, prod, and generally keep the program active. Rarely does this person have line authority to order supervisors and workers to take a particular safety conscious action. Thus the responsibility for safety and health also must be assumed by the supervisor, and even the workers. Some organizations establish employee committees to reinforce safety as an ongoing concern of every worker as an integral part of the day-to-day operation.

Prevention Focus

The key to any safety program is prevention. Hazards must be identified and removed from every workstation, and good housekeeping rules must be established. Low-accident-rate organizations exhibit much better housekeeping and cleanliness standards than do high-accident-rate agencies.[17]

Consideration should also focus on providing a healthy work environment, which includes well-ventilated and lighted workstations with no dangerous noise levels, good temperature controls, and clean and functional bathrooms.

OSHA has prepared thousands of standards that provide guidance for employers. Appropriate standards for equipment maintenance, work methods, and protective clothing should be written down and communicated to respective supervisors and employees. For example, construction workers should be told to wear hard hats, machinists should know to wear goggles, and welders should always wear face shields and gloves.

Because so many park, recreational, and leisure employees work out of doors, particular care should be taken to ensure that their bodies are not overexposed to heat and the sun. Other potential hazards for these employees include insect and snake bites, contact with poisonous plants, and improper work methods for operating equipment or hand tools.

One park maintenance supervisor heard a worker gunning the engine and peeling the tires on a pickup truck, throwing gravel all over the maintenance yard. She immediately told him to slide over to the passenger's side in the front seat and directed another worker to drive the vehicle that day. Although there was no specific rule prohibiting the abuse of the truck's engine and tires, the gravel thrown all over the yard as a result of the horseplay was a temporary hazard for other employees loading their vehicles. Enforcement means not only formally and routinely inspecting work procedures equipment and housekeeping conditions, but also means taking immediate disciplinary action when an employee violates a rule or acts in an unsafe manner.

Preventing accidents means continually focusing on safety. Awareness can be accomplished on the first day of the job by including safety in orientation and on-the-job training. Ongoing training and education are equally important. Campaigns, contests, posters, and commendation letters for safety records are some of the techniques used to keep the spotlight on safety. Supervisors should include accident and safety-related incidents in employee performance appraisals.

As data are collected on accidents and injuries, the safety director (or the supervisor in small organizations) will need to analyze the descriptive reports and statistics to determine where additional preventative measures are needed.

Prompt Response

There is no doubt that every organization should have well-known procedures for handling injuries. These procedures can reduce the element of surprise and prevent confusion. Employees injured on the job must receive first aid or medical treatment immediately. If the supervisor is present following minor injuries, he or she should know these procedures, provide first aid, or make sure that the worker receives medical care. Many organizations provide a first-aid room with adequate supplies for treatment of injuries.

Because the supervisor may not be present all the time, every employee should know the procedures and how to get help for an injured coworker. For emergency medical treatment, the number for an ambulance or a physician should be readily available. A strong case has been made that key personnel in every work unit should receive first aid and cardiopulmonary resuscitation (CPR) training so that they may be able to render help to injured coworkers.

All injuries, no matter how minor, must be reported. Documentation is essential in establishing workers' compensation claims if medical complications develop later. Almost every organization has its own employee accident–injury report form.

If the injury results in a doctor's attention or time lost from work beyond the day of the injury, the supervisor must complete the *Employer's Report of Industrial Injury* within 24 hours. Workers' compensation will not pay the expenses or make disability payments if this report is not submitted.[18] Once treatment is begun, the injured employee should be told that he or she cannot change doctors without the permission of the insurance carrier for workers' compensation.

The Supervisory Role

The line supervisor has daily contact with the employees, knows the working environment, and knows each worker's behavior. This makes the supervisor the key person in a health and safety program. The supervisor may not develop the standards, but is the supervisor who makes sure that they are followed. Even if a safety director has been assigned the responsibility for the overall safety program for the organization, it is the supervisor who most influences the employee's attitude toward safety. The following summarizes those responsibilities.

1. *Sets a good example* by following proper work methods and using safety devices and protective clothing.
2. *Develops safety inspection schedules,* and follows them.
3. *Takes corrective action* when areas or equipment become unsafe or when employees fail to follow safe procedures.
4. *Trains each employee* to use proper work methods, safety devices, and protective equipment and clothing. Makes employees safety conscious.

5. *Investigates accidents* even if they do not result in injuries to determine how they might have been prevented.
6. *Completes and submits all safety-related reports* and records on time.
7. *Seeks* outside help and advice when necessary.
8. *Knows what to do in case of injuries;* preferably knows first aid and CPR.

In the private sector, OSHA also places certain responsibilities on supervisors to keep very specific records. These include a log summary of occupational injuries and illnesses recorded within six working days from the time the supervisor learns of the illness or accident. This is a detailed form explaining the nature of each injury. Injuries requiring temporary first aid do not have to be recorded. In addition, supervisors are asked to accompany OSHA officials when they inspect an organization's physical facilities.

The responsibility for safety and health is shared by the employer, OSHA and its investigators, state agencies implementing workers' compensation laws, and the immediate supervisor. But it cannot be mentioned too often that it is the supervisor who carries the day-to-day responsibility for health and safety in the work environment.

Burnout and Distress

Pressure in the leisure field is inevitable. Employees face the ongoing challenge of frequent program deadlines, demanding patrons, public abuse of parks and facilities, shortages of funds and resources, and too frequently, lower salaries than comparably trained and educated workers. Furthermore, recreation workers suffer from "career identity," as they continuously explain to the public, season after season, what the recreation occupation is all about. All these conditions produce continuous stress. It is not surprising to learn that some leisure employees experience the debilitating and costly behavioral and physical symptoms of burnout and distress.

Before discussing how to control prolonged stress in our lives and how to recognize a coworker or subordinate who is experiencing the symptoms of prolonged stress, we need to answer three questions:

1. What is the difference between stress and distress?
2. What is the relationship of apathy, tedium, and burnout to stress?
3. What happens to the body that makes prolonged stress undesirable?

Stress and Distress

Stress, according to Hans Selye, *is a response to any demand made on the body which required readjustment.* Stress is neither good nor bad. Only unpleasant or prolonged stress is bad and that condition is called "distress."[19]

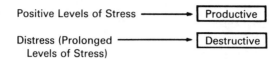

Figure 14.3   Defining stress and distress.

Rollo May, the renowned psychiatrist, has stated that the anxiety of stress is good because it is the propulsion that moves us toward new possibilities.[20] Stress is the energy of a productive life, resulting in stimulation and creativity. It primes us to reach peak performance (see Figure 14.3).

But stress is paradoxical. When stress becomes too great or lasts too long, distress and conflict arise. Distress is destructive. It can interfere with our ability to think and act, and it leads to behavioral changes (see Figure 14.4).

Apathy, Tedium, and Burnout Lead to Distress

Apathy takes the form of prolonged frustration and eventual emotional detachment. The young professional begins his or her career in the clouds, full of enthusiasm and idealism. Then along comes frustration. It may come suddenly in the announcement that the public recreation department is being eliminated and all the programs and parks are being placed under the custodial care of the public works department. Frustration might come slowly—after years of scrounging resources to meet institutional recreation needs.

Apathy also can be felt as boredom, not finding meaning in one's life or work.[21] A 30-year-old athletic supervisor, scheduling games for men's softball teams, finds his mind wandering. A recreation director, age 51, gazes out the window at 9:00 in the morning and thinks about early

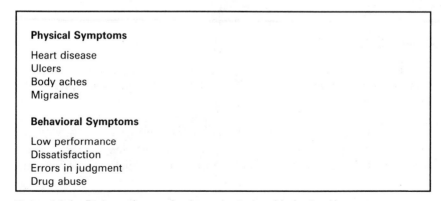

Figure 14.4   Prolonged stress leads to physical and behavioral symptoms.

Nakonis

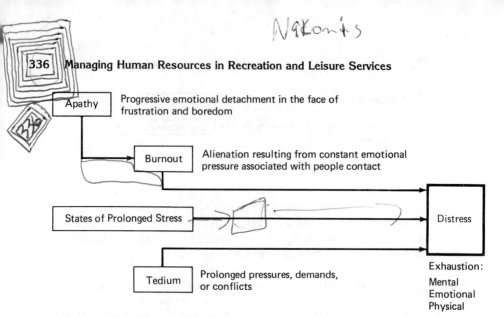

Figure 14.5 Stages of prolonged stress leading to distress.

retirement. Research suggests that underutilization of abilities and skills, and little intellectual stimulation, are potentially important causes of apathy—and apathy leads to burnout in the so-called "helping" fields such as recreation.[22] Similar to burnout, *tedium* actually has the same symptoms. It is a condition resulting from prolonged, chronic pressures, conflicts, or demands and too few accomplishments (see Figure 14.5).

The constant emotional pressure associated with involvement with people over a long period of time can result in *burnout*. People who start out caring for others and liking the recreation field can end up caring mainly about their own health and peace of mind. They experience a loss of concern for the people with whom they are working—a loss of the sense of mission in recreation work. Burnout is almost synonymous with "alienation." It begins with stress that cannot be alleviated. The prolonged stress results in changes in attitude and behavior, which might be noticed as fatigue and irritability. The last stage of burnout is emotional detachment or cynicism. Both tedium and burnout lead to distress: physical, mental, and emotional exhaustion.

Why Distress Is Undesirable

Distress results in an outpouring of hormones and chemicals into the body which the body cannot safely absorb. Initial stress stimulates the brain and the hypothalamus to activate the autonomic nervous system and the pituitary gland. The autonomic nervous system controls the involuntary muscles and readies the body for fighting or fleeing. Blood vessels under the skin constrict, preparing for possible injury. Nose and throat open up to move air more readily. Pupils dilate, and heart rate and blood pressure rise. The lungs breathe more deeply and perspiration increases.

All this internal activity places the body in a position to make quick decisions, perform vigorous acts, or defend itself against injury. But all this internal activity is rarely appropriate, much less healthy, in today's society. The body is locked into a visceral–vascular readiness for combat with minimal opportunity for release. It does not help a recreation manager to "sweat" over a budget deadline or have quick-clotting blood and a dry mouth. If stress continues over a period of time, we begin to experience resistance to further stimuli and eventually reach a state of exhaustion.

According to Robert S. Eliot, foremost research scientist on stress and the body, prolonged stress is the principal cause of coronary heart disease, which is the number-one killer in the United States. Over 1,200 persons die every day from this disease. Forty million other Americans have high blood pressure, which could lead to heart disease. Three-fourths of the visits to family doctors are related to prolonged stress.[23]

Add to heart disease the ailments of peptic ulcers, hypertension, backaches, indigestion, neckaches, migraines, diarrhea, and insomnia, and we see how debilitating and costly the physical symptoms of distress have become to society. The estimated cost of ulcers and cardiovascular disease alone in this country totals $45 billion annually.[24] Although doctors may argue whether or not stress causes all these ailments, they agree that it certainly aggravates them. The costs of the emotional and behavioral symptoms of prolonged stress are equally devastating. Drug abuse, alcoholism, absenteeism, depression, forgetfulness, dissatisfaction, low performance, errors in judgment, and accidents cause critical problems for employing organizations (see Figure 14.4).

Today's society places great demands on human adaptability and consequently, contributes to the incidence of employee distress. Although we agree that stress is the vigor of life, there are finite boundaries in our biosystems. Our adaptive mechanisms can and often do collapse.

Managing Stress: Awareness and Action

Awareness of those factors that can influence stress is the first step in getting control of one's personal life, in recognizing another's distress, or in anticipating the possible distress of employees. The second step is to initiate action to reduce the factors that produce distress.

Awareness of Life Events.   A number of studies over the past twenty years have documented that certain events in our lives will lead to stress. In their research on stress, Holms and Rake developed the Social Read-

Figure 14.6

SELF-ASSESSMENT EXERCISE ON ADAPTION

Below are listed events that occur in the process of living. Place a check in the lefthand column for each of those events that have happened to you during the last twelve months.

Life Event	Point Value	Life Event	Point Value
Death of spouse	100	Son or daughter leaving home	29
Divorce	73	Trouble with in-laws	29
Marital separation	65	Outstanding personal achievement	28
Jail term	63	Spouse begins or stops work	26
Death of close family member	63	Starting or finishing school	26
Personal injury or illness	53	Change in living conditions	25
Marriage	50	Revision of personal habits	24
Fired from work	47	Trouble with boss	23
Marital reconciliation	45	Change in work hours, conditions	20
Retirement	45	Change in residence	20
Change in family member's health	44	Change in schools	20
Pregnancy	40	Change in recreational habits	19
Sex difficulties	39	Change in church activities	19
Addition to family	39	Change in social activities	18
Business readjustment	39	Mortgage or loan under $10,000	17
Change in financial status	38	Change in sleeping habits	16
Death of close friend	37	Change in number of family gatherings	15
Change to different line of work	36	Change in eating habits	15
Change in number of marital arguments	36	Vacation	13
Mortgage or loan over $10,000	31	Christmas season	12
Foreclosure of mortgage or loan	30	Minor violations of the law	11
Change in work responsibilities	29	Score _____	

After checking the items above, add up the point values for all the items checked. A high reading would be 300 or more points and a low would be 150 or fewer. The authors of this rating scale found that people with a high rating are more susceptible to illness that are those with a low rating.

justment Rating Scale shown in Figure 14.6. The self-assessment questionnaire gives weights to each of forty-three life events. The weights were assigned according to the stressful impact these events have on a person's life. People who score high on this rating scale are more susceptible to illness because they have experienced the most recent changes. The more change, the more stress, and the more adaptive the body must become to regain equilibrium. Adaptation consumes energy and when energy becomes depleted, susceptibility to illness increases.

A sensitive supervisor should know if a significant number of these events have occurred to any one employee within a twelve-month period. An employee may not be exhibiting symptoms of distress on the job, but the supervisor should be aware that the stress exists for the subordinate. The presence of enough events to attain a score of 150 points indicates that the employee is having to consume much energy in order to adapt to all lifes changes and faces exhaustion.

Awareness of Symptoms of Distress.   One needs to recognize the numerous symptoms of prolonged stress. Many of these have already been mentioned. The following include some of the most distressful and dangerous symptoms: sleepless nights, loss of appetite, muscular aches, stomach pain, migraine headaches, rashes, constipation, high blood pressure, bad temper, depression, and fatigue. The reader is reminded that distress is only one of many possible causes of these symptoms, but the presence of several of these symptoms simultaneously suggests the possibility of a distressed person.

Awareness of Working Environment Stressors.   In addition to life event changes, the working environment also contributes to distress. A job that presents conflicting demands on an employee, offers little variety and autonomy, and produces poor supervision will generate much job stress.[25] The following eight factors have been found to cause distress.

1. Heavy work loads with unrealistic deadlines.
2. Employer's inability to respond quickly because of poor internal communications.
3. Poor feedback on performance.
4. Lack of control over one's work environment and job.
5. Assigned responsibility without authority.
6. Ambiguity in job assignment or role definition.
7. Work location far from central decision making.
8. High competition for fewer positions at the top of an agency.

Park, recreation, and leisure employees and their supervisors should understand the ambiguous roles that the job and the public place on them. They should determine if they are over- or underworked, determine if they are frustrated by the employer's organizational structure, and recognize stressors in their physical work environment.

Awareness of Personal Support Systems.   People are social beings and need interpersonal relationships. These personal support systems are necessary in order to receive love, esteem, and value, and they tend to protect us in times of life crises.[26] Ideally, we should belong to several different support systems: one at work, one at home, one during recreation, and one with an outside organization in which we hold membership. All our support systems together should collectively provide *listening* persons, *technical support* persons, *emotional support* persons, and *social reality* persons.

Listening persons are usually good friends who will listen to our problems without judging or giving advice unless they are asked. Technical persons are those whom we believe to be very skilled or qualified in a particular area of endeavor. Appreciation from them challenges and motivates us. A supervisor on the job might fill this support need, but certainly not our mothers—parents (or spouse) give us emotional support. No matter what we do, we count on their unconditional love. During times of distress and confusion when we feel isolated in thought or behavior we need someone to agree with us: a person who shares our opinions. Such people give us a sense of reality and keep us in touch with the real world.

When all personal support functions are not in place, the risk of burnout is greater during distressful situations. The fewer and weaker the support systems, the higher the risk of burnout and distress. Research findings show significant correlation between personal support systems as buffers in times of prolonged stress.[27]

The lesson here for the supervisor is to recognize that workers who have lost a loved one or new hirees who have moved a great distance to take the new job may be experiencing a loss of support systems. Recreation careers in the armed forces, state parks, the National Park Service, or large leisure industries may be particularly vulnerable to weakened support systems during times of transfer.

Act to Change Attitudes.   It is also helpful to examine our attitudes about life, our work, and ourselves in order to alleviate prolonged stress. We need to:

1. *Live in the present* and not worry about things in the past we can no longer change or things in the future we cannot control. Even in the present we must learn not to worry about things beyond our control.
2. *Learn to relax* and do nothing at times—and not feel guilty. This applies to on-the-job moments, also. Libraries and bookstores offer many good

selections on breathing exercises to relax. Taking five to ten minutes each day to breathe deeply in a relaxed state has a positive effect on reducing stress.
3. *Learn to laugh.* If negative feelings produce bad chemical changes in our bodies, good feelings produce positive changes. We should seek out those who make us laugh, and laugh every day.
4. *Be a positive person* who sees the best in situations and people.

Act to Change Work Habits.   Volumes have been written about time management and how to reduce on-the-job stress. We could write a chapter about changing work habits, but here we offer the reader only the three following suggestions:

1. *Reduce information overload.* Eliminate environmental "noise" which competes for your attention. Noise can include visual distractions such a people walking by, as well as audio distractions such as ringing telephones or clacking typewriters. Visual distractions also include a cluttered desk and other symptoms of poor housekeeping. Having fewer items on a desk enables the worker to concentrate better on one item at a time.
2. *Use memory aids.* Things-to-do lists, calendars, and diaries are not only helpful but are essential to a busy manager. Schedule similar functions together each day in the same time period, such as letter writing, telephoning, and face-to-face communications. Handle a piece of paper *only once.* Write responses right on the letter and give the letter to a secretary for typing.
3. *Concentrate on one thing at a time.* When a person tries to concentrate on too many things at once, he or she cannot process any one item effectively. The maximum number of unrelated items the brain can recall simultaneously is seven—and for most of us, the maximum is between four to six.[28] If an overload condition persists over a long period of time, the person will start to make errors, become forgetful, have less tolerance for frustration, and will build resentment toward coworkers. Eventually, tedium or burnout will result.

Act to Recreate and Stay Fit.   You would not be reading this text if you did not already know that everyone needs to recreate and exercise regularly. Recreation and fitness are vital to the well-being of the employee.

Walking or climbing a flight of steps several times a day offers a healthy outlet for all the hormones and chemicals the body produces under stress. Physical exercise of any kind reduces the symptoms of prolonged stress.

Recreation is also a stress reducer if it is a regular part of one's life. The annual vacation or the occasional weekend trip to the beach is not adequate to reduce stress. A balanced recreation program should offer social interaction, physical exercise, variety, creative expression, intellectual expression and stimulation, and solitary relaxation. Unfortunately, few persons engage in such a balanced program, however. Too many people under stress watch television as their only recreational activity. The employer and the supervisor may not have much control over an employee's recreational outlets, but they can counsel workers on the importance and value of a well-balanced fitness and recreation program.

Problem Employees

Everyone experiences personal problems from time to time, and occasionally during one's life a personal problem becomes so great that it may temporarily interfere with job performance. Divorce, death, or illness of a loved one can affect people this way. Other conditions may continue over months or years, forcing the individual either to cope with the distressful situation or turn to unacceptable behavior in the form of alcohol or drug abuse.

When an employee turns to unacceptable behavior on the job to reduce the distress of personal problems, we refer to this employee as a *problem employee*. He or she is characterized by not responding favorably to performance appraisals and mild forms of discipline which point out to the employee a deterioration in interpersonal relationships and work performance. In addition to reduced quality and quantity of work, problem employees usually experience increased absences and greater incidents of insubordination.[29] The National Council on Alcoholism estimates that problem drinkers work at 60 percent of their potential.[30]

Organizations should attempt to help the problem employee. It is good business and it is the humanitarian thing to do. Studies show that help for the problem employee will reduce absenteeism, on-the-job accidents, workers' compensation premiums, and accident benefits.[31]

Employee programs to help problem employees are referred to as Employee Assistance Programs (EAPs). These vary considerably depending on the size of the organization or political jurisdiction. Some EAPs provide complete diagnostic and treatment assistance. Most EAPs only offer the employee counseling and referral information to appropriate clinics or agencies.

Problem Drinkers

The following facts on early- and middle-stage alcoholic workers provide evidence that problem drinkers are a serious problem in the working environment.

- Ninety-nine percent of industry's alcoholic employees are between 30 and 55 years of age and have been on their jobs for twelve to twenty years.
- Studies show that problem drinkers at all levels of responsibility experience absenteeism two and one-half times greater than that of non-problem drinkers. These employees have six to ten times more accidents.
- The average problem drinker costs the employer 25 percent of the worker's salary in absenteeism, reduced productivity, accidents, and use of medical benefits.[32]
- According to one study, one in every ten employees has a drinking problem.[33]
- Drinking problems may take from ten to twenty years to result in actual addiction.
- Few late-stage alcoholics are employed because the symptoms at this stage are so acute that they are not tolerated by most employers.

In the early stages of alcoholism, the work pattern varies and may be excellent, poor, or anything in between. Sometimes nervous and irritable, the worker may try to avoid the supervisor. He or she may sometimes come in late, leave early, and take long lunch hours.[34]

During the middle stage of alcoholism the worker may be untalkative but appears all right in the morning, and then will not return from lunch, phoning in sick. The eyes will appear bloodshot or bleary, the hands will shake, and the worker will act depressed. Speech may be slurred or sloppy. Moods will fluctuate, judgment is impaired, and personality changes are noted.

In the last stage, long-term regular drinking increases physiological tolerance so that the employee must drink more to achieve the same effects.[35] The worker may be arrested for drinking or is caught drinking on the job. Eventually, the employee is usually fired.

At one time alcoholism was treated as a moral and legal problem in our society, but the modern theory holds that it is a disease and must be considered as a medical and social problem. The causes of alcoholism are not known, but help is readily available in every community.

Drugs in the Workplace

From the mailroom of the Justice Department to the recreation community center, drugs have found their way into the workplace. It is a serious and growing problem reflecting a national trend. In 1981, drug use cost employers $16.4 billion.[36]

Within any thirty-day period 7 million people overuse legal drugs such as stimulants (amphetamines), barbiturates (phenobarbitol), or tranquilizers (valium). One out of two graduating high school seniors admits to some illegal drug use and one in three acknowledges use within the previous thirty days. More than 25 million Americans use marijuana.[37] At a minimum, 1 percent of the labor force is addicted to hard drugs and 3 percent regularly engaged in legal and illegal drug abuse.[38]

Like alcoholics, drug users have higher absenteeism, turnover and accident rates, and overall lower productivity than do nonusers. In addition, their tendency toward theft is greater, a consequence of having to support their expensive drug habits.[39] Generally, drug addicts are between ages 20 and 25 and have less than four years' experience with the organization. Unlike alcoholics, management usually has only a minimal investment in drug users and will take swifter action to terminate employees with illegal habits.

Halloran suggests that drug addicts hold a variety of jobs and can mask their addiction through careful manipulation of drug intake to prevent withdrawal symptoms. They simply go into the bathroom, experience the initial "rush" undisturbed for up to twenty minutes, and then return to work. If questioned, they provide many acceptable excuses, such as hangover or fatigue caused by family problems or anxiety.[40] Organizational procedures to detect and confront drug abusers are similar to those taken with alcoholics. But unlike alcoholism, drug abuse is illegal. This fact requires management to establish a clear and communicated policy which includes disciplinary action for use, sale, or possession of drugs on the employer's property. The policy should also include off-the-job illegal drug use, which could adversely affect job performance and safety. To do otherwise signals to the public, the users, the dealers, and the employees that the organization will ignore illegal drug use.

Adopting a policy is not enough, however. It must be enforced. Managers should show they are willing to invest time and money to ensure that rules are not broken. Many young employees routinely use marijuana or cocaine and believe that "recreational" use of drugs on their own time is a personal matter, just as the consumption of alcohol by supervisors and managers is no one's business. They think that policies and rules exist only for public show. Information must be provided which explains the different off-duty rules and risks of using drugs versus those of using alcohol. These might include the following facts.

- Marijuana's THC remains in the bloodstream for several days, even weeks, whereas alcohol is usually eliminated within twelve hours.[41]
- Neither drugs nor alcohol belong in the workplace, but alcohol is legal. Possession of any amount of illegal drugs violates state and federal laws.
- Both alcohol and drugs kill on the highway. They could kill on the job.

The legal, physical, psychological, and symptomatic consequences of drug use should be carefully explained to all employees. They should know, for example, how the overuse of barbiturates affect the worker driving a tractor and mower or how the overuse of amphetamines can affect the sport specialist's negotiations with quick-tempered league officials.

Although much more is known about occupational alcoholism than about work-related drug abuse, all evidence points to the fact that the overuse of legal drugs has also become a serious problem for the employer.

Role of the Supervisor

It is the supervisor who must identify the problem worker, confront the worker with decline in performance, and then refer the problem worker for assistance. But that is not all. The supervisor must follow up to ensure that the worker is striving to become rehabilitated. The objective of follow-up is to determine whether job performance improves satisfactorily.

Detection and Confrontation.   Detecting and confronting a problem employee are not easy tasks. Many supervisors have mixed feelings about alcoholic workers, for instance. They view the alcoholic as a difficult problem, but too often, they tend to look the other way or try to cover up for the worker. Supervisors rationalize that the problem will get better. Frequently, they know all about the employee's tragic personal problems. They may know the family and even have spent time drinking with the employee. But sympathy for the problem drinker is not a good reaction to the problem. It only delays corrective action.

The supervisor who spots the problem drinker or drug abuser must confront him or her with specific deterioration of performance, reviewing previously documented incidents. Reviewing this documentation during the disciplinary interview helps the employee to face the problem.

Comments should be only job related. The supervisor is not a professional counselor. Moralizing, diagnosing the cause of the problem, or offering any advice other than referral should not be attempted. It is only when the use of alcohol or drugs interferes with work that the supervisor is obligated to confront the problem employee.

Referral.   Once the supervisor confronts the problem employee, counseling or assistance should be recommended. If the employer does not have access to an EAP, the names and telephone numbers of local agencies offering assistance should be provided. Some employers offer the employees insurance coverage for counseling. Public agencies use public EAPs. The supervisor should be aware of all the alternatives and make these options known to the affected employee.

This step is also difficult for the supervisor because problem employees often will not admit that they have a serious problem. They may become defensive, hostile, or blame their problems on the supervisor or on situations beyond anyone's control. These common reactions should not be taken personally, nor should they elicit supervisor sympathy. During this entire interview the supervisor should remain calm and very supportive. It is important that the problem drinkers and drug abusers know that seeking help will not jeopardize their jobs and that outside assistance will be kept confidential. To ensure confidentiality, organizations will not record such assistance in the employee's personal file.[42]

Discussion of Consequences.   Most important, the employee must understand that there is need for job improvement. Continuation of poor performance will lead to discharge. The statement to this effect should not be made threateningly, but it must be made firmly. Knowing that job loss is possible frequently helps the employee face the problem and want to seek help. Like every other worker, problem employees must continue to work in order to survive.

Follow-up.   Once an employee accepts outside help the supervisor can strengthen the rehabilitation process by taking certain actions:

1. Continue to monitor and document job performance. Look for improvement and encourage the worker through positive reinforcement and praise. Corrective discipline should be applied when performance fails to meet expectations or if the employee does not take EAP seriously. Both continued problems as well as improvements should be documented.
2. Know the EAP guidelines for rehabilitating problem employees. Be patient and do not expect immediate improvement.
3. Preserve the confidentiality of the employee's personal problem and any specific details that may surface. Only a few parties within the organization need to know about participation in the EAP.

Summary and Recommendations

1. In addition to moral and legal reasons, it is economically advantageous for employers to provide a work environment that supports good health, safety, and employee well-being. To do otherwise costs the employer billions of dollars in insurance premiums, medical claims, and lost productivity.
2. There are three basic causes of accidents: unsafe conditions in the work environment, unsafe employee acts, and acts of nature. By far

the major cause of occupational injuries is unsafe human actions.

3. OSHA, state workers' compensation laws, the employer, and the immediate supervisor all share the responsibility for safety and health. OSHA acts to prevent work-related accidents by establishing very detailed standards which are enforced by inspectors who can issue citations and recommend penalties. State workers' compensation laws protect workers from economic hardships by providing financial benefits after the workers have been injured. These laws also provide incentives to the employer to want to improve job safety.

4. To reduce job accidents, employers need to be committed to and involved in a comprehensive safety–health program. The key to any safety program is prevention.

5. Managers should know what their respective workers' compensation about "who" is covered, and under "which" circumstances. Most laws provide broad coverage and include part-time employees and some volunteers.

6. Supervisors play an important role in safety. They must motivate employees to want to act safely, inspect the workplace for unsafe conditions, maintain safety records required by OSHA and state workers' compensation laws, and ensure that prompt medical attention is provided for an injured worker.

7. Stress is any response to a demand made on the body which requires adapting to the demand. Stress is desirable. Distress is stress that lasts too long or becomes so intense that it causes discomfort, interferes with our ability to think and act, and leads to behavioral changes. It is destructive.

8. Prolonged stress is common in the recreation and leisure field. Management, supervisors, and workers need to understand the nature and symptoms of distress in order to eliminate or reduce job-related stressors. Stressors that cannot be eliminated can be managed through awareness and productive action.

9. Balanced recreational activities, regular exercise, positive attitudes, and efficient work habits can help alleviate prolonged stress.

10. About 10 percent of any work force tend to be problem employees, with at least 5 percent of them alcoholics and 3 percent involved in drug abuse. Drug addiction is a growing problem on the job. Organizations should have a definite and communicated policy on drug abuse because it violates state and federal laws.

11. Problem employees do not work up to their potential capacity and experience increased absences and greater incidents of insubordination. Employee programs to help problem employees are called employee assistance programs.

12. The alcoholic is perhaps the most protected problem employee, as many of his or her coworkers and the supervisor tend to ignore or

hide the drinking problem. But when drinking prevents the employee from doing the job properly, it is the supervisor's responsibility to take corrective action.

13. Problem employees must be confronted with documented incidents of deteriorating performance to help them face and accept their problem. Then counseling and assistance should be recommended. The employee must understand that there is a need for job improvement because continued poor performance will lead to discharge. If the employee accepts help, the supervisor will need to monitor and document work performance until the work becomes satisfactory— or until the worker is fired.

Discussion Topics

1. Why is employee well-being so important to the employer?
2. What is an accident? What is an occupational injury, and what are occupational health hazards?
3. What causes most job-related injuries? What are some examples of poor housekeeping?
4. Give the components of a good safety–health program and discuss the role the immediate supervisor plays in achieving good safety performance.
5. What role do OSHA and workers' compensation laws play in employee well-being?
6. If you are the maintenance supervisor and have a small crew working out in a park without a supervisor or crew leader with them, how can you make sure that they comply with safety rules? Is this your responsibility or the safety officer's job?
7. If the supervisor disobeys a safety rule and there is an accident, is the park and recreation organization responsible?
8. Why has employee drug abuse become a major problem? As a supervisor, would you be equally willing to help an alcoholic, a drug addict, and one who is considering suicide?
9. If you were a supervisor and someone came to you needing emotional assistance, how would you respond? Would you feel compelled to give advice or just listen? Do you think people should express their feelings or try to keep them under control?
10. Could you recognize someone who is experiencing distress? Someone with a drinking problem? Someone who uses illegal drugs or abuses the use of legal drugs? Explain why or why not for each of these questions.
11. If stress is productive and desirable, how can prolonged stress be considered destructive?

12. Is it better to fire problem employees than to rehabilitate them?
13. Can supervisors rehabilitate problem employees? What can a supervisor do when he or she detects a problem employee?

Notes

1. Glenn Stahl, *Public Personnel Administration*, 8th ed. (New York: Harper & Row, Publishers, Inc., 1983), p. 346.
2. Jack Halloran, *Supervision: The Art of Management* (Englewood Cliffs, N.J.: Prentice-Hall, Inc., 1981), p. 410.
3. Leslie Rue and Lloyd Byars, *Supervision: Key Link to Productivity* (Homewood, Ill.: Richard D. Irwin, Inc., 1982), p. 284.
4. Dale Beach, *Personnel: The Management of People at Work*, 4th ed. (New York: Macmillan Publishing Company, 1980), p. 625.
5. Halloran, *Supervision*, p. 410.
6. National Safety Council, *Public Employee Safety Guide—Parks and Recreation*, 1974, cited in Robert E. Sternloff and Roger Warren, *Parks and Recreation Maintenance Management*, 2nd ed. (New York: John Wiley & Sons, Inc., 1984), p. 99.
7. Ibid.
8. Rue and Byars, *Supervision*, p. 286.
9. Beach, *Personnel*, p. 640.
10. Ibid.
11. Ibid., p. 634.
12. Stahl, *Public Personnel Administration*, p. 346.
13. Arthur Frakt and Janna Rankin, *The Law of Parks, Recreation Resources, and Leisure Services* (Salt Lake City, Utah: Brighton Publishing Co., 1982), p. 244.
14. Ibid.
15. Herbert Heneman and Donald Schwab, *Perspectives on Personnel/Human Resource Management* (Homewood, Ill.: Richard D. Irwin, Inc., 1982), p. 316.
16. Rue and Byars, *Supervision*, p. 286.
17. Heneman and Schwab, *Perspectives on Personnel/Human Resource Management*, p. 314.
18. Halloran, *Supervision*, p. 397.
19. Hans Selye, *Stress Without Distress* (Philadelphia: J.B. Lippincott Company, 1974), p. 17.
20. Rollo May, *A Psychology Today* (New York: Zin-Davis Publishing Co.), Cassette Tape 42.
21. Jerry Edelwich and Archie Brodsky, *Burnout: Stages of Disillusionment in the Helping Professions* (New York: Human Sciences Press, Inc., 1980), p. 166.
22. Carry Cherniss, *Staff Burnout: Job Stress in Human Societies* (Beverly Hills, Calif.: Sage Publications, Inc., 1980), p. 45.
23. Robert Eliot, "Is It Worth Dying For?" *American Medical News* 24(May 15, 1981): 16.
24. Ibid.
25. Cherniss, *Staff Burnout*, p. 127.

26. Ayala Pines, Elliot Aronsen, and Ditace Kabey, *Burnout: From Tedium to Personal Growth* (New York: Free Press, 1981), p. 130.

27. Ibid., p. 132.

28. Martha Radar, "Dealing with Information Overload," *Personnel Management* (May 1981): 373.

29. Rue and Byars, *Supervision*, p. 200.

30. Ibid.

31. Ibid., p. 198.

32. Randall Schuler, *Personnel and Human Resource Management*, 2nd ed. (St. Paul, Minn.: West Publishing Co., 1984), p. 284.

33. Ibid.

34. Halloran, *Supervision*, p. 341.

35. Beach, *Personnel*, p. 652.

36. Peter Bensinger, "Drugs in the Workplace," *Harvard Business Review* (November–December 1982): 48.

37. Ibid.

38. Arthur Sloane, *Personnel: Managing Human Resources* (Englewood Cliffs, N.J.: Prentice-Hall, Inc., 1983), p. 387.

39. Ibid.

40. Halloran, *Supervision*, p. 349.

41. Bensinger, "Drugs in the Workplace," p. 54.

42. Rue and Byars, *Supervision*, p. 202.

Appendix A: Laws and Orders Affecting Employment Practices

Law/Order (Date)	Applies to:	Objectives/Provisions	Monitoring/Enforcing Agency
1. U.S. Constitution, Fourteenth Amendment (1868)	Federal, state, and local governments	Guarantees equal protection of the law for all persons	
2. Civil Rights Act of 1870 (Sec. 1881)	Private employers, unions, employment agencies	Guarantees all persons same rights as "white citizens" to make and enforce contracts	
3. Civil Rights Act of 1871 (Sec. 1883)	State and local governments	Protected persons from being denied constitutional rights because of state laws	
4. Railroad Labor Act of 1926	Railroad workers, and eventually included airline employees	Recognized the right of employees to organize; prohibited "yellow dog" contracts	National Labor Relations Board (NLRB)
5. Norris–LaGuardia Act (1932)	All employers and labor organizations	Limited use of injunctions in labor disputes, and outlaws "yellow dog" contracts	Labor Department
6. National Labor Relations Act of 1935 (Wagner Act)	Private industry and unions	Established National Labor Relations Board; guarantees the right of employees to organize and bargain collectively; prohibits five unfair labor practices of management	National Labor Relations Board (NLRB)
7. Social Security Act of 1935	All employers	Established a federal tax on payrolls to provide for retirement benefits	Social Security Advisory Council and Social Security Administration
8. Unemployment compensation (1935)	All employers	Provides unemployment benefits to laid-off or fired employees	States and U.S. Labor Department

Appendix A *(continued)*

Law/Order (Date)	Applies to:	Objectives/Provisions	Monitoring/Enforcing Agency
9. State workers' compensation (state laws differ, and passed on different dates)	All employers	Provides benefits to employees injured on the job and to survivors of workers killed on the job	States
10. Fair Labor Standards Act of 1938 (FLSA)	Most employers	Established minimum wages, overtime pay, child-labor standards	Labor Department
11. Executive Orders 8802 and 9346 (1941 and 1943)	Companies with federal defense contracts.	Established Fair Employment Practices Committee to investigate complaints of employment discrimination.	Fair Employment Practices Committee
12. Labor–Management Relations Act of 1947 and 1974 (Taft–Hartley Act)	Private industry and labor unions	Amended Wagner Act, giving employees the right to refrain from joining unions; prohibits six unfair labor practices of unions	NLRB
13. Labor–Management Reporting and Disclosure Act (1959) (Landrum–Griffin Act)	Labor organizations	Reform act to regulate union activities	Secretary of Labor NLRB
14. Equal Pay Act of 1963, 1972 and 1978 (amends FLSA of 1938)	All employers and labor organizations	Guarantees equal pay for equal work, regardless of sex	Equal Employment Opportunity Commission (EEOC)
15. Civil Rights Act (1964) as amended by the Equal Employment Opportunity Act of 1972	Private employers with 15 or more employees, unions, educational institutions, state and local governments, and employment agencies	Prohibits discrimination in places of public accommodation and in employment practices based on race, color, sex, religion, or national origin	EEOC, Office of Personnel Management (OPM), Merit System Protection Board (MSPB)

Law	Covered Employers	Description	Enforcement Agency
Title VI	Employers receiving federal financial assistance	Established EEOC; bars federal assistance to schools, public housing projects, hospitals, and state agencies (and recreation and park agencies) that practice discrimination	EEOC
Title VII	Most all employers with 15 or more employees and state local governments	Established EEOC to enforce Civil Rights Act; prohibits employment discrimination based on race, color, sex, religion or national origin	EEOC
16. Executive Orders 10988 (1962), 11491 (1969), 11616, 11636, and 11838 (1975)	Federal government employers	Authorized and covered collective bargaining for federal employees; prohibited strikes; limited scope of grievance and arbitration procedures; ordered elections	OPM; MSPB
17. Executive Order 11141 (1964)	Federal contractors and subcontractors	Prohibits age discrimination by government contractors	Office of Federal Contract Compliance Programs (OFCCP)
18. Executive Orders 11246 (1965) and 11375 (1966)	Federal contractors and subcontractors working on projects of $10,000 or more; U.S. Postal Service, federal government agencies	Prohibits employment discrimination based on race, color, sex, religion, or national origin	OFCCP
19. Freedom of Information Act of 1966 (amended in 1974)	All government agencies	Guarantees individuals the right to see their personal records held by agencies	Congress
20. Age Discrimination in Employment Act of 1967, as amended in 1978	Private employers with 20 or more employees; unions with 25 or more members; state, local, and federal governments	Prohibits arbitrary age requirements for hiring, promotion, discharge, retirement, pay, conditions, and privileges of employment	EEOC

Appendix A (continued)

Law/Order (Date)	Applies to:	Objectives/Provisions	Monitoring/Enforcing Agency
21. Executive Order 11478 (1969)	Federal government employers	Prohibits discrimination in federal employment based on race, color, religion, sex, national origin, political affiliation, marital status, and physical disability	OPM and MSPB
22. Occupational Safety and Health Act of 1970 (OSHA) (1970)	Most employers	Establishes regulations and standards covering health and safety in the working environment	Occupational Safety and Health Administrations, Department of Labor
23. Vocational Rehabilitation Act of 1973	Federal contractors and subcontractors, federal government employers	Prohibits discrimination against physically and mentally handicapped workers	OFCCP
24. Vietnam-Era Veterans Readjustment Act of 1974	Federal contractors; federal government employers	Prohibits discrimination against disabled veterans and Vietnam-era veterans	OFCCP
25. Employee Retirement Income Security Act of 1974 (ERISA)	Most employers with pension plans (no employer is required to have such a plan)	Protects the participants in employee benefit plans by establishing standards of participation, vesting of benefits and funding of plans; establishes responsibility and obligations for fiduciaries	Department of Labor

26. Federal Privacy Act of 1974	Federal government	Restricts access to governmental files containing personal information about individuals; specifies the procedures and conditions under which personal information can be obtained	Congress
27. Civil Service Reform Act of 1978	Federal employers	Incorporates Title VII and mandates federal "workforce reflective of the nation's diversity"; established Federal Labor Relations Authority	Federal Labor Relations Authority
28. Pregnancy Discrimination Act of 1978 (amendment to Civil Rights Act)	All employers	Prohibits discrimination in employment based on pregnancy, childbirth, or subsequent complications; defines pregnancy as a disability	EEOC

Appendix B: Court Cases Involving Employment Practices

The courts interpret the words of the laws in settling disputes over whether or not organizations have violated the law. When the written words of the laws are not clearly understood, the courts are guided by the *Congressional Record,* which documents the history of debate and testimony leading to the passage of the laws. This provides the courts with the intent behind the law, as offered by statements from lawmakers. Courts are also guided by the decisions given in previous court cases that pertain to the same laws and principles. Thus the courts are not arbitrarily deciding matters, but rather interpreting events from the past.[1]

It is also important for the reader to understand the federal judicial process.

1. Most disputes pertaining to federal legislation are first filed in a federal district court where the judge will review all the evidence and arguments and then render a written opinion justifying the decision. This opinion may state what action must be taken to meet the so-called "letter of the law."
2. If the person filing the complaint (the complainant) does not like the decision of the district court, he or she can appeal in one of twelve federal circuit courts of appeal in this country, depending on the state in which the dispute occurred. Usually, a panel of three or more judges will review the lower court decision and then agree with it, reverse it, or send it back for further investigation.
3. The final step in the appeals process is the U.S. Supreme Court, if the Court decides that it wants to hear the case. The judges may refuse an appeal and will do so if they think they cannot add anything legally significant to a lower court decision.

Griggs v. Duke Power Company (1971)

New employees were required to have a high school diploma and achieve satisfactory scores on aptitude tests. Several blacks could not meet these requirements and filed charges of racial discrimination. The court challenged the employer's use of tests and educational requirements unless the employer can prove that the requirement is job related and predicts behavior necessary to perform the job. Intent to discriminate was not necessary to prove, only adverse impact.

Albemarle v. Moody (1975)

Employer used two national standardized tests to select employees from the unskilled labor pool for various skilled positions. Four blacks chal-

356

lenged the use of these tests. The court required the employer to prove that such tests were job related, permitted job analysis as evidence, and especially endorsed EEOC Guidelines on Testing, which reaffirmed the *Griggs* decision.

Washington v. Davis (1976)

A police department used a verbal-ability test for the selection of police recruits. A higher percentage of blacks than whites failed the test and challenged the test, not under Title VII, but under the Fifth Amendment. The Supreme Court settled the dispute among lower courts and held that intent to discriminate must be established when a test is challenged under Constitutional law, whereas under Title VII, the plaintiff need only show the effect of the test having an adverse impact on protected groups.

Dothard v. Rawlinson (1977)

A female was refused employment because she did not meet a minimum weight and height requirement established for correctional-counselor trainees. The requirement excluded more women than men. The Supreme Court ruled that if strength was a job requirement, a test to measure strength should be adopted. Height and weight requirements are illegal if they are not job related and exclude a greater proportion of minority-group members.

Diaz v. Pan American World Airways, Inc. (1971)

The airlines used a sex hiring criterion claiming that women made better flight attendants. The court struck down the sex criterion, stating that the primary function of an airlines is transporting passengers. Hiring male flight attendants did not jeopardize the business of transporting passengers. Therefore, hiring only women discriminated against men. This case established the principle of "business necessity" as a reason for practicing preferential treatment.

Richardson v. Hotel Corporation of America (1972)

Furthered the principle of "business necessity" by finding that dismissal on the grounds of a conviction record is legal when it is related to business operation, even if it results in adverse impact. The issue is not one of job performance.

Bakke v. Regents of the University of California (1978)

To increase the number of minority students, the University of California Medical School at Davis set aside a specific number of places for minorities. A white male applied for admission and was turned down, even though he scored higher on the admissions criteria than did the minorities who were admitted. The white male charged that he was a victim of discrimination (reverse discrimination). The Supreme Court's decision was that (a) special quotas were unconstitutional unless prior discrimination had been demonstrated, (b) reverse discrimination is prohibited, and (c) race can be a consideration in selection decisions.

Kaiser Aluminum and Chemical v. Weber (1979)

A white worker charged discrimination when he was denied entry into a training program designed to increase the number of blacks in skilled craft jobs. Two blacks with less seniority had been accepted. The Supreme Court declared that voluntary affirmative action giving preferential treatment to minorities is legal, even when there is no evidence of past discrimination.

Usery v. Tamiami Trail Tours, Inc. (1976)

The court ruled that age is a BFOQ requirement for hiring bus drivers based on evidence that the greater the safety factor, the more stringent may be the job qualification to ensure safe driving. (The following year, the Supreme Court rejected age as a BFOQ on the grounds of safety, in the testing of supersonic jets).

Marshall v. Barlow's, Inc. (1979)

The Supreme Court ruled that OSHA inspectors must have a search warrant in order to enter business sites, although inspectors are entitled to warrants when either an employee complains or there is an OSHA administrative policy to conduct reasonable inspections of specifically identified potentially dangerous industries.

Atlantic and Gulf Stevedores, Inc. v. OSHARC (1976)

Employees refused to wear hard hats on the job. OSHA fined the company. The company appealed, stating that every measure had been taken to obtain compliance, short of discharge, which would have led to a wildcat strike. The court ruled that it was the responsibility of the employer to get the violators to comply. This decision implies that it is the obligation of the employer to discipline employees.

Buckner v. Kennedy's Riding Academy (1976)

A teenage female was injured by a horse while performing minor chores around the stable. Because she received a free lunch, free use of the horses, and was occasionally paid a few dollars, the courts ruled that this was compensation enough for her to be awarded workers' compensation.

Norton v. Macy (1969)

A male NASA employee was interrogated by the security chief until he admitted to homosexual tendencies, but denied being a homosexual. NASA fired him for "immoral, indecent and disgraceful conduct." The court ruled that he be reinstated because NASA had said the employee was a good worker and that there were no security risks involved in his job. Firing the employee was arbitrary since the man did not flaunt his behavior and, thereby, risk disgrace.

Note

1. James Ledvinka, *Federal Regulation of Personnel and Human Resource Management*, Kent Human Resource Management Series, Richard W. Beatty, University of Colorado at Boulder, Colorado, Series Consulting Editor (New York: Van Nostrand Reinhold Company, Inc., 1982), p. 12.

Appendix C: Excerpts from Title VII, Civil Rights Act

Section 703

(a) It shall be an unlawful employment practice for an employer

(1) to fail or refuse to hire or to discharge an individual, or otherwise to discriminate against any individual with respect to his compensation, terms, conditions, or privileges of employment, because of such individual's race, color, religion, sex, or national origin; or

(2) to limit, segregate, or classify his employees or applicants for employment in any way which would deprive or tend to deprive any in-

dividual of employment opportunities or otherwise adversely affect his status as an employee, because of such individual's race, color, religion, sex, or national origin.

. . .

(3) Notwithstanding any other provision of this title, (1) it shall not be an unlawful employment practice for an employer to hire and employ employees . . . on the basis of his religion, sex, or national origin in those certain instances where religion, sex, or national origin is a bona fide occupational qualification reasonably necessary to the normal operation of that particular business or enterprise.

. . .

(h) Nothwithstanding any other provision of this title, it should not be an unlawful employment practice for an employer to apply different standards of compensation, or different terms, conditions, or privileges of employment pursuant to a bona fide seniority or merit system, or a system which measures earnings by quantity of production or to employees who work in different locations, provided that such differences are not the result of an intention to discriminate because of race, color, religion, sex, or national origin, nor shall it be an unlawful employment practice for an employer to give and to act upon the results of any professionally developed ability test provided that such test, its administration or action upon the results is not designed, intended or used to discriminate because of race, color, religion, sex, or national origin.

. . .

(j) Nothing contained in this title shall be interpreted to require any employer . . . to grant preferential treatment to any individual or to any group because of the race, color, religion, sex, or national origin of such individual or group on account of an imbalance which may exist with respect to the total number or percentage of persons of any race, color, religion, sex, or nationl origin employed by any employer . . . in comparison with the total number or percentage of persons of such race, color, religion, sex, or national origin in any community, State, section, or other area, or in the available work force in any community, State, section, or other area.

Section 704

(a) It shall be an unlawful employment practice for an employer to discriminate against any of his employees or applicants for employment . . . because he [the employee or applicant] has opposed any practice made an unlawful employment practice by this title, or because he has made a charge, testified, assisted, or participated in any matter in an investigation, proceeding, or hearing under this title.

Appendix D: Excerpts from the Age Discrimination in Employment Act of 1967, as Amended in 1978

Section 4

(a) It shall be unlawful for an employer

(1) to fail to refuse to hire or to discharge any individual or otherwise discriminate against any individual with respect to his compensation, terms, conditions, or privileges of employment, because of such individual's age;

(2) to limit, segregate, or classify his employees in any way which would deprive or tend to deprive any individual of employment opportunities or otherwise adversely affect his status as an employee, because of such individual's age; or

(e) It shall be unlawful for an employer . . . to print or publish, or cause to be printed or published, any notice or advertisement relating to employment by such an employer . . . indicating any preference, limitation, specification, or discrimination, based on age.

(f) It shall not be unlawful for an employer, employment agency, or labor organization

(1) to take any action otherwise prohibited . . . where age is a bona fide occupational qualification reasonably necessary to the normal operation of the particular business, or where the differentiation is based on reasonable factors other than age:

(2) to observe the terms of a bona fide seniority system or any bona fide employee benefit plan such as retirement, pension, or insurance plan, which is not a subterfuge to evade the purpose of this Act, except that no such employee benefit plan shall excuse the failure to hire any individual, and no such seniority system or employee benefit plan shall require or permit the involuntary retirement of any individual specified by section 12(a) of this Act because of the age of such individual.

Section 12

(a) The prohibitions in this Act shall be limited to individuals who are at least 40 years of age but less than 70 years of age.

Appendix E: Sample Application for Employment*

APPENDIX E

APPLICATION FOR EMPLOYMENT

CITY OF GREENSBORO, NORTH CAROLINA

ONE GOVERNMENTAL PLAZA

DRAWER W-2, GREENSBORO, NORTH CAROLINA 27402

QUALIFIED APPLICANTS ARE CONSIDERED FOR POSITIONS WITHOUT REGARD TO RACE, COLOR, RELIGION, SEX, NATIONAL ORIGIN, AGE, MARITAL STATUS, OR THE PRESENCE OF A NON-JOB-RELATED MEDICAL CONDITION OR HANDICAP.

ANSWER ALL QUESTIONS - PLEASE PRINT OR TYPE YOUR NAME

POSITION APPLIED FOR _____ DATE _____

NAME _____ SOCIAL SECURITY NUMBER _____
     (Last)   (First)   (Middle)   (Maiden, if applicable)

PRESENT MAILING ADDRESS _____
                        (Street & No.)   (City)   (State)   (Zip Code)

PERMANENT MAILING ADDRESS _____
(If Different)   (Street & No.)   (City)   (State)   (Zip Code)

TELEPHONE _____
          (Area Code if other than 919)   (Home)   (Business)   (Other   Indicate whose number)

DO YOU HAVE A VALID DRIVER'S LICENSE?   YES ___ NO ___   STATE _____ NUMBER _____

DATE OF BIRTH _____

PLEASE BE SURE THAT YOU COMPLETE ALL SECTIONS OF THIS APPLICATION COMPLETELY AND ACCURATELY TO THE BEST OF YOUR ABILITY. YOUR APPLICATION WILL BE USED AS A PART OF THE EXAMINATION PROCESS AND, THEREFORE, SHOULD REPRESENT YOUR BEST EFFORT. (FOR SOME POSITIONS YOU MAY BE ASKED TO COMPLETE A SUPPLEMENTAL APPLICATION.)

AN EQUAL OPPORTUNITY/AFFIRMATIVE ACTION EMPLOYER

*Courtesy of the City of Greensboro, N.C.

Skills Data

Please indicate your clerical skills:

Typing WPM_____ Shorthand WPM _____

Kind of office equipment operated: _____

_____

_____

Military Data

Are you a veteran? Yes _____ No _____

Branch of service:_____

Dates of active duty: _____

Service number: _____

Rank upon separation: _____

EDUCATION (GIVE COMPLETE EDUCATIONAL HISTORY BELOW)

Elementary School: Name _____ Location _____
High School: Name _____ Location _____

Circle highest school year completed: 1 2 3 4 5 6 7 8 9 10 11 12

Ending date: Month _____ Year _____

If you did not graduate, do you have
a High School Equivalency?_____

Education beyond High School	Name and Location	Attended From-To	Circle No. Years Completed	Did you Graduate?	Degree/ Certificate	Major Subject
College or University			1 2 3 4			
Graduate or Professional			1 2 3 4			
Other Education			1 2 3 4			

EMPLOYMENT DATA: In the space below, give your employment history beginning with your present or most recent employer and list all positions held, including military, part-time, summer, and significant volunteer work for the last 10 years. Details on any period of unemployment must be included. Experience acquired more than 10 years ago may be summarized in one block if not applicable to position for which you are applying.

Title of present or most recent position _____ Starting Salary _____ Final Salary _____

Date employed
Date separated
Full time   Yrs.   Mos.
Part time   Yrs.   Mos.
If part time, number of hours worked per week.

Name and address of employer:_____

Description of duties, responsibilities, and accomplishments:

_____

_____

_____

Number of employees supervised by you: _____
Name of immediate supervisor: _____
Phone number of supervisor : _____
Reason for leaving: _____
May we contact your present employer? _____
If no, please list the name and phone no. of someone knowledgeable of your work. _____

PERSONAL DATA

Are you a citizen of the United States? yes☐ o☐
If no, give country of which you are a citizen and
your alien registration number.

_____

_____

Have you ever been convicted of any offense
against the law (including minor traffic violations)? If so, please explain the nature of the
conviction and the final disposition of the case.

_____

_____

_____

Do you have any relatives currently employed
by the City of Greensboro? If so, who, in what
position, and in what department are they employed? What is the relationship?

_____

_____

_____

Please indicate any special skills, accomplishments, special training or publications you have
which are relevant to the position for which
you are applying.

_____

_____

_____

REFERENCE DATA

Please list three persons who are not related to
you and who have a definite knowledge of your
work. Do not repeat the names of supervisors
listed in the Employment Data Section of this
application.

Name_____

_____
Business or Home Address (Street)

_____
City   State   Zip

_____
Home Phone   Business Phone

Name _____

_____
Business or Home Address (Street)

_____
City   State   Zip

_____
Home Phone   Business Phone

Name_____

_____
Business or Home address (Street)

_____
City   State   Zip

_____
Home Phone   Business Phone

DECLARATION OF APPLICANT

I certify that all statements made in this application are true, complete and correct to the best of my knowledge
and belief, and that any false statements shall be considered sufficient cause for employment disqualification or
dismissal.

_____
Signature of Applicant

Please indicate how you found out about this vacant position.

The City's Employment Opportunities list? _____

From a City employee?_____From a friend?_____

From a newspaper?_____What newspaper?_____

From radio?_____ From TV?_____ Other (specify)_____

364

Title of next position _____

Starting Salary _____ Final Salary _____

Name and address of employer: _____

| Date employed |
| Date separated |
| Full time   Yrs.   Mos. |
| Part time   Yrs.   Mos. |
| If part time, number of hours worked per week. |

Description of duties, responsibilities, and accomplishments:

_____

_____

_____

Number of employees supervised by you: _____

Name of immediate supervisor: _____

Phone number of supervisor: _____

Reason for leaving: _____

Title of next position _____

Starting Salary _____ Final Salary _____

Name and address of employer: _____

| Date employed |
| Date separated |
| Full time   Yrs.   Mos. |
| Part time   Yrs.   Mos. |
| If part time, number of hours worked per week. |

Description of duties, responsibilities, and accomplishments:

_____

_____

_____

Number of employees supervised by you: _____

Name of immediate supervisor: _____

Phone number of supervisor: _____

Reason for leaving: _____

Title of next position _____

Starting Salary _____ Final Salary _____

Name and address of employer: _____

| Date employed |
| Date separated |
| Full time   Yrs.   Mos. |
| Part time   Yrs.   Mos. |
| If part time, number of hours worked per week. |

Description of duties, responsibilities, and accomplishments:

_____

_____

_____

Number of employees supervised by you: _____

Name of immediate supervisor: _____

Phone number of supervisor: _____

Reason for leaving: _____

If additional space is needed, please ask for a continuation sheet, or use a sheet of paper.

365

Appendix F: National Certification in Recreation, Park Resources, and Leisure Services

The National Certification Board (NCB) established in 1981 by the National Recreation and Park Association (NRPA) Board of Trustees is an independent body charged to determine standards for professional recognition in the recreation, park resources, and leisure service profession. The mechanism that recognizes those individuals who have met those standards is called the Model Certification Plan. Persons recognized under this plan qualify for inclusion on the National Roster of recreation, park resources, and leisure service personnel, thus guaranteeing employers that certified personnel have attained stated education and experience qualifications.

The Model Certification Plan requires that park and recreation practitioners who apply for "professional" recognition after November 1, 1986, must be graduates of a park and recreation curriculum that has been accredited by NRPA and the American Association for Leisure and Recreation. The practitioner must also have no less than two years of full-time working experience in a recreation, park resources, and leisure position. For certification as a "provisional professional," the practitioner must have a bachelor's or higher degree from an accredited education insitution but does not need two years' working experience.

There is a third category in which practitioners may be certified. The "technician" may be certified with a two-year associate degree from an accredited educational institution; or have an associate degree in any field and at least two years' experience working full-time in a recreation, park resources, and leisure position; or have a high school diploma or equivalency certificate and at least four years of full-time employment with a park, recreation, or leisure employer.

Each state has the option of adopting the NCB model plan or developing its own certification plan. Practitioners who reside in states that do not have NCB approved plans can apply directly to the national certification program for recognition and certification.

One of the requirements for maintaining active certification is satisfactory completion of two continuing education units (CEUs) or equivalent academic course work from an accredited university in each 24-month period from the date of the initial certification.

Index